Glenn McKee.
15 April, 2013.

THE IRISH LORD LIEUTENANCY, C. 1541–1922

In memory of Peter Jupp

★

The Irish Lord Lieutenancy

c. 1541–1922

edited by

PETER GRAY AND OLWEN PURDUE

UNIVERSITY COLLEGE DUBLIN PRESS

PREAS CHOLÁISTE OLLSCOILE
BHAILE ÁTHA CLIATH

First published 2012
by University College Dublin Press
Newman House
86 St Stephen's Green
Dublin 2
Ireland

www.ucdpress.ie

ISBN 978-1-906359-60-7

Cataloguing in Publication data available from the British Library

Typeset in UK in Plantin and Fournier by Ryan Shiels
Text design by Lyn Davies
Printed on acid-free paper in England by Antony Rowe,
Chippenham, Wilts

Contents

Acknowledgements

This volume originates in a conference on the Irish lord lieutenancy, held at Dublin Castle and Academy House, Dublin, in September 2009. The editors would like to thank the Royal Irish Academy, the Academy's Committee for the Historical Sciences, and in particular Vanessa Carswell and Professor Nicholas Canny, for supporting the conference, as well as all who contributed from the platform and the floor. We are grateful to the Office of Public Works in Dublin for permission to reproduce portraits from the Dublin Castle art collection in this volume. Thanks are due also to Noelle Moran of UCD Press for her care and patience in seeing this volume through to publication.

The authors and editors would like to thank HM the Queen for permission to use and cite material from the Royal Archives, to the duke of Northumberland for permission use the Northumberland Papers at Alnwick Castle, to the marquess of Normanby for use of the Normanby Papers at Mulgrave Castle, to the duke of Devonshire for use of the Devonshire Papers at Chatsworth House, to the Hon. Simon Howard for use of the Carlisle Papers at Castle Howard, to the marquess of Salisbury for use of the Salisbury Papers at Hatfield House and to the duke of Bedford for use of the Bedford Papers at Woburn Abbey. We would also like to thank the archivists and librarians of the following institutions for permitting access to and usage of the collections in their care: Beinecke Library, Birmingham University Library, Bodleian Library, Borthwick Institute, British Library, Cambridge University Library, Centre for Kentish Studies, Churchill College, Cambridge, Devon Record Office, Dublin City Library, Durham University Library, Gloucestershire Record Office, Haddo House, Imperial War Museum, Irish Architectural Archive, John Rylands Library, Lambeth Palace Library, Liverpool Record Office, McGill University Library, National Archives of Ireland, National Library of Ireland, National Library of Scotland, Parliamentary Archives, Public Record Office of Northern Ireland, Royal Dublin Society Library, Scottish Record Office, Sheffield City Library, Somerset Record Office, Southampton University Library, Staffordshire Record Office, Surrey History Centre, The National Archives, Kew, Trinity College Dublin, West Sussex Record Office, Wiltshire and Swindon Archives.

Illustrations

Contributors to this Volume

TOBY BARNARD is a lecturer in history and fellow of Hertford College, Oxford. His publications include *Irish Protestant Ascents and Descents, 1641–1770* (Dublin, 2003) and *Cromwellian Ireland* (Oxford, 2000).

CIARAN BRADY is associate professor of history at Trinity College Dublin. His publications include *The Chief Governors: The Rise and Fall of Reform Government in Tudor Ireland, 1536–1588* (Cambridge, 1994), and *A Viceroy's Vindication: Sir Henry Sidney's Memoir of Service in Ireland, 1583* (Cork, 2002).

PETER GRAY is professor of modern Irish history and head of the School of History and Anthropology at Queen's University Belfast. His publications include *The Making of the Irish Poor Law, 1815–43* (Manchester, 2009) and *Poverty and Welfare in Ireland, 1833–1948* (ed., Dublin, 2011).

K. THEODORE HOPPEN is professor emeritus of history at the University of Hull. He is the author of *The Mid-Victorian Generation 1846–1886* (Oxford, 1998), and co-editor of *Gladstone: Ireland and Beyond* (Dublin, 2011).

KEITH JEFFERY is professor of British history at Queen's University Belfast, and author of *Ireland and the Great War* (new edn, Cambridge, 2011), and *Field Marshal Sir Henry Wilson: A Political Soldier* (Oxford, 2006).

JAMES KELLY is professor of history and head of the history department at St Patrick's College, Drumcondra. His many works on eighteenth-century Ireland include *Poynings' Law and the Making of Law in Ireland, 1660–1800* (Dublin, 2008) and *Henry Flood: Patriots and Politics in Eighteenth-Century Ireland* (Dublin, 1998).

JAMES LOUGHLIN is a reader in history at the University of Ulster. His publications include *The British Monarchy and Ireland: 1800 to the Present* (Cambridge, 2008) and *Ulster Unionism and British National Identity since 1885* (London, 1995).

PATRICK MAUME is a researcher on the Royal Irish Academy's *Dictionary of Irish Biography*. He is the author of *The Long Gestation: Irish Nationalist Life 1891–1918* (Dublin, 2000).

CHARLES IVAR MCGRATH lectures in Irish history at University College Dublin. He is the author of *The Making of the Eighteenth-Century Irish Constitution: Government, Parliament and the Revenue, 1692–1714* (Dublin, 2000).

GILLIAN O'BRIEN is a lecturer in history at Liverpool John Moore's University. She is the co-editor of *Georgian Dublin* (Dublin, 2008).

OLWEN PURDUE is a lecturer in Irish social and economic history at Queen's University Belfast. She is the author of *The Big House in the North of Ireland: Land, Power and Social Elites 1878–1960* (Dublin, 2009).

Abbreviations

ADC	Aide-de-Camp
BL	British Library, London
Bein.	Beinecke Library, New Haven
Bodl.	Bodleian Library, Oxford
CH	Castle Howard
ChH	Chatsworth House
CIGS	Chief of the Imperial General Staff
CJI	*The Journals of the House of Commons of the Kingdom of Ireland*
CKS	Centre for Kentish Studies, Maidstone
CSPD	*Calendar of State Papers, Domestic*
CTB	*Calendar of Treasury Books*
CTP	*Calendar of Treasury Papers*
CUL	Cambridge University Library
DIB	*Dictionary of Irish Biography*
DCL	Dublin City Library
DRO	Devon Record Office, Exeter
DUL	Durham University Library
FJ	*Freeman's Journal*
GRO	Gloucestershire Record Office, Gloucester
HatH	Hatfield House
HH	Haddo House
HMC	Historical Manuscripts Commission
IVA	Irish Vigilance Association
IRA	Irish Republican Army
IWM	Imperial War Museum, London
LRO	Liverpool Record Office
MC	*Morning Chronicle*
MuC	Mulgrave Castle, N. Yorkshire
NHI	*New History of Ireland*
NAI	National Archives of Ireland, Dublin
NLI	National Library of Ireland, Dublin
NPG	National Portrait Gallery
NUI	National University of Ireland
NVA	National Vigilance Association

NW	*Northern Whig*
ODNB	*Oxford Dictionary of National Biography*
OPW	Office of Public Works
PA	Parliamentary Archives, London
PRONI	Public Record Office of Northern Ireland, Belfast
QUB	Queen's University Belfast
RA	Royal Archives, Windsor
RC	Roman Catholic
ScRO	Scottish Record Office, Edinburgh
SF	*Sinn Féin*
SHC	Surrey History Centre, Woking
SP	State Papers
SRO	Staffordshire Record Office, Stafford
SUL	Southampton University Library
TB	Tuberculosis
TCD	Trinity College Dublin
TNA	The National Archives, Kew
UCD	University College Dublin
UI	*United Irishman*
UVF	Ulster Volunteer Force
WRO	Wiltshire Record Office
WSA	Wiltshire and Swindon Archives, Chippenham
WSRO	West Sussex Record Office, Chichester

CHAPTER I

Introduction

The Irish Lord Lieutenancy, c.1541–1922

Peter Gray and Olwen Purdue

This volume aims to address a significant gap in our understanding of the history of Irish governance and British-Irish relations in the early-modern and modern eras. For more than 300 years the government of Ireland was headed by a chief governor commonly titled (almost invariably so after 1660) the lord lieutenant of Ireland. The holder of this senior office of state was from the Restoration always a peer – albeit occasionally a man ennobled for the purpose – and was expected to combine the 'efficient' direction of the Irish executive on behalf of the British government with the 'decorative' ceremonial required of him as viceroy or surrogate of the Crown presiding over the Irish court at Dublin Castle. These overlapping but potentially antagonistic roles were poorly defined in the constitutional form of the lord lieutenancy and were interpreted in different ways by incumbents and by the monarchs and ministries they served. If there was tendency over time for the 'decorative' aspects to attain ascendancy over the 'efficient', this process was never linear; the political importance of public symbolism, extravagant display and patronage in Irish governance also tended to conflate what might at first appear distinct elements. This volume intends to explore the multiple dimensions of the lord lieutenancy as an institution – in its political, social and cultural aspects – and how these changed in the extended period between the royal proclamation of Ireland as a distinct 'kingdom' under the English Crown in 1541 and the break-up of the United Kingdom of Great Britain and Ireland in 1922, which was accompanied by the formal abolition of the office.

A study of the lord lieutenancy is facilitated by recent research into the historical relationship between the British monarchy and Ireland, which has highlighted, particularly for the nineteenth century, the fluctuating and often contested reactions of the Irish of different degrees and persuasions to the pomp of royal visits, the state- and nation-building strategies of royal advisers and ministers and the reputed or proclaimed views of occupants of the throne towards their Irish subjects.[1] Royal expeditions across the Irish Sea were rare events. Between Henry VIII's formal assumption of the Irish 'crown' in 1541 and the dissolution of the Irish parliament in 1801 only two reigning monarchs visited the country, when William III campaigned against his deposed predecessor James II on Irish soil in 1690. Despite the consolidating intentions of the Act of Union (and more significantly the communications revolution accelerated from the 1820s by the introduction of steam propulsion on land and sea), royal visits remained relatively sporadic after 1801. George IV made a brief but remarkably popular appearance in Dublin in 1821; Victoria came four times in her long reign – in 1849, 1853, 1861 and 1900 – while her son, Edward VII, visited on a number of occasions as prince of Wales and again as king in 1903 and 1907. George V's visits of 1911 and 1921 occurred at moments of acute constitutional crisis, with his appearance in Belfast in the latter year setting the seal on partition. In the absence of the monarch except during these brief excursions, and with Ireland lacking (unlike Scotland and Wales) regular royal residences or associations, the majesty of the Crown in Ireland was represented principally by the lord lieutenant in his dual role as viceroy. After a period of erratic residence in the early eighteenth century, incumbents were mostly present in Dublin after 1767, acting as a proxy monarch with greater or lesser degrees of success.

As both royal surrogate and, in theory if not always in practice, the working head of a subordinate administration, the Irish lord lieutenant was increasingly an anomalous office within the United Kingdom. Neither the Welsh (1536) or Scottish (1707) unions maintained a separate executive or court for those territories, although – as Theo Hoppen has observed – the retention of both in Dublin attracted remarkably little attention on the part of most of the framers of the Irish measure of 1800.[2] Criticism of the utility of the lord lieutenancy as a governing instrument multiplied as the century progressed. To the Irish Whig Henry Brooke Parnell in 1834, it was the apogee of a structure that inhibited the reforms that Ireland desperately required.[3] By 1849 the prime minister Lord John Russell had come to agree that the viceregal office was politically dysfunctional and inhibited both good governance and the full integration of Ireland into the Union. However, his abolition bill of 1850 aroused strong opposition in Ireland and was quickly abandoned.[4] In the face of disagreement over what could replace it, the long-serving and influential under-secretary Thomas Larcom defended the lord lieutenancy on exceptionalist grounds in the 1850s–60s – Ireland was an old country but lacked the deep traditions of local self-governance that had evolved in other parts of the UK and lagged far behind them in its political development; so long as Irish government remained 'in advance of the people', he concluded, a strong resident viceroy would remain essential to stability, security and economic and educational progress.[5]

Perhaps not surprisingly, nineteenth-century critics of the institution (both Irish and British) likened the lord lieutenancy to the colonial governorships characteristic of the expanding British Empire, and stigmatised it as representing the subordinated, even colonised, place of Ireland within the UK and the non-completion of a genuine political union.[6] This perception was reinforced by the movement of some Irish incumbents to or from other imperial posts (Cornwallis and Wellesley had previously served as governor general of Bengal; Mulgrave had been the governor of Jamaica; Aberdeen was governor general of Canada between his stints in Dublin, and Dudley went on to be governor general of Australia after leaving Ireland), although in fact relatively few incumbents were drawn from the colonial or diplomatic service. The title of 'viceroy' had been widely used by the Spanish and Portuguese crowns in the governance of their subordinate European and overseas territories since the fifteenth century (and was subsequently also employed in similar a vein by Austrian, Russian and Ottoman rulers), but in the English and British context the term was restricted to the chief governor of Ireland (as an informal alternative to 'lord lieutenant') until the creation of the Indian viceroyalty in 1858. Although the resources and power of the latter office were to vastly exceed those of the Irish lord lieutenant, the ornamentalist character of the new Indian office drew in part on the older Irish model as well as on indigenous Indian forms such as the princely Durbar.[7] Comparisons (usually adverse) were drawn between the two viceroyalties by Irish and British unionist critics of what appeared to them the indefensible 'colonial' institution surviving in Dublin.[8]

Irish supporters of the lord lieutenancy, anxious to distance it from such contemporary colonial associations, drew attention instead to the antiquity of the office and its surviving medieval peculiarities, such as the 'battle-axe guards' (before their abolition in a cost-cutting drive in the 1830s). Nineteenth-century Dublin opinion, both moderate nationalist and Conservative, tended to coalesce around a defence of the office as the manifestation of 'the ancient right of this kingdom to a separate local executive' in the face of 'centralising' British tendencies, and as the guarantor of the city's retention of the status of a national capital.[9] This defensiveness in the face of abolitionist threats may in part contextualise the first serious attempt to trace the office's origins, in Sir John T. Gilbert's *History of the Viceroys of Ireland*, published in 1865.[10] Gilbert, who was the librarian of the Royal Irish Academy, and had been awarded the Academy's prize for his earlier *History of Dublin*, addressed the period from the Anglo-Norman conquest of Ireland to Henry VIII's accession in 1509 (a proposed second volume bringing the history forward to the present appears not have been completed), and adopted an antiquarian approach typical of the gentlemanly scholarship of his day. At the same time, it appears unlikely to be accidental that he chose this topic for his 600 page tome at a time when the very survival of the lord lieutenancy was in question in the wake of serious abolitionist initiatives in 1850, 1858 and 1864, during which attacks on its 'colonial' characteristics were common.[11] In utilising the term 'viceroy' throughout his book to describe the various titles associated with the chief governorship of Ireland, Gilbert equated the medieval offices of 'justiciar' and 'king's lieutenant' with the contemporary lord lieutenancy, thus rendering it a part of the ancient and organic constitution of Ireland.

Gilbert's history was self-consciously 'completed' in 1912 by Charles Kingston O'Mahony in his book *The Viceroys of Ireland*, a much less scholarly and more partisan account that took the story from 1171 through to the then incumbent, the earl of Aberdeen.[12] O'Mahony (1884–1944), who was subsequently a popular crime fiction writer, was in 1912 a committed Liberal Home Ruler, who regarded the viceroyalty (especially as embodied by the genial Aberdeen) as a crucial lynchpin which would continue to connect a self-governing Ireland to Great Britain through the active presence of a royal representative in Dublin. His unreferenced narrative account concluded with an encomium on Lord and Lady Aberdeen's efforts in promoting political reconciliation and on their active philanthropy, undertaken in the face of both bigoted Orange and extreme nationalist hostility.[13] His defence of the institution they occupied drew on an essentialising ethnography and anticipated the realisation of the ideal of a wholly depoliticised viceroyalty under Home Rule:

> [I]f ornamental it is also useful, because the Irish instinctively respect royalty, and a country populated by the descendants of kings could not be expected to have an instinctive respect for any form of government savouring of Republicanism, or one that left wholly to the imagination the majesty of the Sovereign ruler. To satisfy all classes, to tolerate the intolerant, and to represent the non-political King of England, are the duties of the Lord-Lieutenant. . . . When Liberalism has achieved its ambition, the Irish bureaucracy will cease to hold the power that makes or mars every viceroyalty.[14]

The events of the succeeding decade would starkly expose the wishful thinking behind such claims. The viceroyalty was abolished, largely unmourned, in 1922, albeit with the successor office of governor-general being created for both the Irish Free State and Northern Ireland.

There is no modern academic text which addresses the history of the Irish lord lieutenancy in its entirety. The closest to a survey is Joseph Robins,

Champagne and Silver Buckles: The Viceregal Court at Dublin Castle 1700–1922, a work of popular history that uses a number of primary sources to outline a narrative account of the officeholders for that period alongside a more detailed discussion of the 'dining, wining, ceremonials and fashion' of the viceregal household.[15] As a consequence of its focus on ceremonial, this text gives only superficial attention to the political significance and development of the office of lord lieutenant. Robins's principal concern is to sketch the pageantry and conspicuous consumption of the Dublin Castle court. This phenomenon he traces to the lavish entertainments initiated by Essex and Ormond in the 1670s–80s, later revived in emulation of the growing extravagances of the Georgian court of St James by courtier-viceroys such as Grafton and Carteret in the 1720s. As the eighteenth century progressed and incumbents began to spend longer sojourns in Dublin, viceregal entertainments came to play an ever-greater place in the Dublin season around which Ascendancy social life revolved. Robins describes the years 1782–94 as the 'golden era' of the viceregal court in both the opulence of its ceremony (epitomised by the establishment of the Order of the Knights of St Patrick in 1782) and the frequency and hedonism of its balls, levees, feasts and other courtly entertainments.[16] The intense political crises of the later 1790s, and the reconstitution of Dublin Castle as a military citadel encircled by revolutionary dangers, cast a pall over its previous excesses. Although the Castle was refurbished and courtly entertainments revived there and at the Viceregal Lodge in Phoenix Park under Hardwicke and Richmond in the early nineteenth century, the depleted post-Union Dublin season, the developing social aspirations of the Catholic nouveau-riche bourgeoisie, and the growing tensions between the Protestant Ascendancy and the British executive, tended in Robins's view to render the Dublin court a more contested space as well as a pale imitation of its previous self. Despite the flamboyance of free-spending figures such as Marquess Wellesley and the earl of Eglinton, and the increasing formalisation and reinvention of viceregal ritual under the direction of the Ulster king-at-arms from the 1850s, Robins concludes that it never recovered its former glories before its ignominious extinction.[17]

Many studies of Irish politics and of British-Irish relations address the activities of individual holders of the lord lieutenancy, and there are a number of biographies of some of the more prominent incumbents, although scholarly discussions of the institution in its own right and its constitutional relationship with the British government are sparse.[18] Overviews of the structures and shifting dynamics of the Irish executive, including brief attempts to define the role of the lord lieutenant, are to be found for the later seventeenth century in a short but focused study by J. C. Beckett, and for the eighteenth century in J. L. McCracken's contribution to the *New History of Ireland*, and in R. B. McDowell's monograph study of post-1760 politics.[19] The administrative structure in the Union period, which saw radical fluctuations in power relationships between lords lieutenant, chief secretaries and under secretaries, is introduced in McDowell's *The Irish Administration*, while the developing tensions within the Dublin Castle executive in the second half of the nineteenth century have been skilfully dissected by Kieran Flanagan.[20] In addition to these surveys, a few detailed accounts of individual viceroyalties, including those of Wharton, Townshend and Eglinton, have appeared in article form.[21]

With a few exceptions, literature on the social and political activities of the vicereines is also limited. Ishbel, Lady Aberdeen, has attracted most attention, due in part to both the independence and strength of her character as well as to the existance of an extensive archive and the colourful autobiographical publications she co-authored with her husband.[22] She plays a prominent role – as the 'Lady Microbe' of separatist polemics – in Patrick Maume's contribution to this volume. Diane Urquhart has written on the role of Theresa, sixth marchioness of Londonderry (like several of the 'ladies of Londonderry' a significant political actor in her own right), in securing the viceroyalty for her husband in 1886 and shaping the agenda of his tenure and subsequent political career.[23] Not all viceroys were accompanied by vicereines – a number were unmarried or widowers and relied on other female relatives or connections to fulfill certain courtly functions and promote charitable and 'patriotic' objects – but the viceroyalty clearly incorporated a familial dimension unusual in the great offices of state. This is an area that needs further research.[24]

The essays in the current collection approach the lord lieutenancy from a number of different directions, some emphasising the political, others the cultural and philanthropic aspects of the office; a number trace its development over a *longue durée*, others illuminate it through more focused attention to particular moments in its history. What unites them is an attempt to answer the question posed by Theo Hoppen – 'what was the lord lieutenancy for?' It is hardly surprising that no single answer can be identified for the entire period, reflecting the range of facets of the office over time and its differing meaning to a range of constituencies in Ireland and Britain.

Although the principal *raison d'être* of the lord lieutenancy was always to represent the English and later British monarch in Ireland, this did not always entail unpopularity (whether personal or institutional) on the part of those outside the traditional political and social elite of Ireland. Republican separatists may have denounced the viceroyalty as an emblem of oppressive and discriminatory colonial rule, but their moments of political ascendancy (in the later 1790s and after 1916) were brief, if ultimately decisive, in reshaping constitutional relations between the islands. The very intensity of anti-viceregal invective manifested against conciliatory incumbents such as the 7th earl of Carlisle and Lord Aberdeen highlights not universal antagonism on the part of Irish Catholics, but a perceived need to combat the ambivalence towards the office of lord lieutenant on the part of many through strident propaganda. Catholic enthusiasm for a Jacobite viceroy had been demonstrated under Tyrconnell in 1687–9, and while this memory may have faded in the penal era that followed, elite Catholic engagement with reformist lords lieutenant developed in the latter half of the eighteenth century, and the potential for a 'pro-Catholic' viceroy to be lauded as a popular hero was demonstrated in the Fitzwilliam episode of 1795. Similar moments of unlikely popularity, sometimes involving tumultuous street politics, were witnessed in the next century at various points during the incumbencies of Bedford, Wellesley, Anglesey, Mulgrave and Bessborough. Daniel O'Connell gave viceregal functions his imprimatur when he believed engagement best served his political objects, while reserving the right to excoriate (mostly Tory) lords lieutenant as local tyrants enforcing the will of Westminster. Constitutional nationalists as well as 'patriotic' Irish Tories rallied to the defence of the institution as a distinctly 'Irish' constitutional form in the face of abolitionist initiatives in the 1830s–60s, and if Home Rulers were more wary of the office in the aftermath of the strong association of Lord Spencer with coercive policies during the land war, Aberdeen in 1886 and the 'constructive Unionist' viceroys who followed made great efforts to regain Catholic confidence. If the slur 'Castle Catholic' was one of the most potent in the separatist arsenal, it was deployed with such frequency precisely because the Castle had – at least superficially – moved so far from the religious and political exclusivity it had once embodied. Nevertheless, as the formal apogee of a governing structure that many Catholics continued to regard as tainted by the stain of colonialism and religious partiality, and as the ultimate upholder of the sword of coercion (as had been manifest in the 1790s, 1848, 1867, 1881–2 and 1916–22), the relationship between the lord lieutenant and the majority community in Ireland remained ambivalent at best.[25]

The title of 'lord lieutenant' and the chief governorship and viceroyalty of Ireland were not always synonymous, and the delineations of the office evolved over a prolonged period. In the opening contribution to this collection, Ciaran Brady notes that the title of 'king's lieutenant' had been employed very sparingly in the medieval period, and in the century following 1541 the specific commission of 'lord lieutenant' was restricted to only four of the sixty appointments, the great majority holding the inferior title of 'lord deputy'. This reflected concern in London about the greater aggregation of autonomous power implied by the lieutenancy. Despite this sensitivity over titles, the chief governors of Ireland were, in this period, in possession of extensive prerogative powers and expected to be the active agents of Crown policy in political, judicial and (when required) military affairs. Brady's review concludes with a study of the policies of a prominent and controversial lord lieutenant, the earl of Strafford (although he was elevated to that distinction from the deputyship just three months before his impeachment), which plunged the kingdoms of Ireland and England into constitutional crisis in 1640–1.

The narrative of the development of the lord lieutenancy is taken forward by Charles Ivar McGrath from the Restoration of 1660 to the accession of George I in 1714. These unsettled years witnessed a number of different phases. The first saw the emergence of the primacy of the office of lord lieutenant in the practical governance of Ireland, particularly through the formative role played by an Irish magnate, James Butler, marquess of Ormond. Initially appointed lord lieutenant in 1643 and subsequently the upholder of the royal interest in Ireland during the civil wars, Ormond returned from exile in 1661 and was in office for fourteen of the next 23 years. The pattern of appointing high-ranking executive officers for sustained periods as the king's representative in Ireland was broken by the Glorious Revolution and the brief personal appearances of the rival monarchs on Irish soil in 1689–90. Abandoning Stuart modes of governance, William III and his ministers subsequently preferred to rule Ireland through panels of lords justices or short-term deputyships, thus avoiding the concentration of power in the hands of one man. This proved to be not entirely satisfactory, and from 1700, with the appointment of the earl of Rochester as lord lieutenant, the practice of promoting a prominent political figure to the sole governorship was revived. As McGrath concludes, a different pattern, which continued for much of the eighteenth century was established in the reign of Queen Anne; although the second duke of Ormond was to hold his father's office (one he greatly desired) in 1703–7 and 1710–13, her other appointees were English noblemen of high rank, who were often reluctant and brief visitors to Dublin and who transferred their authority to deputies or lords justices during their extended periods of absence.

James Kelly then takes the history of the viceregal office forward through the eighteenth century and several distinct periods of development. For the first few decades after 1714, incumbents were essentially non-resident part-timers, grandees and often courtiers, who were content to leave the practicalities of governance to Irish subordinates and make only occasional forays to Dublin. Their mid-century successors, such as the 3rd and 4th dukes of Devonshire and the 4th duke of Bedford, may have had more substantial political weight, but reliance on Irish undertakers (including the speaker of the Irish Commons as one of usually three lords justices) had become entrenched in the management of the Irish parliament and patronage. This pattern was radically altered from 1767 with the appointment of a resident, active and executively minded lord lieutenant, Lord Townshend, charged with dispensing with the 'undertakers' and taking Irish governance into his immediate hands. If not all his successors were equally capable, and the chief secretary emerged as the viceroy's principal agent in managing an increasingly restive parliament, residency nevertheless became the established norm, with important consequences for the Irish court as well as politics.

Toby Barnard, who has published elsewhere on the development of the post-Restoration Irish court in comparative context, focuses in this volume on the role of later seventeenth and eighteenth-century viceroys in promoting Irish cultural life.[26] His conclusion is that, despite the attentions of eulogists and other seekers of viceregal patronage, the incumbents in this period tended to lack both the understanding of the Irish environment they might have acquired through a settled residency and usually also the inclination to take a leading role in promoting cultural endeavour. While this may have changed to a certain extent in the era of viceregal residency that began with Townshend in 1767, and certain nineteenth-century incumbents such as Mulgrave and Carlisle certainly saw themselves as cultural innovators, the Irish court played only a limited part in cultural development at the best of times.

Gillian O'Brien brings the pre-Union section of the book to an end with a detailed study of the lord lieutenancy in the political and social turmoil that characterised the 1790s. The four viceroys of this decade encountered, with varying degrees of success, the revival of the 'Catholic question' in Irish politics, sectarian polarisation, and a popular republican movement that ultimately resorted to open rebellion supported belatedly by French military intervention. After the spectacular failure of Fitzwilliam's attempt to act autonomously of both Westminster and the Ascendancy elite as a reforming proconsul, Lord Camden reverted to close reliance on the prime minister's wishes, and when these could not be ascertained, the views of his clique of Dublin Castle advisers. With Dublin Castle fortified and aggressive military 'pacification' authorised by the viceroy, the role of lord lieutenant appeared by 1797 to have reverted to that of quasi-military governor of a rebellious island. This appeared to be confirmed by the appointment in 1798 of the first military viceroy for over a century (and one who had been previously governed a conquered colony to boot). However, Cornwallis – along with Prime Minister Pitt and able chief secretary Castlereagh – was fully committed to what they hoped would be a constitutional settlement to the Irish question, a legislative (but not executive) union.

An analytical overview of the lord lieutenancy between the Union and its eventual abolition in 1922 is provided next by Theo Hoppen. The very survival of the institution was, he argues, emblematic of the ambiguities of the Anglo-Irish relationship under the Union, and its functions fluctuated radically in consequence of both the vagueness of the instructions issued to viceroys and the endemic power struggles within the Castle and between London and Dublin. His essay ranges widely across the period, addressing themes such as maintenance of law and order (and the frequent resort to coercion by viceregal proclamation); administrative oversight and efficiency (or more commonly the lack thereof); display, entertainments and patronage; appointment policies and the often poor relations with the prime minister, home secretary and cabinet. Hoppen is struck by how many of the Union viceroys appear totally unsuited for the position, singling out Wellesley, Carlisle and Aberdeen in particular for criticism of their executive weakness. At the same time, it was the structural imbalance resulting from both cabinet and parliament being located in London (and hence the growing importance of the chief secretary who attended the latter and sometimes also the former) that rendered the lord lieutenancy increasingly dysfunctional. What kept it going, he concludes, was a combination of the failure of elites to agree on a workable replacement system, and the ingrained conservatism of British political culture that preferred to tolerate anachronism rather than engage in rational innovation.

The remaining four chapters consider a number of moments in the Union era, addressing with greater detail some of the themes raised in Hoppen's overview. Peter Gray considers the attempts made by Whig viceroys in the period 1835–47 to popularise the institution through engaging with Catholic mass politics. The strategy of seeking to render the governance of Ireland religiously 'neutral' through dispensing with reliance on the Protestant political elite began after 1767 as the administration sought to manage Ireland directly without resort to 'undertakers' (with mixed success). Fitzwilliam's attempt to bid for the support of the resurgent Catholic political movement in the mid 1790s was poorly considered and catastrophic in outcome; later attempts to conciliate majority opinion by Wellesley and Anglesey were half-hearted and counterbalanced by more conservative political forces. The Mulgrave and Ebrington lord lieutenancies of 1835–41 stand out as a rare moment in which a united Irish administration, with support from London, engaged in a concerted campaign to build Irish Catholic political support for a reforming Union state around the slogan of 'justice to Ireland', at the cost of widespread alienation of much (but not all) of Irish Protestant opinion. This essay considers the centrality of the viceroyalty to this initiative – not least in deploying an element of theatricality under Mulgrave. Although it was undermined by Whig loss of office in 1841 and subsequently by the ravages of the Famine and the resort to coercion against agrarian and republican unrest in 1848, the popular support manifested towards the Irish Whig Lord Bessborough during his brief lord lieutenancy in 1846–7 indicates that this attempt to popularise the institution might not have been entirely doomed.

Attempts to revive the ideal of a 'popular' viceroyalty were made in the 1850–60s under the former chief secretary Lord Carlisle, and in a rather different and short-lived Tory-populist mode under Eglinton. As James Loughlin demonstrates in his essay, this approach was again essayed, and not without some success, by the constructive Unionists Cadogan and Dudley, and then by the Liberal Lord and Lady Aberdeen, in the later 1890s and Edwardian period. Loughlin traces a late flowering of a 'welfare viceroyalty' in Ireland, echoing the development of a welfare monarchy in England and connected to it through the promotion of a number of successful 'non-political' royal visits to the island. The period after 1886 saw the abandonment of any attempt to revive the model of the executive lord lieutenancy so strongly associated with Lord Spencer in Gladstone's first and second ministries, which had drawn the office into political contestation with nationalists and strongly associated it and Dublin Castle with coercion. Although the contest for real executive authority in Ireland had finally been abandoned by the post-Spencer viceroys, they retained their ceremonial and patronage roles – and these, Loughlin concludes, became ever more important in both the moderate Unionist and Liberal strategies to retain the British-Irish constitutional tie (with or without Home Rule). This was recognised as a threat and challenged by separatist nationalists. The sheer volume of the press and verbal vitriol cast at the Aberdeens by Arthur Griffith and his allies after 1905, the subject of Patrick Maume's contribution, indicates the intensity of hostility aroused by their version of viceregal welfarism. The energetic if rather eccentric viceregal couple worked hard to make themselves popular (with limited success in Ulster, despite the lord lieutenant's Presbyterianism), but were subjected to sustained lampooning and denunciations. Like much separatist propaganda, this assault on the viceroyalty probably had less public impact before 1914 than its authors would have wished, but it did highlight the existence of a distinct and growing political faction that would tolerate neither lord lieutenant nor the British constitutional link the office embodied.

The last chapter, by Keith Jeffery, considers the end of the lord lieutenancy amid the rapid radicalisation of Irish politics following the Easter Rising and the Sinn Féin electoral victory of 1918. The crisis provoked a final abortive attempt to restore the viceroy to the role articulated by the duke of Wellington in 1850 as its ultimate rationale, as the principal guarantor of security against domestic insurrection.[27] The appointee of 1918, Field Marshall Lord French, former commander of the British Expeditionary Force in France, proved incapable of overseeing the introduction of conscription or of quelling the republican political and military insurgency, and was quickly sidelined (and he narrowly escaped assassination by the IRA on several occasions). The final throw of the die brought to office the only Catholic incumbent since the seventeenth century, the English Tory aristocrat Lord FitzAlan, in 1921.[28] A conciliatory figure, FitzAlan's principal role was to oversee the endgame brought about by the Treaty negotiations and the implementation of partition. When he stood down in December 1922, transferring any residual duties to the governor generals of the new Irish Free State and of Northern Ireland, an institution which had been at the centre of British governance of Ireland since the sixteenth century, and whose antecedents can be traced back to Henry II's Irish intervention in 1171, came unceremoniously to an end.

Notes

1 See especially James Loughlin, *The British Monarchy and Ireland: 1800 to the Present* (Cambridge, 2007); James H. Murphy, *Abject Loyalty: Nationalism and Monarchy during the Reign of Queen Victoria* (Washington, DC, 2001).

2 K. Theodore Hoppen, 'An incorporating union? British politicians and Ireland, 1800–30', *English Historical Review*, 123 (2008), pp 328–50.

3 H. B. Parnell, Memo on the abolition of the lord lieutenancy, 1834, Southampton University Library, Congleton Papers, Ms 64/18/7.

4 See Peter Gray, '"Ireland's last fetter struck off": the lord lieutenancy debate 1800–67', in Terrence McDonough (ed.), *Was Ireland a Colony?* (Dublin, 2005), pp 87–101.

5 Larcom memo on Irish government, 21 Mar. 1858, National Library of Ireland, Dublin, Larcom Papers, Ms 7504/47; Larcom memo 'Query – can Ireland be governed out of Ireland?', 1 Oct. 1860, ibid., 7504/77.

6 Gray, 'Ireland's last fetter struck off'.

7 Miles Taylor, 'The Irish lord lieutenancy and the imperial viceroys', unpublished paper, 2009.

8 See for example, an argument welcoming the rationalisation of British rule in India while rejecting the continuing viceroyalty in Ireland as an expensive anomaly, [Anon.], 'Double government', *Dublin University Magazine*, 51 (April 1858), pp 460–70.

9 *Freeman's Journal*, 6 Feb. 1858; Thomas H. Tracey, *The Irish Viceroyalty* (Dublin, 1864).

10 J. T. Gilbert, *History of the Viceroys of Ireland; With Notices of the Castle of Dublin and its Chief Occupants in Former Times* (Dublin, 1865).

11 For the context, see Gray, 'Ireland's last fetter struck off', and T. Hoppen's chapter, pp 132–57.

12 Charles O'Mahony, *The Viceroys of Ireland: The Story of the Long Line of Noblemen and their Wives who have Ruled Ireland and Irish Society for over Seven Hundred Years* (London, 1912).

13 For a discussion of the latter, see Patrick Maume's chapter, pp 199–214.

14 O'Mahony, *Viceroys of Ireland*, p. 342.

15 Joseph Robins, *Champagne and Silver Buckles: The Viceregal Court at Dublin Castle, 1700–1922* (Dublin, 2001).

16 Ibid., pp 66–9; for the former, see also Peter Galloway, *The Most Illustrious Order: The Order of St Patrick and its Knights* (London, 2002).

17 Robins's discussion of the emergence of the heraldic office of Ulster king-at-arms,

occupied by Sir William Betham (1820–53), Sir J. Bernard Burke (1853–92) and Sir Arthur Vicars (1893–1908), as the interpreter and enforcer of a code of courtly etiquette at Dublin Castle, is a particularly valuable aspect of his text, Robins, *Champagne and Silver Buckles*, pp 125–31, 143–4, 156–60.

18 Modern biographical studies of incumbents include: Christopher Robbins, *The Earl of Wharton and Whig Party Politics, 1679–1715* (Lewiston, 1991); J. V. Beckett, *The Rise and Fall of the Grenvilles: Dukes of Buckingham and Chandos, 1710 to 1921* (Manchester, 1994); E. A. Smith, *Whig Principles and Party Politics: Earl Fitzwilliam and the Whig Party, 1748–1833* (Manchester, 1975); Iris Butler, *The Eldest Brother: The Marquess Wellesley, the Duke of Wellington's Eldest Brother* (London, 1973); Marquess of Anglesey, *One-Leg: The Life and Letters of Henry William Paget, first Marquess of Anglesey* (London, 1961); Diana Davids Olien, *Morpeth: A Victorian Public Career* (Washington DC, 1983); Richard Holmes, *The Little Field-Marshal: Sir John French* (London, 1981); Biographical sketches of a number of viceroys can also be found in the *Dictionary of Irish Biography* and *Oxford Dictionary of National Biography*.

19 J. C. Beckett, 'The Irish viceroyalty in the Restoration period', *Transactions of the Royal Historical Society*, 5th series, 20 (1970), pp 53–72; J. L. McCracken, 'The political structure, 1714–60' in T. W. Moody and W. E. Vaughan (eds), *New History of Ireland, IV: Eighteenth-Century Ireland* (Oxford, 1986), pp 57–6. To this can be added J. L. McCracken, 'The Irish viceroyalty, 1760–73', in H. A. Cronne, T. W. Moody and D. B. Quinn (eds), *Essays in British and Irish History in Honour of James Eadie Todd* (London, 1949), pp 152–68; R. B. McDowell, *Ireland in the Age of Imperialism and Revolution, 1760–1801* (Oxford, 1979), pp 94–100.

20 R. B. McDowell, *The Irish Administration 1801–1914* (London, 1964), pp 52–77; Kieran Flanagan, 'The Chief Secretary's Office, 1853–1914: a bureaucratic enigma', *Irish Historical Studies*, 24 (1984), pp 197–225.

21 Lewis A. Draile, 'The Irish viceroyalty of the earl of Wharton, 1708–1710', *Huntingdon Library Quarterly*, 15: 4 (1952), pp 393–431; Thomas Bartlett, 'The Townshend viceroyalty', in Thomas Bartlett and D. W. Hayton (eds), *Penal Era and Golden Age: Essays in Irish History, 1690–1800* (Belfast, 1979), pp 88–112; Alex Tyrell, 'A card king? The earl of Eglinton and the viceroyalty of Ireland', *The Historian*, 72: 4 (2010), pp 866–87.

22 Val McLeish, 'Sunshine and Sorrows: Canada, Ireland and Lady Aberdeen', in David Lambert and Alan Lester (eds), *Colonial Lives across the British Empire: Imperial Careering in the Long Nineteenth Century* (Cambridge, 2006); Maureen Keane, *Ishbel: Lady Aberdeen in Ireland* (Newtownards, 1999).

23 Diane Urquhart, *The Ladies of Londonderry: Women and Political Patronage* (London, 2007), pp 78–81.

24 There is some discussion of the role of vicereines in formal entertainments and promoting the consumption of Irish goods in Robins, *Champagne and Silver Buckles*, pp 14, 45, 54–5.

25 The case made by Lawrence McBride that the Dublin Castle administration was effectively Catholicised in the period after 1892 has recently been challenged by Fergus Campbell in *The Irish Establishment 1879–1914* (Oxford, 2009).

26 See Toby Barnard, 'The viceregal court in later seventeenth-century Ireland', in E. Cruikshanks (ed.), *The Stuart Courts* (Stroud, 2000), pp 256–65.

27 *Speeches of the Duke of Wellington on the Presentation of the Petitions against the Bill for the Abolition of the Lord Lieutenant of Ireland* (London, 1850).

28 It had been rumoured in 1910 that the Catholic Liberal Lord Granard might succeed Aberdeen, with his American-born wife becoming vicereine, but this had come to nothing, *New York Times*, 16 Jan. 1910.

CHAPTER 2

Viceroys? The Irish Chief Governors 1541–1641

Ciaran Brady

I

If one were to follow the title of this volume precisely, there is a sense in which this chapter is of little relevance to its primary concerns. For while the title of lord lieutenant began to become more common in the years after 1660, and became standard after the appointment of the earl of Rochester to that post in December 1700, in the period between 1541 and 1660, during which some eighty commissions of appointment to the Irish chief governorship were recorded, no more than nine of the appointees (or little more than ten per cent) were accorded the privileged title of lord lieutenant. When, moreover, the period under review is further refined, the irrelevance of the title to the Irish office is even more marked. Fully five of the nine commissions of lord lieutenancy were issued after 1641 (two of them being granted to the Cromwells, father and son), leaving only four especially privileged personages who had been granted the title from a total of sixty commissions to the chief governorship in the century before.[1]

The privilege enjoyed by these four should not, moreover, be exaggerated. For of the four, two (the earls of Essex and Strafford) were executed for treason, one (the earl of Devonshire) died under a cloud, and the fourth (the earl of Sussex) was almost ruined by his experience in Ireland. The title, though much sought after, was also most grudgingly given. Thus Sussex, the first governor to be so elevated in the period, secured the title only on his fourth commission of appointment after he had held office almost continually for over four years, and even then was given the ambiguous title of 'lieutenant general and lord deputy', a formulation that suggested a divergence between the roles of the lieutenant and those of the conventional title of the chief governor. Similarly, the commission received by Essex in 1599 recognised him as 'lieutenant general and general governor of Ireland', a title which, though more grandiose than that accorded Sussex, still maintained a separation of roles.[2] Lord Mountjoy was the first to be given the clear title of lord lieutenant upon his creation as earl of Devonshire, but also only on his fourth appointment to office; while Strafford was made lieutenant only after seven years in office, and three months before his recall. And then there were those who sought for the title and failed to get it. The several early drafts of instructions drawn up for Sir Henry Sidney on his nomination to the viceroyalty in 1565 assumed that he would retain the title of his predecessor Sussex, but when he was finally sworn in to office in the following year it was in the humbler status of lord deputy.[3] He didn't give up; several years later when, in the midst of the crisis of the Desmond rebellion, Sidney's name was again canvassed for the Irish governorship he made it a condition that this time he should have the title of lieutenant. He was never offered the job.[4]

The reticence of the Crown in according such an honour to its Irish chief governors was due to several factors. Considerations of court politics and court protocols played a role. It is significant that the title was conferred only upon senior peers and those whose position at the centre of court was already (apparently) established. To have granted it otherwise to ambitious aspirants such as Sidney or Wentworth, who would have used it to enhance their standing at the centre of power, might easily have proved a source of disturbance and suspicion at the royal court. But the ambivalence of the titles conferred upon Sussex and Essex also suggests a somewhat unresolved attitude on the part of the Crown toward the role of its chief Irish office. As deputies or governors, the viceroys were understood to be invested with the mix of political, administrative, judicial and policing powers traditionally associated with the office of the chief governor. To have added a title of lieutenancy to this might, in view of the largely military duties allotted to the county lords lieutenant in provincial England, have given an indication of the special military powers and authority required in exceptional and temporary circumstances, not intended as a permanent addition to the work of the chief governors .[5]

Two historical inheritances, one from the later middle ages, the other more recent, further contributed to this nervousness about the chief governor's title, especially in the later sixteenth century. Though it was almost equally rare in the middle ages, when the term 'justiciar' was most commonly used in denominating the principal Irish office, formulations not unlike 'lord lieutenant' were occasionally used.[6] Edward II's favourite Piers Gaveston, for example, was appointed the 'king's lieutenant of Ireland' in 1308. But this appointment was a sinecure, and Gaveston, who held the office for less than a year, was of course an absentee. As this suggests the title was normally an honorific one granted to a great – or favoured – courtier, or to a member of the royal family. Henry VII, for example, appointed his uncle Jasper to the office as a gift on his accession to the Crown in 1485 and then conferred it on his younger son Henry while he was still a baby in 1494, while Henry VIII himself bestowed it upon his illegitimate son Henry, duke of Richmond.[7] But there were some exceptions to this pattern. On rare occasions the title was conferred on a figure who was willing to take on the entire government of Ireland as a sub-contract from the Crown. Such was the case with the appointment of Roger Mortimer in the 1380s.[8] And it is possible that it was similar thinking that underlay the 9th earl of Kildare's impudent action in having himself appointed lieutenant to 'Edward VI', the impostor Lambert Simnel.

The last case of an appointed lord lieutenant in the years before 1541 is also the most interesting. Appointed king's lieutenant in March 1520, Thomas Howard, earl of Surrey, a senior and most trusted courtier to Henry VIII, was granted almost plenipotentiary powers to reassert Tudor rule in Ireland by all means necessary. At first the means seemed to be by force and Surrey's title appeared to sanction an overwhelmingly military approach. But as his viceroyalty developed and the realisation of the unlikely success of such a course became evident, Surrey's experience led him to take a marked turn toward conciliation, the 'sober drifts and politic ways' that was to issue finally in the grand constitutional initiative centring around the establishment of Ireland as a kingdom in 1541.[9]

This 'constitutional revolution' of 1541 was the second and more immediate historical development which rendered the concept of the 'lieutenancy' more problematic. Signalling the end of the long war of conquest and proclaiming the equality of native Irish and English colonists under a common Irish sovereign who was also independently king of England, the act for the kingly title seemed to render the notion of a lieutenancy in any of its previous manifestations quite redundant. The idea that it should be an honorific sinecure conferred upon a relative or favourite was, of course, unacceptable. And similarly suggestions that the new Irish sovereign was in need of an intervening person separating him from his Irish subjects, or, again, that Ireland might be taken out on indenture by a powerful magnate, were not to be entertained. And finally, the conception of the lieutenancy as a specifically military office charged with the particular duty of making war against the king's Irish enemies was hardly to be entertained in an era where conciliation and assimilation were supposed to have replaced confrontation and conquest.[10]

Such reasons underlay the reticence with which the great title was conferred and more importantly the manner in which the inferior title of deputy was considered honourable enough in itself. For in the new environment the role of the Irish chief governor as deputy was immeasurably enhanced. No longer the deputy of the lord of Ireland, or of the lieutenant of the lord of Ireland, he was in a real sense a viceroy – a proxy for a king of Ireland who was represented in his person.[11]

Thus whether the title conferred was lieutenant, deputy or merely lord justice, the office of the chief governor of Ireland was one of immense and incomparable authority. It was indeed the single most powerful office in the entire English governing structure, surpassing in its range of formal administrative, fiscal and judicial powers (though not, of course in its political influence) even the highest offices of state in the English central administration.

II

The Irish chief governor was, to begin with, head of the largest civil and military establishment within the Tudor regime outside central government. His powers of executive appointment extended through a whole range of military appointments – garrison commanders, constableships, senechalships, ordnance officers, and temporary military commissions – as well as through an equally large range of lesser appointments in the civil, legal and financial administration of the government in Dublin. Major executive appointments in Ireland – those of lord chancellor, vice-treasurer, chief justices, and other senior positions in chancery and exchequer – remained formally in the hands of the Crown; but even here, an Irish viceroy could, if he played the game deftly, exercise a decisive influence over these appointments as well.[12]

The political, military and diplomatic powers of the governor were remarkably extensive. He might proclaim rebels, make outlaws, make war, negotiate peace, extend pardons and levy support from the English community in Ireland for all his efforts. In all of such decisions the viceroy was supposed to take advice from the Irish council. But the diverse and diffuse nature of that body, which officially included noble, ecclesiastical and judicial members of the old colonial community (not all of whom were regular attendees) as well as English administrative and legal appointees, usually allowed the governor ample opportunity for manipulation and management. Such control was by no means guaranteed, and there were critical occasions of dispute between the governors and their council which shall be noted below. For the greater part, however, most governors of this period demonstrated an assured ability to exert their will over the council.[13]

As chair of the council the governor also exercised extensive judicial powers. The Irish council did not formally sit as a court of equity, along the lines of the early Tudor English innovation, Star Chamber, until the establishment of the parallel institution of Castle Chamber in 1560. Prior to this it sat frequently to hear and determine important cases; and while the governor was expected in these circumstances to take council from his law officers, his personal influence over the determination of cases and the enforcement of judgments could, if shrewdly deployed, be decisive.[14]

Independently of the council, and indeed of the treasury and exchequer, the governor also enjoyed considerable autonomy in matters of finance. The management of his household, which normally included a substantial element of the garrison, was entirely a private matter concerning which the vice-treasurer or other Crown officials lacked any role. And while the governors usually complained that the running of their household was a cause of huge financial loss, it also gave them remarkable freedom in negotiating victualling, maintenance and other service contracts with the local community in a manner that offered both financial and political opportunity.[15] In addition to his private affairs, the governor enjoyed the power to issue grants and leases and reversions of leases of Crown lands, though his decisions had to be registered in the exchequer. More importantly, as the Crown's principal military officer, the governor enjoyed by delegation the power to exact purveyance and scutage, the prerogative rights to commandeer goods and demand payment in lieu of military service.[16] And finally, though less often noticed, the governor had acquired over time the right through custom and practice to issue concordatums, or orders authorising the issue and receipt of payments of often substantial sums for particular purposes.[17]

In the decades before 1534, Irish governors had occasionally been granted license to summon parliament and to prorogue it at will. Such an extraordinary constitutional power was, however, in large part an historical anachronism derived from the governor's role as the protector of the lordship of Ireland and the promoter of the original conquest. Long before the permanent resumption of English control over Irish government in the 1530s such a power had been significantly diminished both by statutory restrictions, most notably Poynings' Law, and by practical political intervention from England.[18]

The establishment of continuous rule from Whitehall, which occurred in the wake of the Kildare rebellion, thus resulted in a permanent reduction of the Irish governor's autonomy. After 1534 no governor would henceforth assume the right to summon a parliament without express instruction from the Crown. And with the increase in the number of English-born administrators and soldiers serving the Crown, the viceroy's potential to exercise autonomy in his decision making was correspondingly reduced. The creation in 1560 of a new office of secretary of state, with responsibilities to report directly to the privy council in Whitehall, was also intended as a check on the governor's executive independence. But such restraints were irksome only in exceptional cases. In their initiation and development of legislative programmes the governors usually enjoyed the full support of Whitehall, which normally acted as means of constraining the effects of parliamentary opposition rather than supplementing it. The addition to the Irish council of newly arrived English Crown servants, suspicious of and suspected by the local political elites, usually added to rather than diminished the practical influence of the viceroy. Epitomising this process, the Irish secretary remained for most of the period highly supportive of (and frequently submissive to) the governor.[19]

Such potential restraints were in any case also accompanied by a massive increase in the character and extent of responsibility which was then imposed on the English chief governor in Ireland. After the attainder and destruction of the house of Kildare in 1536–7 the governor was, in the first place, charged with the responsibility of re-imposing English government in the land without the support and in face of the hostility and suspicion of the single most powerful political forces in the island, the nationwide Geraldine network of alliance and clientage. In this he might count on the support of the equally widespread but rather less powerful network centring on the house of Ormond, but any such aid would come at a price.[20] In addition the new English governor was at exactly the same time charged, along with the newly appointed archbishop of Dublin, with the unprecedented task of overseeing and enforcing major changes in the organisation and character of the church in Ireland attendant upon King Henry's break with Rome, the establishment of royal supremacy over the church in his dominions and the introduction of several liturgical and procedural changes within the structure of the church in Ireland.[21]

It was in the context of this obligation to undertake an unparalleled experiment in innovation – the enforcement of a nationwide policy of conformity and uniformity over the church – that a further exceptional responsibility was placed in the hands of the governor in the 1540s. This was the task of rolling out an extensive and complex diplomatic initiative under which all of the great provincial and local dynasties in Ireland would be peacefully assimilated as subjects of the king of England, equal under the law to their old English-Irish rivals, under the aegis of a dual monarchy proclaimed in the act for the kingly title of 1541.

The desirability of establishing a new and direct relationship with the great powers of provincial Ireland had been in Henry VIII's mind since early in his reign. But it was the compound crisis of the political vacuum created by the destruction of the Geraldine leadership and the need to repudiate the sanction given by Rome under the papal bull *Laudabiliter* (1154) to Henry II to conquer Ireland, that gave renewed urgency to this project. Under the terms of the act for the kingly title passed in the Irish parliament the ancient war of conquest, long abandoned in practice, but still legally operative, was completed. The native Irish had surrendered and offered allegiance, and the lord of the conquerors had not only received them to mercy and pardon but had graciously condescended to be their Irish sovereign, independently of his sovereignty of the people of England. This new Irish sovereignty was, however, to be far from independent of England. The two kingdoms were from henceforth to be indissolubly linked in the person of the English monarch. And all of the laws, institutions, social structures, religious practices and cultural mores which were distinctive to England were gradually to be introduced into Ireland, wholly displacing any alternative forms that existed there. The aim of the new project was not the revival and continuation of the old military conquest, but the inauguration of a sustained programme of acculturation whose ultimate purpose was the fabrication of a little England in Ireland.[22]

The constitutional necessities and strategic advantages of this 'revolution' in royal policy were clear, but the practical ramifications of the aspiration peacefully to absorb the native and colonial elites of the island under the auspices of a new united Irish kingdom were formidable in the extreme. Such a massively ambitious exercise in political change would have been demanding under any conditions, but given the highly unfavourable conditions obtaining in the country in the wake of the Geraldine rebellion and the rising disaffection within the English Pale with the ecclesiastical changes of the early Reformation, it could hardly have been introduced under less auspicious circumstances. And given furthermore the extremely rudimentary, under-financed, unstable and endemically corrupt nature of the English administrative system which was charged with the execution of the project, it is surprising that anyone thought the matter feasible in the first place.[23] That so many figures sought and accepted appointment to the Irish office, and that, following the failures of their predecessors, so many continued to devise ways of bring it to completion, is a testimony not only to the audacity, ambition and fool-hardiness of the early-modern English political elite, but also to their continued confidence in the special capacity of the Irish viceroyalty to serve its purpose.

III

In the century following the inauguration of the kingdom of Ireland as a legal entity, a number of distinct strategies may be seen to have been adopted by the English chief governors in order to establish it as a reality. The first was the great diplomatic initiative launched by Sir Anthony St Leger, the viceroy under whose government parliament had been summoned and the act for the kingly title passed. Known subsequently to historians (but not by contemporaries) as the policy of 'surrender and regrant', this initiative required St Leger to traverse the island, initiating – and in several cases concluding – negotiations with the greater and lesser lords in each of the four provinces. As part of these treaties the Lords agreed to surrender all their lands, seigneuralties and feudal rights on one side of an indenture, only to have these returned to them in full on the other side with the royal imprimatur, usually with a new title of nobility (or in some cases a knighthood) and sometimes with a personal audience with the king at court.

Though the speed and urgency with which this flurry of diplomatic activity occurred rendered it impossible for St Leger and his local advisers fully to address or even appreciate the political, social and cultural complexities of the dynasties with which they were dealing, 'surrender and regrant' was neither as naive nor as crudely cynical as has sometimes been assumed. St Leger was a shrewd political operator with considerable experience at the white-hot centre of Henrician court politics and his service as a royal commissioner in Ireland in 1537–8 had given him a real grasp of the difficulties of post-Geraldine Irish politics. His choice of figures with whom to come to terms was deliberate – he elected to conciliate O'Neill (made earl of Tyrone in 1542) rather than O'Donnell, O'Toole rather than O'Byrne, and most importantly to recognise the highly dubious claims of the de facto earl of Desmond against the protests of the closest allies of English government in Ireland, the house of Ormond. In manoeuvres of this kind St Leger can be seen to have been exploiting the instability of Irish politics in order to gain maximum influence for himself which, given the minuscule nature of his own military forces, was the only practical strategy available. In addition to the diplomatic opportunities afforded by the unstable nature of Irish dynastic politics in the early 1540s, St Leger was able to exploit the powers given to him under the royal supremacy to conduct a lavish and generous distribution of confiscated monastic lands to the local elites (mostly in Leinster and Munster) in a manner that was intended to reassure these powers that, far from challenging them, royal government was intent on securing and advancing their position.[24]

St Leger's measured exploitation of diplomatic and financial influence in order to construct a loyal following to the Irish king from among the indigenous elites was deftly executed during the reign of Henry VIII, and his special relationship with the king enabled him not only to establish a direct relationship between major Irish powerbrokers such as Con Bacach O'Neill and the king, but also to withstand a number of challenges both from within his own administration (in classic viceregal style) and from his disappointed former allies among the Butlers of Ormond.

The strength of St Leger's strategy of reconstructing the dynastic politics of Ireland around the concept of the king's loyal following lay in the fact that it centred around a particular king, and a very forceful monarch at that. During the mid-1540s St Leger's success in encouraging the emergence from within the former factional divisions of Ireland of a king's party was substantial. But after King Henry's death in 1547 and for the rest of the remaining century the kingdom of Ireland was without a king, that is a monarch who was willing to assume a direct and sustained connection with the notional Irish kingdom. In this context St Leger's hopes of nurturing an embryonic king's party in Ireland withered. The immediate consequence of the disappearance of an Irish king in the mid-Tudor years was the alteration and diminishment of the role of the Irish viceroy. In the ten years between 1548 and 1558 no less than thirteen commissions of appointment to the Irish chief governorship were issued.[25] Appointments to the office, such as those of Sir Edward Bellingham and Sir James Croft, were frequently made on an emergency basis, to curb the threat of rebellion and forfend against invasion. As the political status of the viceroys diminished, and their priorities were altered, so their capacity to win loyalty through largess disappeared, and the governors became a positive drain on the resources of the country.

Yet, while the new pressures acting upon the viceroyalty rendered the diplomatic methods of St Leger impossible and plunged his personal style of factional manipulations, flexible arrangements and secret deals into disrepute, they did not deter the mid-Tudor holders of the office from the principal viceregal task of making Ireland English. From the mid-1550s a new approach to the enforcement of the policy of anglicisation associated with the viceroyalties of two young and ambitious courtiers, Thomas Radcliffe, earl of Sussex, and Sir Henry Sidney, emerged. Sometimes attributed (without much foundation) to the growing influence of Spanish colonial practices in the New World, and sometimes to the onset of a hardening Protestant nationalism in England, the new approach grew directly out of a continuing determination to see the original Henrician aim of establishing English legal, administrative and social structures in Ireland completed in a manner that was informed by the failures of the 1540s, and by an acute awareness of the unstable and deficient nature of Tudor government as a whole.[26] In the eyes of the new governors, it was imperative that politics – the deals negotiated and re-negotiated by St Leger – should be subordinated to law, and that conciliation – through reward and opportunist manipulation – should be replaced by authority. The key to achieving this managerial revolution lay in institutionalism, in the reform and revival of existing institutions and in the creation of new institutions to fill special needs. The restocking of the central courts with new personnel, the revival of circuits and assizes, the establishment of Castle Chamber as a new central court of equity modelled on Star Chamber to enable the Irish council to hear and determine the cases of powerful subjects, and the introduction of regional councils in each of the four provinces – modelled on the council in Wales and in the north of England – were all considered to be central to the programme of institutional reform. In addition, the Irish parliament was to be employed as a means of introducing a large body of legislation designed to further the aim of anglicisation. As part of the determination of enforcing respect for law and the forms of law, all existing treaties with the leading dynasties of provincial Ireland were to be applied to the letter, and those who broke or rejected them were not to be bargained with but vigorously opposed and subjected to exemplary punishment. As a means of underlining this point exceptional miscreants, such as the O'Mores and O'Connors of the midlands, who took advantage of the crisis of the mid-Tudor period to launch a revolt against the Dublin government, were to be outlawed and their lands confiscated for plantation by loyal subjects.[27]

From the high perspective of the English nobility this was perhaps an honourable and commendable approach, and its combination of institutional reform with occasional exemplary displays of authority could also be seen as being quite consistent with the character of the earlier Henrician regime in England.[28] But it foundered spectacularly in practice on several grounds. First, despite the attempt to raise the viceroyalty above the level of political intrigue to that of forceful executive action, the viceroys themselves found it impossible to escape the web of factional machination either at the English court or in Ireland itself. The part which Sussex, as a scion of the old aristocracy, played in the campaign against the ascent of the royal favourite Lord Robert Dudley, though quite independent of his Irish service, inevitably affected assessment of the quality of that service at Court, as Dudley and his supporters moved to damage his reputation.[29] And, conversely, as one of Dudley's supporters, Sidney, once in office, found his service similarly exposed to a continuing stream of hostile comment from Dudley's enemies.[30]

Even without this inescapable complication the viceroys would have found it impossible to avoid engagement with the great Irish connections, the Geraldines and the Butlers. The rudimentary nature of the Tudor administration in Ireland, its military and financial weakness, its inability to source independently accurate political intelligence and effective practical support rendered them, as St Leger would have happily reminded them, ultimately dependent on the cooperation and complaisance of some elements within one or other of the great connections for which some form of recompense in the form of favour or protection would be required. Similarly, given the limitations of the regime's independent resources, any hope that they might keep their reformed and renewed institutions free from the taint of favour was naive; as in reality office holders were compelled to choose between the effectiveness of factional connection, and the impotence of splendid isolation.

Aside from all of these complexities, the viceroys, despite occasional successes, simply lacked the power to impose their authority by force. In the midlands the leadership of the O'Mores and O'Connors caved in before an unprecedented and unrepeated show of force organised by Sussex in the later 1550s. But the dispossessions ordered there were not fulfilled and the region remained a war zone for decades to come. Elsewhere, in regard to the O'Briens, the Fitzgeralds of Desmond, the Burkes of Clanrickard and Mayo, and above all the O'Neills, the governors' attempts to exert military intimidation proved repeatedly to be disappointing. In addition to all this, their chronic inability to stem a genuine invasion – the gradual extension of the Scottish MacDonald settlements in the Glens and Route of Antrim – was a further embarrassment.

In the mid-1560s Sussex's government was paralysed by a combination of factional intrigue and military failure – in particular his inability to subjugate the chief of the O'Neills and contestant to the earldom of Tyrone, Shane. But while Sidney succeeded in resolving (temporarily) the problem of O'Neill by intrigue and murder rather than by military defeat, he was to suffer in 1569–70 the humiliation of confronting an extraordinary combination of the great Irish factions in common revolt against him – a fate which all previous viceroys since the 1530s had avoided – even as he was introducing into the Irish parliament the most ambitious programme of institutional reform so far envisaged.[31]

Ironically, however, the revolt against Sidney and the defeat of institutionalism which it heralded was not quite fatal for the project of anglicisation. The extent to which Sidney learned from his ordeal was impressive. Having experienced the revolt of the Geraldines and the Butlers against Dublin rule, he fully appreciated the hugely destructive power of the great feudal alliances. Having likewise witnessed the wreck of his parliamentary programme, and the destruction of the first classically designed regional council introduced in Connacht, he recognised immediately the weakness of the policy of institutional reform. Yet in also registering the unmistakable success of Humphrey Gilbert and Sir John Perrot, the military commanders he had appointed to subdue the combined rebellion in Munster, who had quelled revolt by brutality, terror and atrocity, Sidney's mind gradually moved toward a boldly innovative way of addressing the problem of English rule in Ireland. Politics, law and authority had failed, he began to see, because each had been applied island-wide as a uniform solution to England's general problem. If a more carefully modulated address were developed based upon an analysis of the location of real power in the provinces and localities of Ireland, according to the practices conventionally deployed by the operators of the existing systems of clientage and faction, then the chief governor could exercise a direct and conclusive influence in regional politics. Acting neither as the representative of the English monarch, nor as the upholder and enforcer of English law, but as another player in the conventional game, prepared to employ the traditional techniques of violence, intimidation and protection to a degree that equalled or exceeded that employed by the lords, the governor might, as Gilbert and Perrot had shown, establish a position of real authority in any region.[32]

For the viceroy to have behaved in this way would have entailed, of course, a radical departure from the definition of his status as established by the kingship act of 1541. But for Sidney, developing his new plan for government in the mid-1570s, this was merely a necessary but temporary expedient. Unlike the military governors and the lesser captains acting in time of rebellion, the viceroy, having established his practical ability to determine affairs in each region, would use it to stabilise and consolidate existing power relations in a series of detailed agreements known as 'compositions'. At the heart of these compositions was taxation. Operating in the manner of the great lords themselves, the governor would interpret a willingness on the part of the lords and their subordinates to pay an agreed annual tax as a sign both of their professed allegiance and of their real power and standing in their communities. On this basis he would proceed to recognise political and social standing by the award of titles, and confirmations of tenurial legitimacy in the manner equal to (and by far more realistic than) that which had been essayed in the 1540s.[33]

The idea of using power – the threat of force rather than its application – in order first to measure and then to confirm the existing realities of power distribution amidst the lordships of provincial Ireland was audacious. Some may speculate that it signaled the creeping influence of Machiavelli over the development of Elizabethan policy in Ireland.[34] But whether such an influence is discernible or not, it is clear that this kind of policy was moving far beyond the conventional assumption of English political thinking into a position that seemed distinctly at odds with it. A political regime in which social standing and property ownership was measured by a prior demonstration of an ability to pay tax seemed to be in total contradiction to fundamental principles of the English constitution. The fact that such taxes would be measured and collected on an individual basis by viceregal order rather than by parliamentary consent was no less disturbing, and the assumption that such revenue raised would be used permanently to fund the institutions of central and regional administration and justice was laden with implication for the freedoms granted to all property-holding individuals under English law.[35]

Concerns that Sidney was moving to take viceregal government in Ireland toward a position that later commentators would identify as absolutism were further intensified by the approach which he adopted toward the implementation of that major but frequently neglected policy responsibility, the enforcement of the Reformation in Ireland. The division of responsibility for the management of ecclesiastical and religious change between the viceroy and the archbishops, which had been left undetermined from the outset, exercised a seriously debilitating effect on the advance of the process. Clashes between the viceroys and the archbishops were not uncommon, but they tended to arise over the viceroys' insistence that their secular responsibilities should take precedence over their ecclesiastical ones; and beyond accepting their constitutional responsibilities in the management of parliamentary legislation and the promulgation of proclamations, the viceroys were for the most inclined to leave the archbishops to their work. Sidney, however, was exceptional in his determination to address the problem of religious reform. His draft parliamentary programmes of the middle and later 1560s were heavily concerned with the matter, and Sidney expressed particular disappointment when his proposal to establish a university – a move which he regarded as essential to the success of the Reformation – was rejected by parliament. By the mid-1570s his impatience had intensified, and even as he was introducing his bold political strategy in regard to 'compositions', he also launched a radically new approach toward the advance of religious change which included a striking exposé of the state of the church of Ireland, and the establishment of a powerful ecclesiastical commission and a court of faculties both of which were designed to take real power for the enforcement of religious conformity over the laity and the clergy away from the archbishop of Dublin and place it in the hands of the viceroy.[36]

Sidney's dual threat to the constitutional rights of those who regarded themselves as the English-Irish and to the independent authority of the Church of Ireland generated a political crisis in 1578 that led to his recall. But the continuing attractions of his strategic démarche, especially for those with genuine experience of the nature of Irish political society, is evidenced in the programme for government devised by his former subordinate, Sir John Perrot, when he was appointed viceroy six years later. Perrot took over Sidney's idea of power-based compositions though with some modifications – he negotiated a compromise with the English-Irish of the Pale and, to accelerate progress, he chose to concentrate first on the most difficult challenge of all, the dynastic complexities of Gaelic Ulster. Like Sidney, Perrot also sought to advance the Reformation independently of the archbishop of Dublin, with whom he too came into violent conflict, by enforcing the oath of supremacy and by seeking the foundation of a university. Yet the radical implications of the Sidney-Perrot style of viceregal government once again proved too alarming, and Perrot also provoked a coalition of opposition from among the native Irish and English of Ireland, including, ominously in his case, a substantial number of the English members of the Irish council.[37]

The charge raised against Perrot after his recall that he had plotted treason against the Crown, was, though it ruined him, preposterous, even more so than the allegation earlier made against Sidney that he had sought 'to take the land to farm'. But exaggerated and politically motivated as they were, such accusations contained a grain of truth. For whether they had consciously acknowledged it or not, the adoption of the power-based strategy of reform by Sidney and Perrot entailed an acceptance of the disturbing fact that any successful attempt to establish a real and united kingdom in Ireland necessarily involved taking steps that would ultimately make it constitutionally and politically very different from the kingdom of England upon which it was supposedly modelled.

Though they were clear to the most perceptive minds – most notably and notoriously Edmund Spenser – the frightening implications of this realisation that England could only gain Ireland either peacefully by abandoning English culture, or violently by conquest were largely obscured in the storm of controversy that the reforming viceroys provoked around themselves.[38] The relative ease with which Sidney and Perrot were recalled helped stifle the most radical interpretations of what they had been about. More importantly, the major political crises which ensued upon their departure – the Munster rebellion of 1579–83, the threat of the Armada in 1588 and the deterioration of conditions in Ulster immediately thereafter – rapidly shifted attention both in Dublin and in Whitehall to more urgent matters.

That there was a direct connection between these crises and the composition strategies of the two viceroys is, however, clear. It was the sudden abandonment of Sidney's composition deal with the house of Desmond months after the earl had agreed to it that completely destabilised the fragile earldom and plunged most of Munster into rebellion. Even more seriously, it was the abandonment of Perrot's ambitious scheme for the restructuring of power-relations in Ulster which exacerbated existing tensions both within and between the great lordships of the region and precipitated the series of local revolts that were to combine into the great rebellion of the 1590s.[39] For the most part the connection between political dissolution and the abandonment of forceful reform was largely ignored at Whitehall, and to the extent that any connection was made at all, it was based upon a far more simple reassertion of another vice-regal priority which, it was believed in Whitehall, was both antecedent to and far more important than the commitment to anglicisation. This was the preservation and defence of England's territorial dominion in Ireland.

IV

That the defence of the English lordship from invasion and rebellion was the prime responsibility of the viceroy was an indisputable principle in the years before the great changes of the 1530s, even if it was frequently more honoured in the breach. But while the assumption of the reformist programme in the decades thereafter widened the powers and responsibilities of the viceroy, the idea that the defence of the realm was a pre-eminent duty which might have been regarded as inseparable from the constructive elements in the viceroy's work in the optimistic phases of a reform initiative, continued to be perceived as distinct and fundamental. It was this unresolved question of the relationship of the ancient priority of defence with the modern task of reform which contributed greatly to the destabilisation of the office throughout the sixteenth century. In the late 1540s and again in the early 1550s it was Whitehall's fear of rebellion in the midlands and of invasion from France and Scotland that led to St Leger's replacement with governors charged with military priorities.[40] In the later 1560s Sidney was compelled to abort his parliamentary programme in order to suppress rebellion in the midlands. In 1588 it was Whitehall's anxiety that Perrot was too engaged with his own reform project in Ulster to pay sufficient attention to an imminent Spanish invasion that precipitated his recall.

The alternating character of the Irish viceroy between being a representative of reform and an agent of English military security was seriously damaging to its political influence in several respects. At best it was sharply disappointing. Hard-line soldiers such as Bellingham, Lord Arthur Grey de Wilton (1580–2) and later Sir William Russell (1594–7) and Sir Thomas Burgh (1597) professed a very different view of their role than the pretensions of the reformers. These were military men sent to Ireland to conclude a military mission, but at least their attitude was unambiguous, and their tenure of office brief. A greater disturbance was provoked by viceroys such as Croft and, most notably, Sussex who claimed to be discharging both roles at once without any sense of incongruity. In this regard the ambiguous titles conferred upon Sussex in the early 1560s, referred to at the opening of this paper, were a disturbing sign of the degree to which the strategic and political priorities of the principal English office in Ireland remained incoherently perceived and unresolved at Whitehall.

This ambiguous view of the character of the viceroyalty was made even more acute by the conduct in office of a figure who occupied the chief governorship for longer than anyone since the resumption of English control over the office in the 1530s. This was Sir William Fitzwilliam (1560, 1571–5, 1588–94).[41] Having been among the vanguard of the young men who displaced the subtle and politic ways of the discredited St Leger, Fitzwilliam served as lord justice on a number of occasions in the late 1550s and early 1560s. It was not until 1571 that he attained to the honour of lord deputy. By then, having served for almost a decade as the Crown's vice-treasurer and treasurer-at-wars in Ireland (the latter another title with unresolved ambiguities), Fitzwilliam was a man in trouble. A long overdue audit of government expenditures in Ireland concluded in 1569 revealed a massive deficit, for a portion of which Fitzwilliam was, despite his personal connections (his sister was married to Secretary Cecil) held personally responsible.[42]

Nevertheless, his personal connections helped Fitzwilliam, despite his embarrassment, to office in the early 1570s and the late 1580s, and he used the position to reduce and eventually to recoup his losses by the adoption of a distinctive style. Eschewing any gesture toward the continuance of reform, in his first deputyship Fitzwilliam abandoned Sidney's plans for legislative reform, and in his second systematically dismantled Perrot's complex compositions. But while Fitzwilliam was averse to launching any great military initiative, he was nonetheless anxious to generate an atmosphere in which some emergency might imminently demand such an urgent military response. The advantages of such a stance to a viceroy in need of funds were obvious: his warnings of imminent danger required that the garrison over whose finances he retained control should be kept at a high level of preparedness and some expense, while indefinitely deferring the likelihood of actual expenditure. During his first term as deputy Fitzwilliam was required to generate his own emergencies; successively he provoked crises with the house of Desmond and the house of Kildare, and on one desperate occasion felt obliged to report an imminent invasion from the Ottoman Empire.[43] But in his second term of office he was presented with the superlative opportunity of a genuine invasion scare in the form of the Armada which enabled him to continue in his fabrication of an illusory crisis while a genuine catastrophe was, thanks to his own neglect, emerging before him.

Fitzwilliam's responsibility for the degeneration of political relations between the English government and the lordships of Ulster and Connacht was recognised even in his own time, but the extent to which it irreparably damaged the character of the viceroyalty was made clear only in the brief lord lieutenancy of the earl of Essex. Understandably neglected because of its short and ineffective character, Essex's viceroyalty epitomised the dilemma that had been implicit in the Irish chief governorship since the 1530s.[44] Appointed in the aftermath of the Ulster rebels' greatest victory, Essex was expected to make the appropriate military response. But as the head of a major English political connection he was also a figure of immense political potential most especially at this critical point when the death of the queen and a new succession was imminently expected. Driven between the immediate military imperatives and the powerful political potential of his office, Essex became paralysed by indecision – his only hope of resolving his dilemma resting apparently on the death of Elizabeth and the succession of James VI.

This inherent conflict between the viceroys' role as defender of England's security and promoter of England's culture in Ireland, which did so much to diminish the potential of the office, was accompanied by a further but more subtle contradiction in their position. Despite their title as monarch's deputy or lieutenant and despite the constitutional ambitions of some (such as Sidney and Perrot), the Irish chief governors were never in a real sense proxies for the king. As there never really was an Irish king distinguishable from the English monarch, so the king's representative could never reproduce the trappings of an Irish kingdom. There could be, in the first instance, no permanent Irish court. But even the prospect that such an environment might be occasionally and temporarily produced was precluded by the accident of the Tudors' dynastic succession. After 1553 there was no king, only a queen who was, or in the case of Elizabeth was for long expected to be, joined by marriage to a foreign sovereign with no direct interest in Ireland. Whether married or not, neither queen was expected to reside for long in or even to visit her Irish sovereignty. Equally serious was the fact that after 1547 the Tudor dynasty was without a prince of Wales (or possibly a prince of Ireland) who might have functioned occasionally to project the image of royalty in Ireland and to represent the interests of Ireland at the English court.

In the absence of any semblance of a royal presence, however illusory, some of the viceroys can be seen to have attempted to replicate something of the atmosphere of a royal court. In the 1540s, in the frenetic activity surrounding the sale and leasing of confiscated monastic properties, St Leger briefly reproduced the heady speculative days of the 1530s in the English court, and with similar though short-lived results: in both cases the bonanza was soon exhausted. In different ways Sussex and Sidney also attempted a projection of the majesty of the court, the former through official ceremonies, proclamations and printed proclamations; the latter through maintaining an hospitable house at Kilmainham, through majestic viceregal progresses and through the promotion of such exercises in literary propaganda as Campion's *Historie of Ireland* and Derricke's *Image of Ireland*.[45] For the most part, however, the viceroys didn't bother with such expensive initiatives, and no matter how forceful they might have been as individuals, the dignity of the office *per se* was rarely enhanced by their actions.

The authority of the viceroys' position was further depleted by the operation of Poynings' Law. Originally conceived in the 1490s as a curb on the autonomy of the viceroy, when it was assumed that the office would remain largely in the hands of local magnates such as Kildare and Ormond, this provision that no law passed in the Irish parliament would receive royal approval without prior ratification by the royal (later the privy) council at Whitehall proved something of a hindrance and an embarrassment after 1534 when the office was in the control of English officers. The delays in transmitting and ratifying bills were at least a nuisance and a temptation to further opposition and negotiation, and it was this reason that several viceroys charged with holding parliaments sought for and generally succeeded in getting a suspension of the law during the time of their parliament, but even this move, frequently contested in the Irish parliament, was not executed without difficulty.[46]

The concern of the viceroys to have Poynings' Law suspended was reflective of a deeper insecurity felt by all holders of the office in regard to the court at Whitehall. Though they occupied the most powerful post outside the court and the offices of central government, they were to a greater or lesser degree creatures of that system and dependent for their effectiveness in office on its support, which they could rarely count on for long without making due concessions to the interests of that system. The extent to which Sussex's and Sidney's very different strategies of reform were wrecked by the workings of court politics has already been alluded to, but this was a pattern common across the period between the 1530s and the 1600s. Lord Leonard Grey, the first post-Geraldine governor, survived against considerable opposition in Ireland, as long as he enjoyed the protection of the formidable Thomas Cromwell. But when Cromwell fell, so did he. St Leger enjoyed the confidence of Henry VIII himself and of the duke of Norfolk, but when Somerset came to power as regent he fell from office. His successor Bellingham, Somerset's appointment, did not survive the latter's eclipse. Fitzwilliam was badgered from office in 1575 by the court-based criticisms and insinuations mounted by Sidney. Perrot was ruined by the enmity which he aroused at Whitehall because of his perceived hostility toward the well connected undertakers and servitors of the Munster plantation. Essex's decision to abandon his post in 1599 was the result of his awareness of the machinations being applied behind his back by his great enemy Sir Robert Cecil.

The intensity of factionalism at court may not have been as sustained as earlier historians have assumed – though it often appears to be so from the point of view of the periphery. But even when such pressures did not issue in the recall or disablement of the viceroy, they did contribute greatly to the retardation of the office's potential. In the sixty-three years between the appointment of St Leger and the death of Elizabeth some fifty-five commissions of appointment to the office were issued, offering an average period of tenure of less than eighteen months. This simple statistic is somewhat misleading since those who wished to do most with the office were those who strove to stay longer in it, and those who had little interest in stayed for least time. However, the extent of chronic discontinuity is nonetheless remarkable, and the negative effect of low expectations of tenure in office on those necessary preconditions for the successful development of policy, such as the establishment of sustained modes of funding and supply, and the cultivation of a stable *cadre* of administrative and executive subordinates, though often unnoticed by historians, was of enormous significance.

The cumulative effect of these restraints upon the potential of the office as a vehicle for long-term political and cultural reform was necessarily to diminish that aspect of the post in contrast to its original defensive character, as successive failures in the reformist programme led to a gathering political and military crisis throughout the island. Thus in the closing years of the reign of Elizabeth, despite Essex's ineffectual gestures, it was this primary role that characterised the chief governorship.

Even after the suppression of the national revolt, it was, moreover, this characterisation of the post that prevailed. Significantly, Mountjoy, a figure whose connections in the country and whose view of its condition best placed him to resume a reformist role, elected instead to abandon the office almost as soon as military victory had been secured and to reserve for himself the role of representing Irish interests from within the Jacobean court.[47] In his absence, Sir Arthur Chichester, first as his deputy and soon as his successor as governor, revived the techniques of the security state as first practiced by Fitzwilliam in the 1570s and 1590s. Espying sedition, revolt and invasion everywhere, Chichester sought to sustain an environment where soldiers – the seneschals, garrison commanders and captains of bands who had defended the Crown and defeated the rebels – should not only be rewarded for their service, but continued to be recognised as the vital protectors of the English presence in Ireland. Presiding over an exhausted and defeated native population, and freed from the pressures of the intensive social dislocation which, thanks to Perrot's abortive efforts at reform in Ulster, had destroyed Fitzwilliam's last term in office, Chichester initially experienced little difficulties in promoting his concept of a garrison state. But it wasn't long before external forces began to intrude on this conservative (and repressive) idyll. The unexpected flight into exile of the earls of Tyrone and Tyrconnell in 1607 paved the way for a far more ambitious and capital intensive resettlement of Ulster than Chichester, with his care for the modest resources and horizons of the soldiers, had preferred to contemplate. He soon found himself in confrontation with the interests at Whitehall in much the same way as Perrot (with whom he had little else in common) had twenty-five years previously in regard to Munster. But whereas Perrot with his high views of the Irish office had resisted, Chichester yielded, working toward a compromise in which the soldier – or servitor – interest, including his own personal one, was given some place along with the big investors in the plantation of Ulster.[48]

A figure who was to occupy the viceregal office for almost eleven years, Chichester was also the first occupant of the post since 1534 to acquire any substantial interest in Irish land. The substantial estate which he was granted under the Ulster plantation gave him a more permanent stake in the management of the country's affairs, but also, unlike any of his predecessors, it identified him directly and permanently with a particular interest group within the politically and culturally divided kingdom of Ireland. During his unprecedentedly long term in office, the viceroyalty came to be seen primarily not as the means of uniting all of the island's inhabitants under a common sovereignty, but as a vehicle for the advancement of a particular, relatively novel and highly ambitious social group, the recently arrived English settlers, soldiers and administrators who now became known pejoratively as 'the New English'.

Reinforced by his promotion of less ambitious plantation projects in Wexford and elsewhere and his willingness to exploit the defective titles of natives in order to transfer parcels of land to small-scale English investors, the perception that Chichester was transforming the viceroyalty as a means for the advancement of the New English interest over that of the native Irish and Old English was sharpened by his determination to pursue another of the viceroy's major responsibilities – the enforcement of religious change. Though Sidney and Perrot had made efforts in this regard, the question of advancing reformation had been largely neglected in the crisis of the Nine Years War. While Sidney had concentrated his efforts on the reform of the clergy, Chichester was the first governor directly to attack the laity. By a rigorous enforcement of the oath of supremacy he forced many central and municipal officeholders to resign. By the issuing of mandates – letters under the royal prerogative – to leading figures within the community of the Pale demanding their attendance at church services he compelled many more to declare their recusancy and expose themselves to punitive fines. Those who have studied Chichester's conduct in regard to the enforcement of reformation are inclined to accept the sincerity of his intentions. Just as he was concerned to preserve the security of the state by means of garrisons and servitor-settlers, so, it is suggested, he was determined to suppress subversion hiding under the cloak of religious freedom. But however sincere his intentions, and despite the fact that the new English settler community also contained some secret Catholics, Chichester's religious policy was inevitably associated with his policy in relation to plantation and defective titles and interpreted as yet another exploitation of his office to undermine one community within the kingdom and advance the interests of another.[49]

Though Chichester both deliberately and inadvertently altered the character of the Irish chief governorship in relation to the political and social communities of Ireland, he was unable to modify its almost equally difficult relationship with Whitehall. Conscious that he had been unable to withstand the opposition which his originally modest plans for servitor plantations had aroused at court, Chichester, who before his appointment had had little contact with the centre of power, rapidly made his peace with the first great ministers of the Jacobean court, the earl of Salisbury and later the earl of Northampton. Chichester's compliance, his willingness to respond to the demands of the great courtiers in regard to land and office, and his lack of connection with any other potential rivals enabled him in his first years in office to enjoy a freedom from criticism and intrigue which would have been the envy of his Tudor predecessors.[50]

Chichester's good fortune was more the result of fortunate conditions at court than his own efforts. In the mid-1610s, as the power of Northampton waned, and the prospects of the new royal favourite, George Villiers, waxed, as the continuing expense of the Irish administration became an issue of increasing debate at court, and the viceroy's ability to offer promising projects to courtly speculators diminished, so Chichester's privileged status evaporated. Unlike his predecessors there was no coup or radical change of direction. Chichester went sick; his offer to resign was warmly accepted, and he was allowed quietly to retire to his Irish estates with the promise (not reneged on) of some favour in the future.

The ascendancy of Villiers (as duke of Buckingham) affected the character of English government in Ireland as it did everywhere else.[51] On the surface little difference in the post-1603 viceroyalty as established by Chichester could be seen. Chichester's successor, Oliver St John (1616–22), master of the ordnance in Ireland at the time of his appointment and a figure who had experience of service in the country since the 1590s, continued the practice of favouring the servitor interest. A sometime critic of Chichester, St John had previously made vague commitments to the reform of administrative and financial abuses, but owing his appointment to Buckingham, such aspirations always took secondary place to the requirement of satisfying the increasingly voracious demands of the English court.[52] His inability in these circumstances to stem the rising costs of Irish administration led to his denunciation in the English parliament of 1621, but Buckingham succeeded not only in protecting him from further criticism but in securing the appointment of another client, Henry Carey, Viscount Falkland, (1622–9) as his successor, under the pretext that he would oversee a root and branch reform of Irish government by means of a major royal commission.

Under St John and Falkland, and thanks largely to the ascendancy of the favourite Buckingham, the diminution of the status of the Irish viceroyalty seemed complete. No longer an office with great potential for the making of an Irish kingdom, nor even a means for the construction from within that kingdom of a dominant settler and soldier elite, it appeared to have been degraded into an occasional and disposable tool of English court politics. The final degradation of the office seemed to have been achieved when Falkland, following a desperate attempt to summon parliament without following the procedures of Poynings' Law, was recalled in disgrace and replaced by two of his principal New English opponents serving as joint lords justice.[53] But with the appointment in 1631 of Sir Thomas Wentworth a complete reversal in the status of the office seemed to be about to take place.

Already as lord president of the north a figure of major influence within the court of Charles I, Wentworth took the Irish office and enjoyed more support from his monarch than any of his predecessors,[54] allowing him extensive discretionary powers, including the right to return to court for consultation. Wentworth was thus able to establish his independence of Irish vested interests in a manner that would have been the envy of his Tudor predecessors and would have shocked such New English servitors as Chichester and St John. Wentworth too enjoyed the remarkable advantage of sharing complete agreement with his monarch on the specific agenda of his term in office which was to reform the finances and establish the authority of royal government in Ireland.

It was this unprecedented set of privileges that enabled Wentworth to operate with such extraordinary force in his dealings with the leading political and social interests in Ireland, playing off Old English and New English groups while maintaining his independence of both. In the short term Wentworth was remarkably successful in pursuing his priorities. A series of successful confrontations with the leaders of both the Old English and New English groups, in which Wentworth's continued influence with the king was repeatedly demonstrated, consolidated his authority as viceroy, while a substantial parliamentary subsidy, reform of the customs, and the extensive resumption of land titles all promised a much-needed improvement in royal finances. In collaboration with the archbishop of Armagh, John Bramhall, who had taken office with Wentworth, the viceroy also undertook a substantial reform of the finances and an improvement of the authority of the Church of Ireland.[55]

Nothing symbolised more clearly Wentworth's high view of the viceregal office than the elaborate ceremonial protocols which he insisted upon on all public occasions. More than any of his predecessors Wentworth invested heavily in the establishment of viceregal courts, both in Dublin and in his planned country residences at Jigginstown and Shillelagh. In the deliberate and the extreme seriousness with which he comported himself in his dealings with the king's subjects Wentworth appeared to be deliberately elevating the governor into a genuine viceroy, and not surprisingly he was charged by his critics with presenting himself as a king.[56]

In Wentworth's hands, the Irish chief governorship might therefore be seen to have begun to realise its full potential as a true viceroyalty. But the experiment was less pure, and the achievement less complete, than it might appear. In the first place Wentworth himself, despite his high view of the office and his pretensions to high-minded royal service, was not altogether unlike his immediate predecessors in seeking to use his office as a means for personal gain.[57] He invested heavily in land speculation and development, in monopolies and, despite his boasts to be without any entangling alliances among the country's political interests, was not beyond betrothing his daughter to the eldest son of the most powerful representative of the New English elite, the earl of Cork.[58] Such engagements not only diluted his claims to impartial royal service, they also rendered him personally vulnerable to special influence, and later to personal attack. At the same time the support of the Crown, though general, was never complete. Under pressure from the governor, leading figures from all sides, including the earl of Cork and the earl of Clanrickard, still found it possible to get a sympathetic hearing before the king, sometimes through exploiting channels which went through the queen.[59]

Most seriously of all, the potential of developing the Irish governorship into a genuine viceroyalty was from the beginning seriously inhibited by the king's own conception of how his deputy was to operate in Ireland. Conceived in the later 1530s and the early 1540s under the inspiration of the reformist optimism of English commonwealth thought, the idea of constructing an Irish kingdom within which all subjects would be equal in professing allegiance to a common sovereign was an aspiration rather than an achievement. But from the beginning it had been assumed that the Irish viceroy was to play a central role in converting this ideal of a genuinely united polity into a practical reality. Over time, as we have seen, perceptions of the manner by which this polity was to be constructed developed significantly in the minds of those charged with responsibility for its realisation. In the later sixteenth century the troubling recognition dawned that, if the kingdom was to be truly united, it could no longer be recognisably English. But in the subsequent period this disturbing implication was displaced by the ideologically more comforting (but no less divisive) view that the polity could be created only as an entity in which all other interests were to be subordinated to a new English colonial elite – a polity that would be English, but never a kingdom.

In this context the revival of royal authority under Wentworth might be seen as a rejection of this colonialist drift, and a resurrection of the sixteenth-century commonwealth ideal. But this was far from the case. Instead what Wentworth was undertaking for Charles was merely a logical extension of the colonialist tendencies of the early seventeenth century rather than a return to the constitutionalist aspirations of the Tudor era. His agenda was nothing less than a wholesale takeover of the colonial elite, in which the current practices and future ambitions of the servitors, planters and clients of some court favourite would be overridden in the interest of the greatest colonialist of them all – the king of England.[60] Thus, the kingdom of Ireland did not come full circle in the 1630s, and the role of the viceroy within it was not at last realised. Rather, as the ideal of a united kingdom was stifled in the masquerade of royal ceremony, the Irish chief governorship revealed its true function as a colonial agency.

Notes

1 Authoritative lists of the Irish chief governors are conveniently available in T. W. Moody et al. (eds), *A New History of Ireland (hereafter NHI), ix: Maps, Genealogies, Lists: A Companion to Irish History, ii* (Oxford, 1984), pp 469–98; an earlier, less authoritative and less convenient set of lists which frequently contain detailed information on the nature and terms of individual appointments can be found in Rowley Lascelles (ed.), *Liber Munerum Publicorum, or the Establishments of Ireland* (Dublin, 1824), pt ii, pp 1–19, 197–201.

2 *Liber Munerum Publicorum*, p. 17.

3 Compare early drafts of his instructions at The National Archives, Kew (*hereafter* TNA), SP.63/ 14/2,3,7 with later versions at 15/4.

4 Sidney's 'Notes to be imparted to Sir Philip Sidney', in Arthur Collins (ed.), *Letters and Memorials of State* (2 vols, London, 1746), i, p. 295.

5 On the English office of lord lieutenant see G. Scott Thomson, *The Lords Lieutenant in the Sixteenth Century* (London, 1923).

6 A. J. Otway-Ruthven, 'The chief governors of medieval Ireland', *Journal of the Royal Society of Antiquaries of Ireland*, 95 (1965), pp 227–36, Herbert Wood 'The office of chief governor in Ireland, 1172–1509', *Proceedings of the Royal Irish Academy*, 36, Sect. C (1923), pp 206–38; idem, 'The titles of the chief governors of Ireland', *Bulletin of the Institute of Historical Research*, 13 (1935–6), pp 1–8.

7 On the possibilities of Henry's abortive move in this direction, see D. B. Quinn, 'Henry Fitzroy, duke of Richmond and his connexion with Ireland, 1529–30', *Bulletin of the Institute of Historical Research*, 12 (1935), pp 175–7.

8 J. T. Gilbert, *History of the Viceroys of Ireland; with Notices of the Castle of Dublin and its Chief Occupants in Former Times* (Dublin, 1865), p. 249.

9 On Surrey's viceroyalty see Brendan Bradshaw, *The Irish Constitutional Revolution of the Sixteenth Century* (Cambridge, 1979), ch. 3.

10 Ibid., pp 187–257.

11 This was certainly the clear implication of the act, as Lascelles noted in relation to the appointment of St Leger, 'he was the first Irish viceroy', *Liber Munerom Publicorum*, pt ii, p. 1.

12 In addition to Otway-Ruthven, 'Chief governors' see Steven G. Ellis, *Ireland in the Age of the Tudors: English Expansion and the End of Gaelic Rule, 1447–1603* (Harlow, 1998), ch. 6.

13 On the relations between the governor and his council see in addition to Ellis, Jon G. Crawford, *Anglicising the Government of Ireland: The Irish Privy Council and the Expansion of Tudor Rule, 1556–1578* (Dublin, 1993).

14 Jon G. Crawford, *A Star Chamber Court in Ireland: The Court of Castle Chamber, 1571–1641* (Dublin, 2005).

15 The management of the governor's household in the sixteenth and early seventeenth centuries is a topic which, though neglected, may yield very important insights into the viceroy's role, as an analysis of the household accounts of Lord Deputy Sidney seems to show, Historical Manuscripts Commission (*hereafter* HMC), *De Lisle and Dudley Mss* (2 vols, London, 1934–6).

16 Though such powers which were of far greater significance in Ireland before 1541 when the lordship of Ireland was still officially designated as a land of war, they continued to be exerted, though with increasing difficulty in the later sixteenth century: see Steven G. Ellis, 'Taxation and defence in late medieval Ireland: the survival of scutage', *Journal of the Royal Society of Antiquaries of Ireland*, 107 (1978 for 1977), pp 5–28 and Ciaran Brady, *The Chief Governors: The Rise and Fall of Reform Government in Tudor Ireland, 1536–88* (Cambridge, 1994), pp 215–19.

17 The viceroys' liberal use of concordatums as methods of payment became a matter of some controversy in the later sixteenth century, see 'An information of points to be given in instructions to the lord deputy, 20 Sept. 1589', TNA, SP 63/146/48, Queen Elizabeth to lord deputy and council, 7 Jan. 1596, SP 63/186/6; 'Instructions to the earl of Essex', *Calendar of Carew Mss, 1589–1600* (London, 1873), pp 272–8.

18 D. B. Quinn, 'The early interpretation of Poynings' Law, 1494–1534', *Irish Historical Studies*, 2 (1941–2), pp 241–54.

19 Judith Barry, 'Sir Geoffrey Fenton and the office of Secretary of State for Ireland, 1580–1608', *Irish Historical Studies*, 35 (2006–7), pp 137–59.

20 On the dilemma faced by the first post-Geraldine viceroy, Lord Leonard Grey, see the sketch by Mary Ann Lyons in *Oxford Dictionary of National Biography* (*hereafter ODNB*) [www.oxforddnb.com] and Brady, *Chief Governors*, pp 1–25.

21 James Murray, *Enforcing the English Reformation in Ireland: Clerical Resistance and Political Conflict in the Diocese of Dublin, 1534–1590* (Cambridge, 2009), ch. 3.

22 Bradshaw, *Constitutional Revolution*, pt iii; Brady, *Chief Governors*, pp 25–44.

23 Ciaran Brady, 'Court, castle and country: the framework of government in Tudor Ireland', in Ciaran Brady and Raymond Gillespie (eds), *Natives and Newcomers: The Making of Irish Colonial Society, 1534–1641* (Dublin, 1986), pp 22–49, 217–21.

24 Bradshaw, *Constitutional Revolution*, pt iii.

25 *NHI*, ix, pp 486–7.

26 For classic statements of these views see N. P. Canny, 'The ideology of English colonisation: from Ireland to America', *William and Mary Quarterly*, 30 (1973), pp 575–98, and Brendan Bradshaw, 'The Elizabethans and the Irish', *Studies*, 65 (1977), pp 38–50.

27 Brady, *Chief Governors*, chs 3–4; Nicholas P. Canny, *The Elizabethan Conquest of Ireland: A Pattern Established, 1565–76* (Hassocks, 1976), chs 3–5.

28 See in particular the important comparative study by S. G. Ellis, *Tudor Frontiers and Noble Power: The Making of the British State* (Oxford, 1995).

29 Wallace MacCaffrey, 'Place and patronage in Elizabethan politics', in S. T. Bindoff et al. (eds), *Elizabethan Government and Society: Essays Presented to Sir John Neale* (London, 1961), pp 95–126; idem, *The Shaping of the Elizabethan Regime* (London, 1968); Simon Adams, 'Eliza enthroned? The court and its politics', in Christopher Haigh (ed.), *The Reign of Elizabeth I* (London, 1985), pp 55–78.

30 Brady, *Chief Governors*, pp 115–34.

31 Ciaran Brady, *Shane O'Neill* (Dundalk, 1996); David Edwards, 'The Butler revolt of 1569', *Irish Historical Studies*, 28 (1993) pp 228–55.

32 Brady, *Chief Governors*, pp 136–58; for Sidney's own account of these developments see Ciaran Brady (ed.), *A Viceroy's Vindication?: Sir Henry Sidney's Memoir of Service in Ireland, 1583* (Cork, 2002).

33 Ibid., pp 29–35.

34 On the growing influence of Machiavelli over Elizabethan political thinking, see Markku Peltonen, *Classical Humanism and Republicanism in English Political Thought, 1570–1640* (Cambridge, 1995), ch. 2, and Vincent Carey, 'The Irish face of Machiavelli: Richard Beacon's *Solon his follie* and republican ideology in the conquest of Ireland', in Hiram Morgan (ed.), *Political Ideology in Ireland, 1541–1641* (Dublin, 1999), pp 83–109.

35 This was the central contention of the representatives of the Pale who protested against Sidney in 1577: 'Submission of the gentlemen of the Pale, June 1577', Lambeth Palace Library, Carew Mss 638/128; 'Submission of Netterville and Burness, June 1577', TNA, SP 63/58/42.

36 Murray, *Enforcing the English Reformation in Ireland*, pp 294–303; Ciaran Brady and James Murray, 'Sir Henry Sidney and the reformation in Ireland', in Elizabethanne Boran and Crawford Gribben (eds), *Enforcing Reformation in Ireland and Scotland, 1550–1700* (Aldershot, 2006), pp 14–39.

37 David Mathew, *The Celtic Peoples and Renaissance Europe* (London, 1933), ch. 11: 'The fall of lord deputy Perrot'; Hiram Morgan, 'The fall of Sir John Perrot', in John Guy (ed.), *The Reign of Elizabeth I: Court and Culture in the Last Decade* (Cambridge, 1995), pp 109–25.

38 This is the central argument of Spenser's *View of the Present State of Ireland*, c. 1596; the most accessible modern edition *is A View of the State of Ireland: From the First Printed Edition (1633)*, edited by Andrew Hadfield and Willy Maley (Oxford, 1997).

39 Ciaran Brady, 'Faction and the origins of the Desmond rebellion of 1579', *Irish Historical Studies*, 22 (1981), pp 289–312; Hiram Morgan, *Tyrone's Rebellion: The Outbreak of the Nine Years War in Tudor Ireland* (Woodbridge, 1993).

40 Christopher Maginn, 'A window on mid-Tudor Ireland: the "matters" against Lord Deputy St Leger, 1547–8', in *Historical Research* 78 (2005), pp 465–82; and the references cited in note 38 above.

41 Fitzwilliam, the most experienced English administrator in Tudor Ireland, still awaits detailed study; see the sketch by Mary Ann Lyons in *ODNB*, and Morgan, *Tyrone's Rebellion*, ch. 4.

42 'Brief of the account of Sir William Fitzwilliam for ten whole years ended at midsummer, 1569', TNA, SP 63/28/53.

43 Abundant materials for Fitzwilliam's first term in office are now readily available in Mary O'Dowd (ed.), *Calendar of State Papers, Ireland, Tudor Period 1571–1575* (Dublin, 2000).

44 L. W. Henry, 'Contemporary sources for Essex's lieutenancy in Ireland, 1599', *Irish Historical Studies*, 11 (1958), pp 8–17; idem, 'The earl of Essex and Ireland, 1599', *Bulletin of the Institute of Historical Research*, 32 (1959), pp 1–23; Paul E. J. Hammer, *The Polarisation of Elizabethan Politics: The Political Career of Robert Devereux, Second Earl of Essex 1585–1597* (Cambridge, 1999), Alexandra Gaida, *The Earl of Essex and Late Elizabethan Political Culture* (Oxford, 2012).

45 Sussex appointed an official herald to narrate and celebrate his 'progresses' in a grand manner, Trinity College Dublin Library (hereafter TCD), Ms 581; he also used the preambles of parliamentary statutes to proclaim the grandeur of his office; in the event Campion's *Historie* was not published until 1633; but its publication, clearly intended for more immediate use during the term of Sidney's viceroyalty, was suppressed on the exposure of Campion's Catholicism, see A. F. Vossen (ed.), *Two Bokes of the Histories of Ireland* (Assen, 1963); Vincent Carey, 'John Derricke *Image of Irelande*, Sir Henry Sidney, and the massacre at Mullaghmast, 1578', *Irish Historical Studies*, 31 (1999), pp 305–27; John Bradley, 'Sir Henry Sidney's bridge at Athlone, 1566–7', in Thomas Herron and Michael Potterton (eds), *Ireland and the Renaissance, 1540–1660* (Dublin, 2007), pp 173–94.

46 Quinn, 'The early interpretation of Poynings' Law', pp 241–54; R. D. Edwards and T. W. Moody, 'The history of Poynings' Law, part 1: 1494–1615', *Irish Historical Studies*, 2 (1941), pp 415–24; Brendan Bradshaw, 'The beginnings of modern Ireland', in Brian Farrell (ed.), *The Irish Parliamentary Tradition* (Dublin, 1973), pp 68–77.

47 F. M. Jones, *Mountjoy 1563–1606: The Last Elizabethan Deputy* (Dublin, 1958).

48 John MacCavitt, *Sir Arthur Chichester: Lord Deputy of Ireland, 1605–1616* (Belfast, 1998); also Peter Roebuck, 'The making of an Ulster great estate: the Chichesters, barons of Belfast and viscounts of Carrickfergus, 1599–1648', *Proceedings of the Royal Irish Academy*, 79C (1979), pp 1–27. R. D. Edwards (ed.), 'The letter-book of Sir Arthur Chichester', in *Analecta Hibernica*, 8 (1938), pp 5–177, is a valuable primary source.

49 MacCavitt, *Chichester*, ch. 7; idem, 'Lord Deputy Chichester and the English government's "mandates policy" in Ireland, 1605–1607', *Recusant History*, 20 (1991), pp 320–35; Alan Ford, *The Protestant Reformation in Ireland, 1590–1641* (Dublin, 1997).

50 On Chichester's awareness of the importance of court factions, see 'Letter-book of Sir Arthur Chichester', pp 27–8, 151–2; Linda Levy Peck, *Northampton: Patronage and Policy at the Court of James I* (London, 1982), esp. pp 89–94.

51 Victor Treadwell, *Buckingham and Ireland, 1616–1628* (Dublin, 1998).

52 Vera Rutledge, 'Court-Castle faction and the Irish viceroyalty: the appointment of Oliver St John as lord deputy of Ireland', *Irish Historical Studies*, 26 (1989), pp 233–49; and idem, 'The politics of reform in Ireland under Oliver St John' (unpublished MA thesis, McGill University, 1976).

53 On Falkland see the sketch by Sean Kelsey in *ODNB* and Aidan Clarke, *The Old English in Ireland 1625–42* (London, 1966), chs 2–3.

54 Wentworth is perhaps the most studied of the Irish viceroys in this period, see *inter alia* Hugh Kearney, *Strafford in Ireland, 1633–41: A Study in Absolutism*, 2nd edn (London, 1989); T. O.

Ranger, 'Strafford in Ireland: a revaluation', *Past and Present*, 19 (1961), pp 26–47; J. F. Merritt (ed.), *The Political World of Thomas Wentworth, Earl of Strafford, 1621–1641* (Cambridge, 1996).

55 John McCafferty, *The Reconstruction of the Church of Ireland: Bishop Bramhall and the Laudian Reforms, 1633–1641* (Cambridge, 2007).

56 D. Shaw, 'Thomas Wentworth and monarchical ritual in early modern Ireland', *Historical Journal*, 49 (2006), pp 331–55; Wentworth's regal pretensions are a central complaint in A. Clarke (ed.), 'A discourse between two councillors of state, the one of England, and the other of Ireland (1642)', *Analecta Hibernica*, 26 (1970), pp 161–75.

57 J. P. Cooper, 'The fortune of Thomas Wentworth, earl of Strafford' and 'Strafford and the Byrnes' county', in G. E. Aylmer and J. S. Morrill (eds), *Land, Men and Beliefs: Studies in Early-Modern History* (Cambridge, 1983), pp 148–75, 176–91; Ranger, 'Strafford in Ireland'.

58 Patrick Little, 'The earl of Cork and the fall of Strafford, 1638–41', *Historical Journal*, 39 (1996), pp 619–35.

59 P. J. S. Little, 'Family and faction: the Irish nobility and the English court, 1632–42', (unpublished M. Litt. thesis, TCD, 1992); Terry Clavin, 'Court, faction and government in Ireland: the high politics of Wentworth's deputyship of Ireland, c.1631–1636' (unpublished MA thesis, University College Dublin (hereafter UCD), 1999).

60 M. Perceval-Maxwell, 'Ireland and the monarchy in the early Stuart multiple kingdoms', *Historical Journal*, 34 (1991), pp 279–95.

CHAPTER 3

Late Seventeenth- and Early Eighteenth-Century Governance and the Viceroyalty

Charles Ivar McGrath

There are certain accepted understandings of the office of viceroy and its role in governance in the second half of the seventeenth and the eighteenth centuries. The chief governor or viceroy was the monarch's representative in Ireland, otherwise known (in most cases) as the lord lieutenant. In his absence, the office could be executed by his deputy – titled a lord deputy – or a commission of lords justices, with diminishing degrees of power and remuneration for each office from lieutenant to deputy to justice.[1] However, as J. L. McCracken pointed out in the *New History of Ireland*, a degree of inconsistency in governing practice was evident in the period 1690–1700, and again in 1715–17.[2] This essay examines the late seventeenth- and early eighteenth-century governance of Ireland in order to uncover and explain those inconsistencies, and the reasons behind them, and to clarify and explain the evolution occurring in the office of viceroy in Ireland in that period.

In 1970 J. C. Beckett pointed to a significant alteration in the office of viceroy before and after the interregnum:

> The viceroys of the early Stuarts were administrators, royal servants whose importance derived from the office that they held. Even [Thomas] Wentworth is hardly an exception to this rule, for he had neither following nor influence except as a minister of the crown. But the viceroys of the Restoration period were all, at the time of their appointment, established political figures, who might expect to carry some weight in the world, quite apart from the influence attached to their office.[3]

He also noted that

> whereas the viceroys of the earlier part of the century had ruled Ireland as lord deputies, all these [Restoration] men held the more dignified title of lord

> lieutenant. The change of practice might mean little or nothing in terms of actual power; but it is indicative of the new importance attached to Ireland and its government.[4]

The only minor caveat, which Beckett made himself, was that Charles Blount, Lord Mountjoy, after serving in Ireland as lord deputy for several years, was eventually made lord lieutenant in 1603, while Thomas Wentworth, as earl of Strafford, was made lord lieutenant in 1640, more than six years after first being appointed lord deputy.[5]

The salient point, however, is that the Restoration period saw the emergence (or re-emergence, if one looks back to the fifteenth century) of the primacy of the office of lord lieutenant in the practical governance of Ireland.[6] It was also the case that the office of lord lieutenant was dominated by one man, the leading Irish peer of the time, James Butler, 1st duke of Ormond.[7]

In June 1660 George Monck, duke of Albemarle, was appointed lord lieutenant of Ireland by the recently restored Charles II. Albemarle's royal appointment came about because he had had the title conferred on him in the first instance by the English Convention parliament earlier that year. He had no interest in going to Ireland and neither did his deputy, John, Baron Robartes, so Albemarle governed through lords justices until succeeded by Ormond in November 1661. It was not, however, Ormond's first time in that office, having been appointed by Charles I in 1643. Ormond had continued thereafter as the royalist appointee throughout the 1640s and 1650s, even in exile, and had in fact only resigned the office in June 1660 in a politic move aimed at facilitating the appointment of Albemarle by royal authority, thereby confirming rather than rescinding the earlier actions of the Convention parliament.[8] However, although Ormond's royalist service during the 1640s and 1650s could in theory be viewed as the progenitor for the Restoration reliance upon established political figures as lords lieutenant, the reality was that it had been parliamentarian appointees and commissioners, and not Ormond, who had governed Ireland for most of the interregnum period.[9]

Ormond's first Restoration term as lord lieutenant lasted for more than seven years until February 1669, and he was appointed to a further term from 1677 to 1684. When not resident in the country, he governed through his sons as lord deputies: first Thomas, earl of Ossory, in 1664 and 1668; and then Richard, earl of Arran, in 1682. Ormond was recalled by Charles II in late 1684, but the king died before these orders could be acted upon. Three other men served as lord lieutenant during the reign of Charles II: John, Lord Robartes, 1669–70; John, Baron Berkeley of Stratton, 1670–2; and Arthur Capell, earl of Essex, 1672–7.[10] The re-established importance of having a governing lord lieutenant in situ in Ireland seemed to transfer into

James II's reign. Ormond's recall was confirmed by the new king, and an interim commission of lords justices was put in place while a new lord lieutenant was found. In October Henry Hyde, 2nd earl of Clarendon, was appointed to the post, arriving in Ireland the following January.[11]

The reasons for placing the office of lord lieutenant in the hands of an established politician and making it a more active instrument of Irish governance during the Restoration period seem to have been tied to the increasing incursion of Irish affairs into England, and of English affairs into Ireland. As Toby Barnard has stated,

> It is clear that they were appointed as a result of changing configurations in England and to implement different policies. Looking at the [Restoration] viceroys reminds of the interdependence of England and Ireland.[12]

This apparently new policy may also have stemmed from the need to reassert royal authority more generally following the restoration of the monarchy in 1660. As Sean Connolly has pointed out, it could still be claimed in the seventeenth century that the connection between Ireland and England 'lay in the person of the monarch: Ireland was not a dependency of England, but a separate possession of the English crown.' Hence, 'the lord lieutenants who governed Ireland in the name of Charles II after 1660 were in a real sense his representatives, carrying out his instructions'.[13] It would therefore assist in securing the restored monarchy more generally if the prestige and standing of the king's representative in Ireland was re-established.

The initial impetus for placing greater reliance upon prestigious lords lieutenant seemed to be the Gracious Declaration of November 1660 and the ensuing drive for a land settlement in Ireland. Thomas Carte concluded that Ormond's appointment in November 1661 was because Charles II, having heard 'all the debates in his council upon the bill for the settlement of Ireland, and observing the great difficulties attending that affair, resolved to send over a lord lieutenant'.[14] As Charles II's reign progressed, other pressing matters seemed to require the presence of illustrious political figures to head the Irish government. The desire to make Ireland financially self-sufficient has been identified as the reason for Robartes' appointment, while Essex followed his time in Ireland with a stint as first lord of the treasury in England, during which he endeavoured to exert as much control as possible over Irish finances towards the same end.[15]

Yet, to some degree counter-intuitively, the apparent desire to infuse the office of chief governor with greater prestige and authority coincided with growing external interference in the realm of viceregal authority. Ormond, Essex and the other lords lieutenant found themselves fighting a losing battle against direct incursions by the English treasury into Irish financial affairs.[16] Likewise, the peculiar and changing demands of royal policy with regard to religion saw the chief governors being sidelined on key issues, or in Ormond's case in 1669, completely removed.[17] The one area that seemed immune from interference was the office's role as commander-in-chief of the army, but even that was only until the reign of James II, when Clarendon found himself undermined in relation to the army by the Old English Catholic, Richard Talbot, newly created earl of Tyrconnell.[18] However, when considered from a broader perspective, it would appear that to some extent the diminution in the military role of the lord lieutenant was already under way by the late seventeenth century, a 'trend' which was 'masked' only for a while by the personal interest in such matters of Ormond, and later by his grandson, the 2nd duke.[19]

The evolving pattern of Restoration viceregal appointments was thrown into disarray by the Glorious Revolution of 1688. Already the seeds of discontinuity had been sown in 1687 when James II appointed Tyrconnell as lord deputy, not least because he was the first Catholic chief governor since the sixteenth century. However, the other significant discontinuity in his appointment was that he was not deputy to an absent lord lieutenant, as Clarendon had most definitely been recalled from his post at the same time.[20] To some extent Tyrconnell's appointment could be seen as simply a return to the early Stuart pattern of government by lord deputy, without an absentee lord lieutenant in existence. Indeed, as lord deputy he had been bestowed 'with similar powers as contained in Letters Patent' to Clarendon, and their official instructions were exactly the same.[21] Tyrconnell also eventually received the more prestigious title of lord lieutenant in January 1691, but by that time his and his Jacobite master's circumstances had deteriorated so greatly that the majority of the country was de facto being governed by a Williamite commission of lords justices.[22] But if Tyrconnell's terms of appointment of 1687 might be explained by reference to the early seventeenth century, the decisions made under William III with regard to the Irish viceroyalty were most certainly discordant with the recent and more distant Stuart, and even Tudor, past.

Prior to leaving Ireland in September 1690, William III had appointed two lords justices, Henry, Viscount Sydney, and Thomas Coningsby, to govern in his absence. At the end of the month he added a third, the lord chancellor, Sir Charles Porter, to their number.[23] No intermediary lieutenant or deputy was appointed at any point during this time. Though not apparent at the time, those appointments marked the beginning of a relatively short experiment in the 1690s, and again in 1715–16, with the idea of investing greater authority and responsibility in the office of lord justice. Indeed it could be claimed to have been a policy of reinvesting authority, as the position of lord justice as 'a temporary or emergency appointment' had evolved in the fifteenth and sixteenth centuries from the more authoritative thirteenth- and fourteenth-century position of 'justiciar'.[24] Likewise, it could also be construed as an attempt to return to the early Stuart policy of appointing able, middle-ranking administrators rather than high-ranking, but very often incompetent, politicians.

The reasons for this brief dalliance with the idea of reconfiguring the office of chief governor were complex. In part, there may have been a sense of a lost institutional history owing to the Glorious Revolution itself. Similarly, the Revolution was seen by some as an opportunity to meddle with the existing arrangements for government in Ireland in order to facilitate both personal and official interests.[25] At the same time, there was the question of suitable candidates for the particular office of lord lieutenant. James Butler, 2nd duke of Ormond, was, primarily owing to his grandfather's reputation, ambitious to hold the office, to the extent that it was suggested he almost believed he had a hereditary right to it. From as early as 1690 it was rumoured that he would be appointed at some point in time, and he certainly made known his interest in the post during the following decade, though he was not to be deemed suitable until the reign of Queen Anne.[26]

William's difficulty in finding a suitable candidate was evident from very early on. In August 1689 his military commander in Ireland, Friedrich Herman, duke of Schomberg, expressed his concern that 'so long as the general in Ireland and the lord deputy are two persons', William would not be 'well served by those who have the government of the country, either in peace or war'.[27] That Schomberg referred to the chief governor's post as that of lord deputy rather than lord lieutenant, almost a year before the first Williamite chief governors were actually appointed, hinted at a lack of clarity among those in authority within the Williamite forces as to the constitutional make up of government in Ireland. The following month Schomberg responded to his having been 'consulted [by the king] . . . as to the government of Ireland' by stating that 'at present, the conduct of the war occupies my entire attention. The title of "lord lieutenant" will not much take my fancy when your majesty does me the honour to call me by it'.[28] In the event, Schomberg was not to be appointed to the office, even if in advance of William's arrival in June 1690 he was as good as performing its functions. As was also soon to become evident, Schomberg could not have held the office anyway because he was neither an English or Irish subject, which was seemingly a prerequisite for the post.[29]

William's first attempt at a solution to the problem – the appointment of lords justices in September 1690 – was certainly not perceived at that time in government circles as anything more than an interim measure. In early February 1691 Thomas Osborne, marquess of Carmarthen, 'despair[ed] of any good' in Ireland 'unless the king can find somebody of quality to send thither who is big enough to expect obedience, and who may be assisted by some officer experienced in the military part'.[30] The problem was, as Carmarthen himself pointed out to the king later that same month, the absence of anyone of such quality:

> you have no English subject who is fitly qualified for the employment; and yet you can employ no other. But I do believe your affairs would do better in an indifferent hand of such quality, assisted with good councilors [*sic*] and some good military assistants, although those were foreigners, than they can do by any commission of justices as the present state of things are in that kingdom.[31]

Carmarthen was clearly imbued with the practices of the Restoration period, during which he had risen to prominence as lord treasurer in England in the 1670s.[32] For him, government could only function if someone was sent to Ireland as lord lieutenant, armed 'with the accustomed powers of that place, whose quality, as well as authority, may give a countenance to his actions, and may make him more willingly obeyed than these lords justices are or will be'. In the acknowledged absence of any candidates of suitable quality and ability, he recommended the presumably 'indifferent' talents of, among others, two future lords lieutenant under Queen Anne, Charles Talbot, earl of Shrewsbury, and Thomas Herbert, earl of Pembroke, both of whom at least had the requisite rank.[33]

The subject remained topical in England. Rumours circulated in late 1691 that the lords justices were to be removed, but it was unclear whether they were to be replaced by a sole chief governor or another commission.[34] By early 1692 the rumour mill had come good, as it became known that Henry, Viscount Sydney, who had vacated his post as lord justice and departed Ireland in December 1690 leaving Porter and Coningsby to govern together, was to return to Ireland as sole chief governor, with the title, power and authority of lord lieutenant.[35] It seemed as if the practice of the Restoration was to be resumed, along with the military role of the chief governor, as Sydney's official title was 'lieutenant-general, and general governor' of Ireland,[36] which was reported in one newsletter as being 'lord lieutenant of Ireland and lieutenant-general of the forces in that kingdom and lord high admiral in the Irish seas'.[37]

Sydney's tenure in office, however, was to be brief and tempestuous. Having been central to the creation of a political conflict between the executive arm of government and the Irish legislature in October–November 1692 over the competing rights of parliament and the Crown to initiate supply legislation, Sydney was seen to react in a high-handed manner to parliament's claim to have a 'sole right' in such matters when he utilised the power of his office to its full extent by dismissing several opposition MPs from public office and by refusing to listen to, or allow dissent from, his particular perspective on the matter at hand.[38] Having brought the weight of judicial opinion in Ireland and England to support his view on the subject, by mid-1693 Sydney had discovered that for all his apparent authority, he was unable to resolve the political impasse that had arisen. The Irish political community, which had been exceedingly vocal in both Ireland and England in the intervening months, to the extent that they had prompted the English parliament towards censure of the Irish administration, had demonstrated that it did have some say in such matters.[39]

The solution to the impasse was a variation on an emerging theme. Sydney was removed from office in June 1693. He was replaced by a commission of lords justices rather than another lord lieutenant.[40] The new lords justices, Sir Cyril Wyche, William Duncombe and Henry, Baron Capell of Tewkesbury, were not acting in Sydney's absence, but were clearly appointed to act on their own authority. Such an occurrence had been on the cards for several months. In January 1693 it had been rumoured that Capell was to go to Ireland as lord lieutenant.[41] Further rumours emanated from England during the ensuing months.[42] By early May Sydney was reporting that he heard 'from all sides that their majesties are resolved to have me replaced by lords justices'.[43] Later that month the change was confirmed to Sydney.[44]

Some concerns were raised over the appointment of lords justices. Sydney himself had wondered if a new parliament should be convened in Ireland, 'besides to doubt in point of law whether this parliament can be held before lords justices', which the English secretary of state, Daniel Finch, earl of Nottingham, credited with being 'a good argument'.[45] It is unclear whether Sydney was trying to imply that lords justices did not have the power to convene parliament on their own authority, or whether his concern related only to the parliament convened by himself as lord lieutenant.

A more specific concern was raised by Lord Chancellor Porter, who pointed out to Nottingham in May 1693 that it 'is usual for the chancellor to be one' of the lord justices. His fear was that 'being left out will cause great discourse to my prejudice, and would seem as if I were in the king's displeasure'.[46] Porter had a valid point: the lord chancellor was usually appointed as an interim or temporary lord justice when a lord lieutenant or deputy was absent from the country. Also, Porter's time as lord justice in 1690–2 had become a focal point for much anger in Protestant Ireland, and he was right to be concerned that any sign of loss of favour might encourage activities to his prejudice. His time in government had already come under the gaze of the committee of grievances in the 1692 parliament, and at the time of his writing in May 1693, Coningsby and himself had requested a royal pardon for the time of their service as lords justices, a request which prompted a petition against such a pardon and the preparation of charges intended to be brought before the English parliament. In 1695 a further attempt to impeach him was made in the Irish parliament.[47]

However, the problem for Porter may not have been a loss of royal favour, but rather that the commission of lords justices was not intended as a temporary or interim appointment until a new lord lieutenant was found. Hence, a group of individuals were appointed with a view to undertaking a longer period in government, which amounted to a new use of the office of lord justice. Such a view may be corroborated by the fact that at the beginning of June, Sydney, in his urgency to leave Ireland, had suggested that he 'name a deputy [to govern], if only for a month', until the lords justices arrived.[48] Governing in the absence of her husband, Queen Mary at first did not think he needed to appoint a deputy 'for so short a time', but she soon changed her mind, as a warrant to Sydney of 13 June for appointing two lords justices or a lord deputy attests.[49] Sydney decided that it was better to leave an interim government of lords justices, and appointed Porter and Wyche to the job.[50] These proceedings confirmed that lords justices were normally appointed as an interim measure, and that the incoming commission of Capell, Wyche and Duncombe was breaking that mould.

In part the reason for appointing the commission of lords justices in 1693 would appear to have been that it provided a variety of personalities that would appeal to various sections of the Irish political community, and therefore would have more chance of resolving the political impasse. Capell possessed the most obvious appeal for the Whig-inclined members of the 1692 opposition, not just because his Whig credentials went back as far as the Exclusion Crisis of 1679–81, but also because he was the younger brother of Essex, the well remembered Restoration lord lieutenant. Wyche, although having served as secretary to Sydney in 1692–3, was considered to be a reliable administrator and man of learning who had also served as secretary to both Essex and Ormond. Duncombe had no previous association with Ireland, a fact which in itself made him acceptable to many.[51]

The plan worked, if not quite as had been intended. The Irish political community certainly reacted favourably to the new governors, but after an initial period of harmonious relations, the lords justices themselves began to diverge in opinion, primarily over whether or not an Irish parliament, if convened, would meet in good enough temper to do the king's business. Capell was the only advocate among the three for a parliament, and, with strong backing in both Ireland and England, his views eventually won out.[52] His reward was appointment as sole governor in 1695 with instructions to oversee the convening of a new parliament.[53] However, he was not to do so as lord lieutenant, but rather as 'lord deputy and chief governor '.[54] Once again, there was no absentee lord lieutenant appointed above him.

The king's justification to Wyche and Duncombe was that he required 'the administration of the government of Ireland to be put in one hand'.[55] At the same time Shrewsbury assured Capell that:

> I do not doubt but it will be indifferent to you that the king has only given you the title of lord deputy, since you have with it all the powers of a lord lieutenant, with a reserve only as [to] the disposal of commissions in the army, which has been an exception even in a lord lieutenant's commission, and the king therefore thinks it so much the more reasonable now as this war has bred a greater number of officers to be provided for by his majesty.[56]

However, it has also been suggested that William's decision was motivated by personal dislike of Capell.[57] Whatever the justification for the bestowal of the lesser title of lord deputy on Capell as a sole governor, in terms of governance it was once again more in keeping with early Stuart practice and with the Williamite raison d'être for the new-found use of the office of lord justice.

Capell's biggest challenge as lord deputy proved in the end to be his ill health. His death in office in May 1696 threw the whole process of appointments into the melting pot once again. Lurking in the wings as ever was Lord Chancellor Porter. In 1694, when Capell was just one of three lords justices and it was rumoured that he had died, Porter had pressed to replace him, utilising the same arguments he had advanced for his appointment in 1693.[58] Porter was quick to renew his claims when in early 1696 Capell went into a slow terminal decline. In March Porter began to express his concerns that Capell was too ill to act, and should in accordance with the powers in his commission appoint temporary lords justices until his health was restored.[59] When Capell did just that, Porter began to find fault with the two individuals appointed, William Wolseley and Murrough Boyle, Viscount Blessington, not least because he himself had once again been overlooked for the office.[60]

Porter also began to raise concerns that Capell's commission did not empower him to appoint lords justices in the event of his death. According to Porter, by an act of Henry VIII's reign it was required that following the death of a chief governor while in office, temporary lords justices were to be elected by the council until the monarch's decision on a more permanent replacement was made known.[61] Capell on the other hand defended his choice of lords justices to Secretary of State Shrewsbury in London, and claimed that they should also continue in office if he died, as the Henrician statute required 'writs [to] . . . be issued and returned from the several counties for choosing a justice', which would leave the government vacant for too long at a dangerous time.[62] Shrewsbury in reply politely informed

Capell that 'upon the death of a chief governor the council must elect for the interim as that statute appoints'.[63]

Events in Ireland had overtaken such decisions however, as Capell died before word from Shrewsbury arrived. Wolseley and Blessington demonstrated discretion by immediately agreeing not to act in an official capacity until the king's views were made known, and in the interim Porter summoned the council to hold an election to elect one or more lords justices 'according to the statute'.[64] Several members of the council opposed an election on the grounds that they had not received word from England yet, but the majority felt any further delay was unacceptable, and the election went ahead by thirteen votes to five. Porter was then elected sole lord justice by twelve votes to three.[65] He immediately looked to determine Wolseley and Blessington's commission, placing himself in sole charge of government. His actions prompted much discontent within Irish political circles as people continued to argue over the validity of both Capell's commission and the Henrician statute as a means of appointing a temporary chief governor.[66] The only hope for a resolution was a quick decision by the king on a permanent replacement.[67]

The difficulty with a quick decision related to the same problem raised by Carmarthen in 1691. On 23 June Shrewsbury informed William III's secretary, William Blathwayt, that when the English lords justices appointed to govern in the king's absence had come 'to propose persons for that government [of Ireland], they were so little fond of the employment, and sat today so late . . . on that end' that other business did not get done.[68] At the same time, Shrewsbury told the king directly that it was difficult to propose any one for the post, as individuals of the required quality were scarce, 'the more so, upon this occasion, when one could not mention it to any, with a prospect of remaining long there'.[69] So instead the English lords justices recommended a commission of lords justices, to which the king agreed, with Porter being joined in office by Charles Coote, earl of Mountrath, and Henry Moore, earl of Drogheda.[70]

The new commission had a temporary feel to it, having been appointed at short notice and with two Irish peers of little note who were certainly not the type of men of quality desired for the office within English political circles. The fact that they were Irish peers below the level of duke was probably sufficient in itself to exclude them from serious consideration for the post in the long term. The death of Porter in December 1696 heralded the beginning of the end for Mountrath and Drogheda.[71] In January they were joined as lords justices by Henri de Massue de Ruvigny, Viscount Galway.[72]

Galway's appointment was the precursor to a short-lived return to a policy of employing lords justices for the longer term and empowering them with greater authority and responsibility. In April 1697 Mountrath and

Drogheda were removed and Galway (who was created earl in May), was joined in commission by Charles Powlett, marquis of Winchester, and Edward, Viscount Villiers.[73] As with the two previous long-term commissions of lords justices in 1690–2 and 1693–5 and with Capell's lord deputyship in 1695–6, there was no absentee lord lieutenant appointed to oversee their government. More uniquely, and only to occur once again in 1715–16, the lords justices were to have the sole responsibility for overseeing the meeting of parliament – in the first instance, managing two sessions, in 1697 and 1698–9, from start to finish. In the past, when lords justices had overseen sessions of parliament, they had been acting for absentee lords lieutenant.

Villiers never actually came to Ireland, so the practicalities of the job devolved upon Galway and Winchester. Both men had an appeal for certain sections of the Irish political nation. Winchester was a Whig, while Galway was a Huguenot soldier and courtier who had fought in William III's army in Ireland. Of these appointments, David Hayton has said that 'since neither Winchester nor Villiers was particularly bright, leadership was expected to fall to Galway'.[74] Galway was also a natural choice for William, being, as Patrick Kelly has put it, 'a member of that small, intimate, supra-national elite of close friends and advisers' to the king, who was 'determined to acquit his debt of gratitude to the Huguenot soldiers who had served his cause so faithfully during the nine years war'.[75] However, Galway was also French and, as Carmarthen had pointed out in 1691, it was understood that only Englishmen (and the occasional Irish duke) could be sole governor in Ireland. The best William could hope for was that his reliable Huguenot could govern in Ireland as part of a commission of lords justices, but with most of the power in reality vested in his hands. He was certainly the only Frenchman to serve in the office, and does seem to have been employed for his ability as an administrator more than anything else.[76] Hayton's observation that Winchester was chosen for his 'personal wealth, . . . rank and prestige', and was otherwise 'second-rate, . . . henpecked and easily led, perpetually casting about for advice', would suggest that Galway was the able one who had to be coupled with individuals whose faces were a better fit.[77]

The new lords justices' instructions included orders for summoning parliament.[78] Capell had convened a new parliament in 1695, though the first session had only been adjourned rather than prorogued so that its recall would in theory represent the continuation of the same session. However, Capell's death and the delay in reconvening until 1697 meant that in practice it was treated for all intents and purposes like a new session, including the delivery of an opening speech from the throne by Winchester and Galway on 27 July 1697.[79] Among other things, the session saw the passing of the Bishops' Banishment Act, as it became known, and the passing of a mutilated version of the Treaty of Limerick, both of which were crucial milestones in the development of the penal code against Catholics. Indeed, Catholic contemporaries in Ireland and on the continent quickly blamed both on Galway, who was portrayed as the 'persecuted turned persecutor with a vengeance'.[80] In reality, the 1697 act for banishing bishops and regular clergy had its immediate origins as unsuccessful heads of a bill in 1695, which were reintroduced by the government in 1697, though the real antecedents of the measure can be traced back to proclamations issued in the 1670s.[81] As from the Treaty of Limerick, Galway's only expressed concern was whether incomplete ratification would cause problems when pleading the cause of Protestants in Catholic territories on the continent. Ultimately, he was, in Kelly's words, 'content to follow royal policy' – the efficient administrator getting on with the job at hand.[82] Neither was 1697 unique for anti-Catholic measures in the Irish parliament – at least one act was passed in every session from 1695 to 1709, from the prohibition of foreign education and disarming acts of 1695 through to the cornerstones of the code in 1704 and 1709.[83]

The 1697 session was concluded by prorogation in December of that year. In the lead-up to the next session in 1698, William III demonstrated his continuing confidence in Galway when he expressed his personal sentiments on the subject to his Huguenot lord justice:

> it was never of such importance . . . to have a good session . . . not only with respect to my affairs of that kingdom, but still more with respect to my affairs [in England] . . . after this . . . I should be very glad not to be obliged, for a good while, to have another parliament in Ireland.[84]

The 1698–9 session proved even more difficult than that of 1697 for Galway and Winchester. The parliament failed to assuage English concerns over the competitive Irish woollen industry, and a long-feared prohibition on Irish exports was enacted at Westminster in April 1699.[85] Apart from 1692, it was the most troubled session of William's reign. Yet the blame was not laid at the feet of the lords justices. Galway remained a confidant of the king, who bemoaned to him in June 1699 how he 'could hardly get the estimates of Ireland passed [at the treasury board], as it will be sent you; there are retrenchments which I was forced to make, though I like them not'. Thus 'the estimates of the next year must absolutely be reduced, that my ordinary revenue may serve to pay it; and a parliament in Ireland must not be thought of so soon'.[86] To that end parliament was dissolved in June 1699.[87]

By that time, changes had started to take place within the commission of lords justices. In April Galway, Villiers (since October 1697 earl of Jersey), and Winchester (since February 1699 duke of Bolton) were joined in commission by Archbishop Narcissus Marsh, primarily so that Bolton could leave Ireland.[88] In June, Jersey was finally removed from the commission, while Charles, earl of Berkeley, replaced Archbishop Marsh.[89]

Such tinkering was a precursor to the return to the Restoration tradition of appointing established leading political figures to the more prestigious office of lord lieutenant. The first step in that direction occurred at the end of 1700 when Galway, Bolton and Berkeley were replaced by Laurence Hyde, earl of Rochester, as sole chief governor.[90]

Rochester's term in office as lord lieutenant has been dismissed as unimportant in the past, in part because he only came to Ireland for three months at the end of 1701, and did not oversee a parliament, being removed from office in February 1703.[91] However, there are certain significant aspects to Rochester's service. At a rather mundane level, Rochester's receipt of his official instructions confirm that they were rather formulaic and offered little insight into the differences between various governorships. Rochester was sent 'the copies of instructions that have been given to several lord lieutenants and lords justices' so that he could peruse them and 'direct wherein you think they ought to be altered'.[92] The rather formulaic nature of these official instructions was further borne out by the regularity with which new sets of instructions issued earlier in the 1690s to new governors had simply been duplicates of those issued to predecessors, with the occasional addition.[93]

Of much greater significance however was the fact that, after eleven years of flux in relation to the way in which the chief governorship was entrusted to various commissions of lords justices, a lord lieutenant and a lord deputy, Rochester's viceroyalty marked the commencement of a pattern of appointment that personified eighteenth-century governance. When not resident, Rochester was represented in Ireland by a commission of lords justices made up from senior Irish office holders, peers and archbishops, who communicated primarily through him and were answerable to him. At all times, whether in England or Ireland, he remained the head of the Irish government.[94]

For the rest of Anne's reign the same pattern was adhered to. James Butler, 2nd duke of Ormond, finally realised his wish to be lord lieutenant in 1703 and went on to oversee three sessions of parliament – in 1703–4, 1705, and again in 1711 on his return to office. While out of the country he was represented by lords justices. Ormond's replacement in 1707, Thomas Herbert, earl of Pembroke, only lasted one session, being replaced on his transfer to the office of first lord of the admiralty by Thomas, Lord Wharton, who oversaw two sessions in 1709 and 1710, with lords justices serving when he was absent in England. Wharton was replaced by Ormond in late 1710, and Ormond was in turn replaced by Shrewsbury in 1713, who oversaw one session later that year and was represented after his departure in June 1714 by lords justices, conforming to a pattern established from 1700.[95] Such a regular pattern of practice was not readily identifiable at any earlier stage of viceregal government in Ireland. During the Restoration, the absence of parliament after 1666 mitigated against the existence of such an evident corollary as emerged in Anne's reign: lords lieutenant governed in person during parliamentary sessions, and through lords justices at other times. The pattern was to be adhered to without any divergence from 1717 onwards until permanent residency became the norm for lords lieutenant in the 1760s.[96]

At the same time, the office of lord justice became much more regularised after 1716. From the appointment of Bolton as lord lieutenant in 1717 the system of appointing lords justices in the absence of the serving lord lieutenant became the norm, as the undertaker system came to the fore as the mainstay of governance in Ireland in the eighteenth century.[97] With a lord lieutenant in the country for only six months every two years during the parliamentary session, the regularity with which commissions of lords justices were appointed was almost monotonous. After the re-establishment of permanent residency for the lord lieutenant in the 1760s, the need for commissions of lords justices diminished, the next not being appointed until the death of Charles Manners, duke of Rutland, in office in 1787.[98]

The uniqueness in the pattern of governance in the 1690s, and the more settled practice thereafter, is clarified when the salaries and other payments of the various lords lieutenant, lord deputies and lords justices are examined. The post was always considered to be a great expense to the incumbent, but that was balanced by the fact that, as Beckett put it for the Restoration period:

> the most obvious, and most readily measurable, attraction of the viceroyalty lay in the emoluments attached to it. These, though they cannot be stated with precision, were very considerable. The viceroy's allowances on the military list amounted to more than £11,000; he received almost £7,000 more in other regular payments; fees on licenses for the export of wool (one of the perquisites of the office) yielded, in the 1670s, between £3,000 and £4,000 a year.[99]

These payments can be stated more accurately for the 1690s and thereafter, and though not quite as generous as Beckett believed, they were still very substantial. The basic annual salary for a lord lieutenant was £6,593, 6*s*. 8*d*. This was the salary granted to Sydney in 1692, to Rochester in 1700 and to Ormond in 1703, and to the others that followed thereafter.[100] It was also, however, the salary granted to Capell as lord deputy in 1695, and to Capell, Wyche and Duncombe in 1693 and to Galway, Winchester and Villiers in 1697 as lords justices.[101] In the latter two instances the salary was divided in three, much to the annoyance of Galway, who objected to the fact that Villiers had never come to Ireland yet still benefited from the salary and other financial perquisites without incurring any of the many costs associated with carrying out the job.[102] Even those lords justices appointed as interim governors in the 1690s, such as Porter, Mountrath, Drogheda, Marsh and Berkeley received the full shared salary of a chief governor.[103]

There were also additional sources of income, which once again were received by all incumbents in the 1690s. On entering into the office a new lord lieutenant received a once-off payment of £3,000 for his equipage, or an equivalent share thereof for lords justices.[104] Hence Wyche, Duncombe and Capell each received £1,000 in 1693, as did Galway, Winchester and Villiers in 1697, though the latter's payment seemed dependent upon him actually travelling to Ireland.[105] Other lords justices such as Porter, Drogheda, Mountrath and Berkeley received equivalent amounts as well.[106] Occasional exceptions occurred. In 1695 Capell only received £2,000 for his equipage. Whether this was because he was already serving in Ireland, or because he was lord deputy rather than lieutenant, is not evident,[107] though other incumbents appointed in the 1690s who were already in Ireland did receive their equivalents for equipage money.[108] The only exception, it seems, occurred in 1699 when Marsh was excluded from the £1,000 equivalent equipage payment, much to Galway's annoyance. However, it appeared to have been withheld not on residence grounds but rather because he had served for so short a time.[109]

A further lucrative source of income for all those appointed in the 1690s, whether lieutenants, deputies or justices, was the 'fees of licenses for exporting wool'.[110] Usually, this was paid as an equivalent annual lump sum of £4,000,[111] which accounts for the chief governor's salary occasionally being recorded as £10,593, 6*s.* 8*d.*[112] In 1699 the lords justices feared they would lose this perquisite of office following the passing of the English act prohibiting Irish woollen manufacture exports. Instead, they received orders from England that they were to continue collecting the fees for export licenses from merchants and to prosecute any who did not pay.[113] The £4,000 equivalent continued to be paid into the eighteenth century.[114]

Other perquisites of office included not having to pay poundage on any of their income.[115] In 1695 this amounted to a saving to Capell, Wyche and Duncombe of the not insubstantial amount of £854, 1*s.* 2*d.*[116] There were also less formal, though not inconsequential, sources of income for chief governors. In June 1699 a royal warrant was issued to Bolton and Galway to pay themselves £1,500 each as the king's gift and royal bounty, ostensibly for additional costs incurred by them during the preceding parliamentary sessions.[117] In February 1702 Rochester received a royal gift of £4,000 as compensation when William III decided to remove him from office, though in the event the king's death resulted in Rochester retaining the post for another year.[118] Galway also received a pension of £1,250 per annum when he was replaced.[119] Chief governors could also bring goods in and out of the country duty free,[120] a perquisite that was intended to cover their personal and household goods but one which was certainly utilised by some chief governors for other ends, as evidenced by Rochester's request in 1702 for a hogshead of wine to be entered duty free at Chester 'on my account' even though it was intended for another person.[121]

While the salary and perquisites of the lord lieutenant remained the same into the eighteenth century, the situation changed dramatically for lords justices from 1700 onwards, which in many ways was the most stark contrast between the relative power and prestige of the lord justiceship in the 1690s and its greatly diminished role before and after that decade. On acceding to the office of lord lieutenant at the end of 1700, Rochester appointed lords justices to serve in his absence. For their pay, they were to receive £100 each a month. The remainder of the salary and perquisites, including all the equipage money and wool licenses fees were to go directly to Rochester.[122] With three lords justices, the annual cost to an absentee lord lieutenant was only £3,600 out of a total income in excess of £10,000 per annum plus the once-off equipage money. While the comparison with the salaries of lords justices in the 1690s is stark, it is not evident whether Rochester's actions constituted a new innovation in relation to normal practice in the Restoration period. However, by the time Shrewsbury became lord lieutenant in 1713, the payment of a total salary of £100 a month to each of his lords justices was considered to be the 'usual' allowance for that office.[123]

There was, however, one final experiment with the office of lord justice before the 'usual' became wholly unassailable in the eighteenth century. In September 1714 Shrewsbury was replaced as lord lieutenant by Charles Spencer, earl of Sunderland. Without ever having journeyed to Ireland, in September 1715 Sunderland was replaced by a commission of lords justices, rather than actually being represented in Ireland by them. At that time the preparations for a new parliament were already well advanced. But the management of that parliament was now to be entrusted to two lords justices, Sunderland instead remaining at the centre of power in London in his new position of lord privy seal.[124] Patrick McNally has stated that, in a unique occurrence, the fact of the matter was that Sunderland refused to go to Ireland, thereby necessitating the hasty appointment of lords justices in his place.[125]

On the face of it, it was a surprising turn of events, for it was not an unimportant parliament – the Hanoverian succession was still to be secured, the Jacobite threat remained very real, and Ireland seemed a possible point of conflict.[126] However, on examination the surprise is lessened because returning for a second term of office was the ageing Galway, once again in commission with a younger English peer in the person of Charles Fitzroy, duke of Grafton.[127] Galway had certainly earned the right to reappointment given his success before, his military knowledge at a time of danger, and his acquaintance with key Irish politicians. Grafton was a surprise to all because of his youth and inexperience. The assumption was made that he would 'agree with Lord Galway in everything' and was appointed only because Galway was old and his health uncertain.[128] As with Bolton before, Hayton has observed of Grafton that he was chosen for his personal wealth, rank and prestige, was 'second-rate', and was 'permanently immature'.[129]

Galway's knowledge of the government of Ireland was an important reason for his appointment.[130] Likewise, the younger Grafton was mindful of the experience of his older associate.[131] The parliament that met under their governorship was dominated by events associated with the Jacobite rising in Scotland. With that in mind, they also oversaw the introduction of a national debt in Ireland, following their request to parliament in January 1716 for money to cover the cost of raising new regiments.[132] Whatever the real reason for their appointment, Galway and Grafton managed well at a pivotal moment in Irish history.[133] The evidence would suggest Galway was the main reason for that success. However, at the end of 1716 the decision was taken to appoint a lord lieutenant for Ireland once again, bringing to an end the final experimentation with empowered lords justices.[134]

A number of conclusions can be drawn. The eighteenth century saw a greater formalisation of the way in which the office of chief governor was perceived and managed. It was a formalisation that occurred as a result of a process of experimentation that unfolded during the 1690s. That experimentation had occurred in part because of the break in continuity for Irish government as a result of the Glorious Revolution, in part because of the absence of suitable candidates for the position of sole governor, and in part because of the new demands placed upon chief governors in the political arena as parliament began to meet on a more regular basis. In the process, the office of lord deputy ceased in practice to exist, Capell being the last to hold that post, and parliament experienced its last two periods of governance by a commission of lords justices. While the period of experimentation could be construed as a return to early Stuart practices or even to medieval modes of governance, it was also the catalyst for the greater formalisation of the way in which the office of chief governor was utilised in the eighteenth century. That model of governance emerged during Anne's reign and became firmly settled upon in the reign of George I. But even then, a backward glance for precedents was warranted to the Restoration period, when established political figures had lent their prestige and standing to the office of lord lieutenant and, when absent, had governed via lord deputies and lords justices.

Notes

1 J. G. Simms, 'The Restoration, 1660–85' and 'The war of the two kings, 1685–91' in T. W. Moody, F. X. Martin and F. J. Byrne (eds), *A New History of Ireland (hereafter NHI), iii: Early Modern Ireland, 1534–1691* (Oxford, 1976), pp 420–2, 478–80; J. L. McCracken, 'The political structure, 1714–60', in T. W. Moody and W. E. Vaughan (eds), *NHI, iv: Eighteenth-century Ireland* (Oxford, 1986), pp 57–63.

2 McCracken, 'Political structure', pp 57, 61; J. C. Beckett, 'The Irish viceroyalty in the Restoration period', *Transactions of the Royal Historical Society*, 5: 20 (1970), pp 53–72; J. I. McGuire, 'Why was Ormond dismissed in 1669?', *Irish Historical Studies*, 18 (1972–3), pp 295–312.

3 Beckett, 'Irish viceroyalty', p. 55.

4 Ibid, p. 56.

5 Ibid, p. 56, fn. 1; T. W. Moody, F. X. Martin, and F. J. Byrne (eds), *NHI, ix*: *Maps, Genealogies, Lists: A Companion to Irish History* (Oxford, 1984), ii, pp 487–8. Mountjoy held the office of lord lieutenant until his death in 1606, acting via deputies throughout that time. Strafford on the other hand held it for little more than a year, being executed in May 1641. He did, however, spend some time in Ireland as lord lieutenant, overseeing parliament in March 1640. See Christopher Maginn, 'Blount, Charles, eighth Baron Mountjoy and earl of Devonshire (1563–1606)' and Ronald G. Asch, 'Wentworth, Thomas, first earl of Strafford (1593–1641)', *Oxford Dictionary of National Biography* (hereafter *ODNB*) [www.oxforddnb.com/view/article/2683, /29056].

6 *NHI, ix*, p. 469.

7 Simms, 'Restoration', p. 421.

8 Michael Perceval-Maxwell, 'Butler, James, 12th earl and 1st duke of Ormond', *Dictionary of Irish Biography* [www.dib.cambridge.org/viewReadPage.do?articleId=a1259]; Beckett, 'Irish viceroyalty', p. 55; McGuire, 'Why was Ormond dismissed', p. 295, fn. 2. While the *NHI, ix*, p. 489, gives the date of Ormond's appointment as February 1662, both Perceval-Maxwell and Thomas Carte state the warrant was first issued in November 1661. See Thomas Carte, *The Life of James, Duke of Ormond* (Oxford, 1851), iv, p. 74.

9 *NHI, ix*, pp 488–9; McGuire, 'Why was Ormond dismissed', p. 295, fn. 2.

10 *NHI, ix*, pp 489–90; Simms, 'War of the two kings', p. 479.

11 Simms, 'War of the two kings', pp 479–80; idem, *Jacobite Ireland, 1685–91* (Dublin, 2000), pp 18–22; David Dickson, *New Foundations: Ireland 1660–1800* (Dublin, 1987), p. 22; *NHI, ix*, p. 490.

12 Toby Barnard, 'Conclusion: Restoration Ireland', in Coleman A. Dennehy (ed.), *Restoration Ireland: Always Settling and Never Settled* (Aldershot, 2008), p. 180.

13 S. J. Connolly, *Religion, Law and Power: The Making of Protestant Ireland 1660–1760* (Oxford, 1992), p. 106.

14 Carte, *Ormond*, iv, p. 74. See also Simms, 'Restoration', pp 422–4; L. J. Arnold, *The Restoration Land Settlement in County Dublin, 1660–1688* (Dublin, 1993), pp 37–52.

15 Sean Egan, 'Finance and the government of Ireland, 1660–85' (unpublished PhD thesis, 2 vols, Trinity College Dublin (hereafter TCD), 1983), i, pp 161, 188–9, 192–7; ii, pp 99–100, 107–8; Simms, 'Restoration', pp 421–2.

16 Egan, 'Finance', i, pp 49–50; ii, pp 98–100, 108, 117–18, 124–6, 143–5, 150–1, 162–6, 168–71; Dickson, *New Foundations*, pp 14–15, 17, 20–1; Toby Barnard, *A New Anatomy of Ireland: The Irish Protestants, 1649–1770* (New Haven, 2003), p. 163.

17 McGuire, 'Why was Ormond dismissed', pp 304–12; Dickson, *New Foundations*, pp 13–14.

18 Simms, *Jacobite Ireland*, pp 20–6; John Childs, *The Army, James II, and the Glorious Revolution* (Manchester, 1980), pp 60–79; Dickson, *New Foundations*, pp 20, 23–4; Egan, 'Finance', i, p. 194.

19 Barnard, *New Anatomy*, p. 180.

20 *Calendar of State Papers, Domestic* (hereafter *CSPD*), *1686–7*, pp 332, 335–6; Simms, *Jacobite Ireland*, p. 32.

21 *CSPD, 1686–7*, pp 335, 339; *CSPD, 1685*, pp 110–14, 397.

22 *CSPD, 1690–1*, pp 132, 176–80.

23 Ibid.

24 *NHI, ix*, pp 469, 486.

25 *CSPD, 1690*, pp 201–6; *CSPD, 1690–1*, p. 512; Historical Manuscripts Commission (HMC), *Various Collections, viii, Clements MSS*, p. 216; J. I. McGuire, 'The Irish Parliament of 1692', in D. W. Hayton and Thomas Bartlett (eds), *Penal Era and Golden Age: Essays in Irish History 1690–1800* (Belfast, 1979), pp 2–3; C. I. McGrath, *The Making of the Eighteenth-Century Irish Constitution: Government, Parliament and the Revenue, 1692–1714* (Dublin, 2000), p. 74.

26 HMC, *Ormond MSS*, new series, viii, pp xxiv, xxviii; HMC, *Le Fleming MSS*, p. 279; *CSPD, 1696*, p. 207; D. W. Hayton, *Ruling Ireland, 1685–1742: Politics, Politicians and Parties* (Woodbridge, 2004), p. 37.

27 *CSPD, 1689–90*, p. 232.

28 Ibid., p. 257.

29 *CSPD, 1690–1*, p. 270; Harman Murtagh, 'Massue de Ruvigny, Henri de, earl of Galway, and marquess of Ruvigny in the French nobility (1648–1720)', *ODNB* [www.oxforddnb.com/view/article/18309].

30 HMC, *Finch MSS*, iii, p. 10.

31 *CSPD, 1690–1*, p. 270.

32 J. R. Jones, *Country and Court: England, 1658–1714* (Cambridge, 1978), pp 18–19.

33 *CSPD, 1690–1*, p. 270.

34 See for example HMC, *Portland MSS*, iii, pp 480, 487, 489.

35 —— to Bishop William King, 16 Dec. 1690, TCD, Lyons Collection, MSS 1995–2008, f. 106a; Newsletters, 15, 17 Mar. 1691/2, Bodleian Library, Oxford, Carte MS 76, ff 76–7, 79; *CSPD, 1691–2*, pp 161, 168–9; HMC, *Portland MSS*, iii, p. 489.

36 *CSPD, 1691–2*, pp 168–9.

37 Newsletter, 15 Mar. 1691/2, Bodleian Library, Carte MS 76, ff 76–7.

38 McGuire, 'Irish parliament', pp 13, 23–4; C. I. McGrath, 'Securing the Protestant interest: policy, politics and parliament in Ireland in the aftermath of the Glorious Revolution, 1690–1695' (unpublished MA thesis, University College Dublin (hereafter UCD), 1992), pp 118–22; idem, *Irish Constitution*, pp 75–91; Anon., *An Account of the Sessions of Parliament in Ireland, 1692* (London, 1693), pp 1–28.

39 McGuire, 'Irish parliament', pp 24–6; McGrath, 'Securing the Protestant interest', pp 123–7; idem, *Irish Constitution*, pp 91–2.

40 *CSPD, 1693*, pp 134, 186, 237.

41 Dean John Richards to Wyche, 8 Jan. 1693, National Archives of Ireland, Dublin (hereafter NAI), Wyche Papers, 1/1/65.

42 —— to Bishop William King, 13 May 1693, TCD, Lyons Collection, MSS 1995–2008, f. 275; *CSPD, 1693*, p. 6.

43 *CSPD, 1693*, p. 121.

44 Ibid., p. 134.

45 Ibid., pp 134–5.

46 Ibid., pp 145, 148.

47 McGrath, 'Securing the Protestant interest', pp. 105–12; idem, *Irish Constitution*, pp 87, 107–13.

48 *CSPD, 1693*, pp 166–7.

49 Warrant to Sydney, 13 June 1693, NAI, Wyche Papers, 1/2/34; *CSPD, 1693*, pp 176, 179.

50 *CSPD, 1693*, p. 192.

51 McGrath, *Irish Constitution*, pp 92–3.

52 C. I. McGrath, 'English ministers, Irish politicians, and the making of a parliamentary settlement in Ireland, 1692–5', *English Historical Review*, 119 (2004), pp 593–610; idem, *Irish Constitution*, pp 93–8.

53 *CSPD, 1694–5*, pp 455–61, 468; *CSPD, 1695 & Addenda*, p. 331; HMC, *Buccleuch MSS*, ii, p. 183.

54 *CSPD, 1694–5*, p. 468.

55 Ibid., p. 471.

56 Ibid., p. 461.

57 William Coxe (ed.), *Private and Original Correspondence of Charles Talbot, Duke of Shrewsbury, with King William, the Leaders of the Whig Party, and other Distinguished Statesmen* (London, 1821), p. 65; E. L. Ellis, 'William III and the politicians', in Geoffrey Holmes (ed.), *Britain After the Glorious Revolution 1688–1714* (London, 1969), p. 122.

58 Porter to Coningsby, 26 May 1694, Public Record Office of Northern Ireland, Belfast (hereafter PRONI), De Ros MSS, D638/18/25.

59 Porter to Coningsby, 13 Mar., 22 Apr. 1696, PRONI, De Ros MSS, D638/18/43, 65.

60 Bishop of Kildare to John Ellis, 2 May 1696, British Library, London (BL), Add. MS 28880, f. 126; Porter to Coningsby, 29 Apr. 1696, PRONI, De Ros MSS, D638/18/66; HMC, *Buccleuch MSS*, ii, p. 328. See also Alan Brodrick to St John Brodrick, 20 May 1696, Surrey History Centre, Woking, Middleton Papers, Brodrick MSS, 1248/1, ff 284–5; *CSPD, 1696*, pp 184–6, 191, 194, 197–8.

61 Porter to Coningsby, 29 Apr. 1696, PRONI, De Ros MSS, D638/18/66.

62 HMC, *Buccleuch MSS*, ii, pp 328–9.

63 Ibid., ii, p. 332. Similar problems arose in 1706–7 with the terminal illness and death of one of the lords justices, John, Baron Cutts. See BL, Add. MS 38154, ff 88–9, 102, 128, 142, 144, 146–8, 152, 154, 160.

64 Porter to Coningsby, 31 May 1696, PRONI, De Ros MSS, D638/18/68; *CSPD, 1696*, pp 207–8.

65 Porter to Coningsby, 31 May 1696, PRONI, De Ros MSS, D638/18/68; Minutes of the Irish privy council, 2 June 1696, NAI, M2453.

66 *CSPD, 1696*, pp 209–11, 226, 229–30, 243, 246; HMC, *Buccleuch MSS*, ii, pp 344, 358–9; PRONI, De Ros MSS, D638/18/70–1.

67 HMC, *Buccleuch MSS*, ii, p. 348.

68 Ibid., ii, p. 354.

69 *CSPD, 1696*, p. 239.

70 Ibid., pp 242, 260–2; PRONI, De Ros MSS, D638/18/72; HMC, *Buccleuch MSS*, ii, p. 365; HMC, *Downshire MSS*, i, p. 676.

71 *CSPD, 1696*, pp 457–8.

72 *CSPD, 1697*, p. 19.

73 Ibid., pp 129, 132, 134; HMC, *Buccleuch MSS*, ii, p. 460; *NHI, ix*, pp 490–1.

74 Hayton, *Ruling Ireland*, p. 63.

75 Patrick Kelly, 'Lord Galway and the penal laws', in C. E. J. Caldicott, Hugh Gough and J. P. Pittion (eds), *The Huguenots and Ireland: Anatomy of an Emigration* (Dublin, 1987), p. 244.

76 In general see Murtagh, 'Massue de Ruvigny'.

77 Hayton, *Ruling Ireland*, p. 215.

78 *CSPD, 1697*, p. 134.

79 *The Journals of the House of Commons of the Kingdom of Ireland* (8 vols, Dublin, 1753) (hereafter *CJI*), ii, pp 833–4, 836; *CSPD, 1697*, p. 281.

80 Kelly, 'Galway and the penal laws', p. 240.

81 McGrath, 'Securing the Protestant interest', pp. 72–7; Kelly, 'Galway and the penal laws', pp 239–40.

82 Kelly, 'Galway and the penal laws', p. 241.

83 C. I. McGrath, 'The provisions for conversion in the penal laws, 1695–1750', in Michael Brown, C. I. McGrath and Thomas P. Power (eds), *Converts and Conversion in Ireland, 1650–1850* (Dublin, 2005), p. 58.

84 William III to Galway, 16–26 July 1698, in Paul Grimblot (ed.), *Letters of William III and Louis XIV and of their Ministers, 1699–1700* (London, 1948), pp 84–6.

85 McGrath, *Irish Constitution*, pp 134–52.

86 William III to Galway, 1–11 June 1699, in Grimblot (ed.), *Letters of William III*, pp 334–5.

87 *CJI*, ii, p. 1,123.

88 *CSPD, 1699–1700*, p. 131.

89 *NHI, ix*, p. 491.

90 *CSPD, 1700–2*, pp 173–4.

91 Dickson, *New Foundations*, p. 52.

92 *CSPD, 1700–2*, p. 353.

93 For examples see *CSPD, 1694–5*, pp 445–59; *CSPD, 1696*, pp 265–6; *CSPD, 1697*, p. 134; *CSPD, 1699–1700*, p. 240; *CSPD, 1700–2*, pp 390–1.

94 *CSPD, 1700–2*, pp 187, 192–3, 197, 205–6, 209; Rochester to Thomas Keightley, 11 Feb.,

6, 29 Mar., 5 June 1701, 13, 20 Jan. 1702, National Library of Ireland, Dublin (hereafter NLI), Inchiquin MSS, Keightley Papers, fols 2,596–9.
95 For government and parliament in Ireland in Anne's reign see McGrath, *Irish Constitution*, pp 153–283.
96 *NHI, ix*, pp 492–5.
97 Hayton, *Ruling Ireland*, pp 106–30.
98 *NHI, ix*, pp 492–5.
99 Beckett, 'Irish viceroyalty', p. 70.
100 See, for example, Military Establishment, 1692, NAI, Wyche Papers, 2/51; *Calendar of Treasury Books (hereafter CTB), 1703*, pp 124–5.
101 *CSPD, 1694–5*, pp 27, 490; *CSPD, 1697*, pp 52, 162; *CTB, 1693–6*, pp 498, 1107; *CTB, 1697*, p. 179.
102 *CSPD, 1698*, p. 164; *CSPD, 1699–1700*, p. 161; *CTB, 1697–8*, pp 89, 379.
103 *CSPD, 1693*, p. 431; *CSPD, 1696*, p. 275; *CTB, 1696–7*, pp 206, 421; *CTB, 1698–9*, p. 414.
104 *CTB, 1700–1*, pp 87–8, 310, 318.
105 H. Guy to Wyche, 17 June 1693, NAI, Wyche Papers, 1/1/78; *CSPD, 1693*, p. 175; *CSPD, 1697*, p. 137; *CTB, 1696–7*, p. 421; *CTB, 1697*, pp 158, 162; *Calendar of Treasury Papers (hereafter CTP), 1697–1702*, p. 34.
106 *CSPD, 1690–1*, p. 138; *CSPD, 1696*, p. 275; *CSPD, 1699–1700*, pp 236–7; *CTB, 1696–7*, pp 205–6; *CTB, 1698–9*, p. 383.
107 *CTB, 1693–6*, pp 1,068, 1,102.
108 For examples see H. Guy to Wyche, 17 June 1693, NAI, Wyche Papers, 1/1/78; *CSPD, 1690–1*, p. 138; *CSPD, 1696*, p. 275.
109 *CSPD, 1699–1700*, pp 183, 218, 221.
110 *CTB, 1693–6*, pp 498, 1107; *CTB, 1696–7*, pp 206, 421; *CTB, 1697*, p. 179; *CTB, 1698–9*, p. 414; *CSPD, 1694–5*, p. 490.
111 See for example *CTB, 1693–6*, p. 433.
112 An account of the annual payments to be made for subsisting the army, and for the paying the general officers and others on the Establishment, [1690s], BL, Add. MS 4761, f. 244.
113 *CTB, 1698–9*, pp 94–5, 416; *CTB, 1699–1700*, p. 35; *CTP, 1697–1702*, p. 350.
114 Rochester to Keightley, 11 Feb., 5 June 1701, NLI, Inchiquin MSS, Keightley Papers, fols 2,596, 2,598.
115 *CSPD, 1695 & Addenda*, p. 203; *CTB, 1693–6*, p. 826.
116 Royal Warrant, [1695], NAI, Wyche Papers, 2/98.
117 *CSPD, 1699–1700*, pp 162, 199, 216; *CTB, 1698–9*, p. 378.
118 Rochester to Keightley, 17 Feb. 1702, NLI, Inchiquin MSS, Keightley Papers, fol. 2,599; *CTB, 1702*, p. 150; W. A. Speck, 'Hyde, Laurence, first earl of Rochester (bap. 1642, d. 1711)', *ODNB* [www.oxforddnb.com/view/article/14332].
119 *CTB, 1700–1*, p. 70.
120 *CSPD, 1691–2*, p. 251; *CTB, 1693–6*, pp 1,090, 1,148; *CTB, 1700–1*, pp 330, 353.
121 Rochester to Keightley, 20 Jan. 1702, NLI, Inchiquin MSS, Keightley Papers, fol. 2,599.

122 Ibid., 6, 29 Mar. 1701, ibid., fol. 2,597; *CTB, 1700–1*, pp 69, 210, 244, 274; *CTB, 1702*, p. 128; *CSPD, 1700–2*, pp 295, 336.

123 English lords justices to Shrewsbury, 14 Sept. 1714, TCD, MS 2023, f. 79.

124 Privy council minutes, 15 Sept. 1715, TNA, PC 2/85/146, pp 283–4.

125 Patrick McNally, *Parties, Patriots and Undertakers: Parliamentary Politics in Early Hanoverian Ireland* (Dublin, 1997), p. 47.

126 R. E. Burns, *Irish Parliamentary Politics in the Eighteenth Century* (2 vols, Washington, DC, 1989–1990), i, pp 48–9.

127 *NHI, ix*, p. 492.

128 Burns, *Parliamentary Politics*, i, p. 48.

129 Hayton, *Ruling Ireland*, p. 215.

130 See, for example, Galway to Secretary Stanhope, 21 Oct. 1715, TNA, SP 63/373/189–90.

131 Galway and Grafton to Secretary Stanhope, 26 Oct. 1715, TNA, SP 63/373/183–4.

132 *The Statutes at Large passed in the Parliaments held in Ireland* (20 vols, Dublin, 1763–1801), iv, pp 325–7; C. I. McGrath, 'The Irish experience of "financial revolution", 1660–1760', in C. I. McGrath and Chris Fauske (eds), *Money, Power and Print: Interdisciplinary Studies on the Financial Revolution in the British Isles* (Newark, 2008), pp 166–8; C. I. McGrath, 'Money, politics and power: the financial legislation of the Irish parliament', in D. W. Hayton and James Kelly (eds), *The Eighteenth-Century Composite State: Representative Institutions in Ireland and Europe, 1689–1800* (Basingstoke, 2010), pp 29–30.

133 Burns, *Parliamentary Politics*, i, pp 48–67; McNally, *Parties, Patriots and Undertakers*, pp 102–4.

134 Burns, *Parliamentary Politics*, i, pp 67–9; *NHI, ix*, p. 492.

CHAPTER 4

Residential and Non-Residential Lords Lieutenant – The Viceroyalty 1703–1790

James Kelly

I

By the mid-eighteenth century, the status of the lord lieutenancy of Ireland had fallen so far in the estimation of the British aristocratic elite from whose ranks appointees to that office were drawn that few would have concurred with the second duke of Bolton who announced his intention in 1715 'of retiring for good and all into the country' when his expectations of the viceroyalty were dashed.[1] As the deputy of the king in Ireland, the lord lieutenant was formally possessed of an extensive array of powers: 'its honours are many; its privileges are numerous', the second edition of the *Royal Register* reported encouragingly.[2] Moreover, the occupant of the office was, Henry Penruddocke Wyndham observed on a visit to Ireland in 1759, accorded greater 'respect . . . than his king receives in London'. Yet, as Wyndham also noted, the lord lieutenant possessed fewer powers than his predecessors 'a century' previously.[3] As exemplified by the instructions given the earl of Carlisle, who was sworn in on 23 December 1780, the lord lieutenant was formally responsible for the wellbeing of the Church of Ireland by ensuring that 'pious and orthodox persons . . . of good repute' were appointed to church livings. He was required to ensure 'the equal and impartial administration of justice' by monitoring the courts of justice and the officials who manned them. He was obliged to support the officials tasked with the administration of the revenue, and it was his duty to ensure that public moneys were properly expended. It was also his responsibility to ensure the Irish army establishment was maintained and disciplined, that the trade laws were enforced, the currency regulated, and, among a range of other functions, he was empowered to call parliament. Saliently, he could only exercise his authority in the latter respect with the king's prior permission, and the main civil, religious and military appointments were also made by the king, albeit on the lord lieutenant's recommendation.[4]

Though these administrative responsibilities were sufficient, the earl of Chesterfield confided in 1745, to ensure 'that the business of this place . . . is continual', the 'chief task which confronted every lord lieutenant was the management of the Irish parliament and the acquisition of a sufficient majority in the House of Commons'.[5] A cooperative parliament was necessary to ensure the authorisation of the funds required to pay for the administration of the kingdom, and to maintain a smooth and untroubled Anglo-Irish nexus. As a result, the lord lieutenant's time was primarily taken up with political issues, which obliged him during the era of non-residential viceroys, 1701 to 1767, to accommodate the aspirations, personal and political, of the various factions and interests that comprised the Anglo-Irish elite, and to retain sufficient credibility with ministers and officials at Whitehall to ensure they responded expeditiously and sympathetically to dispatches and delegations from Dublin. Because these tasks required considerable personal and political judgment, energy and patience, many lords lieutenant deemed the task of overseeing the government of Ireland to be 'extremely disagreeable', and some responded, like Lord Chesterfield in 1746, by avowing that their 'stay . . . shall be as short as I can possibly make it, though it cannot be half so short as I would wish it'.[6] The duke of Grafton arrived at a similar conclusion in 1724; he observed then that 'the king's service . . . make[s] me willingly submit to do some *penance* here, knowing well that it will be no longer than the present circumstances of affairs absolutely require'.[7]

Since most lords lieutenant found the position demanding, and some even deemed it disagreeable, the average incumbency between 1701 and 1767 was a modest thirty-five months. Only nine of the twenty-three men who held the office then remained *in situ* for more than three years,[8] and while they account for forty-three of the sixty-seven years, a further nine occupied the position for less than two years (four served for less than twelve months).[9] Moreover, as the disinclination of peers of the first rank (dukes) to accept the office in the 1760s indicates, it became increasingly difficult to convince ambitious, able and well connected politicians to accept what Lord Hervey described as 'this honourable Irish exile', and Lord Northington denominated as 'an honourable banishment'.[10] The utilisation, during the early decades of the eighteenth century especially, by those in power of the office to marginalise political rivals helped to foster and to perpetuate this impression, though the effectiveness of this tactic was diminished considerably by the fact that the holder of the office was in a position to exercise his right to sit at cabinet when not in Ireland. This helped to sustain the impression of the lord lieutenancy as an invitingly 'splendid station', but because most lords lieutenant eagerly surrendered the position after a relatively short incumbency, and few maintained a special interest in Ireland thereafter, the predominantly negative image that the office obtained among the British ruling elite during the early decades was fixed firmly by mid-eighteenth century.

It is hardly surprising therefore, following the earl of Rochester's decision in 1701 not to take up permanent residence in Ireland, that the fifteen men who succeeded him in the lord lieutenancy between 1703 and 1760 determined that they need only be present in Ireland when peers and MPs gathered to meet in parliament.[11] Since parliament met biennially for approximately six to eight months from 1703, the lord lieutenancy was essentially a part-time position. This suited the duke of Ormonde (1703–7, 1710–13), 'a generous, good natured, fine gentleman', who was more at ease with the gentility of the royal court than the rough and tumble of provincial politicking.[12] Non-residence also suited the duke of Dorset (1730–7), who was so unskilled in the practical arts of politics and uncomfortable with the interpersonal demands of the position when he was first appointed that he sought to compensate by entertaining 'with [such] great magnificence' that it was concluded 'he seems to love show and grandeur more than business'.[13] And it appealed to practising politicians like Pembroke (1707–8), Wharton (1708–10), Shrewsbury (1713–14), Sunderland (1714–17), Townshend (1717), Bolton (1717–20), Grafton (1720–4) and Cartaret (1724–30), who did not conceive of the Irish viceroyalty as the summit of their ambitions.[14]

Non-residency had major implications for the lord lieutenant as, first, the lords justices appointed to oversee Irish affairs when the incumbent was not in the kingdom, and, second, the parliamentary managers, who assumed responsibility for forging a working majority in the House of Commons, exercised influence that would otherwise have rested with the viceroy. This state of affairs was not without consequence for the office of lord lieutenant, but advantages were so obvious, when compared with the alternatives, that successive lords lieutenant declined to change it, as Lord Chesterfield recalled over a decade after he had handed on the baton:

> A lord lieutenant may if he pleases govern alone, but then he must, as I know by experience, take a good deal more trouble upon himself than most lord lieutenants care to do, and he must not be afraid; but as they commonly prefer *otium com dignitate*, their guards, their battle-axes and their trumpets, not to mention perhaps the profits of their post, to a laborious execution of it, they must necessarily rule by a faction, of which faction for the time being they are only the first slaves. The condition of the obligation is this: your excellency or your grace wants to carry on his majesty's business smoothly, and to have it to say when you go back that you met with no difficulties; this we have sufficient strength in

> parliament to engage for, provided we appear to have the favour and countenance of government; the money, be it what it will, shall be cheerfully voted; as for the public you shall do what you will, or nothing at all, for we care for that no more than we suppose your grace or excellency does, but we repeat it again, our recommendation to place, pensions etc must prevail, or we shall not be able to keep our people in order. These are always the expressed, or at least the implied conditions of the treaties, which either the indolence or the insufficiency of the governors ratify: from that moment, these undertakers bury the governor alive, but indeed pompously.[15]

Chesterfield's negative perceptions notwithstanding, most lords lieutenant contrived to govern Ireland in partnership with, rather than in deference to the lords justices and undertakers upon whom they depended. Moreover, this arrangement largely worked successfully, because it ensured that the money required for the maintenance of the civil and military establishments was routinely voted, and, since most differences were defused rather than fought out, that the Anglo-Irish nexus functioned after a satisfactory fashion, which was the ministerial priority.[16] However, it also had a downside, which was adverted to repeatedly in the 1750s; it permitted a *corps d'elite* of Irish politicians to exercise more power over the governance and direction of the kingdom than many English officials deemed prudent, and it sustained what by then had become debilitating factional rivalries. With the advantage of hindsight, George Vernon explained in 1766 to the marquess of Granby:

> It must have been evident to [every] man, since it was so to me, that fixed lords justices so frequent and long in power, to whom the Irish looked up for their preferment, so far attached all parliamentary interest to themselves, that our lords lieutenant could have no independent weight, but must be under the control of the Irish governors, who, having also their separate interests, embarrassed the lieutenant, and threw the nation into factious parties, to the obstruction of all public business, and the support of private jobs.[17]

This potentially deleterious situation did not excite concern during the long viceroyalty of the fourth duke of Devonshire (1737–45) because the protagonists then ensured that differences were resolved by compromise and accommodation. However, this cooperative outlook was contingent on the principals of the main interests – governmental and factional – acknowledging that there was more to be gained by maintaining existing arrangements than by pressing their own agendae, and this was no longer the case by the 1750s.

In the early 1750s the combination of a weak lord lieutenant (the duke of Dorset, 1750–5), a wilful chief secretary (Lord George Sackville), and an assertive lords justice (the primate, Archbishop George Stone) who concurred that the influence Irish politicians had been permitted to accrue was at the expense of English authority in Ireland caused the Irish administration to embark on a policy aimed at bringing government back to Dublin Castle. Their juncture with the Ponsonbys, an ambitious political connexion that had been manoeuvring for some time to supplant the long dominant Boyle interest, provided them with the numbers to take the struggle into the House of Commons, which set in train the sequence of events that precipitated the Money Bill dispute.[18] It also highlighted the limitations of the existing undertaker system, and encouraged wildly exaggerated claims that the Irish parliament aimed at independency when the most Irish representatives aspired to, as Thomas Pakenham, the MP for Longford, pointed out, was 'the benefit of those restrictions [*lege* rights] obtained at the [Glorious] Revolution'.[19]

In the absence of the restraint exercised by the main protagonists, and the unwillingness of the British government to alter its essentially conservative attitude to the administration of Ireland, inimitably defined by Robert Walpole as *quieta non movere*, the Money Bill dispute might have shattered the equilibrium that had prevailed in Irish politics since the early 1730s. Yet there was no going back to the *status quo ante*, and the fact that the lord lieutenant, the marquess of Hartington (1755–7), who negotiated the compromise settlement that brought the dispute to a close chose to remain in Ireland through the summer of 1755, though parliament was not in session and he itched to return home, indicated that the key issues of power and authority that lay at the root of the dispute had not been resolved.[20] This was confirmed by the different political and administrative options for the future governance of Ireland that were floated in the 1750s. Signally, these included a legislative union, which Irish public opinion visibly and memorably made clear it would not wear in the winter of 1759.[21]

This option excluded, attention focused on the terms upon which individuals served as lords lieutenant. Hartington's acknowledgement that his decision to stay in Ireland in 1755 was 'best for the service' as well as his 'reputation' might have recommended the immediate inauguration of a system of residential lords lieutenant, but his return to England, after an incumbency of less than two years, was testament to the fact that this was not an arrangement he was content to initiate.[22] His successor, the duke of Bedford (1757–61), was equally unwilling; he had to be convinced to accept the lord lieutenancy, and the fact that he was obliged, 'after a short struggle . . . to follow the example of his predecessors, to return to the old system, and to put himself in the hands of the parliamentary undertakers' suggested to some that it was business as usual. But this was not the case since he recommended the appointment of a lord deputy rather than lords justices when the lord lieutenant was not resident.[23] In practice, the overwhelming desire on the part of British ministers not to alter the foundations of government in Ireland, continuing political instability in Britain, and the realisation that peers of appropriate stature were not queuing up to accept an Irish posting, encouraged caution. Both Earl Temple and Lord Hardwicke declined the opportunity before Bedford was succeeded in office in 1761 by the earl of Halifax, an experienced politician with a good knowledge of imperial policy, who cannily ingratiated himself with the Irish public by declining to accept the augmentation of his salary sanctioned by the Irish parliament. In addition, he vowed 'to do all the good he can to Ireland, . . . to govern you [Ireland] well himself, and . . . not [to] be governed by *undertakers*'. Yet, he too was not long in the country when he 'put himself into the hands' of the rehabilitated primate, George Stone.[24]

Halifax's priority was to do nothing that would create waves, which he contrived successfully to do for one session, but 'tired of the kingdom', he let it be known in the summer of 1762 that he would not return.[25] His successor the duke of Northumberland was more of a political makeweight; he was offered the position when (among others) the marquess of Granby declined. Convinced, like the duke of Dorset in the 1730s, that he could spend his way into the affections of politicians and public, Northumberland relied heavily on the superior political skills of his chief secretary – the grasping and ambitious William Gerard Hamilton, the administrative knowledge of Primate Stone, and the influence with MPs of Lord Shannon and Speaker Ponsonby. He was enabled thereby successfully to negotiate the 1763–4 session without major embarrassment, but his dependence on Hamilton caused those who expected more from his 'jovial magnificence' to dismiss him as 'a poor weak man, [who] means no harm, . . . but [who] is entirely under the government of his secretary'.[26]

Northumberland was less ineffectual than his critics perceived, but, in common with his immediate predecessors, he was unwilling either to extend his stay in Ireland beyond one session or to assume the responsibility for bringing about the administrative changes many now deemed necessary.[27] These included the cabinet, which determined at a meeting on 1 February 1765 attended by three recent lords lieutenant – Northumberland, Halifax and Bedford – that future lords lieutenants 'should be directed to reside ~~almost~~ constantly, and, in case of necessity, that there should be a short leave of absence given to him and a Lord Deputy appointed to the government during that absence'. However, the instability that gripped British politics in the mid-1760s meant that this decision was not acted upon.[28] Indeed, instead of a residential lord lieutenant of appropriate *gravitas*, the direction of the kingdom was entrusted in June 1765, largely for financial reasons, to the earl of Weymouth, 'a man of dissipated and extravagant tastes' who was expected in some quarters to spend five years in Ireland. In fact, Weymouth held the office for such a short period that he contrived to surrender the seals of office having never even visited the kingdom of which he was titular head.[29] His successor was an Irish peer, the earl of Hertford, who had previously sought the office, and been passed over on more than one occasion. His primary motive in accepting the position was familial rather than political, and he was both uninspiring and widely disliked. In addition, he did nothing to disabuse those who perceived he was another in a long sequence of lords lieutenant who possessed few of the personal and political skills required to lay the foundations of an improved system of government in Ireland headed by a residential lord lieutenant.[30] As a result, the deficiencies and defects of current arrangements were a common cause of complaint by the mid-1760s, as Charles O'Hara senior lucidly elaborated:

> This kingdom hitherto has been governed by [lord] lieut[enan]ts who neither knew its constitution nor its interests. Willing to jog on quietly, they have therefore put themselves into the hands of the prevailing interest of the place to carry on business for them. When some have attempted to do without it, as the d[uke] of Dorset in 1751, the prevailing interest has opposed and defeated them. But for the most part, it has been a lucrative composition; the lord lieutenant to provide for his immediate dependents, and the supporting powers to have all the rest. But in the course of the barter, the interests of the kingdom have never been thought of. Its utility to England has never been consulted. The only objects have been jobs, and the only measures expedients.[31]

This was plainly unsatisfactory, and guided by the policy considerations that had prompted the decision to favour residency in 1765, and by the implicit acknowledgement that the recent sequence of uninspiring and abbreviated viceroyalties was not conducive to effective government, the earl of Bristol was appointed lord lieutenant in 1766 on the explicit understanding that he would reside for the full duration of his incumbency. Indeed, he animated the hopes of those patriots (and others) in Ireland who welcomed this very prospect by letting it be known that he 'will be his own minister, that all applications must be addressed directly to him, that he will study the good of the country, and promote it where it clashes with the interest of Gr[eat] Brit[ain]'. Bristol's avowal was a source of 'alarm' for those, interested only in power and in the 'loaves and fishes' of office, who had a vested interest in the maintenance unaltered of the undertaker system, but their concern proved gratifyingly short-lived.[32] Lord Chatham, who headed the ministry of which Bristol was a part, did agree to meet with Henry Flood, who had emerged as one of the most luminous and perceptive younger voices on the Irish political stage, to discuss the future government of Ireland, but

Chatham's idea were insufficiently well worked out to suggest that the promised new era of residential lords lieutenant was about to commence, and he was, in any event, unable to sustain his ministry, with the result that Bristol never even came to Ireland. As a result, seasoned observers of the Irish scene justifiably concluded that the 'project for abolishing the lords justices and taking the government of the House of Commons' and placing it immediately in the possession of a lord lieutenant was simply 'utopian'.[33]

II

In the wake of the fitful nature of the attempts in the mid-1760s to give effect to the 'consensus of opinion [in Britain] from the early 1760s onwards . . . that lords lieutenant should be constantly resident', it is hardly surprising that there were many on both sides of the Irish Sea who doubted if it was every going to happen.[34] Having concluded pragmatically that it was not 'a question of right or wrong, but of practicable or impracticable', Edmund Burke opined in October 1766 that the proposed arrangement would not 'hold five years' even if someone could be persuaded to accept the position on condition that they must reside in Ireland for the duration of their term in office.[35] There was certainly no expectation that Lord George Townshend, who was prevailed upon in August 1767 in a somewhat desperate attempt to attach his still more mercurial brother, Charles, to the newly established Grafton ministry, would remain in the country 'an hour after the sessions'.[36] For one thing, it was widely anticipated, given the tremors of alarm that gripped the undertakers some months earlier when Chatham and Bristol toyed ineffectually with the idea of assembling a Castle party in the House of Commons and implementing a number of popular (patriot) measures, that the next meeting of parliament would be 'as troublesome . . . as any that ever was'. This must make what was in any circumstances 'disagreeable work' still more bothersome. Secondly, because it was expected that Bristol would be the next minister to meet the Irish parliament, a substantial part of the 'salary' normally available to an incoming lord lieutenant had been expended, with the result that the incumbent could calculate on 'losing £8,000 or £10,000'.[37] These were considerations that weighed heavily with most of Townshend's predecessors, but the new lord lieutenant was less exercised by such contingencies.

An experienced soldier, who had served successfully in Canada, Townshend shared the 'fixed and firm ideas concerning the dependence of the British colonies' more usually associated with his brother.[38] As a result, when he discovered on his arrival in Ireland that the 'undertakers', from whom he expected support and cooperation, were determined to extract personal and political concessions greater than what he, and his cabinet colleagues in London, deemed reasonable, and were not prepared to support the scheme, which had strong royal as well as ministerial support, to add three thousand soldiers to the Irish army establishment, he sought and was given permission to stay in Ireland when the tense, but by no means wholly unsuccessful, 1767–8 session concluded.[39] By depriving the speaker, John Ponsonby, and at least one, and perhaps two other leading figures in Ireland of the much coveted opportunity to exercise the authority and influence that came with being a lords justice, Townshend made it apparent that what most Irish politicians had long apprehended was approaching – the day when they would no longer be entrusted with the power and perquisites that flowed automatically in their direction from the undertakers system. Unwilling to contemplate this eventuality, and encouraged by Townshend's volatile personality, which repelled as many as it fascinated, they vowed to resist. And they were encouraged to make a stand by the conclusion of the energetic, if loosely bound, patriot phalanx that Townshend was embarked upon an attempt to augment the power of the monarchy at the expense of parliament.

The fact that he was opposed by two of the most powerful strands in Irish politics placed Townshend in a particularly invidious position. He contrived, as he knew he must, to rally support from independent country gentlemen and smaller parliamentary connections, but he was at a severe disadvantage. Firstly, he had not come to Ireland with a well thought out 'plan for new-modelling' the government of Ireland by pulling 'the present structure . . . down to the ground' and building 'a new one . . . on the same foundation'. And, secondly, as there was no certainty as to what his intentions were, and the most compelling previous attempt to 'bring government back to Dublin Castle' in 1752–5 had failed disastrously, many MPs and their patrons were disposed to sit on the fence and await the outcome.[40] The magnitude of the issues at stake, and the strength of Townshend's resolve were highlighted in the winter of 1769 when, by rejecting the critical privy council money bill that symbolised the submission of the Irish parliament to the authority of the king, the combined weight of Townshend's opponents elevated the matter at issue above that of a struggle for power, upon which ministers could afford (as they had traditionally done) to take different positions, into a dispute with constitutional ramifications, which allowed for far less difference. Townshend did not secure the support from his cabinet colleagues to which he believed he was entitled, and the long-term better governance of the empire demanded, but he was given enough authority, particularly when Lord North assumed the reins of power in Britain in 1770, not only to intensify his efforts to forge a Castle party, but also to take the struggle to his opponents. North's support was crucial in enabling him to deal with potential supporters from a position of some strength, and to keep his opponents on the back foot through 1770 and in the run-up to the 1771 spring session.

He was also assisted by his temperament, for though he was congenitally impatient with the pompous and the self-important, which was not ideal when it came to forging a political connection and to negotiating with peers and MPs, he possessed a soldier's capacity to deal with adversity and to act decisively. This compensated for his moodiness, his erratic work habits, and fondness for raucous company, which the more refined found repellent.[41] As a result, though the Castle 'party' he assembled was far from secure or assured of victory in the sessions of 1771 and 1771–2, when the more controversial aspect of his strategy (the division of the board of revenue) was debated in parliament, such divisions as it lost were embarrassing rather than humiliating defeats. Moreover, he was assisted by the absence of concert between the various interests that constituted the opposition, and by the poor leadership provided by its principals beginning with John Ponsonby, whose decision in 1771 to resign the speakership rather than deliver a complimentary message from the House of Commons to Townshend was a serious error of judgment.

The refusal of Lord Shannon, who had detached himself from the opposition before the end of the 1771–2 session, formally to align his substantial interest behind the new Castle party cautions one against concluding that Irish politics were irreversibly restructured during the five years and two months that Townshend served as lord lieutenant. Nonetheless, the perception that he had repaired some of the 'internal weaknesses' to which government had long been subject by 'numberless follies and faults', and that his decision to reside in Ireland had established a precedent that his successor must follow ensured that a new era in the history of the office and in the government and administration of Ireland was about to begin.[42] It was not a case that Townshend's tenure had established the pattern that his successors were obliged to follow; there was no blue-print, no fixed statement of policy and no plan because matters were worked out essentially after an *ad hoc* fashion, but Townshend's decision to reside in Ireland for the duration of his time in office, and his acceptance that the lord lieutenant personally assumed the responsibility for ensuring the administration had a majority in the House of Commons changed the office and Irish politics irrevocably. There was no going back to the days when lords lieutenant could contentedly delegate the task of government to others. The model of an executive viceroyalty that Townshend had forged for the practical task of ensuring smooth government within a more structured imperial context was the model for the office that was to survive until the Act of Union still more fundamentally altered the constitutional context and the nature of the office.

If the effect of this was to affirm and consolidate the authority of the lord lieutenancy in Ireland, it came at a price. Since resident lords lieutenant were unable to attend cabinet meetings, it was only a matter of time until it was determined that the office was not of cabinet rank. There was no formal decision to this effect. But the denial of a request by the earl of Carlisle that he might be permitted to attend a cabinet meeting in 1780, and the decision that formal contact with the cabinet should proceed through the secretary of state for the southern department (later the home secretary) effectively subordinated the lord lieutenant to the secretary of state.[43] Moreover, because, unlike successive chief secretaries, lords lieutenant were not encouraged to travel to England even on business trips, the chief secretary became the primary point of interaction between the Irish administration and the British government, and, in the aftermath of the ratification of the Act of Union, the *de facto* head of the Irish executive.[44]

This was in the future. Yet, it was already apparent before Townshend left Ireland in 1772 that his decision to assume responsibility for the creation of a Castle party had transformed the fortunes of the office of chief secretary. Prior to Townshend's acceptance of the lord lieutenancy, the chief secretaryship was an intrinsically subordinate administrative post, frequently occupied by political nonentities or dependents of the lord lieutenant, some of whom had little to offer.[45] This was not universally the case; William Gerard Hamilton (1761–4) and Richard Rigby (1757–61) were capable administrators and talented parliamentary performers, but they were a minority, and the skill level brought by those who filled the position was often closer to that of Walter Cary, who struggled as chief secretary to Dorset in the 1730s, and to Lord George Sackville, whose misjudgments contributed to the Money Bill dispute. Alternatively, they were non-entities in the tradition of Sir Charles Bunbury, Francis Seymour-Conway and August John Hervey, who made no impact at all during the mid-1760s.[46]

Townshend's first chief secretary, Lord Frederick Campbell, was constructed in the same mould, but the conjuncture of the appointment of Robert Macartney in January 1769 and the privy council Money Bill crisis later the same year, created a set of conditions wherein the chief secretary had to assume a more active political role. Macartney found this trying at first, but he rose triumphantly to the challenge. Macartney was not the only skilled official in the Irish bureaucratic machine with political knowledge to whom Townshend could appeal, but he was the most important because it fell to him to take the administration's case into the House of Commons; he in effect became the ministerial presence in that chamber and, as a result, the prototype for those who succeeded him. Indeed, as a result of the role he assumed between 1769 and November 1772, the choice of chief secretary thereafter was as vital as that of the lord lieutenant. This was made explicit by Townshend's successor Earl Harcourt who counselled the prime minister in 1776 to alert his putative successor to be 'extremely attentive to the choice of his secretary, on whose prudence, abilities and firmness the success of a chief governor will greatly depend'.[47]

III

Harcourt was prompted to proffer these remarks in 1776 by his concern to ensure that nothing was done that would endanger the present 'system' and allow matters to 'revert to their former channel'. This was unlikely then, but it was a possibility in 1772 because, Archibald Acheson, the MP for county Armagh observed pertinently, 'the work is not finished'.[48] A majority of those in high office was sufficiently convinced of the merits of residence to advise that there should be no 'interregnum', and therefore no lords justices to bridge the gap between Townshend's departure and his successor's arrival.[49] Yet, the admission by Lord North two years earlier 'that it was not to be expected that men of the first rank in this country [w]ould choose to pass their lives in Ireland', and his willingness to leave it to lords lieutenant to determine the duration of their administrations (four to six years was the suggested length), indicated that residence was far from embedded.[50] Indeed, it was still not fully rooted four years later, in 1776, for though the prime minister and the lord lieutenant were strongly of the opinion then that the office could only be offered 'upon conditions of constant residence', they recognised that these terms were unacceptable to many.[51] Lord Nuneham summarised the prevailing attitude well when in 1772 he advised his father, Simon, Earl Harcourt, not to take the position on the grounds that he could not see how anybody would 'accept as a favour, a six years' banishment amongst . . . a wrong-headed and almost rebellious people'.[52] As a result, identifying someone with the skills required for the role proved more challenging than ever in the final decades of the eighteenth century. The task was not made any easier, certainly, by the reinforcement in the 1770s, 1780s and 1790s of the prevailing negative impression that Ireland was a 'wearisome', 'wretched situation'. [53] Reports from successive chief secretaries and lords lieutenant to the effect that they did not receive appropriately 'digested and decided instructions', and that ministers and prime ministers – the earl of Hillsborough, Lord North and William Pitt were singled out – 'too often leave us to fight our own battles at a great disadvantage', added to the sense of isolation that the holders of these offices found trying.[54]

The expressions of exasperation, anger and self-pity that such experiences generated were compounded, on occasion, by the prospect of financial loss. This was not a new phenomenon; few non-resident lords lieutenant were as careful as the earl of Chesterfield, who recalled smugly in 1768 that he had made £500 clear during his stay in Ireland, or as avaricious as the resident Earl Harcourt, who reputedly 'saved during his lieutenancy here upwards of £40,000, exclusive of secret service money'.[55] This is an improbable (but not impossible) figure, since it was commonly acknowledged that the annual financial allowance available to lords lieutenant, which was increased from £12,000 to £16,000 in 1762 and to £20,000 in 1783, was inadequate to meet the coasts of the position. This certainly was the implication of the claim that Townshend had incurred debts of £12,000 by 1771; by the assertion by William Eden, who was chief secretary in 1780–2, that one 'parliamentary winter' had cost him £3,000; and by the recollection of Earl Temple, who served twice as lord lieutenant in the 1780s, that his 'establishment would have required at least £15,000 p.a. added to the present salary of £20,000' to cover his outgoings. It is not clear how the duke of Rutland (1784–7), who was alerted to the likely cost prior to his departure for Ireland, regarded this prospect, but his preparedness to spend generously contributed in no small measure to his personal popularity, whereas the contrary perception that the earl of Westmorland (1790-4) was a 'skinflint' did his reputation no good at all.[56] Furthermore, those lords lieutenant who declined to participate actively in the cultural life of the capital were also perceived as failing the country; the earl of Carlisle (1781–2), for example, was compared unfavourably with the duke of Portland (1782) because he 'made no effort to patronise the city's public entertainments, arts or letters'.[57]

All things being equal, most lords lieutenant would have preferred to pursue a prudent financial course, but few were prepared to do so, either with their own money or with the public purse, if it made life any easier. This was the attitude certainly of Earl Harcourt, who succeeded Townshend in the autumn of 1772. Though an experienced courtier and diplomat, Harcourt was not disposed to exert himself in the same manner as his predecessor. Having served as British ambassador to Paris for four years immediately prior to his appointment to Ireland, he was used to a gentle lifestyle and, determined that this should continue to be the case, he convinced the secretary to the embassy at Paris, John Blaquiere, to accompany him to Ireland to serve in the capacity of chief secretary.[58] Blaquiere was a good choice. Though he was frowned upon in certain quarters in Ireland as 'a man of low birth and of no property', he possessed the talents required to succeed in the role. His critics alleged that he was endowed with 'the sublime faculty of exciting venality, and of making proselytes to their country's ruin by corrupting individuals with the public treasure', but this was a partial as well as a partisan judgment. Blaquiere was undoubtedly skilled in the personal negotiations that were a crucial aspect of the work of residential chief secretaries, but he was also a capable performer in the Commons, and an attentive administrator.[59] These were essential qualities in a good chief secretary, but they were doubly necessary in this instance because, for all 'the gentleness of his manners and the novel obsequiousness of his civility', Harcourt's 'disinclination even to the appearance of business threw everything absolutely into the hands of his secretary'.[60] This was not how it was meant to be, of course, but the Harcourt viceroyalty made it apparent for the first time in the era of executive lords lieutenant that an administration could function efficiently and effectively if the two men at its helm were not equally able, but were possessed of complementary skills and got on well together.

Moreover, one should not underestimate Harcourt. His vainglorious preoccupation with his portrait and the obvious pleasure he gleaned from vacationing at St Wolstans, his country retreat, should not occlude his sound political instincts, and, in particular, his perceptive realisation that, more than any other tactic or strategy he might employ, patronage provided the key to the success of his ministry. To this end, Harcourt gave generously of the resources at his disposal 'to those who contribute[d] most to the support of government'.[61] He was greatly assisted, to be sure, by the eagerness of the leaders of several parliamentary interests, alienated from Dublin Castle during Townshend's administration, to re-engage, and by a series of defections by leading patriots from the politics of opposition. His most notable triumph in respect of the latter was the recruitment was Henry Flood. This was achieved at a high financial cost, but it contributed to the success with which the administration was able not only to ensure that vital financial legislation was approved, but also to oversee the implementation of a series of important revenue raising measures that improved the exchequer's finances.[62] Furthermore, he was able to negotiate the potentially damaging absentee tax controversy in 1773 without major difficulty, and, more significantly, to secure parliamentary authorisation in 1775 for a request to make available 4,000 troops on the Irish army establishment for service in North America. This was probably Harcourt's finest moment, for though he insured himself against embarrassment then, and in the short session convened after the 1776 general election, by engaging in a major splurge in patronage, it meant that when he was finally permitted to leave Ireland in the autumn of 1776, he did so with praise ringing in his ears.[63] 'You will leave the government of Ireland in a state of ease and opulence, which it has not known in twenty years', Lord North effused, while the endorsement provided by George III made the prime minister's words all the sweeter.[64]

Though Earl Harcourt was commonly perceived by those in the corridors of power as having been a particularly successful lord lieutenant, the reality was that his weaknesses were not exposed during the four years that he was in office. Moreover, he was lucky. This notwithstanding, Lord North was properly anxious that he should be succeeded by a man of equal or greater ability. A substantial number of individuals were considered, some were even canvassed to accept the position as a special favour to the prime minister; all declined and, as a result, North was obliged, against his will and 'for want of a better' candidate, to overcome the 'strong political objection' he entertained to nominate John Hobart, earl of Buckinghamshire. 'An ambitious and a proud man, without any particular talents', who had previously served without distinction as ambassador to St Petersburg, Buckinghamshire's primary qualification for the job was that he sought the position. This did not augur well for the smooth government of Ireland at a time when storm clouds were gathering. However, Buckinghamshire's insistence on choosing his own chief secretary suggested that he had a clear idea of what was required.[65]

In practice, as events were to show, Buckinghamshire was not only out of his depth, but also prone to blame others for his own lack of judgment. His task was made more difficult, to be sure, by the fact that the example of the American colonies, a good electoral performance in 1776, and decades of pent-up frustration at the failure of successive British ministers to enhance their commercial and constitutional rights, prompted a surge in popular politicisation that transformed the Volunteers from a mere civil defence force into a potent advocate of change, and the patriots in parliament into a formidable political adversary for the first time. However, Buckinghamshire made a critical error when he chose Richard Heron as his chief secretary. Heron may have been, as Buckinghamshire contended, 'a most excellent chamber council', but the skills required to prosper in that employ and in the minor legal postings he held in England prior to his arrival in Ireland were quite different to those demanded of a chief secretary. Most significantly, he had no parliamentary presence, as Buckinghamshire later acknowledged:

> Sir Richard Heron['s] talents do not enable him to take the least active part in parliament. Consequently, upon every unforeseen motion the house goes wild, those who should support follow their own caprice; the originally intended measure is modify'd away, and many who in fact intended to betray the cause assert that they could not distinguish what was really the wish of government.[66]

This was a serious self-inflicted injury, but it need not have rebounded quite so badly had Buckinghamshire surrounded himself by men of business with the skills required to prop up the most limited of chief secretaries. However, other than Philip Tisdall, the attorney general, whose death in 1777 deprived the administration of its anticipated leader in the House of Commons, Buckinghamshire aspired to construct a working parliamentary majority out of an inchoate collection of family connections (the Conollys and the Leinsters), Castle loyalists and borough interests. This was sufficient to permit the administration to negotiate the 1777–8 session relatively unscathed, but the sharp deterioration in the economic environment that followed was compounded by the radicalising effect on Irish opinion of the refusal of the Westminster legislature to grant a generous measure of 'free trade' in 1778. The consequences of this were brought home in the autumn of 1779 when the administration lost control of the House of Commons, and the patriot interest, led by Henry Grattan, took the unprecedented step of authorising a six-month, rather than the customary two-year, money bill in order to compel the government to concede 'free trade'.[67]

Buckinghamshire endeavoured to explain away the failures of his administration by reference to 'the current state of the Empire', and the weaknesses at the 'heart' of government, but the fact that the Castle party mounted such poor resistance in parliament, and that he sought from February 1780 to replace Heron with a new chief secretary, was an indictment of the lord lieutenant's judgment as well as of his stewardship.[68] His lack of political skill was epitomised by the virtual refusal of otherwise dependable Castle loyalists and committed men of business to work with the administration, and by the disorganisation that gripped its ranks during much of the 1779–80 session. The administration's position was so weak that George Macartney observed ominously in 1780 that 'there seems now to be in most respects as little relations between Ireland and Great Britain as between Great Britain and the Electorate of Hanover'.[69] Indeed, the previous year that government had secretly investigated the possibility of an Anglo-Irish union, and had only jettisoned the idea when it was made clear that any attempt to initiate such a scheme would make an already bad situation worse.[70]

Frustrated on this front, and alarmed by the eagerness of the patriot leadership to pursue an agenda of constitutional reform (legislative independence) that threatened the very foundations of the Anglo-Irish connection, it was decided in the autumn of 1780 not only to replace the ineffectual Heron but also to recall Buckinghamshire. The failure of Lord North to make it clear to Buckinghamshire that this was his intention ensured that the manner in which he was replaced left an enduring legacy of bad feeling. 'Lord North seems determined upon no measure but that of expelling me with humiliation and disgrace from this kingdom', he observed plaintively, but given the many levels on which his administration had failed Buckinghamshire's comment was particularly self-serving.[71]

IV

The maintenance of political authority in Ireland, which was the lords lieutenant's primary responsibility, was contingent on a Castle majority in the house of Commons, and Buckinghamshire and Heron had so far failed in this task in the winter of 1779–80 that a question mark was posed against the future of the Castle executive. This meant that the challenge that greeted Lord Carlisle and his chief secretary William Eden, who then took up office in Ireland late in 1780, was more than usually forbidding. They were tasked, in the words of George Macartney, 'to recover our authority, to restore respect, and conciliate affection'.[72] Significantly, both were better equipped for the task than their predecessors. Having been mooted as a possible lord lieutenant in 1776, and in the interval served as one of the British peace commissioners that attempted, unsuccessfully, in 1778 to negotiate a settlement with the American colonists, the erudite Carlisle was described by admirers as 'young, active and able'. He certainly possessed few illusions as to the order of the task that awaited him in Ireland, but convinced that he must be decisive, and that he had an able ally in William Eden, who had been identified by Buckinghamshire as a suitable replacement for the ineffectual Richard Heron, Carlisle confidently assumed responsibility for the Irish administration in November 1780.[73]

Matters went encouragingly well as the outset, as the administration's combination of firmness and conciliation won over many previously disgruntled men of business.[74] Eden was particularly successful in this respect, as he possessed a natural facility at man management and a capacity for intrigue that were immensely useful to a chief secretary. As a consequence Carlisle was able to stem the drift and disorganisation that beset the Irish administration under Buckinghamshire; indeed, he contentedly observed in advance of the assembly of MPs for the 1781–2 session that 'order and good government will be restored . . . in Ireland'. Carlisle's forecast seemed justified for a time, as divisions within patriot ranks, between those who were eager to press for constitutional reform and influential moderates who were more cautious, inhibited the patriots' extra-parliamentary efforts and diminished their effectiveness in the Commons. As a result, the administration was able to resist disagreeable motions during the first part of the session, but the tide turned against them when the Volunteers of Ulster, who gathered at Dungannon in February 1782, produced a rousing set of resolutions that transferred the fitful campaign for constitutional reform into a forceful national movement. Obliged to acknowledge that 'a nation of armed politicians' could only be assuaged by appropriate concession,[75] Carlisle and Eden sought to convince their ministerial superiors to accede to the moderate proposals advanced by Barry Yelverton to amend Poynings' Law and to repeal the Declaratory Act. But their efforts were set at naught when Lord North was forced to resign in March and the Rockingham Whigs, who came to power shortly afterwards, chose to replace all previous officeholders, including the lord lieutenant, with men from within their own ranks.

Convinced that it had been 'his good fortune to conduct the business of this country at a most critical period without discredit to his majesty's government, and with many increasing advantages to the interests of this kingdom', Carlisle was taken aback by the prospect of his removal. Both Eden and he had anticipated that they might be permitted to remain in Ireland to conclude 'the business of the session and the various public measures and arrangements of some difficulty' then in train, on the grounds that they would, they believed, bring stability to the kingdom.[76] Both could have reconciled themselves to the prospect of being replaced by Rockingham Whigs, but the decision to deprive Carlisle of the lord lieutenancy of Yorkshire was deemed vengeful. Instead of the praise they anticipated for having endured what Carlisle termed 'this seat of thorns', and Eden deemed 'a situation of incessant trouble, . . . not very edifying to health, life or fortune', they felt that they had been treated unfairly, and they declined to cooperate with the incoming administration.[77] It was a virtual repeat of what had happened in 1780, but whereas Buckinghamshire's departure was administratively justified, Carlisle's replacement by the duke of Portland was seen as purely political. It was the first of a sequence of such appointments, as the politics of the senior officeholder in the Irish administration came increasingly to mirror party alignments in Great Britain.[78]

His insistence that he left the Irish administration in a better state than he had encountered it, notwithstanding, Carlisle was acutely conscious of the scale of the problems that awaited his successor, the third duke of Portland:

> I envy not the situation of my successor . . . The junction of the Thames and the Liffey would be as easy an attempt as to enforce a British statute. No juries will find under it, and there are 30,000 men with the arms of government in their hands, who would take the field tomorrow rather than submit to it. These are serious truths.[79]

In practice, neither Portland, nor Earl Temple, who assumed the reins of power when the Rockingham Whig administration collapsed after less than six months in existence, had to deal with problems of the same order of magnitude as Carlisle. Part of the reason for this was that both men were more securely located within the embryonic party system in Great Britain, but it was still more significant that both were in office at a moment when politicians in London accepted the logic of Carlisle's analysis that Irish opinion must be mollified, not defied, and that the only way that this could be done was by meeting Irish demands for greater legislative freedom.

This was not a conclusion that either Portland or Temple, or the governments of which they were members, arrived at entirely willingly. Portland arrived in Ireland in early April 1782 with instructions to lay the basis for a constitutional settlement that would be mutually agreeable.[80] Temple came to Ireland with ambitious plans to put in place a system of 'solid and substantial government'.[81] Both quickly discovered that they possessed neither the authority nor the influence to achieve these goals. Within days of taking up office, Portland was obliged to concede that his plans for a compact that explicitly acknowledged Britain's constitutional primacy would not be realised, and that legislative independence would have to be ceded unconditionally.[82] Temple was accorded a little more time to ponder the implications of the Irish demand that Great Britain formally renounce its entitlement to make law for Ireland, but once he had done so he was still more emphatic that concession was made in a timely fashion. It was a prerequisite, he contended in the winter of 1782–3, not only for his continuing in position, but also for the transition from a situation where 'no efficient government' obtained to the 'firmness' he and others avowed was essential for the preservation intact of the Anglo-Irish connection.[83] As a result, both administrations agreed a number of major legislative initiatives that served rather to weaken than to strengthen the traditional basis of government in Ireland, and to pose a serious question mark against the capacity of future lords lieutenant to impose their will on parliament or on the kingdom at large. Temple summed up the problem of governing Ireland vividly when he observed on 2 December 1782 that 'those to whom the people look up with confidence are not the parliament, but a body of armed men, comprised chiefly of the *middling* and *lower orders*, influenced by *no one*, but leading those who affect to *guide them*'.[84]

This was, as Temple and most others in the corridors of power were acutely aware, not the basis of a strong and secure system of government. The irony was that the three lords lieutenant – Carlisle, Portland and Temple – during whose terms the authority of the Irish executive was most compromised were not weak men or ineffectual viceroys. Quite the contrary; Portland was one of the most influential figures in the Whig party at Westminster, a future secretary of state and prime minister, whose ambitions included the establishment of an Irish Whig party that accepted direction from its senior British partner.[85] Temple was younger and less politically experienced, but he was possessed of a clear idea of what needed to be done. Moreover, like Portland, he dominated his administration; he was so dominant indeed that he was described by one observer as 'both secretary and lord lieutenant'.[86] This was to reflect unfairly on the actual chief secretary, William Grenville, who was an able advocate of the administration's argument in support of renunciation in London, but it accurately captured the public's perception of the roles and performance of the two men.[87]

Though it was acknowledged that the 'frequent and rapid changes' at the head of the Irish administration precipitated by changes in government in Great Britain were a source of 'real and solid mischief', both Portland and Temple recognised that they had little option but to resign their positions when the ministries to which they were attached fell within a year of each other in 1782–3.[88] In truth, neither left with major regret. Portland was convinced that had he stayed longer, he would have laid the foundations for an Irish Whig party, while Temple felt he had lost a glorious opportunity to display his exceptional abilities by putting a system of firm government in place.[89] Both, but Temple particularly, were glad to be relieved of 'a very troublesome and thankless situation'.[90] Unlike Carlisle, of whom it was said prior to his return to England, he 'has not dared to stir out of his Castle, and Eden . . . was near receiving personal violence from the populace as he was setting off', the departures of Portland and Temple prompted genuine shows of public emotion, the like of which had not been seen in decades.[91] Moreover, these positive memories lingered in the public imagination.[92]

Political insiders, conscious of the problems that must arise should Portland's vision of an Irish Whig party be realised and of the practical problems caused by Temple's overweening confidence, were more reserved; some were fiercely critical. William Eden observed tartly prior to the departure of the former:

> The Duke of Portland will embark amidst the praises of all the fools, which are a considerable faction in every kingdom, but his government is already held in execration by many injured and worthy individuals, and in extreme contempt by every man of sense.[93]

This was the view certainly of John Beresford, Edward Cooke and other officeholders who continued to bemoan the drift that had commenced under Buckinghamshire, and who believed that the constitutional changes conceded in 1782 were incompatible with a secure Anglo-Irish connection.[94] As passionate advocates of a firm government, they held out few expectations of Lord Northington and William Windham who succeeded Earl Temple and William Grenville in May 1783 for the simple reasons that, as Whigs, they were guided by the duke of Portland, who counselled that they should look to the Irish patriots for support and direction. Moreover, their worst forebodings seemed about to become true when Windham, characterised insightfully by one acute observed as 'very much a gentleman and very little a minister', resigned the chief secretaryship after only a few weeks because he felt he would simply 'be incapable of the business'.[95] Edward Cooke, the canny under-secretary, who observed this keenly, was more convinced than ever of the qualities required of a secretary:

> Let us have a man of business and of some clearness of head; some nerve, some method, some liberality, some knowledge of the world, some powers of decision, and above all, if possible, let him be a substantial character capable to think and write, and act a little for himself.[96]

Cooke was prompted to make this comment by his perception that Portland wanted only ciphers who would do his bidding, but if so the appointment of Thomas Pelham in Windham's place was a serious error of judgment. Though only at the outset of his career, Pelham was already recognised as a man of ability. Equally importantly, he complemented the earl of Northington, whose sybaritic ways, and predisposition to gout, ensured he had no interest in hard work. Described in one Irish newspaper as a 'bon vivant' and sympathetically by one Irish hostess as 'disposed to be a comfortable creature',[97] Northington arrived in Ireland under the impression that he could delegate much of the responsibility of government, as he was instructed, to Portland's friends. With this in mind, he contentedly surrounded himself with patriots such as John Forbes, Henry Grattan and Barry Yelverton, only to find them wanting. The first hints that this might be the case were provided in the run-up to the meeting of parliament in October 1783, when the perception abroad of a lack of system and 'weak government' prompted those in the know to forecast difficulties in the House of Commons. These fears proved justified, though the administration was enabled to avoid serious embarrassment because of the willingness of John Beresford to come to their rescue. Had this been Buckinghamshire, the situation would have been allowed to drift, and thereby to disimprove, but, belying his reputation for indecision, Northington sought firstly to shake the Whig-patriots, to whom he was well disposed, out of the 'languor and indifference' with which they prepared for the meeting of parliament, and, when this failed, he set in train a process that was to see him replace unreliable patriots and independents with 'men of business' who were able to deliver strong and efficient government. Since this meant replacing Forbes, Grattan and Yelverton with John FitzGibbon, John Scott and John Foster, there was understandable anxiety in Whig and patriot circles at what Northington was doing, but his determination to put in place a system of government that would not break down at every pressure point was compelling.[98] He was assisted to overcome the objections of well meaning patriots by their unease with the campaign orchestrated by a combination of Volunteers and middle-class political activists to reform the representative system, which was seen to pose a threat as serious to the political stability of the kingdom as the earlier campaigns for free trade and legislative independence. Northington was entitled to little personal credit for this, but the decisive rejection by parliament in November 1783 of the reform bill that originated with the Grand National Convention of Volunteer delegates signalled that parliament had regained the political initiative in the political sphere, and, because the administration had effectively regained control of parliament, it meant that a major step had been taken in the restoration of the authority of the Irish executive.[99]

It so happened that Northington was not present to witness the full realisation of what he had brought about. The collapse of the Fox-North coalition in December 1783 provided him with a justifiable reason to tender his resignation, and to escape the 'plague and trouble' of his situation.[100] The identification of his replacement was complicated by the political uncertainty surrounding the establishment of William Pitt's ministry, but once it was clear that Pitt had the backing of the king, the way was soon paved for the appointment of Charles Manners, 4th duke of Rutland to head the Irish executive.

Rutland was widely perceived as a particularly unsuitable choice for the demanding position of lord lieutenant of Ireland. Concern focused in the first instance on his lack of political experience; but still more anxiety was expressed at his lifestyle, and, in particular, his penchant for gambling, whoring and alcohol. It was the opinion of one hostile observer that 'if there is one man more unfit for that situation it is his grace'.[101] However, in marked contrast to many of those who accepted the office, Rutland was a willing appointee. Having been a member with Pitt of the 'society of young ministers' that met at Goostrees Inn in London in the early 1780s, he unhesitatingly let it be known that he was not only determined to accept the position, but also that 'he was going for ten years to Ireland'.[102] This was a remarkable pronouncement, given that the average durations of the terms of his four immediate predecessors was less than nine months, and that even the third duke of Devonshire, who held the eighteenth-century record, had served for two months short of eight years. However, Rutland was devoted to Pitt, and, as he explained to the Lord Chatham in 1785, 'the great attachment which I have to yourself and your family, bind me to my present situation as long as I can render service to our country and strengthen your brother's able and honourable government'.[103] The main obstacles that Rutland identified to his service as an effective lord lieutenant were his 'indolence', and his expressed preference for 'planting and retirement' over politics. He might also have added his bibulousness, which was still more extreme than that of Townshend and which shocked more than one Irish hostess, but he contrived successfully to minimise the implications of these character flaws by choosing Thomas Orde as his chief secretary.[104] Orde had high level administrative experience, having previously served as under-secretary in the Home Office and as secretary to the treasury. However, he was untested in a position as demanding as the chief secretaryship, and, as time was to show, he lacked the qualities of 'decision' that characterised the ablest men of business. 'He talks and talks and talks the whole morning, and he argues and inviles till he wastes his strength and loses his effect, and he writes and writes all the evening till he puzzles his subject and exhausts his spirit', Edward Cooke observed critically.[105] Yet what Orde lacked in decisiveness he made up for in application. Besides, he could, and did, draw freely on the knowledge and expertise of the exceptionally capable men of business elevated to office by Northington and the deep reservoir of goodwill generated by Rutland.

The Duke's amiability and gregariousness gained the administration many friends; in the estimation of John FitzGibbon, 'he governed this country more by the weight of his personal influence than by the patronage annexed to his office'.[106] It did not secure the administration against failure. The most embarrassing was the loss in 1785 of William Pitt's ambitious plan for a commercial union; but the administration safely negotiated the rejection of parliamentary reform in 1784–5, and contrived effectively to take the Volunteers out of politics by approving legislation in 1785 that would have permitted, had they been so minded, the establishment of a government-controlled militia in their place.[107] As a result, the 1786 parliamentary session was the quietest in over two decades – quieter even than those overseen by Harcourt and Blaquiere in the early 1770s. This was a matter of great relief to observers, who a few years earlier had apprehended that Ireland might follow the example of the American colonies, and seek full independence.[108] Indeed, it was confidently anticipated when Orde's health was no longer capable of bearing the strain that Rutland would continue in post.[109] Moreover, he was happy to stay, and so convinced of the importance of having a lord lieutenant *in situ* at all times, he stoutly declined his wife's attempt in the summer of 1787 to persuade him to visit England on the grounds that this would necessitate 'appointing lords justices to govern the kingdom in my absence, which would leave it open to cabal and faction, and might excite an endeavour to restore a system which England at a great expense some years ago abolished'.[110] Ironically, Rutland's health proved more vulnerable than that of his chief secretary and his unexpected, and much lamented, death in November 1787 brought to an end a viceroyalty that in its final years seemed an exemplary manifestation of how Ireland ought to be administered.

If Rutland's viceroyalty stands apart as one of the more successful of the era of residential lords lieutenant, the public expectation was that his successor, the marquess of Buckingham, who as Earl Temple had prior experience of the office, would be still more successful. The ease with which the administration negotiated the 1788 session seems to suggest that the devotion to business he and his chief secretary, Alleyne Fitzherbert, displayed made for an excellent partnership.[111] The lord lieutenant's refusal 'to make a party, trusting entirely to the rectitude of his administration' also seemed well judged, that is until the Regency crisis in the winter of 1788–9 exposed the marquess's 'mean vengeful temper', and demonstrated that he did not possess what George III described as the 'temper, judgment, . . . avowed resolution to avoid partiality and [to] employ the favours he has to recommend to with the justice due to my service and to the public'.[112] It also highlighted the limitations of vice-regal control. Buckingham contrived successfully to frustrate the ambitions of the Irish patriots to offer the regency of Ireland to George, Prince of Wales, and thereby to stave off a still more threatening constitutional crisis, but the episode, and the decision of the vanquished Whigs to form themselves into a quasi political party – the Whig Club – vividly demonstrated that residential lords lieutenant alone were no guarantor to the stability or the security of the Anglo-Irish connection.[113] This was to be revealed all the more graphically in the 1790s.

V

During the twenty-two years between the appointment of Lord Townshend in 1767 and the departure of the marquess of Buckingham, after only two years in office in 1789, there were a total of nine viceroyalties. Since this was only one less than during the preceding twenty-two years (1745–67), it could be argued that the reversion to the practice of requiring lords lieutenant to reside in Ireland made little difference. It certainly did little to enhance the appeal of the office to English politicians, from whose ranks all the residential lords lieutenant were drawn; significantly more individuals declined the opportunity to come to Ireland than took it up. Yet the experiment of the executive residential lord lieutenancy represented a significant change from the situation that obtained between 1701 and 1767 when the lord lieutenant delegated the task of managing parliament to undertakers, and the burden of administering the kingdom of Ireland to lords justice. The removal of both from the scene between 1767 and 1772 meant that lords lieutenant could no longer conveniently evade the duties and responsibilities of the position, and while all were not equally attentive, equally adept, or faced by equal challenges, the practical reality was that decisions they made and the qualities of decision-making they brought to bear greatly shaped the nature and experience of government in eighteenth-century Ireland. It may be an exaggeration to claim that they embodied the Anglo-Irish nexus, but they did have a profound influence upon the manner in which political business was conducted in Ireland and the Anglo-Irish nexus was managed.

Notes

1 Cited in David Hayton, 'The "country" interest and the party system, 1689–1720', in Clyve Jones (ed.), *Party and Management in Parliament 1660–1784* (Leicester, 1984), p. 43.

2 *The Royal Register: With Annotations by Another Hand* (2nd edn, 9 vols, London, 1779–84), ii, pp 149–50.

3 Henry Penruddocke Wyndham to Henry Wyndham, 20 Oct. 1759, Beinecke Library, New Haven (Bein.), Osborn collection, Wyndham Papers, letter 12.

4 British Library, London (hereafter BL), Auckland Papers, Add. Ms 34417, ff 232–40.

5 Chesterfield to Mallet, 27 Nov. 1745, in Bonamy Dobree (ed.), *The Letters of Philip Dormer Stanhope, Earl of Chesterfield* (6 vols, London, 1932), iii, p. 704; Edith M. Johnston, *Great Britain and Ireland 1760–1800: A Study in Political Administration* (Edinburgh, 1963), p. 28.

6 Chesterfield to Newcastle, 18 Feb. 1746, in Dobree (ed.), *The Letters of Chesterfield*, iii, p. 730.

7 Grafton to Townshend, 8 Feb. 1724, in A. P. W. Malcomson (ed.), *Eighteenth-Century Irish Official Papers in Great Britain* (Belfast, [1974]), i, p. 6.

8 These were the duke of Ormonde, Feb. 1703–Apr. 1707; duke of Bolton, Apr. 1717–June 1720; duke of Grafton, June 1720–May 1724; Lord Cartaret, May 1724–June 1730; duke of Dorset, June 1730–Apr. 1737; duke of Devonshire, Apr. 1737–Jan. 1745; earl of Harrington, Nov. 1746–Dec. 1750; duke of Dorset, Dec. 1750–Apr. 1755; duke of Bedford, Jan. 1757–Apr. 1761.

9 These were the earl of Pembroke, Apr. 1707–Dec. 1708; earl of Wharton, Dec. 1708–Oct. 1710; duke of Shrewsbury, Sept. 1713–Sept. 1714; Viscount Townshend, Feb.–Apr. 1717; earl of Chesterfield, Jan. 1745–Nov. 1746; marquess of Hartington, Apr. 1755–Jan. 1757; Viscount Weymouth, June–Aug. 1765; earl of Hertford, Aug. 1765–Oct. 1766; earl of Bristol, Oct. 1766–Aug. 1767.

10 Lord Hervey, *Memoirs of the Reign of George II*, ed. John Wilson Croker (2 vols, London, 1848), i, p. 143; Northington to Payne, 18 Jan. 1784, National Library of Ireland, Dublin (hereafter NLI), Northington-Payne letters, Ms 888, ff 205–7.

11 This includes Ormonde, Feb. 1703–Apr. 1707 and Oct. 1710–Sept. 1713 and Dorset, June 1730–Apr. 1737, Dec. 1750–Apr. 1755, who served two terms.

12 Peter Wentworth to Lord Raby, 20 Oct. 1710, in J. J. Cartwright (ed.), *The Wentworth Papers, 1705–39* (London, 1883), pp 149–50.

13 Bishop Clayton to Mrs Clayton, 9 Nov. 1731, 2 Jan. 1732, Bein., Osborn collection, Sundon letterbook, f.c.110(2), ff 110–12, 118–29.

14 See *Oxford Dictionary of National Biography* (hereafter*ODNB)* for a convenient biographical notice of each of the men named.

15 Chesterfield to Waterford, 23 May 1758, in Dobree (ed.), *The Letters of Chesterfield*, v, pp 2,304–5.

16 See D. W. Hayton, *Ruling Ireland, 1685–1742: Politics, Politicians and Parties* (Woodbridge, 2004).

17 Vernon to [Granby], 27 Oct. 1766 in Historical Manuscripts Commission (hereafter HMC), *Rutland*, ii, p. 288.

18 For the Money Bill dispute see Declan O'Donovan, 'The Money Bill dispute of 1753', in Thomas Bartlett and D. W. Hayton (eds), *Penal Era and Golden Age: Essays in Eighteenth-Century Irish History* (Belfast, 1979), pp 55–87; Eoin Magennis, *The Irish Political System, 1740–1765: Golden Age of the Undertakers* (Dublin, 2000), ch. 3.

19 Memorandum by Thomas Pakenham, 4 Sept. 1755, Public Record Office of Northern Ireland, Belfast (hereafter PRONI), Chatsworth Papers, D3158/852.

20 See J. C. D. Clark, 'Whig tactics and parliamentary precedent: the English management of Irish politics, 1754–56', *Historical Journal*, 21 (1978), pp 275–301; Hartington to Burlington, 27 June, Hartington to Devonshire, 30 July 1755, PRONI, Chatsworth Papers, D3158/733, 796B.

21 James Kelly, 'The origins of the act of union: an examination of unionist opinion in Britain and Ireland, 1650–1800', *Irish Historical Studies*, 25 (1986–7), pp 247–8.

22 Hartington to Burlington, 27 June, Hartington to Devonshire, 30 July 1755, PRONI, Chatsworth Papers, D3158/733, 796B.

23 Walpole to Mann, 8 Dec. 1756 in W. S. Lewis (ed.), *The Correspondence of Horace Walpole* (48 vols, New Haven, 1937–83), xxi, p. 31; Anon, 'A short sketch of the political history of Ireland', NLI, Joly Ms 29, ff 36–8; J. L. McCracken, 'The political structure, 1714–60', in T. W. Moody and W. E. Vaughan (eds), *A New History of Ireland (NHI), iv: The Eighteenth Century* (Oxford, 1986), p. 63.

24 Peter D. Brown and Karl W. Schweizer (eds), *The Devonshire Diary* (London, 1982), pp 81–2; Chesterfield to Waterford, 9 June, 12 Sept. 1761, in Dobree (ed.), *The Letters of Chesterfield*, v, pp 2,378, 2,382; Lord Holland, 'Memoir of events attending the death of George II', in the Countess of Ilchester and Lord Stavordale (eds), *The Life and Letters of Lady Sarah Lennox* (2 vols, London, 1902), i, pp 35–6; Halifax to Egremont, 28 Feb. 1762, in *Calendar of Home Office Papers 1760–75* (4 vols, London, 1878–99), i, pp 160–1.

25 Montagu to Walpole, 17 May 1762, in Lewis (ed.), *Walpole Corres*, x, p. 31.

26 George III to Bute, 7, 10, 15 Apr. 1763, in Romney Sedgwick (ed.), *Letters from George III to Lord Bute* (London, 1939), pp 211, 216, 222; Walpole to Montagu, 14 Apr. 1763, in Lewis (ed.), *Walpole Corres*, x, p. 63; O'Hara to Burke, 26 July 1763, in R. J. Hoffman, *Edmund Burke: New York Agent* (Philadelphia, 1956), pp 311–2; Northumberland to Stone, 18 July, Northumberland to Shannon, 4 Aug. 1763, PRONI, Alnwick Papers, T/2872/8, 17.

27 Walpole to Hertford, 18 Apr. 1765, in Lewis (ed.), *Walpole Corres*, xxxviii, pp 533–4.

28 J. R. G. Tomlinson (ed.), *Additional Greenville Papers 1763–5* (Manchester, 1962), pp 335–6; see Thomas Bartlett, 'The Townshend administration in Ireland, 1767–72' (unpublished PhD thesis, Queen's University Belfast (hereafter QUB), 1976), pp 22–3.

29 News from Brussels, 18 June 1765, in Cathaldus Giblin (ed.), 'Catalogue of Irish material in the Nunziatura di Fiandra, pt 7', *Collectanea Hibernica*, 11 (1968), p. 54; Lady Sarah Bunbury to Lady Susan O'Brien, 22 June 1765, in Ilchester and Stavordale (eds), *Life and Letters of Lady Sarah Lennox*, i, pp 168–70.

30 Hertford to Walpole, 18 Jan. 1765, in Lewis (ed.), *Walpole Corres.*, xxxviii, p. 491; Burke to O'Hara, 21 Oct. 1766, in Hoffman (ed.), *Edmund Burke*, p. 366; James Kelly, *Henry Flood: Patriots and Politics in Eighteenth-Century Ireland* (Dublin, 1998), pp 95–6.

31 Charles O'Hara Sr to Charles O'Hara Jr, [1766], NLI, O'Hara Papers, Ms 20393.

32 Burke to O'Hara, 21 Oct. 1766, in Hoffman (ed.), *Edmund Burke*, p. 366; Northington to Grafton, 31 Aug. 1766, in Sir William Anson (ed.), *Autobiography and Correspondence of Augustus Henry, Third Duke of Grafton* (London, 1898), p. 129; Chesterfield to Waterford, 10 Oct. 1766, in Dobree (ed.), *The Letters of Chesterfield*, vi, p. 2767.

33 Kelly, *Henry Flood*, pp 107–15; Northington to Grafton, 31 Aug. 1766, in Anson (ed.), *Autobiography and Correspondence of Grafton*, p. 129; Sir James Caldwell to Shelburne, 26 Jan. 1768, BL, Lansdowne abstracts, Add. Ms 24137.

34 Thomas Bartlett, 'Introduction', to idem (ed.), *Macartney in Ireland 1768–1772* (Belfast, 1978), pp xvi–ii.

35 Burke to O'Hara, 21 Oct. 1766, in Hoffman (ed.), *Edmund Burke*, p. 366.

36 Augustus Hervey to Grenville, 31 July 1767, in W. J. Smith (ed.) *The Grenville Papers* (4 vols, London, 1852–3), iv, p. 131. Townshend had previously (in 1765) expressed an interest in the office: Burke to O'Hara, 21 Oct. 1766, in Hoffman (ed.), *Edmund Burke*, p. 318.

37 Hervey to Grenville, 31 July 1767, in Smith (ed.) *The Grenville Papers*, iv, p. 131.

38 Thomas Bartlett, 'The Townshend viceroyalty, 1867–72', in idem and D. W. Hayton (eds), *Penal Era and Golden Age*, p. 95. What follows is based on Bartlett, 'The Townshend administration', passim, and Kelly, *Henry Flood*, ch. 4; idem, *Sir Edward Newenham, 1734–1814: Defender of the Protestant Constitution* (Dublin, 2004), ch. 2.

39 Bartlett, 'The Townshend viceroyalty', p. 93.

40 Burke to O'Hara, 12 Mar. 1767, in Hoffman (ed.), *Edmund Burke*, pp 392–3.

41 Waite to Wilmot, 7 June 1769, cited in Bartlett, 'The Townshend viceroyalty', note 18; Horace Walpole, *Memoirs of the Reign of George III* (4 vols, London, 1894), iii, p. 231; Brabazon Noble to [George Shirley], 3 Dec. 1767, PRONI, Shirley Papers, D/3531/A/5, p. 20; Walpole to Mann, 18 Aug. 1767, in Lewis (ed.), *Walpole Corres*, xxii, p. 549; Cory to Townshend, 18 Nov. 1767, Bein., Osborn collections, Townshend Papers, Box 9.

42 Conway to O'Hara, 27 June 1770, NLI, O'Hara Papers, Ms 20391.

43 McCracken, 'The political structure', p. 57.

44 Buckinghamshire's vindication, PRONI, Lothian Papers, T/3502/1; David Lammey, 'A study of Anglo-Irish relations between 1772 and 1782, with particular reference to the "free trade" movement' (unpublished PhD thesis, QUB, 1984), pp 6–9.

45 For an overview, see Johnston, *Great Britain and Ireland*, pp 34–44; Bartlett, *Macartney in Ireland*, pp xiii–v.

46 Bishop Clayton to Mrs Clayton, 9 Nov. 1731, 2 Jan. 1732, Osborn collection, Sundon letterbook, f.c.110(2), ff 110–12, 118–29; Bartlett (ed.), *Macartney in Ireland*, pp xiii–iv.

47 See Thomas Bartlett, 'Ireland', in Peter Roebuck (ed.), *Macartney of Lissanoure* (Belfast, 1993), pp 66–87; idem, *Macartney in Ireland*, pp xiv–v; Harcourt to North, 21 Apr. 1776, Dublin City Library (*hereafter* DCL), Harcourt Papers, Gilbert Ms 93, f. 207.

48 Harcourt to North, 21 Apr. 1776, DCL, Harcourt Papers, Gilbert Ms 93, f. 207; Acheson

to Townshend, 26 Aug. 1772, NAI, Townshend Papers, Ms 654.

49 Rochford to Townshend, 7 Aug. 1772, in *Calendar of Home Office Papers*, iii, p. 531.

50 Allan to Townshend, 26 Dec. 1770, NAI, Townshend Papers, Ms 730/53; Smith to Macartney, 15 Aug. 1772, in Bartlett (ed.), *Macartney in Ireland*, p. 223; Nuneham to Harcourt, [Apr. 1772], in Harcourt (ed.), *Harcourt Papers*, iii, p. 109.

51 Harcourt to North, 8 May, in Harcourt (ed.), *Harcourt Papers*, x, pp 150–1; North to Harcourt, 29 May 1776. NLI, Harcourt Papers, Ms 555 f. 105.

52 Nuneham to Harcourt, [Apr. 1772], in Harcourt (ed.), *Harcourt Papers*, iii, p. 109.

53 Northington to Payne, 18 Jan. 1784, NLI, Northington-Payne letters, Ms 888 ff 205–7; W. D. Griffin, 'The forces of the crown in Ireland, 1798', in Gaetano L. Vincitorio (ed.), *Crisis in the Great Republic* (New York, 1969), p. 175.

54 Buckinghamshire's vindication, PRONI, Lothian Papers, T/3502/1; Eden to Loughborough, 19 July 1781, BL, Auckland Papers, Add. Ms 34417, ff 396–7.

55 Chesterfield to Waterford, 30 Oct. 1768, in Dobree (ed.), *The Letters of Chesterfield*, vi, p. 2,868.

56 Henry Grattan Jr., *Memoirs of the Life and Times of Henry Grattan*, (5 vols, London, 1839–46), iii, pp 170–2; Smith to Townshend, [*c.* 20 Mar.] 1771, Bein., Osborn Collections, Smith letters, c. 41, no. 48; *Finn's Leinster Journal*, 4 Dec. 1776; Temple to Rutland, 11 Jan. 1784, in HMC, *Rutland*, iii, p. 73; Eden to Loughborough, 12 Jan. 1782, in Bishop of Bath and Wells (ed.), *The Correspondence of William Eden, Lord Auckland*, (4 vols, London, 1861–2), i, pp 316–7; *Freeman's Journal*, 10 Jan. 1795. It was rumoured that Rutland owed £30–40,000 at his death: *Dublin Evening Post*, 30 Oct. 1787; *Volunteer Evening Post*, 7 Feb., 18 Mar. 1787; John to Robert Dillon, 27 Oct. [1787], NLI, Dillon of Clonbrock Papers.

57 *Hibernian Journal*, 23 Sept. 1782.

58 Kelly, *Henry Flood*, p. 179; G. E. C., *The Complete Peerage* (13 vols, London, 1910–59), vi, pp 300–1; Harcourt to [Rochford] and replies, 2, 18 June, 2, 3 5, 12 July 1771, The National Archives, Kew (hereafter TNA), SP78/282, f. 255, /283 ff 4–6, 7–10, 26–7, /285 ff 239–40, 267–8.

59 HMC, *Charlemont*, i, p. 35; E. M. Johnston-Liik, *History of the Irish Parliament 1692–1800* (6 vols, Belfast, 2002), iii, pp 202–5.

60 Buckinghamshire to Thompson, 9 Apr. 1779, BL, Mackintosh Collection, Add. Ms 34523 f. 178.

61 NLI, Harcourt Papers, MS 5161; Harcourt to Conolly, 4 May 1774, Irish Architectural Archive, Dublin, Conolly Papers, A/10/2.

62 Lees' review of Earl Harcourt's administration, in Harcourt (ed.), *Harcourt Papers*, x, p. 249; Kelly, *Henry Flood*, ch. 5.

63 Blaquiere to Robinson, 2 Nov. 1775, in William Hunt, *The Irish Parliament, 1775* (Dublin, 1907), pp 84–91; Harcourt to North, 21 June 1776, DCL, Harcourt Papers, Gilbert Ms 93 ff 425–7; Harcourt to Buckinghamshire, 8 Dec. 1776, NLI, Heron Papers, Ms 13034/3.

64 North to Harcourt, 29 June, 24 Nov. 1776, NLI, Harcourt letterbook, Ms 775, ff 109, 112–3; Harcourt to North, 26, 30 Oct. 1776, DCL, Harcourt Papers, Gilbert Ms 93 ff 473–6; Harcourt to Weymouth, 24 Oct. 1766, TNA, SP63/455 ff 121–2.

65 North to Harcourt, 2 Sept. 1776, NLI, Harcourt letterbook, Ms 775, ff 111; Robinson to [Dartmouth], 1 Oct. 1776, in HMC, *Dartmouth*, iii, p. 229; Roebuck, *Macartney*, p. 23; Nuneham to Harcourt, 3 Oct., Blaquiere to Harcourt, 18 Nov. 1776, in Harcourt (ed.), *Harcourt Papers*, iii, pp 121–2, x, pp 204–9; *The Royal Register*, iv, pp 106–10; A. F. Steuart (ed.), *The Last Journals of Horace Walpole* (2 vols, London, 1910), i, pp 589–90; Buckinghamshire to Hotham-Thompson, 4 July 1776, PRONI, Hotham Papers, T/3429/1/1.

66 Buckinghamshire to Eden, 22 July 1780, BL, Auckland Papers, Add. Ms 34417 ff 94–7.

67 R. B. McDowell, *Ireland in the Age of Imperialism and Revolution, 1760–1801* (Oxford, 1979), pp 267–70.

68 Buckinghamshire to Eden, 22 July 1780, Explanatory minutes, 1780, BL, Auckland Papers, Add. Ms 34417 ff 94–7, 98.

69 Macartney to Lady Ossory, [Oct.–Nov. 1780], NLI, Fitzpatrick Papers, Ms 8012/4.

70 Kelly, 'The origins of the act of union', pp 251–3.

71 Buckinghamshire to Germain, 2 Nov. 1780, in HMC, *Lothian MSS*, p. 375.

72 Macartney to Lady Ossory, [Oct.–Nov. 1780], NLI, Fitzpatrick Papers, Ms 8012/4.

73 Blaquiere to Harcourt, 18 Nov. 1776, in Harcourt (ed.), *Harcourt Papers*, x, pp 204–9; Kelly, *Henry Flood*, p. 277; HMC, *Carlisle*, pp 322–97, passim; *Hibernian Journal*, 6 Sept. 1780; Gower to Carlisle, 21 July 1780, in HMC, *Carlisle*, p. 436.

74 A. I. M. Duncan, 'A study of the life and public career of Frederick Howard, fifth earl of Carlisle 1748–1825' (unpublished PhD thesis, Oxford University, 1981), pp 102–38; Kelly, *Henry Flood*, p. 277ff.

75 Eden to North, 3 Mar. 1782, BL, North (Sheffield Park) Papers, Add. Ms 61862 ff 73–4.

76 Carlisle to Shelburne, 31 Mar. 1782, Eden to Shelburne, 5 Apr. 1782, BL, Fox Papers, Add. Ms 47582 ff 54, 56.

77 Carlisle to Gower, 23 Mar. 1782, TNA, Granville Papers, 30/29/1/15; Eden to North, 3 Mar. 1782, BL, North (Sheffield Park) Papers, Add. Ms 61862 ff 73–4.

78 For Portland's explicit affirmation of the Whigs' commitment to this practice, see Portland to Temple, 22 Feb. 1783, in duke of Buckingham (ed.), *Memoirs of the Courts and Cabinets of George III* (4 vols, London, 1853–5), i, p. 163.

79 Carlisle to Gower, 23 Mar. 1782, TNA, Granville Papers, 30/29/1/15.

80 Rockingham to Charlemont, 9 Apr. 1782, Sheffield City Library, Wentworth-Woodhouse Muniments, Rockingham Papers, R1–2037; James Kelly, *Prelude to Union: Anglo-Irish Politics in the 1780s* (Cork, 1992), pp 38–40.

81 Temple to Shelburne, 2 Dec. 1783, BL, Lansdowne Papers, Add. Ms 24238 ff 104–5); Temple to Portland, 2 Mar. 1783, in Buckingham (ed.), *Courts and Cabinets of George III*, i, p. 165.

82 Kelly, *Prelude to Union*, pp 40–1.

83 Peter Jupp, 'Earl Temple and the question of renunciation, 1782–3', *Irish Historical Studies*, 17 (1971–2), pp 299–317; Temple to Shelburne, 2 Dec. 1783, BL, Lansdowne Papers, Add. Ms 24238 ff 104–5; Temple to Grenville, 15 Jan. 1783, BL, Dropmore Papers, Add. Ms 58874 ff 37–8; North to [Temple], 5 Apr. 1783, BL, North (Sheffield Park) Papers, Add. Ms 61862 f. 82.

84 Temple to Shelburne, 2 Dec. 1783, BL, Lansdowne Papers, Add. Ms 24238 ff 104–5.

85 David Wilkinson, *The Duke of Portland* (Basingstoke, 2003).

86 Conolly to Temple, 7 Dec. 1782, BL, Buckingham Papers, Add. Ms 40179. f. 39.

87 Peter Jupp, *Lord Grenville, 1754–1834* (Oxford, 1985), pp 21–9; Ogilvie to Leinster, 26 July 1782, NLI, Fitzgerald Papers, Ms 624 f. 116b.

88 Temple to Portland, 2 Mar. 1783, in Buckingham (ed.), *Court and Cabinets of George III*, i, p. 165; Temple to Beresford, 19 July 1793, BL, Buckingham Papers, Add. Ms 40733, f. 69; Cornwall to Pery, [post 3 May 1783], PRONI, Pery Papers, T3052/161; Sydney to Northington, 2 Feb. 1784, BL, Northington letterbook, Add. Ms 38716 ff 264–6.

89 Temple to Bulkeley, 20 Mar. 1783, in Buckingham (ed.), *Court and Cabinets of George III*, i, p. 223.

90 Temple to [Northington], 29 Apr. 1783, BL, Pelham Papers, Add. Ms 33100 ff 113–4.

91 Romilly to Roget, 12 Apr. 1782, in *Life of Sir Samuel Romilly* (3 vols, London, 1840), i, pp 160–1; Anonymous account, 5 June 1783, TNA, HO100/9 ff 165–7; Cuffe to Temple, 10 July 1783, BL, Buckingham Papers, Add. Ms 40179 f. 91.

92 Buckinghamshire to Elliott, [1783], in HMC, *Lothian MSS*, p. 418; Anon., *A Comparative View of the Portland Administration in Ireland* [Dublin, 1786], p. 3 ff.

93 Eden to Carlisle, 6 July [1782], in HMC, *Carlisle MSS*, pp 631–2.

94 Beresford to Eden, 14 Apr., Cooke to Eden, 30 Apr. 1783, BL, Auckland Papers, Add. Ms 34419 ff 170–1, 186–7.

95 Cuffe to Temple, 10 July, BL, Buckingham Papers, Add. Ms 40179. f. 91; Windham to Northington, 15 July 1783, BL, Windham Papers, Add. Ms 37873 ff 19–21.

96 C[ooke] to Eden, 9 Aug. 1783, BL, Auckland Papers, Add. Ms 34429 ff 248–50.

97 Ibid; Francis Hardy, *Memoirs of Charlemont* (London, 1810), p. 251; *Dublin Evening Post*, 25 Apr., 1 May 1783; Lady Louisa Conolly to [?], 29 Oct. 1783, NLI, Fitzgerald Papers, Ms 614 f. 260.

98 For the Northington administration, see Kelly, *Prelude to Union*, pp 56–75.

99 James Kelly, 'Parliamentary reform in Irish politics, 1760–90', in David Dickson et al. (eds), *The United Irishmen* (Dublin, 1993), pp 80–3.

100 Northington to Temple, 27 Dec. 1783, BL, Northington letterbook, Add. Ms 38716 ff 243–4; Northington to Payne, 27 Feb. 1783, NLI, Northington-Payne letters, Ms 888 ff 209–10.

101 Cornwallis to Ross, 23 Feb. 1784, in Charles Ross (ed.) *Correspondence of Charles, First Marquess of Cornwallis* (3 vols, London, 1859), i, p. 160; duchess of Portland to Mrs Ponsonby, 9 Feb. [1784], PRONI, Grey/Ponsonby Papers, T3393/9; Kelly, *Prelude to Union*, p. 77.

102 George Selwyn to Carlisle, [19 Feb. 1782], HMC, *Carlisle MSS*, p. 581; Duchess of Portland to Mrs Ponsonby, 15 Feb. [1784], PRONI, Grey/Ponsonby Papers, T3393/10.

103 Rutland to Chatham, 14 Feb. 1785, TNA, Hoare (Pitt) Papers, 30/70/3 f. 115.

104 Ibid; Louisa Conolly to Sarah Napier, 17 June [1784], PRONI, Bunbury Papers, letterbook 18, f. 4.

105 William Burton Conyngham to Lord Sydney, [mid-1785], Bein., Osborn collection, Conyngham files; Cooke to Eden, 10 Sept. 1786, BL, Auckland Papers, Add, Ms 34422 ff 237–9.

106 Beresford to Orde, 27 Oct. 1787, NLI, Bolton Papers, Ms 16353/71; FitzGibbon to Eden, 18 Nov. 1787, PRONI, Sneyd Papers, T3229/1/6; David Dundas to Henry Dundas, 27 Jan. 1789, NLI, Dundas Papers, Ms 54/32; *Volunteer Journal* (Dublin), 17 Mar. 1784.

107 Kelly, *Prelude to Union*, ch. 5; James Kelly, 'The politics of volunteering, 1779–93', *The Irish Sword*, 22: 88 (2000), pp 139–56.

108 *Volunteer Evening Post*, 8 Feb., 3 Apr. 1787.

109 He was described by one regular correspondent 'as King of Ireland for life', Pulteney to Rutland, 3 July 1787, in HMC, *Rutland*, iii, p. 395.

110 Rutland to duchess of Rutland, 18 June 1787, in HMC, *Rutland*, iii, p. 394.

111 Scrope Bernard to Grenville, 27 Dec. 1787, 19 May 1788, BL, Dropmore Papers, Add. Ms 58969 ff 9–10, 27; Hely Hutchinson to [?], 19 June 1788, HMC, *Donoughmore*, pp 322–3; Charlemont to Halliday, 4 Jan. 1788, in HMC, *Charlemont*, ii, pp 65–6.

112 Lady Louisa Conolly to duke of Leinster, 29 Dec. 1787, NLI, Fitzgerald Papers, Ms 614 f. 217; George III to William Pitt, 29 Oct. 1787, in Arthur Aspinall (ed.), *The Later Correspondence of George III* (5 vols, London, 1962–70), i, p. 349.

113 For the Regency crisis see McDowell, *Ireland in the Age of Imperialism and Revolution*, pp 339–43.

CHAPTER 5

The Lord Lieutenancy and Cultural and Literary Patronage c. 1660–1780

Toby Barnard

I

An image sums up one argument of this essay. A circle enclosing a blank was printed in lieu of a portrait in a poem addressed to the incoming lord lieutenant in 1669.[1] The viceroy, Lord Robartes of Truro, was one of many holders of the position sent from England and charged with implementing the current agenda of the English government. Robartes was only briefly and unmemorably domiciled in Dublin. The eulogist – William Mercer, a Scottish army officer – does not seem to have intended to insult Robartes, even obliquely, as a nonentity. Nor was Mercer a post-modernist *avant la lettre*.[2] Simply there was no portrait of Robartes to hand with which Mercer might ornament his effusion. In the event, Robartes remained in Ireland for too short a time to generate tangible sycophancy, whether embodied in pigments, engraving or verse.[3]

The welcoming verses for Robartes introduce two themes. The first is the almost fortuitous way in which English peers arrived in Dublin as governors and the speed with which they departed, usually leaving only faint imprints. The social and political leverage these grandees exerted in England was not automatically replicated in Ireland. Yet, viceroys were courted as potential patrons by virtue simply of the office that they occupied. At the same time, omissions and shortcomings were seized upon and magnified.[4] Vacancies inevitably occurred in the civil, ecclesiastical and military establishments over which lords lieutenant would exercise (or attempt to exercise) influence. Results were readily gauged: suitors were either gratified or disappointed. In the cultural and artistic spheres, gains from favours accorded by the lords lieutenant tended to be indirect rather than direct or immediate. Patronising writers, painters, craft-workers and designers other than from crude calculation of self-glorification was an investment undertaken only by lords lieutenant drawn temperamentally to these specialised activities. Robartes, in common with many predecessors and successors, did not bother with these potential but seemingly inessential props to his power.

Sent to do the king's business in Ireland, Robartes interpreted his brief narrowly.[5] A former Cromwellian collaborator and sympathetic to Protestant dissent, he looked a more plausible executor of the indulgent policies now favoured by the Stuart regime than the incumbent Ormond, lord lieutenant since 1661. Arriving as a stranger in Dublin, Robartes lacked the connections of Ormond, the leading peer and landowner in Protestant Ireland. Unfamiliarity with the Dublin scene did not of itself preclude the employment of writers, artists and musicians. Indeed, some of the more astute successors to Robartes appreciated the value of enlisting such helpers. Although Robartes did little or nothing to organise literary and dramatic celebrations of his rule, toadies leapt forward spontaneously. One was Mercer, who – unprompted – eulogised the incumbent ruler. This phenomenon, of unsolicited tributes, recurred under most viceroys.

The motives of eulogists varied. Some who celebrated viceregal authority did so simply to demonstrate an unswerving support for the English monarch, whose deputy in Ireland the lord lieutenant was. The identity and personal characteristics of the incumbent viceroy hardly mattered. While in some cases, a disinterested loyalism was the spur, in other celebrants, the public praise was designed to attract favour either from the distant English regime or locally in Ireland. The resulting favours might be expressed in prestigious sinecures, influence, status or cash. However, there was no guarantee that those who stepped forward unbidden to celebrate a particular viceroyalty would be rewarded. Often they went unnoticed.

In the case of Mercer, the verses to greet Robartes were merely one episode in a career of attempted self-promotion through compulsive versifying. On another occasion, Mercer's published lines sought the backing of the municipal corporation in Cork.[6] As an army officer, disappointed of full recompense for his military services in Ireland and eager for further postings, it made sense in 1669 for Mercer to cultivate the nominal head of the army in Ireland, Lord Lieutenant Robartes. It is possible that Mercer, overlooked by the returned royalist Ormond, hoped that there would be more ideological congruence between himself and the erstwhile Cromwellian, Robartes. Otherwise, it was almost fortuitous that it was Robartes whom he apostrophised. Other viceroys (and their wives) received sundry dedications and were petitioned on behalf of multifarious causes, some pathetically personal, but others at least notionally of public utility.[7] Frequently the addresses were entirely speculative, from aspirants unknown to the lord lieutenant. Many failed in their objectives, being ignored by the recipients. However, the flurries of artistic creativity that inevitably surrounded each viceroy give an impression of cultural activism on the part of the governor. In order to decide whether or not this was more than an impression, it is helpful to try to distinguish between passive and active patronage. From this exercise, it will emerge that a few – but only a few – lords lieutenant did deserve their reputations for forwarding specific causes in Ireland.

II

The often speculative nature of what was dedicated to the occupants of Dublin Castle is exemplified by printed verses of Dorothy Smith. Published in Dublin during 1701, Smith intended her lines as 'a pastoral welcome' to the earl of Rochester on his arrival in Ireland. Smith smoothly alluded to Rochester's predecessors, Galway and Romney, lords justice during the 1690s, who were praised for their support of the theatre. Rochester's brother, Clarendon, lord lieutenant between 1685 and 1686, was also mentioned, as was the viceroy whom many in Ireland remembered with greatest affection, the first duke of Ormond.[8] What prompted Smith to have her pastoral printed is unclear. Possibly she was already connected with the establishment in Dublin Castle or hoped for preferment in it. More obvious, because conventional, was the motive behind George Wilkins's decision to have his verses published in 1699. Wilkins, a recent graduate of Dublin University, suavely chose the duchess of Ormonde as the dedicatee. In addition, he noted that her husband was chancellor of the university. Wilkins's *Chace of the Stagg* was a sustained and contrived description of a stag-hunt and the landscape through which it ran. The cornered stag was likened to the beleaguered Charles I: a demonstration of royalist sentiments likely to commend itself to the Ormondes, and perhaps to entitle Wilkins to preferment.[9] Ormonde, inheritor of the only Irish dukedom and one of the most valuable estates in the kingdom, would be appointed lord lieutenant in 1703. This appointment led others, including Dryden, to laud him in print.[10] But already, as Wilkins's example shows, Ormonde was the focus of literary celebration. Wilkins's oblique approach, through the viceroy's wife, was a tactic adopted by others. Thus, in 1736 William Hammond offered poetic advice to the duchess of Dorset. Hammond wished to check the spreading deism of Isaac Newton and Samuel Clarke, and felt that a contrived connection with the vicereine would strengthen his case.[11]

By the middle of the eighteenth century, lords lieutenant typically arrived from England without extensive knowledge of Ireland and faced patriotic campaigns against the insensitive English policies which they were to implement. Print was becoming increasingly important as a medium through which Irish opposition was orchestrated. The 1720s, with Swift's involvement in the attacks on Wood's Half-Pence, inaugurated the inky spats. They were renewed during the 1750s. Alert viceroys saw the value of skilful defenders. Some – such as Gorges Edmond Howard and William Henry – were retained; others, like Revd John Gast, volunteered. Paid hacks, when their affiliations were uncovered, were ridiculed, and tended to lose influence. Nevertheless, fresh volunteers appeared. Gast may have written a series of pamphlets supportive of the administration during the 1750s from conviction. Even so, these literary services helped him towards lucrative preferment in the Church of Ireland, and allowed him to forsake the drudgery of school-mastering. Also, he abandoned topical polemic in favour of laborious researches into the history of Greece.[12] More unabashedly self-interested than Gast was Sir James Caldwell, a baronet from County Fermanagh.

Caldwell, an inveterate pamphleteer, turned his pen from schemes of improvement addressed to the Dublin Society to apologias for the lord lieutenant, Viscount Townshend. Having aroused hostility in the Irish Parliament during 1769 with proposals to increase the size of the army for which Ireland paid, Townshend needed defenders, but perhaps not of Caldwell's type.[13] Two pamphlets, one a defence of the army augmentation addressed to the Irish House of Commons and the other a vindication of Townshend, appeared late in the skirmishing.[14] Although they were published anonymously, Caldwell's authorship could easily be uncovered. Ponderous and pompous, the contributions were not calculated to affect the outcome of the debates. Caldwell's stance on contentious issues was unpredictable and inconsistent, depending chiefly on whichever attitude was most likely to ingratiate him with the administration of the day. The defence of Townshend was intended to make incontrovertible Caldwell's claims to an Irish peerage. When Townshend failed to reciprocate by recommending Caldwell for ennoblement, not only did Caldwell switch his allegiance (turning abruptly towards Townshend's successor, Harcourt), but he inveighed against his recent hero, Townshend.[15] Caldwell's fickleness was undoubtedly extreme, as indeed was his obsession with securing a peerage (he failed). So, too, it was thought, was his naivete. Caldwell's brother-in-law commented, 'among friends, I feel some wonder that with an understanding above the generality, Sir James's experience has not taught him that the great men of these times are for ninety-nine times in a hundred no more than titled merchants, whose ultimate object is retribution'.[16] Given the brief tenure of most lords lieutenant and the limits to their bounty, with more patronage reserved by the English ministry, the Irish parliament and revenue commissioners, prudence as well as self-interest obliged the hopeful not to rely exclusively on the largesse of any particular viceroy. Eighteenth-century viceroys, ostensibly 'great men of these times', were regarded as unreliable supporters.

How too close an attachment to the lord lieutenant might damage local reputation is illustrated by Gorges Edmond Howard, an acquaintance of Caldwell. Howard had placed his legal and literary skills at the disposal of various paymasters. Eventually he called in some of the debts when, early in the 1780s, he was organising an ambitious edition of his own collected writings. He persuaded the current viceroy and vicereine, Lord and Lady Carlisle, to head the printed tally of subscribers, together with their immediate predecessors, the Buckinghamshires. Yet, contrary to Howard's hopes, these examples did not secure the three hundred subscribers for which he had been aiming. Obsequiousness had failed to bring the expected return, and Howard (wealthy enough) was left to foot the bill for his publication.[17]

Subscriptions were a relatively cheap and easy way in which lords lieutenant could ingratiate themselves with would-be authors. Allowing his name to head the printed list of subscribers implied endorsement of both author and the work. It is doubtful how often a viceroy had read anything more than a sketchy proposal for the project before agreeing to pay over money in advance. Nevertheless, an association of this type was a more active act of patronage than simply being the named recipient of a publication. The intention of an author or publisher in signing up the lord lieutenant was to give an extra *cachet* to the forthcoming work and to lure the sheepish into following the bellwether from the Castle. Yet, Howard's humiliation showed that viceregal endorsement was not always enough to overcome the reservations of others about subscribing. Moreover, the presence of the names of the lord lieutenant and his wife in a subscription list can seldom have made the difference between a work being published or not. Their names as subscribers do sometimes indicate a writer's links with the administration and the Castle set, or the acceptability of the work's contents to those groups. The Revd Thomas Leland, a suave clerical don from Trinity, could advertise the facts that the lord lieutenant, the duke of Bedford, had paid for two fine paper copies of his *Philip of Macedon*, and that Bedford's predecessors, Lords Devonshire and Dorset, had each subscribed. However, the English dukes were eclipsed by the much more substantial patronage of the leading bibliophile in Protestant Ireland. Lord Charlemont had agreed to buy fifty sets.[18] Once the lord lieutenancy was monopolised by interlopers from England, it was easier for local notables to exercise social and cultural leadership, as the examples of the Conollys, Kildares, Charlemont and Mornington show.

III

Much printed work was directed speculatively to the lord lieutenant or his lady. Set alongside Caldwell's and Howard's disappointments, examples of literary flattery yielding obvious rewards are fewer. One is provided by John Wilson, an Englishman whose play, *The Cheats*, brought him celebrity in 1664. The dramatic success may not have been the sole, or indeed the most important, reason why Wilson came to the notice of Ormond, then lord lieutenant. But Ormond ensured the appointment of Wilson to be recorder of Derry in 1666. This was not, perhaps, such a welcome reward as at first it appeared. Wilson was soon plunged into the rancorous civic politics of Derry. He fell foul of the strident Presbyterian and Scottish groups within the corporation.[19] Even so, Wilson repaid his patron, publishing a learned defence of monarchy (against the alleged republican leanings of some Presbyterians in the north of Ireland) and eulogies on Ormond himself.[20] Wilson hymned Ormond as the personification 'of Plato's grand nobility/An inbred greatness, innate honesty . . . You, who almost alone,/Durst grasp a spear and underprop a crown'. Scarred by his own experiences in fractious Derry, Wilson looked to the lord lieutenant 'to tune our jarring harp'.[21] There is no evidence that Ormond requested these services as a price for his earlier promotion of Wilson.

Similarly, the most memorable poetic memorialist of Ormond, John Dryden, did not write to order. The characterisation of Ormond as Barzillai in *Absolon and Achitophel* spontaneously expressed Dryden's admiration. But there were others (notably Sir Robert Southwell) to whom Ormond did entrust a defence of his record and reputation.[22] Moreover, Ormond, as head of a sizeable affinity in Ireland and thanks to his family's long settlement and his own long service there, was the centre of a following the members of which might spontaneously praise him. In this regard the Ormondes differed from their successors in the lord lieutenancy throughout the later seventeenth and eighteenth centuries.[23] The two dukes' grip on the viceroyalty helped each to imprint Dublin Castle with a distinctive physical and cultural stamp. In achieving this they (especially the first duke) were assisted by the forcefulness of their wives.[24] In addition, the Ormondes had extensive connections within Ireland as well as in England and beyond. The benefits that this could yield are indicated when, in 1698, William Philips directed his play *The Revengeful Queen* to Ormond, 'because your family have vouchsafed to be the patrons of mine for several generations'.[25]

Wilson dedicated his treatise on monarchy to Ormond.[26] Its loyalist tenor would have been congenial to the duke, but there is no evidence that he had encouraged Wilson to compose it. The way in which Wilson seems originally to have come to Ormond's notice does, however, suggest one artistic sphere in which the lord lieutenant actively interested himself: the theatre. Wilson's London success with *The Cheats* inaugurated his turbulent career as an office-holder in Ireland.[27] Plays featured prominently in the diversions staged at Dublin Castle during the 1660s. Ormond's enthusiasm for play-going was shared by many at the court of Charles II; nor was it a novelty in Ireland. The lord deputy of the 1630s, Thomas Wentworth, earl of Strafford, is credited with the introduction of the professional playhouse into Dublin.[28] Ormond, in several respects a conscious continuer of Wentworth's approach to the Irish government, became an active patron of theatrical performances during the 1660s. His willingness to attend and applaud was certainly useful to dramatists and impresarios.[29] Yet, there is no evidence of his commissioning specific works. Instead, what has been called 'a Dublin Castle coterie' greatly influenced the choice of plays and set a fashion for play-going.[30] Some only briefly in Dublin, such as the well-connected Katherine Philips, wrote for the theatre, and persuaded others from the office-holding elite to assist. A local notable, the earl of Orrery, although a political rival of Ormond, had his dramas – heavy with topical and historical allusions – acted, sometimes with Ormond in the audience.[31] Both Philips and Orrery were familiar with the conventions of the restoration stage in London, and hardly contributed anything distinctively Irish to the programme available in Dublin.[32] Apart from Philips's and Orrery's contributions, the theatrical seasons quickly settled into re-stagings of London hits. The conventionality of the offerings suggests that neither Ormond nor his successors did anything to prompt the writing of new pieces. Yet he and – perhaps more importantly – his dynamic wife encouraged an atmosphere friendly to theatrical endeavours. The Ormondes' taste for the theatre had been fostered by travel. Foreign journeys, sometimes voluntary and sometimes enforced exile, familiarised successive generations of the Butlers with what was fashionable in continental Europe. Conspicuous among the volumes in the Ormondes' library (kept mostly at Kilkenny) were printed texts of plays, many in French or Italian, picked up on tour.[33]

The theatre in Dublin, while sometimes falling into the doldrums, persisted as an entertainment, popular alike among the fashionable elites and the less elevated. Among the Ormondes' successors in the viceroyalty, the dukes of Devonshire and Dorset commanded numerous theatrical performances (fifty-four and about thirty respectively).[34] Dorset (lord lieutenant between 1730 and 1737) included theatrical entertainments among the spectacles through which he aimed to impress Dublin with his ducal magnificence and viceregal standing. Returning as viceroy in 1751, he commanded twenty-four performances of plays in the ensuing seasons. This contrasted with the four ordered by his immediate predecessor.[35] Useful as the command performances were to theatrical managers, in commercial terms they were not notably more valuable than the occasions when the judges and legal profession or the freemasons paid for special presentations. In 1734, the Boyne Society was also prepared to step in when there was no resident lord lieutenant in order to underwrite the customary staging on the anniversary of William III's birth (4 November) of Rowe's *Tamerlane*.[36]

In any case, what was bespoken by the viceroy was the familiar and popular, such as *Tamerlane* or (by Dorset) Voltaire's *Mahomet* and Shakespeare's pieces, not fresh offerings from Irish dramatists. The hardy perennials were capable of partisan and provocative interpretations, especially when supplemented by topical prologues and interpolations. But these additions were not devised by the lords lieutenant.[37] Moreover, useful as viceregal patronage was to the managers and shareholders since the command performances usually sold out, it did little to help aspiring playwrights. Indeed, in the absence of a guaranteed livelihood dramatists of Irish birth – like other authors – tended to desert the island for London.[38]

By the eighteenth century, the theatrical offerings belonged to a mixed economy of cultural diversions, which included musical concerts and ridottos, but also lectures and improving demonstrations.[39] Much was unashamedly commercial, but a substantial element was intended to raise money for medical and educational charities. Lords lieutenant and their ladies were earnestly solicited to head published lists of subscribers, take tickets and (best of all) grace the events with their presence. Tedious as these obligations might become, conscientious viceroys recognised a duty and discharged it. Once again, instead of showing any initiative, they typically obeyed the strongest pressures exerted by the locals. Important to the success or failure of a performance as the viceregal presence might be, the intervals during which no lord lieutenant resided at the Castle were so frequent and protracted, that the promoters of plays, concerts and exhibitions knew better than to rely on such patronage. Nor did they need to. Although, by the mid-eighteenth century, the calendar of performances was seriously over-crowded, Dublin itself was thronged with permanent and temporary residents. It was to these customers that impresarios and performers looked for backing. In bringing over from England or continental Europe celebrities – whether singers, instrumentalists, dancers or actors – the likely profit was the chief incentive.[40] It has been shown conclusively that the social and cultural scene in eighteenth-century Dublin flourished even in those seasons when the lord lieutenant was absent and parliament did not sit.[41]

In commissioning new music, it might be argued that the viceregal court took a more decisive role. In the cycle of official celebration, accession days and royal birthdays, spectacles were devised, principally as displays of loyalty to the incumbent regime in Britain. Odes set to music were included regularly in these entertainments. They seldom involved noticeable artistic innovation.

Nevertheless, they provided employment to a fortunate few, notably Johann Cousser. By 1716, the Bohemian Cousser was styled 'Master of musick attending His Majesty's state in Ireland'.[42] Furthermore, the state maintained a group of musicians, which numbered eleven in 1725.[43]

The musical event for which eighteenth-century Dublin is most commonly remembered, the première in 1742 of Handel's *Messiah*, exemplifies the dynamics of the cultural scene. Handel's appearance in Ireland owed little or nothing to the lord lieutenant, although the latter (Devonshire) was happy enough to grace performances of Handel's music. But, in a tradition which clouds this subject, sycophants subsequently attributed Handel's arrival in Ireland to an invitation from Devonshire.[44] In this case, the tradition of an explicit invitation was invented in the next century. It did, however, reveal an inclination which astute viceroys might exploit. As the monarch's surrogate in Ireland, the lord lieutenant ranked first in the kingdom. His presence, as well as his backing, was sought eagerly since it conferred prestige. In the 1760s, the then viceroy, the earl of Halifax, recognised this and acted accordingly. Halifax bewailed the tedium of the events over which he had to preside. Yet, by choosing to favour particular occasions with his presence, 'the great advantage the charity got by my company was that it filled the room'.[45] Obedient to these imperatives, in 1777, a successor of Halifax, Lord Buckinghamshire, was recorded as going in state to the Magdalen Hospital chapel and donating £11 *7s 6d* to the charity. Later in the month he went to another event in aid of the Marine School. For marking Queen Charlotte's birthday, Buckinghamshire had the customary assembly at the Castle at which a musical ode was sung, a theatrical performance was commanded and then a ball was given. But later in his incumbency, Buckinghamshire failed to attend an oratorio performed on behalf of Mercer's Hospital.[46]

IV

Sifting through the poems, plays and dedications, it is hard to discover much that was commissioned by a lord lieutenant. Once in office, many became associated with a particular grouping, and accordingly became butts for the invective and satire of the disappointed and disgruntled. Numerous lords lieutenant – Grafton, Dorset, Harrington, Bedford and Townshend – charged with implementing contentious measures, blundered between imperiousness and bibulous accessibility. Unwittingly, they thereby stimulated Irish literary vitality. The viceroyalty certainly inspired a good deal of ribald and sometimes memorable commentary, but this was inadvertent, not planned, and not the kind of creativity with which most governors wished to be associated.

The administration in Dublin Castle, subjected to attacks in print and parliament, gradually moved from trying to silence critics to answering them. As has been made clear from a series of studies, viceroys varied dramatically in their deployment of the arts of political management. Normally success depended on their good judgment in choosing those to whom these functions were to be delegated. In addition, viceroys wooed members of both houses of the Irish parliament. Throughout the 1750s and 1760s, peers and commoners were invited to dine at the Castle. Those who declined invitations or received none were noted methodically.[47] Familiar political arts could be supplemented by oblique approaches to the business of embedding the dynasty and systems of Hanoverian Britain in Ireland. That few lords lieutenant tried hard to do so is hardly surprising. As has been emphasised, most alighted only fleetingly in the Castle for the duration of the parliamentary session. Increasingly, the incumbents in Dublin hoped to enhance their reputations so as to secure higher office in England. Reputations for magnanimity and cultural innovation were not irrelevant to that quest but generally counted for less than political acumen. In addition, those whom the viceroys represented, the later Stuart and Hanoverian monarchs, were seldom renowned for cultural ardour. Nevertheless, some assisted collective initiatives; for example, Charles II with the Royal Society of London and George III with the Royal Academy and Royal Society of Arts. In several instances, women, either as queens regnant or consorts, offset the prevailing philistinism.[48]

Any assessment of comparable influence in Dublin through the vicereine is hampered by frequent uncertainty as to whether or not the viceroy was accompanied by his wife. The predominantly masculine aura of the Castle, with secretaries, stewards, chaplains, aides de camps, gentlemen of the bedchamber and gentlemen at large, is dispelled by accounts of the lavish entertainments on the state holidays at which women vied through their dress and dancing to be noticed.[49] Another sign of a regime more receptive to cultural diversity – at least temporarily – is the inclusion of women at the formal viceregal dinners. The invitations may have acknowledged belatedly that women other than the vicereine enjoyed political influence in Ireland. Dorset's gatherings occasionally included women, but it was only under the earl of Northumberland's viceroyalty between 1763 and 1764 that four or more were regularly present. The earl of Hertford invited even more: on 17 November 1765, half of the dozen who dined were women; on 14 March 1766, eight of the twenty guests. Later in the same decade, Townshend reverted to men only.[50]

The monarch's deputies in Ireland rarely gave priority to intellectual and cultural ventures. Thereby they copied their Stuart and Hanoverian leaders. Most viceroys preferred the hunt, the turf, the dance and the bordello. Here, probably, the most notable acts of patronage occurred, with the duke of

Rutland (lord lieutenant between 1784 and 1787) outstanding for his public resort to houses of ill fame.[51] Nevertheless, institutional endeavours to leaven Ireland interested some viceroys. Three bodies in particular – the Dublin Philosophical Society, the Incorporated Society and the Dublin Society – deserve to be considered as possible examples of effective viceregal interventions. Charles II had endorsed the craze for experiment and speculation when he granted a royal charter to the Royal Society in 1661. Several from Ireland were active in the English organisation, but there was interest in founding a comparable group in Dublin. When the scheme was realised in 1684, it owed almost everything to the energies of the young William Molyneux, a recent graduate of Dublin University. However, a new lord lieutenant, Lord Clarendon, arriving in 1685 proved an enthusiastic patron and adviser.[52] The first phase of the Dublin Philosophical Society scarcely outlasted Clarendon's lord lieutenancy. Clarendon's successor, Tyrconnell, preoccupied with more conventional tasks, had no truck with the Society. Clarendon's predecessor, Ormond, although he professed incomprehension in scientific matters, could be a benevolent patron.[53] However, he showed no favour to the infant Society. When the Society was revived in 1693, one of the lords justice, Sir Cyril Wyche, was an active participant. As well as offering an official endorsement, Wyche supplied continuity, since he had attended the earlier meetings.[54] However, such support was not enough to save the Society from decline. For a third time, in 1707, it sprang – briefly – to life. Now, the lord lieutenant, Pembroke, was happy to accept the presidency.[55] Once more, though, even the example of Pembroke, 'a man of great curiosity, reading and judgment', was not enough to sustain the Society.[56]

The experience of a group which revived and continued some of the activities of the Philosophical Society again showed that backing from Dublin Castle was not enough for an organisation to survive and succeed. The Dublin Society emerged from a small coterie that had started to meet in Trinity College from 1731. In taking on a more formal and an enlarged identity in 1733, the directors of the Society saw the value of inviting the lord lieutenant to join. It would become standard practice for the lord lieutenant to be named as president of the Dublin Society.[57] Most viceroys came only to one statutory meeting each year. Yet, official recognition of this kind indicated the centrality of the Society to the associational and philanthropic life of Dublin, and (arguably) of Ireland. What enabled the Dublin Society to overcome its early vicissitudes and then to flourish was not its dexterity in enlisting the lord lieutenant but a large membership willing to pay the annual subscription and to participate in the routines of the Society.[58] Nevertheless, the Dublin Society paid tribute to one lord lieutenant as responsible for its good fortune in the second half of the eighteenth century. Lord Chesterfield, while viceroy (between 1745 and 1748), not only accepted nomination as president, but advised the Society to consolidate its corporate status (enshrined in the 1733 charter) by seeking the award of public revenues. With Chesterfield's recommendation, the Society was granted £500 annually from public funds.[59] From the 1760s, the Society, thanks to legislation, received taxes which it was free to disburse in a system of subsidies and prizes for technical and agricultural inventions. The habit of deference led to Chesterfield's role being exaggerated. It was the active members who came constantly to meetings who ensured the well-being and longevity of the institution.[60] Yet, there can be no denying that Chesterfield's advice had been timely and helpful.

Accounts of the establishment of a third institution may have allowed flattery to distort the record. The Incorporated Society, like the Dublin Society, received its charter in 1733. Official recognition was the culmination of a process, at first diffuse, but latterly more coordinated, which aimed to introduce into Ireland a national network of Protestant charity schools. The prime mover behind the programme was Henry Maule, a Church of Ireland clergyman and, from 1726, a bishop. However, it was Maule's superior, the English-born archbishop of Armagh, Hugh Boulter, who was hailed publicly as the contriver of the vital charter.[61] Successive lords lieutenant, although favourably inclined to a project which was designed to strengthen the administration that they headed, were content to leave the lobbying and direction to the clergy.[62] Once the Incorporated Society had been formed, it depended heavily on donations. In common with other charitable ventures, it raised funds by annual services, both in Dublin and London, at which sermons were preached. At least from the 1760s, if not earlier, the lord lieutenant, when in Dublin, was expected to appear at these devotions.[63] In this respect, the Incorporated Society was merely one of the several causes that convention and ideology required the viceroy to own.

V

Given the number of calls for the lord lieutenant's support, discrimination had to be practised. Inevitably, many individuals and some groups felt discriminated against. Moreover, few viceroys were disinterested enough to give their time equally to all the meritorious causes that sought their backing. And indeed it was by showing biases towards specific activities that individual viceroys earned fame and were remembered favourably. While there were exceptions, these do not alter the impression of limited viceregal influence over the cultural, literary and artistic life of Dublin. The insubstantiality was an inevitable consequence of the character of the viceroyalty in the eighteenth century. Lords lieutenant were almost always hampered by their being strangers to the kingdom, stationed there only temporarily and frequently being short of funds. Against such weaknesses must be set a uniquely elevated status, which entitled each incumbent regardless of personal attributes to deference. Moreover, occasional viceroys had close links with Ireland, through estates and kindred there (as in the cases of the dukes of Devonshire) or, with Dorset, thanks to two tours of duty. In addition, the lord lieutenant's unfamiliarity with the personalities and issues could be compensated through the wit, assiduity and connections of the officers of his household. Andrew Fountain, Joseph Addison and Tom Tickell retained friendships in Ireland long after they had returned from their brief stays there.[64] Also, it has to be allowed that now and again lords lieutenant themselves possessed charm. Lord Carteret in the second half of the 1720s seems to have been notable in this respect, as well as adept as a politician.[65] Possibly Harcourt had it too. But in the main, the governors showed their prowess best by being able to hold their drink in the stupendous bouts that occurred on their watches. Townshend became notorious for his inability not to blab out confidences in his cups. Strong heads were not necessarily incompatible with discerning patronage, but, in combination with the other enfeebling factors, greatly diminished the likelihood of most viceroys making a lasting impact on the creative life of Dublin, let alone Ireland.

Notes

1 Anon., *A Welcom in a Poem to His Excellency John Lord Roberts . . . Lord Lieutenant General and General Governour of Ireland* (Dublin, 1669).

2 Andrew Carpenter (ed.), *Verse in English from Tudor and Stuart Ireland* (Cork, 2003), pp 442–6.

3 Later portraits of Robartes, by then earl of Radnor, are known.

4 T. C. Barnard, 'The vice-regal court in the later-seventeenth-century Ireland' in Eveline Cruickshanks (ed.), *The Stuart Courts* (Stroud, 2000), pp 256–65; T. C. Barnard, *Making the Grand Figure: Lives and Possessions in Ireland, 1641–1770* (New Haven and London, 2004), pp 1–20.

5 J. I. McGuire, 'Why was Ormond dismissed in 1669?', *Irish Historical Studies*, 18 (1973), pp 295–312.

6 William Mercer, *The Moderate Cavalier* (Cork, 1675).

7 Petitions addressed to 2nd duke of Ormonde, Bodleian Library, Oxford (Bodl.), Eng. Hist. C 974; National Library of Ireland, Dublin (hereafter NLI), Ms. 2494.

8 Dorothy Smith, *The Shepherds Jubilee, or, a Pastoral Welcome, to His Excellency the Earl of Rochester, &c. on his Arrival in Ireland* (Dublin, 1701).

9 George Wilkins, *The Chace of the Stag: A Descriptionary Poem dedicated to Her Grace the Duchess of Ormond* (Dublin, 1699).

10 John Dryden, *Fables Ancient and Modern; Translated into Verse from Homer, Ovid, Boccace, & Chaucer* (London, 1700), sig. B[1]–[C1v].

11 [William Hammond], *Advice to a Son: A Poem* (Dublin, 1736).

12 T. C. Barnard, 'Writing and publishing histories in eighteenth-century Ireland' in Stephen Paul Forrest and Mark Williams (eds), *Constructing the Past: Writing Irish History, 1600–1800* (Woodbridge, 2010), pp 95–112.

13 Thomas Bartlett, 'The Townshend viceroyalty, 1767–1772', in Thomas Bartlett and D. W. Hayton (eds), *Penal Era and Golden Age: Essays in Irish History, 1690–1800* (Belfast, 1979), pp 88–112; Martyn J. Powell, 'The reform of the undertaker system: Anglo-Irish politics, 1750–1767', *Irish Historical Studies*, 31 (1998), pp 19–36.

14 Anon., *An Address to the House of Commons of Ireland: By a Freeholder* ([Dublin], 1771); Anon., *An Essay on the Character and Conduct of His Excellency Lord Visc. Townshend* ([Dublin], 1771).

15 Sir J. Caldwell to Lady Caldwell, 3, 12 and 22 Nov. 1772, 10 and 15 Dec. 1772, 1, 6, 8, 18, 28 Jan. 1773, John Rylands Library, Manchester, B 3/29/26, 34, 37, 42, 44, 45, 51, 52, 55; Sir J. Caldwell to Lord Townshend, 22 Oct. 1772, ibid., Caldwell letter books, 6, pp 1203 et seq.

16 J. Hort to Lady Caldwell, 5 Jan. 1773, Public Record Office of Northern Ireland, Belfast (hereafter PRONI), D 1634/2/62a.

17 Gorges Edmond Howard, *The Miscellaneous Works, in Verse and Prose*, (3 vols, Dublin, 1782), i, pp vii–iii.

18 Thomas Leland, *The History of the Life and Reign of Philip, King of Macedon* (London, 1758).

19 Milton C. Nahm (ed.), *John Wilson's The Cheats* (Oxford, 1935); Cf. John Kerrigan, *Archipelagic English: Literature, History and Politics, 1603–1707* (Oxford, 2008), pp 305–7.

20 [John Wilson], *A Discourse of Monarchy, more particularly, of the Imperial Crowns of England, Scotland and Ireland* (London, 1684); John Wilson, *To His Grace James Duke of Ormond, &c. Lord Lieutenant of Ireland, on his Return to that Government* (London, 1677).

21 Wilson, *To His Grace James Duke of Ormond.*

22 B. E. Hoffman (ed.), *A Contemporary Account of the Life and Times of James, 1st Duke of Ormonde*, The Butler Society, North American region, publication no. 2 (1980); R. Southwell, 'The life of James Butler, the first duke of Ormond' in Lord Mountmorres, *The History of the Principal Transactions of the Irish Parliament, from the Year 1634 to 1666* (2 vols, London, 1798), i, pp 180–313; Cf. Michael Perceval-Maxwell, 'Sir Robert Southwell and the duke of Ormond's reflections on the 1640s', in Micheál Ó Siochrú (ed.), *Kingdoms in Crisis: Ireland in the 1640s* (Dublin, 2001), pp 229–47; Michael Perceval-Maxwell, 'The Anglesey-Ormond-Castlehaven dispute, 1680–1682: taking sides about Ireland in England', in Vincent P. Carey and Ute Lötz-Heumann (eds), *Taking Sides? Colonial and Confessional* Mentalités *in Early Modern Ireland* (Dublin, 2003), pp 213–30.

23 Frances Elrington Ball, 'Some notes on the households of the dukes of Ormonde', *Proceedings of the Royal Irish Academy*, 38, sect. C, no. 1 (1928), pp 1–20; D. W. Hayton, 'Dependence, clientage and affinity: the political following of the second duke of Ormonde', in T. C. Barnard and Jane Fenlon, *The Dukes of Ormonde, 1610–1745* (Woodbridge, 2000), pp 211–41.

24 T. C. Barnard, 'Introduction', in Barnard and Fenlon, *The Dukes of Ormonde*, pp 33–4; Jane Fenlon, 'The duchess of Ormonde's house at Dunmore', in John Kirwan (ed.), *Kilkenny:*

Essays in Honour of Margaret M. Phelan (Kilkenny, 1997), pp 79–87; Jane Fenlon, 'The Ormonde inventories, 1675–1717: a state apartment at Kilkenny Castle', in Agnes Bernelle (ed.), *Decantations* (Dublin, 1992), pp 29–36; Jane Fenlon, '"Her Grace's closet": paintings in the duchess of Ormond's closet at Kilkenny Castle', *Bulletin of the Irish Georgian Society*, 36 (1994), pp 30–47; Jane Fenlon, 'Episodes of magnificence: the material worlds of the dukes of Ormonde', in Barnard and Fenlon (eds), *The Dukes of Ormonde*, pp 137–60.

25 William Philips, *The Revengeful Queen* (London, 1698).

26 [Wilson], *A Discourse of Monarchy*, sig [A2v].

27 Nahm (ed.), *John Wilson's The Cheats*, p. 19.

28 William Smith Clark, *The Early Irish Stage: The Beginnings to 1720* (Oxford, 1955), pp 26–42; Alan J. Fletcher, *Drama, Performance, and Polity in Pre-Cromwellian Ireland* (Cork, 2000), pp 261–77.

29 Clark, *The Early Irish Stage*, pp 46–61.

30 Ibid., p. 62.

31 Diary of the 2nd earl of Cork, s.d. 17 and 18 Feb. 1662[3], 10 Apr. 1672, Chatsworth House, Derbyshire.

32 M. Choudhury, 'Orrery and the London stage: a loyalist's contribution to restoration allegorical drama', *Studia Neophilologica*, 62 (1990), pp 43–59; Clark, *The Early Irish Stage*, pp 62–6; Marie-Louise Coolahan, *Women, Writing and Language in Early Modern Ireland* (Oxford, 2010), pp 195–218: Kerrigan, *Archipelagic English*, pp 244–67; Nancy Klein Maguire, *Regicide and Restoration: English Tragicomedy, 1660–1671* (Cambridge, 1992); Christopher Morash, *A History of Irish Theatre, 1601–2000* (Cambridge, 2002), pp 21–9.

33 Accounts, 1647–8, s.d. 12 Nov. 1647, Bodl., Carte Ms. 30, f. 342v; inventory of Ormond's goods in his Irish houses, Oct. and Nov. 1684, NLI, Ms. 2554/6, p. 95; catalogue of Ormond's books at Kilkenny, 6 Jan. 1684[5], NLI, Ms. 2554/3; library list of 2nd duke of Ormonde, *c.*1716, The National Archives, Kew (hereafter TNA), FEC1/877.

34 John C. Greene and Gladys L. H. Clark, *The Dublin Stage, 1720–1745: A Calendar of Plays, Entertainments, and Afterpieces* (Bethlehem, London and Toronto, 1993), pp 45, 156; Thomas Snagg, *Recollections of Occurrences* (London, 1951), p. 102; La Tourette Stockwell, *Dublin Theatres and Theatre Customs (1637–1820)* (Kingsport, 1938), p. 183.

35 Helen M. Burke, *Riotous Performances: The Struggle for Hegemony in the Irish Theater, 1712–1784* (Notre Dame, 2003), p. 222; Morash, *A History of Irish Theatre*, p. 35; Esther Keck Sheldon, *Thomas Sheridan of Smock-Alley* (Princeton, 1967), pp 170–2, 337, 356.

36 Greene and Clark, *The Dublin Stage*, pp 136, 140–1, 142–3, 146–7, 151, 161, 165, 167.

37 Burke, *Riotous Performances*, pp 43–51; Morash, *A History of Irish Theatre*, pp 58–66; Sheldon, *Thomas Sheridan of Smock-Alley*, p. 172.

38 Greene and Clark, *The Dublin Stage*, p. 89.

39 Anon., *The Last Time of Performance for the Amusement and Entertainment of Ladies as well as Gentlemen, at the Smiths Hall in Smock-Alley, Dublin* (n.d. [Dublin, 1744]).

40 W. H., 'A letter of Sir W[illia]m Fownes after enjoying the company of two young ladies at a concert of musick at my lodgings [in] Dublin', 1732, British Library, London (hereafter BL), Add. Ms. 846A, f. 171; David Fleming, 'Diversions of the people: sociability among the orders

[40 *cont.*] of early eighteenth-century Ireland', *Eighteenth-Century Ireland*, 17 (2002), pp 99–111; Greene and Clark, *The Dublin Stage*, pp 24–5; Gráinne McArdle, 'Signora Violante and her troupe of dancers, 1729–32', *Eighteenth-Century Ireland*, 20 (2005), pp 55–78; Snagg, *Recollections of Occurrences*, pp 81–4, 95–6, 98–9.

41 Tighernan Mooney and Fiona White, 'The gentry's winter season' in David Dickson (ed.), *The Gorgeous Mask: Dublin, 1700–1850* (Dublin, 1987), pp 1–16.

42 Brian Boydell, *A Dublin Musical Calendar 1700–1760* (Dublin, 1988), pp 36–41, 275. As an example: J. S. Cousser, *A Contest between Mars and Jupiter: A Serenade to be Represented on the Birthday of His Most Sacred Majesty King George . . . at the Castle of Dublin the 28th May, 1721* (Dublin, 1721).

43 Greene and Clark, *The Dublin Stage*, p. 68.

44 David Hunter, 'Inviting Handel to Ireland: Laurence Whyte and the challenge of poetic evidence', *Eighteenth-Century Ireland*, 20 (2005), pp 156–63; Watkins Shaw, *The Story of Handel's Messiah* (London, 1963); Horatio Townsend, *An Account of the Visit of Handel to Dublin* (Dublin, 1852).

45 Halifax's journal, 1761–3, NLI, Ms. 8064; T. C. Barnard, *Making the Grand Figure*, pp 10–11.

46 Lords lieutenant's dinner lists, s.d. 21 Mar. 1777, 6 and 20 Apr. 1777, 3 Feb. 1778, Mar. 1778, 5 Apr. 1778, NLI, Ms. 1471.

47 Lords lieutenant's dinner lists, NLI, Mss 1464–71.

48 Clarissa Campbell Orr (ed.), *Queenship in Britain, 1660–1837: Royal Patronage, Court Culture and Dynastic Politics* (Manchester, 2002); Jane Roberts (ed.), *George III and Queen Charlotte: Patronage, Collecting and Taste* (London, 2004); Hannah Smith, *Georgian Monarchy: Politics and Culture, 1714–1760* (Cambridge, 2006).

49 Barnard, *Making the Grand Figure*, pp 10–11, 16–20.

50 Lords lieutenant's dinner lists, NLI, Mss 1465, 1468, 1469, 1470.

51 Mary Lyons (ed.), *The Memoirs of Mrs Leeson, Madam 1727–1797* (Dublin, 1995), pp 143–7.

52 K. Theodore Hoppen, *The Common Scientist in the Seventeenth Century: A Study of the Dublin Philosophical Society, 1683–1708* (London, 1970), pp 97–8.

53 Barnard, 'Introduction', in Barnard and Fenlon (eds), *The Dukes of Ormonde*, pp 2–3.

54 Hoppen, *The Common Scientist*, pp 96–7.

55 Ibid., pp 192–3.

56 K. Theodore Hoppen (ed.), *Papers of the Dublin Philosophical Society, 1683–1709*, (2 vols, Dublin, 2008), ii, p. 747.

57 Minutes, Dublin Society, 1758–61, s.d. 8 Nov. 1759, Royal Dublin Society Library; Henry F. Berry, *A History of the Royal Dublin Society* (London, 1915), pp 24, 76.

58 T. C. Barnard, 'The Dublin Society and other improving societies, 1731–85', in J. Kelly and M. Powell (eds), *Clubs and Societies in Eighteenth-Century Ireland* (Dublin, 2010), pp 53–88.

59 Berry, *A History of the Royal Dublin Society*, pp 46–8.

60 T. C. Barnard, '"Wedded to old customs": The Dublin Society, John Wynn Baker and agricultural innovation', in Fergus Mulligan (ed.), *Auguri: To Mary Kelleher* (Dublin, 2009), pp 19–35; Barnard, 'The Dublin Society and other improving societies', pp 81–8.

61 T. C. Barnard, 'Protestants and the Irish language, c.1675–1725', *Journal of Ecclesiastical History*, 44 (1993), pp 243–72; D. W. Hayton, 'Did Protestantism fail in early eighteenth-century Ireland? Charity schools and the enterprise of religious and social reformation, *c.*1690–1730', in Alan Ford, James McGuire and Kenneth Milne (eds), *As by Law Established: The Church of Ireland Since the Reformation* (Dublin, 1995), pp 166–86; Kenneth Milne, *The Irish Charter Schools, 1730–1830* (Dublin, 1997), pp 11–33.

62 Rules and Orders, Incorporated Society, 1735–1779, s.d. 3 Jan. 1745[6], Trinity College Dublin (hereafter TCD), Ms. 5301.

63 Board Book, Incorporated Schools, 1761–1775, s.d. 23 May 1766, 17 June 1770, 10 May 1772, 13 May 1774, TCD, Ms. 5225; Isaac Mann, *A Sermon preached at Christ Church, Dublin, on the 15th of May, 1774 before . . . Earl Harcourt, President, and the Rest of the Incorporated Society of Dublin* (Dublin, 1775).

64 'Catalogue of the books to be sold at Dublin Castle . . . part of the library of Secretary Tickell, deceased', *c.*1729, Smythe of Barbavilla Mss, now in TCD; Barnard, *Making the Grand Figure*, pp 4, 14, 19–20, 199, 215; Walter Graham (ed.), *Letters of Joseph Addison* (Oxford, 1941); Hoppen (ed.), *Papers of the Dublin Philosophical Society*, ii, p. 747; John Ingamells, *A Dictionary of British and Irish Travellers in Italy, 1701–1800* (New Haven and London, 1997), pp 376–7; R. E. Tickell, *Thomas Tickell and the Eighteenth-Century Poets (1685–1740)* (London, 1931).

65 Barnard, *Making the Grand Figure*, pp 2–3, 10, 13, 14, 17; D. W. Hayton, *Ruling Ireland, 1685–1742: Politics, Politicians and Parties* (Woodbridge, 2004), pp 215–16, 234–5, 242–55.

CHAPTER 6

Revolution, Rebellion and the Viceroyalty 1789–99

Gillian O'Brien

The position of lord lieutenant of Ireland was rarely coveted, and this was never more true than in the 1790s. Lord Camden referred to his time in Ireland as 'a splendid banishment' while his successor, Lord Cornwallis, declared that 'the life of a lord lieutenant of Ireland comes up to my idea of perfect misery'.[1] Four viceroys served in Ireland between 1789 and 1799: John Fane, 10th earl of Westmorland; William Wentworth, 2nd Earl Fitzwilliam; John Jeffries Pratt, Earl Camden and Charles, Marquess Cornwallis. The decade 1789–99 was a period of enormous upheaval, and the lord lieutenant faced many challenges as military, financial, parliamentary, religious, and administrative crises ebbed and flowed. These challenged the capacities of the viceroys, and inevitably some responded more ably than others.

As the king's representative in Ireland, and the kingdom's most senior political figure, perhaps the role of the viceroy should have been clear. However, the truth is that the parameters of the position were ill defined. The lord lieutenant was expected to be a figurehead, a host, a politician, a mediator, an administrator and a military strategist. He was required to be flexible and adaptable in an environment where the political and military circumstances altered with great rapidity. He was to do all this without clear guidance from London and with limited support in Dublin.

On one point, however, the British administration was clear: the lord lieutenant owed his loyalty to those who had appointed him. This loyalty, according to the *Gentleman's Magazine* of July 1797, rendered the viceroy virtually powerless:

> Although the viceroy of the sister kingdom bears about him the trappings of royalty, he is, in truth, only an officer delegated to discharge the functions of government. In that capacity he must ever be subject to the control, the advice and the mandate of the British cabinet.[2]

Henry Grattan concurred, complaining that 'the viceroy's function was only to obey orders and to be the English agent in the Kingdom of Ireland', and that this situation 'established a monarchy of clerks'.[3] The British government insisted upon its right to control the Irish administration in Dublin, with the Prime Minster, William Pitt, asserting that 'power remained in this country [England] to control the [lord lieutenant of Ireland]'.[4] Yet, in truth the lord lieutenant often felt abandoned by his colleagues in London and sought support and advice from within rather than without the country. This was particularly true of Westmorland and Camden. Fitzwilliam's position was rather different – he thought London excessively interested in his position in Ireland and, by the time of Cornwallis's appointment, Westmorland's complaint that 'England is indifferent where the power is in Ireland' was no longer valid as England was firmly focused, for once, on Irish affairs.[5]

During the 1790s there was considerable continuity within the Irish administration and this was both a strength and a weakness for the viceroys. Key officeholders such as John Foster, John FitzGibbon, Sackville Hamilton, Edward Cooke, Arthur Wolfe and Archbishop Charles Agar were men of great influence – which they used to dominate a succession of lords lieutenant.[6] Viceroys often had limited knowledge of Ireland and limited political experience and so continuity of staff was vital. Nowhere was this continuity more obvious, nor more troublesome, than within the so-called Irish 'cabinet'. John Magee, editor of the *Dublin Evening Post*, complained in 1795 that this 'cabinet':

> have been so long in the habit of living in splendour and opulence at the expense of the public, that they at length begin to think of their places as an inheritance . . . they are too proud, too lazy, and too profligate to betake themselves to honest industry.[7]

The 'cabinet' in the 1790s was comprised chiefly of John Foster, the speaker of the House of Commons; John FitzGibbon (later Lord Clare), the lord chancellor; John Parnell, the chancellor of the exchequer, and the chief commissioner of the revenue, John Beresford. Managing this 'cabinet' was difficult as the 'members' regarded themselves as the rightful administrators of the country and saw the lord lieutenant as a temporary inconvenience to be tolerated rather than respected. What made the 'cabinet' particularly difficult to deal with was the fact that they rarely acted as a unified whole and often placed their personal interests above all else. This was particularly evident when promotions or the use of patronage was involved, provoking Camden's chief secretary, Thomas Pelham, to write that he 'would rather work at the plough all the rest of my days than engage in that dirty traffic of patronage while men like the Speaker act in the manner they do'.[8]

Alongside political and administrative duties the lord lieutenant performed a ceremonial role. An important aspect of the viceroy's entertainment was to provide the Irish elite with a version of the royal court, and the lord lieutenant presided over a series of lavish dinners and flamboyant balls in an attempted emulation of London society. Such extravagance was often a drain on the viceroy's personal finances. At the beginning of the eighteenth century the lord lieutenant's salary was £11,000 p.a., this was increased to £16,000 during Lord Halifax's tenure of office (1761–3) and to £20,000 in 1783. In addition, each lord lieutenant was provided an additional one-off payment of £3,000 on his appointment. However, this was seldom adequate to fund the lavish lifestyle which many enjoyed and a number of viceroys complained of the drain on their resources. Lord Carlisle, lord lieutenant between 1780 and 1782, reckoned that he was £10,000 poorer, while Camden regularly bemoaned the expense of his position, though he prided himself on spending less than Buckingham (1782–3, 1787–9) whose excesses were renowned.[9] Cornwallis's refusal to hold the customary balls, dinners and levees caused Bishop Thomas Percy to complain that, although Cornwallis was 'very civil and pleasant . . . he will not be a favourite here, for he is very sober himself, and does not push the bottle'.[10]

Despite the pomp and ceremony that surrounded Dublin Castle, the efforts made by lords lieutenant to portray the Irish aristocracy as equal to the English were often undermined. Particularly irritating was the tendency of the administration in Whitehall to offer Irish peerages to minor English figures. Interference from London had several negative effects. Firstly, such actions removed valuable patronage from Dublin Castle's control and gave positions of potential influence to men who frequently knew little and cared less about Ireland. Secondly, and most importantly, this practice highlighted the fact that the Irish peerage was held in less regard than its English counterpart. It proved impossible to persuade the Protestant ascendancy that the impression of grandeur they enjoyed in Dublin was even remotely comparable to the reality of that in London.

With a myriad of duties and responsibilities, direct involvement with military affairs was not high on the agenda for any lord lieutenant. The military forces in Ireland were led by a commander-in-chief and in theory the lord lieutenant would be little troubled by military concerns, and certainly play no active part in developing military strategy. Given that Westmorland, Fitzwilliam and Camden had no military experience this was a good thing. However, during the 1790s, as the security situation in Ireland deteriorated and the Irish military command showed itself to be fragile and flawed, the lords lieutenant were obliged to become increasingly involved. Such involvement culminated in June 1798 when Cornwallis, who held the rank of general, was appointed lord lieutenant and commander-in-chief simultaneously.

I

Westmorland was sent to Ireland in the aftermath of the damaging regency crisis of 1789. He was, as was Camden later, a college friend of the prime minister, William Pitt. Westmorland was a political novice; appointed to the office of joint paymaster-general in September 1789, the following month he became a member of the privy council and ten days later was appointed lord lieutenant of Ireland. Westmorland's lack of political experience was immediately apparent to senior members of the Irish 'cabinet', including Foster, Beresford and FitzGibbon, and throughout his tenure he became increasingly reliant on his subordinates in Dublin Castle and the Irish parliament, and increasingly remote from his paymasters in Westminster.[11] To a very large extent Westmorland's viceroyalty was dominated by the Catholic question, which was further complicated by the difficult financial times. From the beginning of 1792, Ireland was in the throes of a recession caused, at least partly, by a bad harvest and the beginning of the French wars. Trade virtually dried up, causing revenue to plummet at a time when funds were in increasing demand as the military situation in Ireland deteriorated throughout the 1790s.[12]

In 1792 the London government was anxious to grant considerable concessions to English Catholics and desired that Ireland would follow suit. Westmorland was torn between following Whitehall's lead and representing the opinion of the Irish 'cabinet'. Personally, he shared the fears of the Irish ascendancy and regarded the proposed concessions as excessive. Convinced that his concerns were being ignored he dispatched his chief secretary, Robert Hobart, to London to appeal for only very limited concessions for Ireland. Hobart was ignored. Pitt and his advisers concluded that if the Irish administration was allowed to dictate Catholic policy, 'it will end in their giving way too late and without either having the credit of liberality or deriving the benefit of attaching to English government that body which composes the effective mass of the people of Ireland'.[13] Westmorland was incensed. Pitt responded to what he regarded as Westmorland's tantrum, commenting 'the idea of our wishing to play what you call a Catholic game is really extravagant; we have only thought of what was the most likely plan to preserve the security and tranquillity of the British and Protestant interest'.[14] It was clear that, of those two priorities, the Protestant interest came a distant second.

Westmorland could postpone the inevitable but not prevent it. Policy would be dictated by London without recourse to his opinion.[15] However, since 1782 Whitehall could not oblige the Irish parliament to pass a bill. As Tom Bartlett has observed, 'a recommendation was as far as London could go, [but] in British circles it carried the weight of a decision'. As far as Pitt was concerned it was up to the lord lieutenant to ensure, using persuasion and promises, that the government would have a majority in parliament and London was prepared to wait.[16] In 1792, reflecting both Westmorland's weakness and the Irish 'cabinet's intransigence', the Irish parliament passed a watered-down bill which granted moderate concessions to Catholics with regard to education, intermarriage and access to the professions but fell far short of offering anything on the contentious issues of the right to bear arms and the county franchise.

In 1793, following intense negotiations, Westmorland and Hobart reluctantly steered a second relief bill though parliament where it was passed alongside a raft of other bills designed to reassure and placate fearful Protestants. The 1793 Relief Act granted Catholics access to all but the most senior state and military positions. In addition they now had the right to bear arms and were granted the parliamentary franchise on the same terms as their Protestant counterparts.[17] Soon after the granting of Catholic relief the Militia Act was passed in a move designed to increase the number of troops in the country. Since the outbreak of war between France and Britain in February 1793 many troops intended for Ireland were instead transferred to fight against the French revolutionary army. Ireland needed additional troops to defend the country from both internal and external threats and the militia were intended to do just that.[18] The county militias were to be officered by the local Protestant gentry while the majority of the rank and file would be Catholic conscripts. If the creation of an additional military force, albeit a largely Catholic one, was intended to reassure Protestants, that effect evaporated quickly with the widespread rioting that followed the establishment of the militia in the spring and summer of 1793.[19]

Westmorland spent almost five years in Ireland. He arrived in Ireland a naive, inexperienced young man and departed disillusioned. His hostility towards Catholic relief broadly reflected the views of the Protestant ascendancy and throughout his tenure of office he, as A. P. W. Malcomson has observed, 'acted more as the Irish cabinet's representative in Great Britain than as the British Government's representative in Ireland'.[20]

II

Westmorland was recalled from Ireland at the end of 1794 as part of an uneasy coalition agreement between Pitt and the Portland Whigs which had been negotiated in July. Given Portland's previous experience of Ireland – he had been lord lieutenant in 1782 – it was no surprise that he was appointed home secretary, a position which gave him responsibility for all policy decisions relating to Ireland. Among other appointments it had been agreed that the position of viceroy of Ireland would be filled by a Whig, and the 4th Earl

Fitzwilliam was nominated. To some extent he was an obvious choice. As the nephew and heir to Lord Rockingham he had impeccable Whig credentials. Allied to these he had an interest in Irish affairs being both an Irish large estate owner and married to a cousin of the Irish Whig leaders William and George Ponsonby. However, his political mettle was unknown: aged forty-six, he had never held political office. The London administration was anxious to ensure that few changes would take place in the Irish administration following Fitzwilliam's appointment, as this would imply dissatisfaction with previous strategy. Aware that Fitzwilliam's appointment would cause unease among the Irish 'cabinet' the prime minister and other senior officials met on 24 November 1794 in Downing Street where they briefed Fitzwilliam about his role in Ireland. Under no circumstances was the Catholic question to be raised, he was instructed, and no dramatic changes of personnel were to be considered.[21]

Fitzwilliam's appointment was crassly handled. Although formal confirmation of his appointment did not take place until December 1794, rumours and speculation were rife through the summer and autumn: in July and September, the United Irish paper the *Northern Star* reported with enthusiasm that Fitzwilliam's appointment was imminent.[22] Fitzwilliam himself informed Henry Grattan of his new position in August while Portland was equally indiscreet when, in the autumn of 1794, he invited both Grattan and the Ponsonbys to London to discuss future plans for Ireland.[23]

It was expected that Fitzwilliam's appointment might herald some alterations in the balance of power, but no one envisaged change to be so immediate and far-reaching. Edward Cooke, under-secretary at the military department, commented that 'Pitt had abandoned Ireland to their [the Whigs'] will and pleasure'.[24] At the formal dinners every new lord lieutenant was obliged to host, William Ponsonby acted as Fitzwilliam's right-hand man and reportedly informed all who cared to listen that Fitzwilliam had arrived in Ireland with the sole purpose of giving effective control of the country to the Ponsonbys and their supporters.[25] And this seemed to be the viceroy's intent. Within days Fitzwilliam had dismissed under-secretaries Hamilton and Cooke and, most significantly, Beresford from his position as commissioner of the revenue. In typical fashion Beresford claimed that he was dismissed because the new administration believed that:

> no Lord-Lieutenant could exist with my power; that I had made a Lord Chancellor, a Chief Justice of the King's Bench, an Attorney-General, nearly a Primate, and certainly a Commander-in-Chief; that I was at the head of the Revenue, and had the Law, the Army, the Revenue, and a great deal of the Church in my possession; and . . . that I was considered the King of Ireland.[26]

However, it was not Fitzwilliam's root and branch assault on those who wielded power in Ireland that caused the greatest consternation in London. Fitzwilliam granted an audience to the Catholic Committee and their supporters and he indicated that he would not oppose the Catholic Relief Bill introduced by Grattan on 12 February.[27] Whitehall may have tolerated the speed and extent of the personnel changes the new viceroy was instigating, it was his blatant disregard of government policy regarding the Catholic question that ensured his dismissal.[28]

III

In the space of six turbulent weeks, Fitzwilliam challenged the political status quo. Those assured of a voice in Irish politics were silenced, while other voices, so often muted, were heard. The self-appointed defenders of the Protestant interest in Ireland regarded Fitzwilliam's viceroyalty as an act of betrayal and believed Pitt had sacrificed Ireland to ensure his own political survival. For Pitt, focused on victory over France, abandoning Ireland to the whims of the Portland Whigs might have seemed an acceptable price to pay for political security at home, but Fitzwilliam's behaviour as viceroy quickly indicated that he had miscalculated. A new, loyal and reliable viceroy was required and Pitt, unwilling to take another risk, focused his attention on another college friend, Lord Camden. Camden, a junior lord of the treasury and son of the highly regarded former lord chancellor, had been previously considered for the position of viceroy in June 1794 but was passed over on that occasion in favour of Fitzwilliam. The *English Chronicle* assessed Camden's strengths and weaknesses concluding:

> As his abilities are rather solid than splendid . . . an ostentatious display of them is not to be expected. Modesty, reserve and diffidence, are the leading peculiarities of his disposition, and all conspire with the natural turn of the endowments to make him an interesting companion in private life than a conspicuous figure in the senate.[29]

Such solid, if unremarkable, qualities made Camden an ideal candidate to replace Fitzwilliam. Camden's loyalty to Pitt was unquestioned, and he was regarded as a capable, if unimaginative, administrator. Camden was also firmly attached to the idea that Ireland should be dependent on England; writing in 1785 he declared: 'Ireland, more especially the Protestant part of it, will come at last to understand that free and independent as she is, she can never hope to enjoy that freedom or independence without the protection of England.'[30]

Camden accepted his new position with great reluctance. He claimed that he could not satisfy his 'conscience in accepting a situation in which I might risque [*sic*] the safety of that country or the peace of this by an error of judgment, a want of resolution or a hasty decision', and he feared that the urgency of the appointment coupled with 'the real state of Ireland not being known, and the sentiments of the English Cabinet not being completely decided, as to the future measures to be pursued' rendered the new lord lieutenant at a disadvantage. Characteristically, Camden was apprehensive not only for the state of the British interest in Ireland but also worried about his own reputation, commenting 'I risque my own credit and character, as well as those who sent me by plunging myself into a government without knowing my support', and concluded, 'I think it is impossible my decision can be other than to decline the proposal'.[31] However, following Pitt's appeal to Camden's sense of duty and the invoking of their friendship, he grudgingly agreed to accept the position of viceroy.[32]

Prior to leaving for Ireland, Camden was carefully briefed on the intended nature of his lord lieutenancy. Portland indicated that Camden was being dispatched 'to moderate, to soothe, conciliate and reconcile'. He was to 'hold a firm and decided language from the first moment of [his] landing in Ireland'. As the representative of the British government in Ireland he was to use his 'own discretion and judgment' on matters which 'relate only to the better ordering and government of that country'. For 'all other matters which may appear to you . . . to affect the policy, the revenue . . . of this country or of the empire at large' the lord lieutenant was to take no action until he 'received the signification of his majesty's pleasure'. Whitehall, not Dublin Castle, would be in charge of any significant Irish policy.[33]

At the outset Camden adhered strictly to the advice offered to him by Portland and Pitt, causing Lord Charlemont to remark: 'instead of a viceroy, [he] is in effect no more than a vice-Pitt'.[34] He made efforts to placate those offended by Fitzwilliam; he reinstated Beresford, Hamilton and Cooke and attempted a reconciliation with the Ponsonbys, who refused his overtures. With regard to the Catholic question, Grattan's Catholic Bill was defeated in the House of Commons in May but some concessions were offered and the establishment of the seminary at Maynooth in June 1795 effectively neutralised any opposition within the Catholic hierarchy.

Camden arrived in Dublin laden down with assurances of support from London and with the experienced and popular Thomas Pelham by his side as chief secretary. But it quickly became apparent that Camden would be left to his own devices. Camden adhered to Portland's desire for close communication and sent regular dispatches to London. There was much private correspondence between Dublin and London but Camden rarely received the official communications he craved, and he wrote despondently to Pitt that 'it really hurts me every week to be obliged to write to you in the language of complaint'.[35]

Pitt, absorbed by the war with France, had little time for Camden's missives. He was confident that if the French were to launch an invasion force the great British navy would easily defeat it. The internal security of Ireland was within the lord lieutenant's remit and Whitehall refused to acknowledge warnings of revolution as anything other than an internal matter.[36] Auckland noted in August 1796 that 'Irish affairs have been for some time under the consideration of the cabinet', but 'the salvation of the country depends infinitely more on the exertions of all of you who are on the spot than upon anything that can be done or suggested from hence'.[37] The Dublin Castle administration accepted responsibility for retaining command of the internal security of the country, but the Irish government was adamant that, if the French attacked Ireland, Britain should assume responsibility for Ireland's defence, both external and internal.

While Camden's pleas for assistance were routinely ignored, Pitt and his ministers received a growing mountain of intelligence indicating that a French attack on England or Ireland was likely. A report on a potential invasion, compiled in 1796 by Dundas, concluded 'there never was a time when the enemy had a prospect of attempting the invasion of Britain with a force so considerable as at present'.[38] Camden began to make his own plans and, by August 1796, the Irish military command had drawn up defence plans in case of an invasion. In a speech to both houses of parliament in October, Camden remarked that 'the ambitious plans of our enemies have threatened to interrupt the happiness and prosperity of his [majesty's] people by making a descent on this kingdom and Great Britain'.[39] Beresford feared that a French invasion force would be 'gigantesque'.[40] In December 1796 the French did launch an invasion attempt but it was not the forces in Ireland or the great British navy that was triumphant. The 'Protestant Wind' that prevented a landing at Bantry Bay proved the most robust defence offered. Perhaps Camden and his advisers were the only group to take some comfort from the failed French expedition. The external defences of Ireland had been threatened but not breached, and, internally, the feared rebellion had not materialised.

Camden's relationships with Whitehall and the Irish 'cabinet' were often fraught, but it was the military that proved to be his Achilles heel. Through much of the 1790s the military command of Ireland was troubled and disjointed. During Camden's administration there were four commanders-in-chief: General Robert Cuninghame, Lord Carhampton (Simon Luttrell), Sir Ralph Abercromby and General Gerard Lake. Camden thought Abercromby the only competent one among them. The elderly Cunninghame was a reluctant commander, who claimed that 'his limbs are so weak he is not fitted for active service'.[41] Camden deemed Carhampton as 'not fit for the command of the army', while Cooke claimed he was unpopular with 'every officer in the whole army'.[42]

Ignored by Whitehall and deprived of the guidance of Pelham, who was frequently ill and, from August 1795, often out of the country, Camden was isolated. He had arrived in Ireland, in his own words, 'a very prejudiced Englishman', but by early 1797 his perspective had changed and he now regarded himself as 'infected with Irish prejudice'.[43] Once Pitt's firm defender, Camden increasingly adopted a hard-line approach, which met with the approval of the Irish 'cabinet'.

The attempted French invasion dramatically altered Camden's attitude to the excesses of the military. Hitherto, he had been reluctant to stray beyond the letter of the law, but from early 1797 he was determined to defend the armed forces in Ireland against any detractors. A series of repressive measures were introduced by Camden during the summer and autumn of 1796, including the Indemnity and Insurrection Acts and the suspension of *habeas corpus*. Initially reluctant to implement these laws, in the spring of 1797 Camden embraced their use along with other measures such as the Convention Act of 1793 and the proclamation of May 1797 which authorised the military to act without waiting for direction from civil magistrates. He approved of the dragooning of Ulster, which took place in the spring of 1797, and assured the commanding officer, General Lake, that he believed his conduct to be both 'spirited and judicious' and tellingly remarked: 'even did I think otherwise, you will always find me the last person who will cease to protect an officer who is acting with me in these difficult times'.[44]

Camden may have felt the military action in Ulster to be justified but many disagreed. The dragooning of Ulster prompted Lord Moira, a peer in both the Irish and British House of Lords, to voice his concerns over the manner in which the Irish government operated. Respected for his military expertise, Moira was often criticised for his liberal political views. In March and November 1797 he used the British House of Lords as his forum to criticise the cruelty of the army in the north, and his criticisms generated enormous publicity in both Ireland and Britain, much to the anger of the Irish administration. The kerfuffle generated by Moira had just died away when the newly appointed commander-in-chief, Sir Ralph Abercromby, also criticised the army, most famously in his general orders of February 1798 where he attacked the 'disgraceful frequency' of court-martials and the poor discipline of the army which, in his memorable phrase, 'must render it formidable to every one but the enemy'.[45] Camden was furious, not least because Abercromby's criticism was public, but also because it contradicted the proclamation of May 1797.

Outrage in Ireland was expected, but Camden had not anticipated the level of discontent emanating from Britain. Cooke acknowledged that

Abercromby's order was irresponsible, but he noted that the affair might have been easily dealt with had the English newspapers and politicians not become involved.[46] Camden hoped to weather the storm and retain Abercromby but, in the face of opposition from Pitt and other senior British politicians allied to Abercromby's determination to resign, this was unlikely. It was seen, at least in London, that Abercromby was overriding the authority of the king's minister in Ireland. The minister was frequently ignored by Whitehall, yet, when the insult came from another source, they were quick to take umbrage on Camden's behalf.

Camden received letters from incensed correspondents. Buckingham described Abercromby's order as 'criminal to the highest degree', while Westmorland regarded it as 'an insult upon the lord lieutenant, parliament and council and a libel on the army'.[47] Lord Abercorn complained that the 'act of the commander-in-chief of Ireland [was] directly in the teeth of a proclamation of the government of Ireland!'[48] Abercromby's behaviour contributed considerably to the escalating crisis. He let it be publicly known that his position in Ireland was untenable, not because of the poor state of the armed forces but because of the opposition of the Irish 'cabinet' to his attempts at reform. He spoke of 'Lord Camden as one of the best men in the world but one of the weakest, and completely guided by a set of violent, hot-headed men'.[49]

In April 1798 Abercromby was replaced as interim commander-in-chief by General Lake. Camden was disappointed, believing Lake had little to recommend him as he was 'easily led and [had] no authority', and complained that he 'was not equal to the situation'.[50] As the country moved towards open rebellion, Camden despaired. Tolerated by the Irish 'cabinet', ignored by the London administration, rejected by the military command, he was desperate to leave the country. The final straw was the outbreak of rebellion on 23 May which prompted Camden to remark that 'no war ever began with such prospect of dreadful slaughter as the present'.[51] With ill-humour and little enthusiasm Camden turned his mind towards quashing the rebellion, but in truth much of his strategic planning centred on orchestrating his return to England.

Camden had first mooted a return to England in the spring of 1797 when he cited his wife's ill-health as the motivating factor.[52] Characteristically, Pitt did not respond to Camden's overture. During the Abercromby affair of March 1798 Camden again raised the issue, this time expressly requesting that Pitt replace him with a military man. Camden outlined the advantages of combining both roles in one person:

> The reason that I have thought a military man should be Lord Lieutenant . . . is that it is scarcely possible to procure a general of experience who will lend himself as much as a commander-in-chief must do to the political situation of the country and act under orders which as a military man he feels to be incompatible with discipline . . . whereas the military and civil responsibility centering in the same person he would be better able to act for the general good of the country.[53]

Cornwallis's name had been bandied about as a future lord lieutenant as early as March 1795, and the possibility of his appointment was discussed in political and social circles in Ireland in May 1797. In March 1798, for the second time, Camden explicitly suggested him as his successor.[54] However, Pitt had voiced doubts about Cornwallis's suitability for the position, claiming he was unconvinced that 'his temper of mind and prejudices on Irish subjects make him qualified for the task'.[55] Yet within two months Pitt's thinking had altered radically. Within a week of the outbreak of rebellion, Pitt had decided to actively pursue a union between Britain and Ireland.[56] Cornwallis's political and military expertise allied to the fact that he was known to be in favour of granting further Catholic relief, was seen as an ideal combination and the prime minister concluded that he, rather than Camden, would more effectively oversee delicate union negotiations.[57] On 11 June, Pitt wrote to Camden informing him that Cornwallis was to be appointed as both lord lieutenant and commander-in-chief. Camden was irritated not by the choice but by the manner of the appointment and was anxious that his reputation not be sullied. To show that he had not fallen from favour and to bolster support for the union within the cabinet Camden was offered a seat at the cabinet table. The inclusion of a figure who had direct and recent experience of Ireland could only serve to endorse Pitt's argument for union. Indeed this endorsement was soon forthcoming; shortly after Pitt's offer Camden composed a detailed memorandum outlining his advice on how the British administration should proceed towards union.[58]

Despite Camden's increasing disengagement from matters military or political, by the time he returned to England in late June much of the rebellion was over. The rebellion in the north had been quashed and in Wexford the rebels had been defeated at Vinegar Hill. The French had not yet landed at Killala nor had Wolfe Tone returned to Ireland, but militarily the government forces had control. The real threat had passed under Camden's stewardship, not Cornwallis's, a fact often overlooked. Cornwallis, as political and military commander, finished the job Camden had begun, and took all the credit for it.[59]

IV

The French invasion at Killala in August persuaded Cornwallis that his primary concern was securing the country and he was prepared to take a personal role to ensure this. However, like Abercromby he had little faith in the Irish troops, describing the Irish militia as being 'totally without discipline, contemptible before the enemy'.[60] He delayed his march towards Mayo until he received additional Scottish and English soldiers and he quickly secured victory over the French forces and their Irish allies.[61]

Like the other lords lieutenant of the 1790s, Cornwallis's appointment was not without controversy. Hardliners were incensed by what they regarded as Cornwallis's weakness when it came to crushing the rebellion and Sir Richard Musgrave dismissed the 'indiscriminate and ill-judged leni[enc]y' of Cornwallis's security policy arguing that 'the rebellion would have been completely put down soon after it broke out if Lord Camden had remained here'.[62] Cornwallis's acceptance of the 'Kilmainham Treaty', whereby United Irish prisoners gave details of the organisation of the United Irishmen in return for no prosecutions and banishment for life was cited as evidence of his leniency, although he argued that it was simply a pragmatic move as, with the exception of Samuel Neilson, there was little evidence to convict the men.[63]

By September 1798 Cornwallis was ready to turn his attention to the pursuit of what he called 'that great question – how this country can be governed and preserved and rendered a source of strength and power, instead of remaining a useless and almost intolerable burthen to Great Britain'. He was reluctant to seek the answer from the 'principal personages . . . who have long been in the habit of directing the councils of the lords lieutenants', as 'they are blinded by their passions and prejudices, talk of nothing but strong measures, and arrogate to themselves the exclusive knowledge of a country of which, from their mode of governing it, they have, in my opinion proved themselves totally ignorant'.[64] Unlike his predecessors in the post in the 1790s, Cornwallis did not have to pander to the Irish 'cabinet' to secure his position. For once Whitehall's attention was firmly focused on Dublin and the lord lieutenant was actively in receipt of its support.

The potential for a union between Ireland and Britain had been acknowledged through the 1790s but little active attention had been paid to it. Pitt was inclined towards the idea but awaited the ideal opportunity. As Edmund Burke had observed to Fitzwilliam in September 1794, the only way a union could be justified was 'in some desperate crisis of the whole empire'.[65] For Cornwallis, as for Pitt, when that 'desperate crisis' came in 1798 the answer to how best to secure Ireland was clear: union. However, he, his chief secretary Castlereagh, and Pitt greatly underestimated the level of opposition the proposal would meet in the Irish houses of parliament and their complacent approach was largely responsible for the defeat of the first effort to secure a union in January 1799. For the second attempt Cornwallis embraced the advice offered by Cooke in September 1798. The union, Cooke wrote, 'must be written up, spoken up, intrigued up, drunk up, sung up and bribed up'.[66] Such an approach proved successful and in August 1800 the act effecting union between Britain and Ireland was passed.

V

A myriad of challenges faced the viceroys of the 1790s but to a large extent it was an external factor that dominated their experiences. Britain's war with France (from the spring of 1793) made the business of the Irish viceroy almost impossible. Fitzwilliam was appointed because Pitt needed to secure a pro-war ally and little consideration was given to how the ascendancy in Ireland would react to having the Whigs in power. The continental war reduced the numbers of regular military stationed in Ireland and increasingly the security of the country was reliant on a combination of regular soldiers, fencibles, yeomanry and militiamen, all commanded by a fragile military leadership. The weakness of the military command was unsurprising as few skilled generals were prepared to serve in Ireland when there was a real war raging in continental Europe. The war raised the hopes and expectations of radicals and revolutionaries while increasing the fears and worries of the Protestant ascendancy. Most significantly for the lord lieutenant, the war with France focused Whitehall's attention across the St George's Channel and not the Irish Sea. Westmorland may have felt ignored by London in 1792 when, exasperated by Pitt's indifference, he fumed: 'If Ireland was at the bottom of the sea it might be one thing, but while she exists you must rule her', but this was nothing compared to the neglect Camden felt as his repeated warnings of imminent French invasion were dismissed. The outbreak of rebellion in May 1798 proved – to London at least – that Ireland could no longer be managed at a remove, that even a carefully-managed lord lieutenant was not sufficient to guarantee a secure relationship with Ireland. Only a union could guarantee that, or so they thought.

The 1790s proved a decisive decade for the relationship between Britain and Ireland. From the regency crisis of 1789 to the Act of Union in 1800 the four viceroys of the 1790s faced a range of challenges. Kevin Whelan has described Westmorland, Fitzwilliam and Camden as a 'series of weak lords lieutenants', by contrast R. B. McDowell observed that 'the lord lieutenants who held office in Ireland during the last decades of the eighteenth century were all men of marked personality, vigorous and intelligent members of a powerful aristocracy.'[67] The truth lies somewhere between these two assessments. Westmorland, Fitzwilliam and Camden were inexperienced politicians with no military experience. Thrown into the turmoil that was Ireland in the 1790s they struggled to secure the British interest in Ireland from both internal and external threats. With no clear definition of their role Westmorland and Camden began by determinedly representing the British government in Ireland but by the time of their recall both men represented the views of the Irish cabinet far more than they represented the British. Cornwallis, the only viceroy of the 1790s to possess extensive military and political expertise, was dispatched to Ireland to crush what remained of the Rebellion and to ensure that no future viceroy would find his loyalties so tested. The passage of the Act of Union removed any ambiguity about the role of the viceroy; from January 1801 he was simply an administrative figurehead.

Notes

1 Camden to Thomas Steele, 18 Mar. 1796, Centre for Kentish Studies, Maidstone (hereafter CKS), Pratt Papers, U840 0194/1; Cornwallis to Major General Ross, 1 July 1798, Charles Ross (ed.), *Correspondence of Charles, 1st Marquis Cornwallis* (3 vols, London, 1859), ii, p. 356.

2 *Gentleman's Magazine*, July 1797.

3 21 Apr. 1795, *Parliamentary Register*, xv, pp 189–90.

4 *Debates in the House of Commons* (Dublin, 1797), p. 226.

5 Thomas Bartlett, *The Fall and Rise of the Irish Nation: The Catholic Question 1690–1830* (Dublin, 1992), p. 139.

6 FitzGibbon was attorney general from 1783 until 1789 when he became lord chancellor, a position he held until 1802. Arthur Wolfe replaced FitzGibbon as attorney general. John Foster was speaker of the House of Commons from 1785. During Fitzwilliam's brief tenure of office in early 1795 the under-secretaries Sackville Hamilton and Edward Cooke, and John Beresford, the chief revenue commissioner, were removed from office, but all were reinstated upon Camden's appointment in May 1795.

7 *Dublin Evening Post*, 25 Mar. 1795.

8 Pelham to Camden, 1 Dec. 1795, CKS, Pratt Papers, U840 C122/6.

9 Camden to George Hardinge, 20 Feb. 1798, National Library of Ireland, Dublin (hereafter NLI) Lord Lieutenant's Correspondence, Ms 886/237; Danny Mansergh, *Grattan's Failure: Parliamentary Opposition and the People in Ireland 1779–1800* (Dublin, 2005), p. 11.

10 Quoted in James Quinn, 'Charles Cornwallis', in James McGuire and James Quinn (eds), *Dictionary of Irish Biography* (9 vols, Cambridge, 2009), ii, p. 863; R. B. McDowell, *Ireland in the Age of Imperialism and Revolution, 1760–1801* (Oxford, 1979), p. 99.

11 A. P. W. Malcomson, *John Foster: The Politics of the Anglo-Irish Ascendancy* (Belfast, 1981), p. 64.

12 Edith Mary Johnston-Liik, *History of the Irish Parliament, 1692–1800* (6 vols, Belfast, 2002), i, p. 175.

13 Bartlett, *Fall and Rise*, p. 138.

14 McDowell, *Imperialism*, p. 399.

15 Bartlett, *Fall and Rise*, p. 131.

16 Ibid., p. 138; Malcomson, *Foster*, p. 388.

17 Johnston-Liik, *Irish Parliament*, i, p. 183.

18 Bartlett, 'Defence, counter-insurgency and rebellion: Ireland, 1793–1803', in Thomas Bartlett and Keith Jeffery (eds), *A Military History of Ireland* (Cambridge, 1996), pp 249–56.

19 Ibid., pp 253–5.

20 Malcomson, *Foster*, p. 64.

21 The meeting was attended by Pitt, Portland, the foreign secretary Lord Grenville, the lord privy seal, Lord Spencer and Windham the secretary of war. No formal record of the meeting took place and no written account existed until March 1795 when all those in attendance (with the exception of Fitzwilliam) agreed to a memorandum confirming the substance of the meeting. 'Memorandum', March 1795, CKS, Pratt Papers, U840 0142A/4; Windham to Fitzwilliam, 5 Mar. 1795; British Library, London (hereafter BL) Windham Papers, Add. Ms 37875.5; Portland to Pelham, 28 Mar. 1795; BL, Pelham Papers, Add. Ms 33101/165.

22 *Northern Star*, 7 July, 8 Sept. 1794.

23 Fitzwilliam to Grattan, 23 Aug. 1794 in R. B. McDowell, 'The age of the United Irishmen: revolution and the union, 1794–1800', in T. W. Moody and W. E. Vaughan (eds), *A New History of Ireland, iv: Eighteenth-Century Ireland, 1691–1800* (Oxford, 1986), p. 341. See also Fitzwilliam to Portland, 10, 15 Aug., 8 Sept., 8 Oct., 14 Oct. 1794, Public Record Office of Northern Ireland, Belfast (hereafter PRONI), Portland Papers. T2905/15/11, 13, 15, 17, 19; D. Wilkinson 'The Fitzwilliam episode 1795: a reinterpretation of the role of the duke of Portland', *Irish Historical Studies*, 29 (1995), pp 321–2; E. A. Smith, *Whig Principles and Party Politics: Early Fitzwilliam and the Whig Party, 1748–1833* (Manchester, 1975), p. 179.

24 Cooke to Pitt, 16 Nov. 1795, in A. Aspinall (ed.), *The Later Correspondence of George III* (5 vols, Cambridge, 1962–70), ii, p. 267.

25 John FitzGibbon to Auckland, 24 Mar. [1795], PRONI, Sneyd Papers, T3229/1/7.

26 Beresford to Auckland, 9 Jan. 1795, in William Beresford (ed.), *The Correspondence of Right Hon. John Beresford* (2 vols, London, 1854), ii, pp 49–52.

27 George III to Portland, 21 Feb. 1795, in *Correspondence of George III*, ii, p. 305.

28 Portland to Camden, 26 Mar. 1796, CKS, Pratt Papers, U840 0142A/3.

29 Lewis Namier and John Brooke (eds), *The House of Commons, 1754–1790* (3 vols, London, 1964), iii, p. 324.

30 Camden to Robert Stewart, 25 Aug. 1785, quoted in Bartlett, *Fall and Rise*, p. 119.

31 Camden to Pitt, 7 Mar. 1795, CKS, Pratt Papers, U840 0142A/1.

32 Note by Camden regarding his appointment as lord lieutenant, March 1795; Pitt to Camden, 8 Mar. 1795, ibid.

33 Portland to Camden, 26 Mar. 1795, ibid., U840/0142A/3.

34 Charlemont to Haliday, 26 July 1795, in Historical Manuscripts Commission (hereafter HMC), *Manuscripts and Correspondence of James, 1st Earl of Charlemont* (2 vols, London, 1891–4), ii, p. 265.

35 Camden to Pitt, 30 Jan. 1796, The National Archives, Kew (hereafter TNA), Chatham Papers, 30/8/326/60.

36 Marianne Elliott, *Partners in Revolution: The United Irishmen and France* (London, 1982), pp 119–20.

37 Auckland to Beresford, 28 Aug. 1796, Beresford (ed.), *Beresford Correspondence*, ii, pp 125–6.

38 Dundas, 'Notes on a possible invasion', 1796, CKS, Pratt Papers, U840 0172.

39 13 Oct. 1796, *Parliamentary Register*, xvii, p. 1.

40 Beresford to Auckland, 4 Sept. 1796, in Beresford (ed.), *Beresford Correspondence*, ii, p. 130.

41 Cunninghame to Camden, 9 May 1795, TNA, HO100/54/110.

42 Camden to Pelham, 2 Oct. 1797, BL, Pelham Papers, Add. Ms 33105/212.

43 Camden to Robert Stewart, 4 Feb. 1793, in Lord Londonderry (ed.), *Memoirs and Correspondence of Viscount Castlereagh* (4 vols, London, 1848–9), i, pp 156–9; Charlemont to Haliday, 26 June 1795, in HMC, *Charlemont Correspondence*, ii, p. 265; Camden to Pitt, 31 Jan. 1797, CKS, Pratt Papers, U840 0156A/8.

44 Lake to Camden, 18 Oct. 1797; Camden to Lake, 20 Oct. 1797, CKS, Pratt Papers, U840 0165/6; /7.

45 [Abercromby], General Order, 26 Feb. 1798, in Henry McAnally, *The Irish Militia 1793–1816: A Social and Military Study* (Dublin, 1949), p. 323.

46 Cooke to [Auckland], 12 Mar. [1798], PRONI, Shannon Papers, D2707/A3/3/51.

47 Buckingham to Camden, 11 Mar. 1798, CKS, Pratt Papers, U840 0198/1; Westmorland to Beresford, 15 Mar. 1798, in Beresford (ed.), *Beresford Correspondence*, ii, pp 152–3.

48 Abercorn to Camden, 12 Mar. 1798, CKS, Pratt Papers, U840 0186/6.

49 Abercromby to [York?], 22 Mar. 1798, NLI, Melville Papers, 54A/124.

50 Camden to Pelham, 6 June 1798, BL, Pelham Papers, Add. Ms 33105/388; Camden to Pitt, 7 June 1798, NLI, Lord Lieutenant's Correspondence, Ms 886/311.

51 Camden to Pitt [late May 1798], NLI, Lords Lieutenant's Correspondence, Ms 885/261.

52 Camden to Pitt, 1 June 1797, CKS, Pratt Papers, U840 0156A/19. In addition to his wife's ill health Camden had an undisclosed reason for wanting to return to England. In April 1797 he had inherited substantial estates in Sussex and Kent and he was anxious to take over the running of these.

53 Camden to Pitt, 7 Apr. 1798, ibid., U840 0156A/30.

54 Camden to Pitt, 26 Mar. 1798, ibid., U840 0156A/29; *Freeman's Journal*, 26 Mar. 1795.

55 Pitt to Camden, 31 Mar. 1798, CKS, Pratt Papers, U840 0190A/4.

56 Patrick M. Geoghegan, *The Irish Act of Union: A Study in High Politics, 1798–1801* (Dublin, 1999), p. 10.

57 Ibid., p. 216; Bartlett, *Fall and Rise*, p. 246.

58 Camden to Pitt, [17?] June 1798, in J. Holland Rose, *Pitt and Napoleon, Essays and Letters* (London, 1912), pp 335–8.

59 Charles Ross, brother of Lord Cornwallis, observed:

> He [Cornwallis] reached Dublin, June 20 and immediately entered upon his office, but the capture of Wexford by General Moore on the 21st and the total overthrow of the insurgents at Vinegar hill relieved him from much of his anxiety. These events indeed more properly belong to Lord Camden's viceroyalty, as all the arrangements had been made during his administration.

There was considerable continuity of opinion between the two viceroys with Cornwallis commenting to Portland that

> you will have received the most ample information of every kind from Lord Camden, with whose general sentiments I perfectly concur and who from his experience is more able to give a detailed account of the situation in Ireland than myself.

Cornwallis to Portland, 28 June 1798, HMC, *Cornwallis Correspondence*, ii, p. 354.
60 Cornwallis to Portland, 8 June 1798, Cornwallis to Ross, 24 June 1798, in ibid., ii, pp 357, 369.
61 Harman Murtagh, 'General Humbert's futile campaign', in Thomas Bartlett et al. (eds), *1798: A Bicentenary Perspective* (Dublin, 2003) p. 183.
62 Musgrave to Percy, 20, 27 Aug. 1798, quoted in James Kelly, *Sir Richard Musgrave 1746–1818 Ultra-Protestant Idealogue* (Dublin, 2009), p. 85.
63 James Quinn, 'The Kilmainham Treaty of 1798', in Bartlett et al. (eds), *1798*, pp 424–5.
64 Cornwallis to Portland, 16 Sept. 1798, in HMC, *Cornwallis Correspondence*, ii, p. 404.
65 Burke to Fitzwilliam, September 1794, quoted in Kevin Whelan, 'The other within: Ireland, Britain and the Act of Union', in Dáire Keogh and Kevin Whelan (eds), *Acts of Union: The Causes, Contexts and Consequences of the Act of Union* (Dublin, 2001), p. 15.
66 Cooke to Auckland, September 1798, quoted in James Quinn, 'Dublin Castle and the Act of Union', in Michael Brown, Patrick M. Geoghegan and James Kelly (eds), *The Irish Act of Union, 1800* (Dublin, 2003), p. 100.
67 Kevin Whelan, 'Introduction to Section V', in Bartlett et al. (eds), *1798*, pp 385–6; R. B. McDowell, *Imperialism*, p. 399.

CHAPTER 7

A Question None Could Answer: 'What Was the Viceroyalty For?' 1800–1921

K. Theodore Hoppen

I

During the long parliamentary debates concerning the Union in 1799 and 1800 when detailed attention was given to finance, customs and excise, when patronage and cash were sprayed about with abandon, when Pitt enlisted Virgil to reinforce the promise that two nations, each unsubjected, were entering an everlasting compact on equal terms,[1] the actual mode of governing Ireland was almost casually overlooked. And thus the lord lieutenant, the chief secretary, the under-secretary and the whole Dublin Castle machine moved seamlessly and virtually untouched into the post-Union world. By the time a new home secretary, Lord Pelham, realised in September 1801 that this was not perhaps a good idea, it was too late.[2] Pelham's arguments for complete incorporation were strongly opposed by those who felt that only the presence of a viceroy could prevent the reappearance of those local 'undertakers' who had governed Ireland before 1770.

The able, if hyperventilating, Lord Redesdale, who came to Ireland as lord chancellor in March 1802, had no doubts on this score. Not least because Emmet's rebellion seemed to show that only an immediate present authority could keep the country quiet, 'a disposition to obey government' being, in his view, 'no part of the Irish character'.[3] In short, the post-Union administration became from the start emblematic of the ambiguities of the Anglo-Irish relationship. As a writer in the *Saturday Review* dismissively put it many years later 'Ireland was, and was not, to be part of the Empire [and] . . . Ireland was to become [a kingdom], but with a proxy king'.[4] Given the initial absence of sustained thinking (indeed of virtually any thinking) about the role of the viceroy and his colleagues in the governance of Ireland after the Union, it is hardly surprising that much depended upon individual inclinations, perceptions of tradition, and the imperatives of political contingency.

Even more important were two sets of fluctuating and highly unstable power relationships: that between Dublin and London, and that between the various members of the Irish administration.

Some viceroys saw their primary role to be that of drumming English (or Scottish) sense into recalcitrant Hibernian skulls. The bluff well-meaning Anglesey declared in 1831 a 'peculiar anxiety' to knock the heads of Catholics and Protestants 'of the higher classes' into a realisation that 'their respective properties depended upon their cordial co-operation'.[5] And, in truth, this was a natural response to the anodyne 'Instructions' which viceroys received on taking office: Anglesey was merely parroting what London had laid down.[6] The staunchly Tory duke of Northumberland was issued with similarly vapid bromides in 1829 about 'equal and impartial administration' as well as hopelessly detailed precepts concerning military and revenue matters.[7] The 'Instructions' of Marquess Wellesley ran to fifty-two pages and were no less formulaic, with much talk of 'mildness and impartiality'.[8] As time went on viceroys began to realise that their powers rarely matched initial expectations. There were of course energetic exceptions, such as Clarendon, Kimberley (Wodehouse), and Spencer, but withdrawal into undemanding geniality proved more common. And while necessity – putting down disorder, distributing patronage, guarding one's back – could sometimes propel even the feeblest into activity, it remains the case that unpredictable oscillations between metropolitan interference and neglect, opaque divisions of responsibility, and tensions between ministers, cumulatively diminished the impact of Castle administrations in general and of lords lieutenant in particular.

Perhaps the most obvious and pressing duty of lords lieutenant was the suppression of those disorders seen by London as a characteristic part of Hibernian life, though here too neither consistency nor a clear identification of aims and processes proved much in evidence.[9] While the lord lieutenant stood at the head of the Irish peace preservation machine, individual viceroys, no less than London ministers, moved restlessly along a spectrum ranging from mildness to repression. Their correspondence reveals an unstable tendency towards mixing boasts that all was calm and quiet with instant admissions that outrage and bestial disorder were burning through the land.[10] Clarendon in the 1840s believed his main role to be that of protecting 'the people against themselves' and pushing them along 'the right path'.[11] So little, however, did the patient respond, that almost seventy years later 'trouble makers' were still being denounced as, quite simply, 'bordering on lunacy or mental degeneracy'.[12]

In the law-and-order field 'Having one's cake and eating it' might well be seen as the viceroyalty's most characteristic motto. Of course circumstances changed, but attitudes changed more quickly still and seem at times to have been generated more by *a priori* belief systems than by concrete realities. On the whole, the rod-of-iron approach created the most emphatic prose. The former diplomat, Whitworth, who was not unusual in stressing 'the distinction to be made between England and this part of His Majesty's dominions', wanted the 'lower orders . . . kept down' by 'military government'. His predecessor, Richmond, had demanded 'strong measures',[13] and Peel, who served as chief secretary with both men and whose obvious youthful cleverness exercised an undoubted influence, made no secret of his belief that 'an honest despotic government would be by far the fittest government for Ireland'.[14] Nor were such opinions confined to die-hard Tories. Wellesley stridently pushed for strong action within a month of his appointment, though towards the end of his second term he had – and this was also not unusual – entirely changed his mind. By contrast, his brother, Wellington – both as chief secretary and prime minister – remained a consistent advocate of harsh measures.[15] And among others Haddington, Anglesey, De Grey, Clarendon (who hankered after a *despotismo ilustrado*), St Germans, Spencer, and Cowper can all be found asking for more soldiers, more police, more legal powers, and more toughness all round, though many of them – sometimes almost simultaneously – presented no less forceful recommendations for conciliation, concession, and presenting the other cheek. No wonder London, let alone the Irish public, became confused.[16]

As time went on sustained reliance on coercion began more and more to strike politicians of all stamps as ineffective in all but the shortest of terms. One finds in the papers of, for example, Gladstone, Kimberley, Clarendon, and Arthur Balfour long lists of 'exceptional' statutes that had proved, at best, mere smoke and mirrors.[17] By December 1881 Spencer (ironically soon to become unusually successful as a viceregal coercer) had become astonished by 'the tremendous powers now at the disposal of the Irish executive' and extremely worried that, if these failed, few even potentially 'efficacious' weapons remained to be tried.[18] And while Arthur Balfour's years as chief secretary between 1887 and 1891 showed that the prefectorial cane could still be usefully deployed, the experiences of its last great proponent, Field-Marshal French, rather more forcefully demonstrated the opposite. Coercion alone was not, in any case, as Austen Chamberlain recognised in 1918, 'a policy, at any rate it is not a permanent policy'.[19]

II

While all this gives the impression of unremitting – at times perhaps even manic – activity in the Viceregal Lodge, this was by no means the invariable impression gained by contemporary observers. In 1838 Melbourne (who before becoming prime minister had served as chief secretary and was himself notoriously indolent) told his lord lieutenant that the 'Augean stables were more easily cleaned' than Dublin Castle, where, as he put it, 'nothing is right'.[20] Subsequent complaints often concerned simple lack of competence. Carlisle, though (as Lord Morpeth) an active and effective chief secretary between 1835 and 1841, having concluded that the lord lieutenancy had become 'comparatively insignificant', devoted himself to low-level geniality and crowd-pleasing displays typified by turning up on St Patrick's Day engulfed in 'an extra-enormous bunch' of shamrock.[21] W. E. Forster – a notably acerbic chief secretary – detected slackness abounding in April 1882.[22] Five years later a shocked Liberal MP visited Dublin Castle and found 'no lord lieutenant [Londonderry], no chief secretary [A. J. Balfour] . . . no permanent under-secretary [Buller]'.[23] But even when the *Mary Celeste* was fully crewed, a feeling of useless busyness seemed to settle on the place. Morley felt as if 'nothing' was actually done, nothing brought 'to an effective head, nor put in the way of being brought to a head'.[24] Carnarvon, musing on his experiences as lord lieutenant, thought viceroys were completely ignored until some crisis arose when either coercion or cash was sprayed heedlessly about.[25] Cadogan, who was actually in the cabinet (despite Arthur Balfour declaring that he lacked 'mental capacity'), hoped that transforming the lord lieutenant into a non-political figure who was not changed with every ministry would render the office at least sentimentally, if not politically, more effective. The lightweight Dudley found the pressure too much and simply decamped to Biarritz for a two-month holiday.[26]

Small wonder that Antony MacDonnell (under-secretary 1902–8), who possessed Indian experience, found the Castle a bit of a joke with 'little or no control over the administration of the country'. By 1916 the viceroy, in the shape of Wimborne, had become an irrelevance ignored by everyone with any influence over events.[27] Four years later a new commander-in-chief found a Castle administration in complete chaos, while English experts judged its members 'woodenly stupid and quite devoid of imagination', its impact 'practically non-existent'.[28]

Yet it had all started with a modest bang designed to prevent post-Union Dublin from looking too much like an abandoned capital. Hardwicke in 1802 tried to convince 'the town that the Union has produced no alteration in the style of living at the Castle'.[29] Thirty year later it was argued in a House of Lords debate that it was only the 'regal display' of the viceroy 'which still invested the metropolis of Ireland with something of a charm . . . [and] made the Irish still think they were an independent people'.[30] Whatever the truth of such dubious claims, successive lords lieutenant threw themselves into the task with, on the whole, surprising degrees of enthusiasm and expense. Hardwicke devoted many days to entertaining 'in a very laudable Hibernian style'. Talbot, though complaining of being 'dragged to an ordinary dinner and ball, without a single soul there beyond a damn corporation member', put on no less than eighty-eight dinners for peers and 196 for commoners at Dublin Castle in 1818 alone, with yet more free food laid out in the Phoenix Park.[31] Anglesey provided fourteen dinners, attended another three, held three levees, two drawing-rooms, and four balls in a single fortnight in April 1828.[32] Even after 1831, when the lavish personnel was reduced and the Battle-Axe Guard (which had garishly adorned formal functions) abolished, viceroys were still surrounded by an army of officials including, as late as 1868, a state steward, chamberlain, comptroller, master of the horse, gentlemen ushers, three paid ADCs (plus several unpaid), and two 'gentlemen at large' ('a nice place with very little to do').[33] Eglinton in the 1850s was so generous that his bankers started to complain and the prime minister to doubt whether Dublin afforded the 'materials for a continuance of such profuse hospitality'.[34] Even the less rich Clarendon regularly put on dinners for fifty guests once or twice a week, while his levee books amount to no less than nine substantial volumes.[35]

Carlisle tried to generate popularity by attempting to learn 'all the national dances'.[36] Northumberland arrived in Dublin in 1829 with £90,000 worth of plate and wearing 'all his splendid outfit as ambassador at Paris', while Mulgrave's first action in Dublin was to consult a tailor and order 'a fancy *green* uniform'.[37] If for Wodehouse the whole business had, by 1864, begun to look farcical ('I put on a very grave face, but it is a hard matter not to laugh'), others still revelled in their 'success' in entertaining on behalf of the British connection. Londonderry boasted of the 'feelings of loyalty' his social activities generated,[38] while Cadogan quickly resigned himself to acting 'as a milch cow for "the season"'.[39]

By then the Dublin season, which took place during the six weeks ending on St Patrick's Day, had degenerated into a gimcrack party battleground. Already in the 1840s jokes were being made about advertisements in the Dublin press for the hire of 'claret-brown court-dress' at half-a-crown a day for 'the approaching levee at the Castle [and for] . . . teetotal and repeal processions, fancy balls etc.'[40] Twenty years later an MP told the Commons that the Castle had come to be regarded as no more than 'a great restaurant – a social and agreeable lounge for barristers and military men'.[41] The correspondence of the duke of Marlborough includes a letter complaining that the viceroy was to be found entertaining 'singing apothecaries, cobblers' sons, rowdy attorneys, corporation whiskey-sellers and seedsmen'. And with the arrival of Home Rule as a viable legislative possibility, Unionists began to boycott Liberal viceregal courts even though they sometimes secretly missed the dancing and the dressing up.[42] Houghton noted the 'pre-arranged absence of the landed classes' and even the Tory Dudley found in 1905 that 'very few of the genuine Irish families come', though he still worried about his ADCs' competence in dancing the quadrille.[43] Aberdeen ushered in a decade of parsimony, achieving the unusual distinction of ruining himself financially while acquiring a reputation as the meanest lord lieutenant of modern times.[44]

Viceroys had few ways of accurately assessing public feeling and tended, rather naively, to read a good deal into the behaviour of crowds at their official entries or departures from Dublin. Anglesey was impressed in 1830 that, despite O'Connell's influence, he was greeted with 'as much enthusiasm as I ever witnessed'.[45] In 1886 Morley, with bland hypocrisy, congratulated Aberdeen (a man he had no time for) on an occasion that would 'take a conspicuous place in the history of our time'. Carnarvon innocently commenting that 'the Irish are a strange people', likened his own departure to that of Fitzwilliam in 1795, what with all the 'visible signs of respect', the bowing and raucous enthusiasm. Cadogan more acutely realised that such things were generated by crowds probably 'four-fifths' of which were 'deadly enemies'.[46] Indeed, the failure of most British politicians and British visitors generally to see through the surface geniality of Irish social discourse at all levels says much for the bluntness of their cultural antennae, though Gladstone proved better attuned than most with a deadpan diary entry for his arrival at Kingstown in October 1877: 'A newsman called "You're welcome to Ireland". A voice from behind "No you're not"'.[47] More tellingly, while during his first viceroyalty Spencer found it possible to go for a solitary ride every afternoon, in May 1885 Charles Dilke accompanied him on his first walk for many weeks, shadowed by police and meeting but one man who lifted his hat while others shouted 'Murderer' and 'Who killed Miles Joyce?'[48]

The occasion on which viceroys most pressingly asked themselves the question 'What is the lord lieutenant for?' was probably when they looked at their own financial accounts, for while their remuneration was high, their expenses were higher still. No one took the job in order to get rich, even though, in the official remuneration stakes, the position lay towards the head of the pack. Between 1784 and 1812 the salary was £20,000 a year Irish or about £18,500 British, then it rose to £30,000, and then fell back to £20,000 British in 1831.[49] A shifting and opaque sum was also provided as a *contribution* towards expenses, as much as £6,232 in 1841. As a result, the whole Castle machine constituted a significant gravy train for the local economy: in 1850 Clarendon reckoned that it generated no less than £100,000 annually.[50]

Finding victims to accept appointment was, in any case, often difficult. To begin with, there was no consensus as to whether viceroys should be of Irish or of English (or Scotch) background. In the early years the emphasis was largely on the danger of Irish appointees who could not, it was claimed, 'divest themselves of native prejudices, partialities, and animosities'. Redesdale in

1802 was convinced that 'in every department Englishmen are more likely to do . . . justice than Irishmen',[51] though Wellesley was unusually willing to admit to Hibernian roots and occasionally referred to Ireland as 'my unhappy country'.[52] Even having Irish relatives (who might demand all kinds of jobbery) was considered a dubious asset as Peel pointed out when Talbot was appointed in 1817.[53] Although as late as 1868 Kimberley (as Wodehouse had become) still maintained that appointing Irishmen was 'against the principle of the Union', opinion had begun to shift.[54] Palmerston had asked Bessborough (whose father had been viceroy 1846–7) to serve before settling on Wodehouse: 'He has many qualifications. He is an Irishman . . . knowing all the peculiar circumstances of Ireland and Irish affairs'. Offering the job to Londonderry in 1886 Salisbury emphasised that 'a great desire' was being 'expressed in many quarters that it should be held by an Irishman', and Londonderry himself claimed that his Irishness provided peculiar insights into what needed to be done.[55] Joseph Chamberlain went so far as to argue (one wonders how seriously) that 'we stupid Englishmen are not fitted for the delicate work of administering the affairs of a quick-witted race like the Irish'.[56] Even those who were, by any definition, entirely English began to claim an Irish identity, as French did on appointment in 1918, an event hailed by that equally bogus 'Irishman', Walter Long, as potentially opening (should they find a 'native' chief secretary) the possibility of having 'for the first time . . . an Irish government composed exclusively of Irishmen'![57]

Often, however, prime ministers simply found it difficult to get anyone at all. Few men wanted to live more or less permanently in Ireland. The job was not, in general, a stepping stone to higher things. And when it was seen as important in itself, this was because it had become onerous, tedious, and dangerous. Those who took it on tended to stress their high-minded sense of sacrifice. Hardwicke felt himself 'divested . . . of influence and patronage' and deprived of ministerial support. Bathurst, thinking Wellington might offer him the post, stressed that 'nothing would induce me to go'.[58] On entering office in 1847 Clarendon boasted of his 'patriotic, uncompensated sacrifice'; on leaving in 1852 he marvelled at his 'consenting to be an exile from England in order to stand in the pillory here'.[59] It would be tedious to specify the many subsequent occasions on which it proved difficult to find anyone even vaguely prepared to become lord lieutenant. However, the fact that we know of serious problems in 1864, 1866, 1874, 1880, 1886, 1889, 1902, 1916, and 1918 suggests that things became no easier, indeed probably more difficult, as time went on.[60]

The majority of viceroys were wealthy souls either on the way down or never again to be so high as when appointed to Dublin. Some were soldiers: Cornwallis, Richmond, Anglesey, French. Some had been professional diplomats: Whitworth and Heytesbury. Some were dazzlingly rich: Bedford, Northumberland, Eglinton, Londonderry, Cadogan, possibly others. Some had enjoyed distinguished careers but were now on the slide: Wellesley, Bessborough, St Germans, Carlisle. A very few were men of distinction with more senior positions in prospect: Clarendon, Spencer, Houghton. Others were simply the best of the bad choices available.

Their views and abilities covered a wide range and suggest that no agreed thinking had ever taken place as to how Ireland should be governed. Indeed, given the difficulty of persuading men to go to Dublin at all, it is not surprising that contingency and accident counted for more than careful selection and planned programmes. Still, it is surprising how many feeble performers were allowed to take the stage. Three examples make the point. The first, Marquess Wellesley – the man with the most distinguished former career of any viceroy – served from 1821 to 1828 and again in 1833–4. The older brother of the duke of Wellington and at first the more notable of the two, Wellesley had worked in the senior reaches of British India's administration, as ambassador extraordinary in Spain, and as foreign secretary in Perceval's government from December 1809 until March 1812. Without office for the next nine years, he seems to have fallen into a fussy self-importance marked by 'vanity, dissipation, want of private and unsteadiness of public character, a ruined fortune, and [worse still] a strong predilection for the Roman Catholic cause'.[61] He was plagued by an army of illegitimate children who hung around the place seeking jobs. He spent hours languishing on a sofa feeling unwell and took an age to compose memoranda in the purest classical prose.[62] Orangemen threw bottles at him in the theatre and his second marriage in 1825 to a Catholic woman solemnised by the Anglican primate and the Catholic archbishop of Dublin became the talk of the town. A man of considerable talents and of liberal views, his obvious decline and self-absorption rendered him strikingly unsuited for a post in which consistency, hard work, and a respected public presence were essential requirements.

The second study in feebleness is that of a lesser, though still notable, figure whose career followed a similar downward trajectory: the seventh earl of Carlisle. As Lord Morpeth he had been a successful chief secretary between 1835 and 1841 when he had encouraged the pioneering activities of Thomas Drummond.[63] Thereafter some tolerably important cabinet posts followed, but after 1852 nothing until the viceroyship in 1855 by which time he had run out of steam. His correspondence reveals an incisive young man gradually turning himself into a genial nonentity. By 1861 a former chief secretary (H. A. Herbert) put into words what all had long known: that Carlisle was 'more unfit for the office than any man he ever had to deal with. He cannot say "No": he grants things he ought to refuse . . . all out of good nature'. When complaints were made about this to the prime minister, Palmerston grandly waved them aside with the quip that 'a lord lieutenant ought to be able to do a job now and then'.[64]

And finally Lord Aberdeen: if Wellesley was the ravaged but once gorgeous roué of the viceregal tribe and Carlisle its amiable valetudinarian, Aberdeen was Mr Pooter incarnate. Notoriously overshadowed by his formidable wife with whom he produced two volumes of reminiscences entitled *We Twa* (1925) and *More Cracks from We Twa* (1929) as well as a book of deliberately non-dirty jokes called *Tell Me Another* (1925), he was known as 'Jumping Jack' because of an inability to stand still and was notorious for an urgent desire to entertain viceregal guests by imitating the sound of train whistles.[65] Undoubtedly the Aberdeens were a worthy pair, but no one thought them especially talented, least of all Mr Gladstone who – a ruthless freeloader in later years – spent many happy days as their guest at Dollis Hill House.[66] No wonder Morley, on again becoming chief secretary in 1892, wanted anyone but Aberdeen as viceroy, though Gladstone's blandly casual agreement to this exclusion seems less than attractive.[67] That Aberdeen, who wore rosy spectacles to the end, was allowed to cling on for more than nine years is a reflection both of the low importance with which the office had come to be perceived and of the influence of the leaders of the Irish Parliamentary Party, who found him pliantly sympathetic to their cause.

III

Shifts in the significance and influence of the viceroyalty can best be understood in the context of its two most important power relationships: with the London government and with the chief secretary. Both relationships suffered from confusion, misunderstanding, lack of definition, ambiguity, casual turns of opinion, and infighting.

From the start London's view of the lord lieutenant was unclear and contested, not least because the Act of Union was silent as to the nature and powers of the 'Irish government'. Although an opening attempt in 1801 by the home secretary, Pelham, to abolish the viceroyalty and incorporate Ireland fully into British administrative structures failed,[68] his successor, Charles Yorke, laid down the cloudy dictum that while 'Ireland must continue to be administered by a lord lieutenant' the very fact of Union must also 'induce a more frequent and more immediate interference of the principal branches of Government here with the Irish administration'.[69] Twelve years later, Lord Liverpool, on being asked about the powers of the Dublin government, confessed that he could hardly define his own or those of the chancellor of the exchequer, let alone those of officials 'I know so little of'.

Peel, while chief secretary, was no clearer. 'The respective duties' of himself and the viceroy, were, he admitted in 1816, 'quite undefined'.[70]

As time went on much began to depend upon the forcefulness and assiduity of the individuals concerned, upon the frequency and nature of communications between the two islands, and upon the visibility of Irish affairs in ministerial minds. One unanalysed hangover from pre-Union times was the 'fact' that Ireland came under the particular attention of the home office, though few chose to define what this amounted to. Portland, a notably lazy home secretary, announced his continuing authority in 1801.[71] Pelham, after failing to push through his incorporation plans, retired into such indolence that Hardwicke complained of a failure to issue 'a single sentence that conveys the least information'.[72] The 'Instructions' received by Bedford in 1806 attempted a greater clarity and laid down that he should communicate 'through the secretary of state; and all measures of importance to be submitted through him for the decision of the cabinet'.[73] But while this emphasis on frequent contact was often insisted upon thereafter, it was much less frequently obeyed in either Dublin or London.[74]

Cornwallis, soon after the passing of the Act of Union, promised high-powered efficiency, 'regular correspondence . . . daily or weekly minutes . . . transmitted from all the departments here . . . duplicates . . . regularly despatched'.[75] This turned out to be no more than hot air. Some Irish officials did indeed keep in close touch, sometimes to good effect, sometimes to metropolitan annoyance as in the case of Wellesley's wordy and tedium-inducing briefs.[76] The real difficulty lay in London's unpredictable and uneven response. Pitt, whose mind was admittedly on other things, hardly responded at all, not even when the viceroy boldly demanded 'an explanation of the neglect and inattention' he had experienced. Talbot in 1819 could never work out with whom he was expected to communicate.[77] Melbourne, both as home secretary and prime minister, was notoriously indolent; Dublin complained that he would 'send nothing that he is not directed to send'.[78] When taxed with this he excused himself for having relied on others to pass on his views and insisted that henceforth no 'steps of importance' be taken without the approval of the home secretary.[79] All this is rendered almost fantastical when it emerges that the home office at this time casually binned correspondence from Ireland, so that Graham, on becoming home secretary in 1841, was driven to writing to Dublin pleading that locked letter-books preserved in the Castle and marked 'The Marquis Wellesley's Ministerial Correspondence' be sent to London without delay. The Famine years too witnessed serious communication problems 'with no clear pattern' emerging from the hailstorm of letters that passed to and fro.[80] In truth, the whole business continued to depend too much on individual commitment. Under Wodehouse communications were brisk, frequent, and to the point. Under

Cowper things got so bad that Gladstone had to send Spencer to Dublin to clarify the situation.[81] But when Spencer himself had again become viceroy and found himself obliged to complain about a lack of news all he got was a cool reply to the effect that, while the prime minister had 'often thought of your isolation . . . I concluded you had an arrangement [for receiving information] with some humane and less occupied colleague'.[82]

For much of the time Ireland was, in any case, little in London's thoughts. Portland when home secretary 'always found Ireland a dinner bell at the cabinet' and when Littleton as chief secretary attended a cabinet in 1833 he found that ministers took 'as little interest in the business discussed [Ireland] as if it had been a turnpike meeting'.[83] Russell could not recall the cabinet ever seeing letters from Anglesey or Wellesley, nor did he himself do much to keep colleagues informed of communications from Mulgrave. When Wellesley and Goulburn were together despatched to Dublin as viceroy and chief secretary in 1821 no 'advantage had apparently been taken by the cabinet . . . to have a general discussion with them on Irish affairs before they departed'.[84] Clarendon, when viceroy during the Famine, knew at first-hand how Irish measures were treated in cabinet: without 'sufficient information upon a state of things so totally unlike any that we know of'. Unsurprisingly, therefore, he sympathised when Wodehouse complained in 1865 of 'the apathy of English ministers about Irish affairs'.[85] Carnarvon in the 1880s thought that viceroys had just enough power to make people think they could influence events but not enough to turn expectations into reality: 'out of sight, out of mind' was his downbeat assessment.[86] The Liberal government of 1892–5 was, Gladstone aside, bored with Ireland: a long cabinet meeting in June 1893 devoted half its time to discussing whether the mayors of certain towns should become lord mayors, then an hour to Indian matters, then eight minutes to Irish finance 'at the fag end of the sitting'. When Rosebery as prime minister received a letter from the lord lieutenant (Houghton) about the land question he quickly passed it on to with the comment 'It is not a subject which interests me, or with which I am thankful to say I have anything to do'.[87] And Asquith too was notoriously wearied by Irish business: 'Birrell [at cabinet] engaged in "unfolding" (a task which never comes to an end) his Irish tale – *plus ça change plus c'est la même chose*. Perpetual movement and no progress could perhaps be an apter description'.[88]

The reasons why and the paths by which things came to such a pass are to be found not only in the changing political landscape of the Union years or in how matters stood between viceroys and imperial governments, but in the internal dynamics of the Irish administration as a whole. What most powerfully made the weather in this respect was the relationship between the viceroy – a peer resident in Ireland – and the other key figure, the chief secretary – responsible for Irish business in the Commons and resident in

London while parliament sat (and thus closer to the ultimate centre of power). After 1800 what had previously been a simple two-sided Dublin/London conversation turned into a triangular discourse in which the chief secretary played an increasingly prominent part. Whatever else this achieved, it certainly made things more complicated.

While a certain amount of thinking did take place concerning the relationship of viceroy and chief secretary, contemporary analyses were fitful and unsystematic. Peel in 1816 made the obvious point when he told the prime minister

> They are offices the respective duties of which are quite undefined. The lord lieutenant is paramount in point of law, and by his commission, but then from his attendance in parliament the secretary is practically . . . made responsible; and really unless there is almost an identity of feeling and of interests, it will be difficult to conduct the business in harmony.[89]

Melbourne made another crucial point when writing to Mulgrave in 1835, namely, that both viceroy and chief secretary could not always avoid having to make decisions without personally consulting the other, something even the arrival of the telegraph between Holyhead and Howth in 1852 did not entirely prevent.[90] On becoming prime minister Peel again talked about the 'indefinite nature of the relation in which' the leading men in the Irish administration stood to one another. Eight years later an MP emphasised this state of 'perfect anarchy. Sometimes the lord lieutenant controlled the chief secretary; occasionally the chief secretary controlled the lord lieutenant. Sometimes the under-secretary controlled both'.[91] And, indeed, it was an under-secretary, Thomas Larcom, who in 1858 produced a memorandum which got to the heart of the problem:

> The Government of Ireland, in fact, centres in the lord lieutenant who has a parliamentary, an administrative and a private secretary. But the importance and power of the House of Commons, growing as it is year by year, renders the chief secretary the real practical centre, and it is in that that the true difficulty and anomaly of the Irish Government consists. The centre is out of the centre, and produces eccentric motions (to borrow a phrase from mechanics).[92]

What kept the 'system' on the road was principally the fact that no one could agree on a replacement. Spencer in 1871 recognised its 'manifest drawbacks' but also its protean qualities – its very lack of clarity permitting a good deal of useful, if confusing, flexibility.[93] While seeking overall agreement, Spencer also insisted upon his right as viceroy 'to act on my own responsibility', an approach which had earlier led Gladstone to deliver a typical (and typically opaque) 'dose of doctrine' about being 'restrained from giving way to influence derived from one quarter or one side of a subject and constrained to make our minds the meeting point (no pleasant process) of all the influences wheresoever derived'.[94] But Gladstone could also be brutally direct when he felt the need, as when telling Aberdeen in 1886 'Well, that's settled. Now as to arrangements. John Morley will be chief secretary. You will look after administration; we will deal with policy'.[95]

What, however, no amount of prime ministerial lecturing could overcome were the endless rows which took place between individual viceroys and chief secretaries. The period opened with fairly general agreement that the viceroy was still the more powerful.[96] This was reinforced by the very rapid turnover of chief secretaries in the years before Peel's appointment in 1812 when no less than ten men held the post.[97] But the rows and disputes were, in part at least, a reflection of growing pains in the relationship produced by gradual (though not always steady) increases in the power of the chief secretary. Tensions were exacerbated by a curious tendency towards 'balance' which involved appointing men with diametrically opposed views, as in the period 1818–27, while in the 1830s severe tensions existed between Anglesey and Stanley and between Wellesley and Littleton (Wellesley's son-in-law).[98] Indeed, Stanley had begun to think this the usual state of affairs and to doubt 'whether it should be possible that Ireland ever should have a lord lieutenant and a secretary completely united in opinion'.[99] In the early 1840s Peel, as prime minister, found it impossible to stop his viceroy, De Grey, and his 'liberal' chief secretary, Eliot, from turning differences over policy into personal feuding.[100] Serious problems are also known to have arisen in the 1850s, 1860s, 1880s, 1900s, and 1910s,[101] with a pinnacle of absurdity being reached in 1918 when French declared himself in favour of creative tension between himself and his chief secretary (Shortt) 'because each side will then know that their claims are kept in view and discussed within the circle of Government'.[102]

What most clearly reflects the growing stature of the chief secretary was cabinet membership. After the Union only five viceroys out of thirty-three combined their office with a cabinet seat: Clarendon,[103] Spencer, Carnarvon, Cadogan, and French. The matter surfaced as a significant 'problem' in June 1831 when Stanley became the first chief secretary to join the cabinet and Anglesey felt hard done by. From then on viceroys complained that they were being made to look like junior partners and were rarely mollified by the meaningless assurance that *in Dublin* they were somehow 'in control'.[104] Wodehouse refused to continue in office if his chief secretary was given a cabinet seat. Marlborough (himself a former cabinet minister) felt that serving with a chief secretary in the cabinet implied a want of confidence in himself.

His complaints were brusquely overruled, as were similar moans about being ignored from Londonderry in 1887 and Cadogan (despite his cabinet membership) in 1899.[105]

After 1830 the direction of travel in the viceroy/chief secretary relationship becomes clear. With a few exceptions (notably Spencer's position between 1882 and 1885) influence and power came more and more to accrue to the chief secretary. Of the thirty-nine men who held that office from 1830 onwards, no less than nineteen did so as members of the cabinet. What many had long known to be the case was brutally articulated when in 1905 Dudley tried to assert his authority by making 'unhelpful' speeches and presuming to have a mind of his own. His rebarbative chief secretary, Walter Long, got the prime minister to lecture Dudley to the effect that a tighter sense of cabinet responsibility together with swifter communications had 'now transferred the leadership of the Irish Government to the minister who happens to be . . . in the House of Commons'.[106]

IV

From the start of the post-Union period one drastic solution to all these problems was again and again canvassed, namely, the complete abolition of the viceroyalty. But, also again and again, this potentially mighty cut of the Gordian knot was blunted by an absence of agreement about possible replacements. Should there be root-and-branch change? Should the chief and under-secretaries also be placed upon the funeral pyre? Should there be an Irish secretary of state in London? Should the home secretary simply take over? What about a member of the royal family either permanently or occasionally located in Ireland? Should there be a royal residence in Ireland? The permutations were endless, but saluted more by repetition than analysis.

In 1823, 1830, and 1844 Joseph Hume, a leading 'economical' reformer, succeeded in mounting Commons debates on motions for abolishing the viceroyalty, in the course of which the arguments that were to inform the issue for the next century were duly rehearsed. Hume saw the office as standing in the way of United Kingdom integration, something desirable, above all, on grounds of efficiency. In 1823 he demanded that 'Ireland should become the same as a county of England', something now possible because it took only thirty-six hours to get from London to Dublin. By contrast, Goulburn (chief secretary 1821–7) believed that the Irish saw the lord lieutenant as a symbol of a nationhood upon which it would be unwise to trespass any further.[107] Almost identical territory was traversed in 1830, when O'Connell strongly opposed abolition, and in 1844, when the chief secretary, Eliot, rather mysteriously argued that the viceroyalty had accustomed the Irish 'to swim with corks; whip away the corks and drown they will and sink'.[108]

Throughout these years a substructure of less formally expressed opinions underpinned the parliamentary set pieces. Wellesley thought abolition would save money and ensure that 'local powers would be moved by the common united principle of action from the mainspring of England'. Stanley kept changing his mind as to whether the lord lieutenancy was a good or a bad thing.[109] In fact few leading politicians presented a consistent front, though Wellington remained firmly and influentially in favour of retention and Disraeli, more enigmatically, followed suit.[110] Peel theoretically wanted, but pragmatically opposed, abolition.[111] Melbourne was generally, though not very strongly, against,[112] while Russell eventually mounted the abolitionist assault that came nearest to success: the parliamentary bill of 1850. Already in 1847 Russell had appointed Clarendon on the understanding that he would be the last holder of an office 'of separation rather than union between the two countries'.[113] But though the Commons motion of 1850 was carried by the huge majority of 295 to 70, it foundered under Wellington's attack in the Lords.[114]

Yet the controversy continued. Only a few months later Earl Grey, the secretary for war and the colonies, was pressing for complete integration with only a junior minister in the home office to look after specifically Irish affairs.[115] The maverick radical, J. A. Roebuck, put on Hume's mantle and introduced Commons motions for abolition in 1857 and 1858.[116] Although these failed, they elicited much discussion in Irish official circles. Carlisle (like Goulburn in the 1820s) believed abolition would 'offend the feeling of nationality among the people' and collide with the Irish propensity for localism, prompt patronage, and face-to-face politics.[117] Memoranda by Carlisle and Larcom and contributions from the chief secretary, Edward Cardwell, and the Irish attorney-general, Rickard Deasy, added little to what had now become an old song, though all inclined against abolition. Deasy again emphasised feelings 'of distinct nationality' and claimed that Ireland could not be governed 'as you do Yorkshire or Devon'.[118]

The year 1871 witnessed renewed discussions about the utility or otherwise of the viceroyalty. A formal cabinet paper on the matter was produced, and what had become (and was to continue to be) the chief trope on the subject – a kind of viceregal version of St Augustine's prayer about wishing to become holy but not just yet – was energetically batted about: abolition in the future, retention for the time being. Gladstone admitted that the question had long defeated the finest minds, including his own.[119] Less surprisingly, the intense discussions of 1885–6 regarding Ireland's status within the United Kingdom again revived the issue. Spencer, thoroughly disenchanted with his second viceroyalty, was now all for abolition, and another cabinet paper was produced. While some Liberal ministers, notably Harcourt, agreed, and while the brief Salisbury government of 1885 made noises to the same effect, a kind of overwhelming inertia once again ensured that nothing was done.[120] Even so, Cadogan embarked for Dublin with severe doubts as to the permanence of his position, and in 1905 Edward VII was reported as privately pronouncing the viceroyalty a 'gimcrack thing at best and difficult now to get proper men for it'.[121]

Especially during the second half of the nineteenth century these endless and inconclusive debates were propped up by a kind of rolling bass in the form of arguments that quietude, loyalty, and even enthusiasm might be generated if only the queen could be persuaded to acquire a residence in Ireland to be inhabited by herself occasionally and more regularly by another member of her family who might then become a sort of non-political viceroy substitute. Things really took off in the 1860s generated by worries that the louche and idle Prince of Wales be found something respectable to do. In 1865 Lord Stanley recorded in his diary that the prince talked of becoming viceroy 'a great deal, neither very sensibly nor the reverse', while two years later Stanley's father, then prime minister (and of course a former chief secretary), rather undermined a well-earned reputation for sharp thinking by telling Disraeli that such an appointment might well have 'a very great effect'.[122]

It was, however, Gladstone who, above all, believed that a royal residence would help strengthen the Union. His tireless efforts in the late 1860s and early 1870s might be seen as a low profile, though deeply-felt, aspect of the mission to pacify Ireland. And the ensuing battle between a prime minister convinced of the value of his idea and a monarch suspicious of all things Irish and even more suspicious of the moral reliability of her eldest son (whose affair with Nellie Clifden at the Curragh in 1861 combined the two in her mind) engendered much heat but little light of any kind. Memoranda were drawn up, conversations held at Windsor, houses in Ireland identified, many senior politicians consulted – all to no effect.[123] In 1885 the queen again rebuffed suggestions from Carnarvon, while attempts to combine an Irish royal residence with the diamond jubilee celebrations of 1897 were similarly repelled.[124]

In the event, viceroys simply soldiered on, becoming, though with occasional hiccups, less important, more marginal, and more than a little ridiculous. But with sensible alternatives hard to identify, the viceroyalty experienced, even among the wreckages of 1916–21, a kind of dingy afterlife, a decrepit and rickety equivalent of the more robust steeples of Fermanagh and Tyrone.

The mere fact that Wimborne succeeded Aberdeen as lord lieutenant in 1915 with the support, indeed almost with the permission, of Redmond does not suggest that the office retained any Tarzan-like muscularity.[125] After the rising of 1916 Birrell, Nathan, and Wimborne were all effectively dismissed. Asquith visited Dublin, talked colourfully of the viceroy as a 'cipher . . . a vice-roi-fainéant,' and vaguely of new 'arrangements'. Yet, in the end, Wimborne was allowed to creep back in August because there was no agreement as to the nature of any new 'arrangements', and also because Wimborne personally was less tainted with neglect for the simple reason that he had possessed little authority.[126] That this smooth reversion to established norms occurred despite the trenchant comments of the *Royal Commission on the Rebellion in Ireland* concerning the viceroy's overall irrelevance and the 'anomalous' and 'unworkable' character of the 'Irish system of government' as a whole says much about the lack of initiative and creativity among a British political elite necessarily preoccupied with a world war.[127] What, however, highlights with particular force the fog of unreality within which the government was then operating is Asquith's own trip down memory lane in the shape of a suggestion that more frequent royal visits would provide a sovereign remedy for the present discontents.[128]

Despite Wimborne's irrelevance in 1916 it was, ironically, the threats of new disorder associated in particular with the possible imposition of conscription in Ireland that generated the viceroyalty's last Hurrah in the shape of Field Marshal French's appointment in May 1918. It all began with firm assertions and promises that this was to be a new kind of arrangement and French understood – and was given to believe – that he would be the 'sole Governor of Ireland', the 'actual and not merely the nominal Head' of a 'quasi-military administration'. But while French was admitted into the cabinet in October 1918, things soon unravelled as violence grew in 1919 and all sorts of political cooks began to dip their spoons into the pot. Thus, while French was in the cabinet, so were the various chief secretaries with whom he served and with whom, after initial cordiality, he invariably fell out.[129] By the summer of 1920 the chief secretary was again clearly top dog and French had become 'little more than a mendacious blusterer, irrelevant to the administration of which he was technically the head'.[130] In April 1921 he was replaced by the intentionally transitional (and Catholic) Viscount Fitzalan, a kind of final whimper to French's initial bang.

V

Few in 1800 would have believed that the office of lord lieutenant would last for as long as it did. Already then observers in general and viceroys in particular were worrying about its role, its (almost certainly receding) powers, and its place within the government of Ireland. What, above all, its survival

Henry Balam (publisher), 'Charles Blount, earl of Devonshire' (1600–3), © National Portrait Gallery, London.

After Sir Anthony Van Dyck, 'Thomas Wentworth, 1st earl of Strafford' (1633–40), © National Portrait Gallery, London.

Michael Dahl, 'James Butler, 2nd duke of Ormonde' (1703–7, 1710–13), © National Portrait Gallery, London.

George Vertue, after Sir Godfrey Kneller, 'Lionel Sackville, 1st duke of Dorset' (1730–7, 1750–5), © National Portrait Gallery, London.

Thomas Hudson, 'Philip Dormer Stanhope, 4th earl of Chesterfield' (1745–6). Permission to reproduce images and copyright courtesy of the Office of Public Works.

Samuel William Reynolds, after Sir Joshua Reynolds, 'George Townshend, 4th Viscount and 1st Marquess Townshend' (1767–72), © National Portrait Gallery, London.

William Owen, 'William Wentworth Fitzwilliam, 2nd Earl Fitzwilliam' (1794–5), © National Portrait Gallery, London.

John Singleton Copley, 'Charles, 1st Marquess Cornwallis' (1798–1801). Permission to reproduce images and copyright courtesy of the Office of Public Works.

Daniel Maclise, 'Constantine Henry Phipps, 1st marquess of Normanby' (1835–9), © National Portrait Gallery, London.

Stephen Catterson Smith, 'William John Ponsonby, 4th earl of Bessborough' (1846–7). Permission to reproduce images and copyright courtesy of the Office of Public Works.

Thomas Cranfield, 'George William Frederick Howard, 7th earl of Carlisle' (1855–8, 1859–64), © National Portrait Gallery, London.

Alexander Bassano, 'John Poyntz Spencer, 5th Earl Spencer' (1868–74, 1882–5), © National Portrait Gallery, London.

Thomas Alfred Jones, 'Charles Stewart Vane-Tempest-Stewart, 6th marquess of Londonderry' (1886–9). Permission to reproduce images and copyright courtesy of the Office of Public Works.

Solomon Joseph Solomon, 'George Henry, 5th Earl Cadogan' (1895–1902). Permission to reproduce images and copyright courtesy of the Office of Public Works.

Charles Wellington Furse, 'John Campbell Hamilton Gordon, 7th earl of Aberdeen' (1885, 1905–15). Permission to reproduce images and copyright courtesy of the Office of Public Works.

H. Walter Barnett, 'The marquess and marchioness of Aberdeen and Temair', © National Portrait Gallery, London.

Walter Stoneman, 'John Denton Pinkstone French, 1st Earl French of Ypres' (1918–21), © National Portrait Gallery, London.

reveals is the profound conservatism of the British political mind when contemplating Ireland and Irish affairs. Of course the history of the viceroyalty records only a small part of a larger incapacity, but amidst the failure to marshal relevant questions and, more importantly, relevant answers concerning its role can be seen a wider failure of perception, understanding, and indeed daring on the part of politicians on the two sides of the Irish Sea. Both with regard to the viceroyalty and to the Anglo-Irish relationship in general after the Union, a policy of clinging to nurse for fear of something worse induced a kind of paralysing stasis. Whether a greater willingness to innovate in this (admittedly) small corner of post-Union government would have produced something 'better' rather than merely 'different' is of course another matter altogether.

Notes

1 *Hansard's Parliamentary Debates*, 1st series, vol. 34, col. 285 (31 Jan. 1799).

2 K. Theodore Hoppen, 'An incorporating union? British politicians and Ireland 1800–1830', *English Historical Review*, 123 (2008), pp 330–4.

3 Redesdale to Long, 7 Nov. 1804, The National Archives, Kew (hereafter TNA), Pitt Papers, PRO30/8/330; also to Hawkesbury, 28 June 1805, ibid.; to Perceval (his brother-in-law), 20 Oct. 1803 and 4 Nov. 1804, Gloucestershire Record Office (hereafter GRO), [1st Baron] Redesdale Papers, D2002/3/1/20; to Wickham, 30 Jan. 1806, Historical Manuscripts Commission (hereafter HMC), *Thirteenth Report, Appendix, Part III: The Manuscripts of J. B. Fortescue, Esq. Preserved at Dropmore*, viii (1912), pp 24–5.

4 *Saturday Review*, 20 Aug. 1864 (cutting in National Library of Ireland (hereafter NLI), Larcom Papers, Ms 7506): 'This fiction suited the Irish mind, because it meant practically many dinners, much drinking and much jobbery.'

5 Anglesey to Melbourne, 2 Jan. 1831, Public Record Office of Northern Ireland, Belfast (hereafter PRONI), [1st marquess of] Anglesey Papers, D619/29B.

6 Melbourne's 'Instructions' to Anglesey, 18 Dec. 1830, in British Library, London (hereafter BL), [1st Marquess] Wellesley Papers, Add. Ms 38103. See also Bodleian Library, Oxford (hereafter Bodl.): microfilm from Royal Archives, [2nd Viscount] Melbourne Papers, 93.

7 Northumberland's twenty-four page 'Instructions', Jan. 1829, Alnwick Castle, [3rd duke of] Northumberland Papers, DNP/70; also Richmond's 'Instructions' of 13 Apr. 1807, NLI, [4th duke of] Richmond Papers Ms 60.

8 In Alnwick Castle, Northumberland Papers, DNP/70.

9 This, even though levels of 'ordinary' crime were certainly no higher – indeed probably lower – in Ireland than in England. See K. Theodore Hoppen, 'Grammars of electoral violence in nineteenth-century England and Ireland', *English Historical Review*, 109 (1994), pp 597–620.

10 For especially striking examples, see Wellesley to Peel, 2 Dec., and Goulburn to Peel, 3 Dec. 1824, TNA, HO100/211.

11 Clarendon to Lansdowne, 18 Aug. 1848, Bodl., [4th earl of] Clarendon Papers, Irish Letter-Book III; and to Russell, 31 July 1849, ibid., Letter-Book IV.

12 General Maxwell (then in effective control of Ireland) to Long, 11 June 1916, Parliamentary Archives, London (hereafter PA), Bonar Law Papers, 53/3/2.

13 Whitworth to Sidmouth, 16 June 1814, TNA, HO100/178, and 18 June 1814, Centre for Kentish Studies, Maidstone (hereafter CKS), [1st Earl] Whitworth Papers, U269/O218/6, and 19 Jan. 1816, ibid., U269/O218/8; Richmond to Hawkesbury, 3 Oct. 1807, ibid., U269/O2128/5.

14 Peel to Gregory (under-secretary), 15 Mar. 1816, in C. S. Parker (ed.), *Sir Robert Peel from his Private Papers* (3 vols, London, 1891–9), i, p. 215.

15 Wellesley to Peel, 31 Jan. 1826, NLI, [1st Marquess] Wellesley Papers, Ms 322; to Littleton, 7 Aug. 1834, ibid., Ms 323; to Goulburn, 5 July 1822, Surrey History Centre, Woking (hereafter SHC), Goulburn Papers, 304/44.

16 See, for example, Haddington to Goulburn, 23 Jan. 1835, SHC, Goulburn Papers, 304/46A; Stanley to Grey, 20 Sept. 1831, Liverpool Record Office (LRO), [14th earl of] Derby Papers 167/1; De Grey to Peel, 6 May 1843, BL, Peel Papers, Add. Ms 40478; H. Maxwell, *The Life and Letters of George William Frederick, 4th Earl of Clarendon* (2 vols, London, 1913), i, pp 281–2; and Clarendon to Russell, 14 Oct. 1849, Bodl., Clarendon Papers, Irish Letter-Book IV; St Germans to Aberdeen, 7 Apr. 1854, BL, [4th earl of] Aberdeen Papers, Add. Ms 43208; Spencer to Gladstone, 9 Mar. 1870, BL, Gladstone Papers, Add. Ms 44306; Cowper to Gladstone, 13 Nov. 1880, K. C. [Countess] Cowper, *Earl Cowper KG: A Memoir* (privately printed, 1913), p. 427.

17 BL, Gladstone Papers, Add. Ms 44722; Gladstone to Queen Victoria, 10 May 1882, TNA, Royal Letters, CAB41/16/24 (also *Hansard*, 3, vol. 304, cols 1041, 1043 (8 Apr. 1886); Bodl., [1st earl of] Kimberley [Wodehouse] Papers, Ms Eng c.4064; Bodl., Clarendon Papers, Irish Box 65; BL, Balfour Papers, Add. Ms 49822.

18 Spencer to Gladstone, 2 Dec. 1881, BL, Gladstone Papers, Add. Ms 44308.

19 French to Long, 17 Apr. 1919, Wiltshire and Swindon Archives, Chippenham, Long Papers, 947/9/230 (where the phrase 'rod of iron' occurs); A. Chamberlain to P. L. Gell, 25 May 1918, Birmingham University Library, Austen Chamberlain Papers, AC31/1/14.

20 Melbourne to Normanby, 4 Aug. 1838, Mulgrave Castle, Normanby Papers, MM/192.

21 Carlisle to Palmerston, 10 Feb. 1855, Southampton University Library (hereafter SUL), Broadlands Papers, GC/CA/447; 'A Native', *Recollections of Dublin Castle and of Dublin Society* (London, 1902), pp 39–40; Castle Howard (CH), [7th earl of] Carlisle Papers, J19/8: Diaries 17, 19 Mar. 1857.

22 Forster to Hartington, 13 Apr. 1882, Chatsworth House (ChH), [8th duke of] Devonshire Papers, 340.1144.

23 The MP (James Stuart) told this to Gladstone on a visit to Hawarden: Morley to Harcourt, 13 Oct. 1887, Bodl., Morley Papers, Ms Eng. d.3574; also Morley to Spencer, 13 Oct. 1887, BL, [5th Earl] Spencer Papers, Add. Ms 76938.

24 Morley's Diary, 24 Oct. 1894, Bodl., Morley Papers, Ms Eng. d.3460.

25 Carnarvon's 'Historical Notes', c.1885–6, BL, [4th earl of] Carnarvon Papers, Add. Ms 60827.

26 Salisbury to Queen Victoria, 18 May 1900, TNA, Royal Letters, CAB41/25/40 (see also Greenwood's Memorandum of 12 Jan. 1921, TNA, Cabinet Memoranda, CAB24/118: C.P. 24444); Andrew Adonis, *Making Aristocracy Work: The Peerage and the Political System in Britain 1884–1914* (Oxford, 1993), p. 221; Dudley to Churchill, 1 Nov. 1905, Churchill College, Cambridge, Churchill Papers, CHAR 2/23/36–7.

27 MacDonnell to his wife, 16 Nov. 1902, Bodl., MacDonnell Papers, Ms Eng. hist. e.216; Carson to Lloyd George, 21 Dec. 1916, PA, Lloyd George Papers, F/6/2/4; Duke to Lloyd George, 16 July 1917, ibid., F/37/4/30; Wimborne to Lloyd George, 29 Mar. 1918, ibid., F/48/1/7.

28 General Macready to Long, 23 Apr. 1920, enclosed in Long to Bonar Law, 27 Apr. 1920, PA, Bonar Law Papers, 103/5/3; Report by Warren Fisher, 15 May 1920, ibid., 102/5/21; Sir John Anderson to Greenwood, 20 July 1920, PA, Lloyd George Papers, F/19/2/14.

29 Hardwicke to Addington, 22 July 1802, TNA, Pitt Papers, PRO30/8/328; also to Hawkesbury, 30 Dec. 1805, TNA, HO100/128, arguing that if such an approach failed there would 'be a revival of the gloom and despondency which the Union at first produced'.

30 Marquess of Londonderry in *Hansard*, 3, vol. 4, cols 944–6 (7 July 1831).

31 Corry to Abbot, 10 Oct. 1802, TNA, [1st Baron] Colchester Papers, PRO30/9/140; Talbot to Gregory, 22 July 1819, PRONI, [2nd Earl] Talbot Papers, D4100/1/1; Talbot's entertainment books, Straffordshire Record Office (SRO), [2nd Earl] Talbot Papers, D649/9/7.

32 Marquess of Anglesey, *One-Leg: The Life and Letters of Henry William Paget, First Marquess of Anglesey* (London, 1961), p. 371.

33 R. B. McDowell, *Public Opinion and Government Policy in Ireland, 1801–1846* (London, 1952), p. 79; Fortescue to Spencer, 11 Dec. 1868, BL, Spencer Papers, Add. Ms 76905.

34 Eglinton to Derby, 14 Apr. 1852 and 18 Mar. 1858, LRO, Derby Papers, 148/2 and 148/3; Derby to Eglinton, 12 Apr. 1852, Scottish Record Office (hereafter ScRO), [13th earl of] Eglinton Papers, GD3/5/1360. Eglinton had already spent a fortune on his famous medieval tournament: see Ian Anstruther, *The Knight and the Umbrella: An Account of the Eglinton Tournament of 1839* (London, 1963).

35 Clarendon to G. Grey, 16 Feb. 1851, Bodl., Clarendon Papers, Irish Letter-Book VI; Levee Books in Clarendon Papers Irish.

36 *Hansard* 3, vol. 146, col. 1982 (7 July 1857). See Carlisle's Diary for 25 Mar. 1857, CH, Carlisle Papers J19/8:

> In the evening a few people came and we had a variety of most delightful music – the 2 Robinsons, Mesdames Macdonnell, Geale, Miss Williams etc. singing, and Mrs Robinson playing beautifully. The quartet from *Lucia* and the Miserere from the *Trovatore* . . . were divine.

37 F. M. L. Thompson, '3rd duke of Northumberland', in *Oxford Dictionary of National Biography* (hereafter *ODNB*); Lord Colchester (ed.), *A Political Diary 1828–30 by Edward Law, Lord Ellenborough* (2 vols, London, 1881), i, p. 310; John Prest, *Lord John Russell* (London, 1972), p. 97. Mulgrave became marquess of Normanby in June 1838. In 1892 the chief

[37 *cont.*] secretary told the incoming viceroy, Houghton, to make sure he ordered his outfits in Dublin, Morley to Houghton, 19 Aug. 1892, Cambridge University Library (hereafter CUL), [1st marquess of] Crewe Papers, C36.

38 Londonderry to Salisbury, 7 Feb. 1887, Hatfield House (HatH), [3rd marquess of] Salisbury Papers, 3M/E. Londonderry also made himself 'popular' (as Eglinton had done) by race-going and agricultural activities. See Hicks Beach to R. Churchill, 24 Oct. 1886, CUL, Randolph Churchill Papers, Ms 9248/16/1920; *Galway Vindicator*, 28 Apr., 25 Aug. 1852; Eglinton to Derby, 21 Aug. 1858, LRO, Derby Papers, 148/3.

39 Cadogan to G. W. Balfour, 21 Jan. 1899, TNA, Balfour Papers, PRO30/60/14.

40 Ralph Bernal (who had been on the viceregal staff) citing *Saunders' News-Letter* of 1 Mar. 1844 in *Hansard* 3, vol. 74, col. 845 (9 May 1844).

41 Ralph Bernal Osborne (son of Ralph Bernal), ibid., vol. 184, col. 1966 (2 Aug. 1866).

42 R. F. Foster, *Lord Randolph Churchill: A Political Life* (Oxford, 1981), p. 34; Lady Clonbrock to Lady Aberdeen, 9 Jan. 1909 and Louisa Arnott to Lady Aberdeen, 9 Jan. and 11 Feb. 1909, Haddo House (hereafter HH), [1st marquess of] Aberdeen Papers, 1/5.

43 Houghton to Sir H. Ponsonby, 8 Dec. 1892, CUL, Crewe Papers, C59; Dudley to A. J. Balfour, 8 Oct. 1905, BL, Balfour Papers, Add. Ms 49802; Brodrick to A. J. Balfour, 27 Oct. 1905, ibid., Add. Ms 49721.

44 Lady Aberdeen to Campbell-Bannerman, 9 Jan. 1905 [*recte* 1906], BL, Campbell-Bannerman Papers, Add. Ms 41210; Joseph Robins, *Champagne and Silver Buckles: The Viceregal Court at Dublin Castle 1700–1922* (Dublin, 2001), pp 153–6.

45 Anglesey to Grey, 29 Dec. 1830, Durham University Library (DUL), [2nd Earl] Grey Papers, GRE/B3/32.

46 Morley to Aberdeen, 6 Aug. 1886, HH, Aberdeen Papers, 1/5; Carnarvon's Diary for 21 Jan. 1886, BL, Carnarvon Papers, Add. Ms 60925; Carnarvon to Queen Victoria, 8 July 1885, TNA, Carnarvon Papers, PRO30/6/53; Cadogan to G. W. Balfour, 22 Aug. 1895, TNA, Balfour Papers, PRO30/60/18.

47 M. R. D. Foot and H. C. G. Matthew (eds), *The Gladstone Diaries* (14 vols, Oxford, 1968–94), ix, p. 258 (17 Oct. 1877).

48 Spencer to O'Hagan, 17 Feb. 1869, PRONI, [1st Baron] O'Hagan Papers, D2777/8/13; Dilke's Memoirs, 23 May 1885, BL, Dilke Papers, Add. Ms 43939.

49 Anglesey, *One-Leg*, pp 268, 380; Hardwicke to Yorke, 7 Nov. 1803, BL, [3rd earl of] Hardwicke Papers, Add. Ms 35704.

50 *Hansard* 3, vol. 59, cols 672–3 (21 Sept. 1841); Clarendon to Russell, 12 Mar. 1850, Bodl., Clarendon Papers, Irish Letter-Book V.

51 Littlehales to Abbot, 20 Sept, 1801, in Lord Colchester (ed.), *The Diary and Correspondence of Charles Abbot, Lord Colchester* (3 vols, London, 1861), i, pp 317–18; Redesdale to Abbot, 15 Aug. 1802, TNA, Colchester Papers, PRO30/9/119. See also Redesdale to Wickham, 30 Jan. 1806 – 'This country will not be well governed until governed by English minds' – HMC, *Fortescue Manuscripts*, viii, p. 25.

52 Wellesley to Littleton, 2 Sept. 1833, SRO, [1st Baron] Hatherton Papers, D260/M/O1/7.

53 Peel to Liverpool, 31 Oct. 1816, BL, Peel Papers, Add. Ms 40292; and to Whitworth, 30

Mar. [1817], Whitworth Papers, CKS, U269/O225/19. Talbot, De Grey, Kimberley, and Marlborough were all married to Irishwomen.

54 Angus Hawkins and John Powell (eds), *The Journal of John Wodehouse First Earl of Kimberley for 1862–1902* (London, 1997), p. 229 (16 Dec. 1868).

55 Palmerston to Grey, 28 Aug. 1864, SUL, Broadlands Papers, Letter-Book I; Salisbury to Londonderry, 26 July 1886, HatH, Salisbury Papers, 3M/D/XVII; Londonderry to A. J. Balfour, 1 Apr. [1887], BL, Balfour Papers, Add. Ms 49802.

56 Chamberlain to Londonderry, 25 Feb. [1898], PRONI, [6th marquess of] Londonderry Papers, D2846/3/10/9.

57 Long to French, 4 Dec. 1918, Imperial War Museum, London (IWM), [1st Viscount] French Papers, JDPF/8/1B.

58 Hardwicke to Redesdale, 15 Apr. 1805, GRO, Redesdale Papers, D2002/3/1/47; Bathurst to Wellington, 29 Dec. 1828, SUL, [1st duke of] Wellington Papers, WP1/973/13.

59 Clarendon to Cornewall Lewis, May 1847, Maxwell, *Clarendon*, i, p. 276; Clarendon to Carew, 28 Feb. 1852, Trinity College Dublin (hereafter TCD), [1st Baron] Carew Papers, Ms 4021.

60 1864: Palmerston to G. Grey, 28 Aug. 1864, SUL, Broadlands Papers, Letter-Book I; 1866 and 1874: Marlborough to Disraeli, 20 Feb. 1874 and 22 July 1876, CUL, [7th duke of] Marlborough Papers, Ms 9271/4; 1868: Fortescue Diary, 7, 8, 12 Dec. 1868, BL, [1st Baron] Carlingford Papers, Add. Ms 6379A; and P. Gordon (ed.), *The Red Earl: The Papers of the Fifth Earl Spencer 1835–1910* (2 vols, Northampton, 1981–6), i, p. 72; 1874: John Vincent (ed.), *A Selection from the Diaries of Edward Henry Stanley, 15th Earl of Derby (1826–93) Between September 1869 and March 1878* (London, 1994), p. 166 (22 Feb. 1874); 1880: 'Cowper', *ODNB*; 1886: E. W. Hamilton's Diary (6 Feb. 1886), BL, Hamilton Papers, Add. Ms 48642; 1889: Zetland to Salisbury, 5 Apr. 1889, HatH, Salisbury Papers, 3M/E; 1902: Cadogan to Ashbourne, 28 July 1902, PA, [1st Baron] Ashbourne Papers, B22/43; 1916: Lord R. Cecil's Memorandum, 30 June 1916, Wiltshire and Swindon Archives, Chippenham (hereafter WSA), Long Papers, 947/9/179; 1918: Midleton's 'Memorandum with regard to Viceroyalty of Ireland', TNA, [1st earl of] Midleton Papers, PRO30/67/38.

61 Bankes to Colchester, 20 Dec. 1821, in Colchester (ed.), *Charles Abbot*, iii, pp 241–2.

62 Littleton (who served as Wellesley's chief secretary and was married to his illegitimate daughter) to Grey, 30 Aug. 1833, DUL, Grey Papers, GRE/B32/7/12; Wellesley to Goulburn, [June 1823], SHC, Goulburn Papers 304/43.

63 See Diana D. Olien, *Morpeth: A Victorian Public Career* (Washington DC, 1983). The only other chief secretary to serve as viceroy was Lord Eliot (1841–5), as earl of St Germans, in 1853–5.

64 John Vincent (ed.), *Disraeli, Derby and the Conservative Party: Journals and Memoirs of Edward Stanley, Lord Stanley 1849–1869* (Hassocks, 1978), p. 169 (18 Apr. 1861).

65 Patrick Maume, 'Aberdeen' in *Dictionary of Irish Biography* (hereafter *DIB*).

66 H. C. G. Matthew, *Gladstone 1875–1898* (Oxford, 1995), pp 241, 288, 359.

67 Morley to Spencer, 28 July 1892, BL, Spencer Papers, Add. Ms 76939.

68 Hoppen, 'An incorporating union?', pp 330–3.

69 Yorke (then secretary at war; he became home secretary in Aug. 1803) to Abbot, 12 Oct. 1801, TNA Colchester Papers, PRO30/9/120.

70 Liverpool to Peel, 4 Oct. 1813, BL Peel Papers Add. Ms 40181; Peel to Liverpool, 31 Oct. 1816, ibid., Add. Ms 40292.

71 Michael MacDonagh (ed.), *The Viceroy's Post-Bag: Correspondence hitherto unpublished of the Earl of Hardwicke* (London, 1904), p. 60; Hardwicke to Yorke, 20 Aug. 1801, BL, Hardwicke Papers Add. Ms 35771.

72 Hardwicke to Pelham, 24 May 1803, BL, [2nd earl of Chichester] Pelham Papers, Add. Ms 33111; and to Yorke, 11 May 1803, BL, Hardwicke Papers Add. Ms 35772.

73 Bedford's 'Private Instructions' [Feb. 1806], Woburn Abbey, [6th duke of] Bedford Papers, Irish Box 2.

74 See, for example, Littlehales to Abbot, 19 Sept. 1801, TNA, Colchester Papers, PRO30/9/124; Peel to Anglesey, 7 Apr. 1828, PRONI, Anglesey Papers, D619/26B; Melbourne to Anglesey, 9 July 1832, ibid., D619/29C.

75 Cornwallis to Portland, 10 Nov. 1800, TNA, HO100/94.

76 For useful communications, see SHC, Goulburn Papers, 304/35 and McGill University Library, Montreal, [1st Viscount] Hardinge Papers, Irish; for Wellesley, see BL, Wellesley Papers, Add. Ms 37298.

77 Hardwicke to Pitt, 3 Feb. 1805, BL, Hardwicke Papers. Add. Ms 35710; Talbot to Sidmouth, 7 and 10 Sept. 1819, TNA, HO100/197; Sidmouth to Talbot, 28 Sept. 1819, ibid.

78 Littleton to Anglesey, 11 June 1833, PRONI, Anglesey Papers, D619/31F.

79 Melbourne to Anglesey, 2 May 1833, Bodl., [microfilm] Melbourne Papers, 94; and to Mulgrave, 20 May 1835, ibid., 99.

80 Graham to De Grey, 1 Dec. 1841, Bodl., [microfilm, now in BL and resorted] Graham Papers, Ir/8; and to Heytesbury, 29 Oct. 1844, ibid., Ir/17; Robin Haines, *Charles Trevelyan and the Great Irish Famine* (Dublin, 2004), p. 124.

81 Kimberley Papers, Bodl., Mss Eng. c.4016–39; Foster to Spencer, 8 Oct. 1880, BL, Spencer Papers, Add. Ms 76923 and Spencer to J. Chamberlain, 21 Dec. 1881, ibid., Add. Ms 76925.

82 Gladstone to Spencer, 24 June 1882, BL, Spencer Papers, Add. Ms 76854.

83 Redesdale to Sidmouth, 24 Sept. 1813, TNA, HO100/172; Littleton's Diary for 21 July 1834, SRO, Hatherton Papers, D260/M/F/5/26/9.

84 Russell to Lansdowne, 7 Sept. 1835, TNA, [1st Earl] Russell Papers, PRO30/22/1E; Norman Gash, *Mr Secretary Peel* (London, 1961), p. 37.

85 Clarendon to Wood, 28 Oct. 1847, Borthwick Institute (York), Hickleton Papers, A4/57; Clarendon to Wodehouse, 16 May 1865, Bodl., Kimberley Papers, Ms Eng. c.4025.

86 Carnarvon's 'Historical Notes', c.1885–6, BL, Carnarvon Papers, Add. Ms 60827.

87 Morley's Diary for 6 June 1893, Bodl., Morley Papers, Ms Eng. d.3454; also Morley to Gladstone, 8 Mar. 1895, ibid., Ms Eng. d.3571; Rosebery to Morley, 20 Nov. 1894, National Library of Scotland, [5th earl of] Rosebery Papers, Ms 10130.

88 Asquith to Bryce, 6 Nov. 1907, Bodl., [1st Viscount] Bryce Papers, Ms 23.

89 Peel to Liverpool, 31 Oct. 1816, BL, Peel Papers, Add. Ms 40292.

90 Melbourne to Mulgrave, 23 May 1835, Bodl., Melbourne Papers, 99.

91 Peel to Graham, 15 Dec. 1842, BL, Peel Papers,Add. Ms 40448; and to Eliot, 20 Dec. 1842, in Parker (ed.), *Peel*, iii, p. 42; *Hansard* 3, vol. 111, col. 209 (17 May 1850).

92 Larcom to Naas, 7 June 1858, NLI, Larcom Papers, Ms 7504.

93 Spencer's Memorandum, 4 July 1871, BL, Gladstone Papers, Add. Ms 44307.

94 Spencer's 'More notes on the functions of the Lord Lieutenant and Chief Secretary', 22 Apr. 1882, BL, Spencer Papers, Add. Ms 76853; Gladstone to Spencer, 26 Jan. 1871, ibid., Add. Ms 76850; also Spencer to Gladstone, 26 Aug. 1884, BL, Gladstone Papers, Add. Ms 44311.

95 Lord and Lady Aberdeen, *We Twa* (2 vols, London, 1925), i, p. 248.

96 Cornwallis to Portland, 10 Nov. 1800, TNA, HO100/94; Redesdale to Hardwicke, 14 Oct. 1803, TNA, HO100/114; Hardwicke to Hawkesbury, 9 July 1804, BL, Hardwicke Papers, Add. Ms 35409; Morpeth to Melbourne, 22 June 1837, Bodl., Melbourne Papers 98.

97 See Hardwicke to Pitt, 14 Dec. 1804, TNA, Pitt Papers, PRO30/8/318; Redesdale to Colchester, 30 Oct. 1823, Colchester (ed.), *Charles Abbot*, iii, pp 302–5.

98 Creevey to Miss Ord, 3 Nov. [? 1832], in H. Maxwell (ed.), *The Creevey Papers* (London, 1923), p. 607; Stanley to Grey, 1 Aug. 1832 and 6 Jan. 1833, LRO, Derby Papers, 169 and 167/2; Littleton to Melbourne, 9 Sept, 1833 and 20 Sept. [1834], SRO, Hatherton Papers, D260/M/O1/2 and 4.

99 Stanley to Anglesey, 19 Jan. 1833, LRO, Derby Papers, 167/2.

100 Peel to Graham, 15 Dec. 1842, BL, Peel Papers, Add. Ms 40448 ('Decisive proof that the government of Ireland cannot be satisfactorily administered under the present constitution'); D. A. Kerr, *Peel, Priests and Politics: Sir Robert Peel's Administration and the Roman Catholic Church in Ireland, 1841–1846* (Oxford, 1982), pp 72–5.

101 St Germans to Aberdeen, 27 Feb. 1855, BL, Aberdeen Papers, Add. Ms 43208; Palmerston to Carlisle, 12 Mar. 1855, CH, Carlisle Papers, J19/1/56; Carlisle to Palmerston, [Dec. 1861], ibid., J19/1/96; Hawkins and Powell (eds), *Journal of John Wodehouse*, p. 180 (8 Dec. 1865); Naas to Disraeli, 29 Aug. [1867] and 18 Aug. [1868], Bodl., Disraeli [1st earl of Beaconsfield] Papers, 90/2 and 3; Spencer to Granville, 9 Apr. 1882, TNA, [2nd Earl] Granville Papers, PRO30/29/29; Spencer to Hartington, 12 Apr. 1882 and 31 July 1884, ChH, Devonshire Papers, 340.1143 and 1493; Cadogan to Ashbourne, 22 May 1900, PA, Ashbourne Papers, B22/19; Wyndham to A. J. Balfour, 20 Sept. 1901, BL, Balfour Papers, Add. Ms 49803 (Talking to Cadogan is 'like speaking through a megaphone with a pudding in its orifice'); Birrell to Nathan, 4 Feb. 1915, Bodl., Nathan Papers, Ms 449.

102 French to Long, 3 Sept. 1918, WSA, Long Papers, 947/9/230; but see French to Lloyd George, 12 Oct. 1918, IWM, French Papers, JDPF/8/1B.

103 Not all authorities list Clarendon as in the cabinet, but he certainly 'retained his key', Maxwell, *Clarendon*, i, p. 278.

104 Anglesey to Grey, 7 Mar. 1831, PRONI, Anglesey Papers, D619/28A; Grey to Anglesey, 13 June 1831, ibid.; Holland to Anglesey, 29 June 1831, ibid., D619/27A; Grey to Anglesey, 13 Aug. 1831, DUL, Grey Papers, GRE/B3/138; Stanley to Grey, 4 Aug. 1832, ibid., GRE/B11/8/51.

105 Kimberley to Fortescue, 1 June 1866, Somerset Record Office, Taunton, [1st Baron] Carlingford Papers, DD/SH/60/232; Marlborough to Beaconsfield, 14 Aug. [1876], CUL, Marlborough Papers, Ms 9271/4; Beaconsfield to Marlborough, 31 Aug. 1876, ibid.; Londonderry to A. J. Balfour, 1 Apr. [1887], BL, Balfour Papers, Add. Ms 49802; Cadogan to G. W. Balfour, 21 Jan. 1899, TNA, Balfour Papers, PRO30/60/14.
106 A. J. Balfour to Dudley, 15 Aug. 1905, WSA, Long Papers, 947/5/65; also Long to Sandars (Balfour's private secretary), 31 Mar. 1905 and 25 Aug. 1905, BL, Balfour Papers, Add. Ms 49776; Dudley to Long, 19 Aug. 1905, WSA, Long Papers, 947/5/68; Dudley to A. J. Balfour, 8 Oct. 1905, BL, Balfour Papers, Add. Ms 49802.
107 *Hansard*, 2, vol. 9, cols 1,212–41 (25 June 1823). See the excellent essay by Peter Gray, '"Ireland's last fetter struck off": The lord-lieutenancy debate 1800–67', in Terrence McDonough (ed.), *Was Ireland a Colony? Economics, Politics and Culture in Nineteenth-Century Ireland* (Dublin, 2005), pp 87–101.
108 *Hansard*, 2, vol. 24, cols 555–80 (11 May 1830); ibid., 3, vol. 77, cols 834–61 (9 May 1844); Eliot to Peel, 7 May 1844, BL,Peel Papers, Add. Ms 40480.
109 Wellesley to Lamb, 5 June 1827, Bodl., Melbourne Papers, 98; Stanley to Grey, [10 Mar. 1831] and 24 Sept. 1832, DUL, Grey Papers, GRE/B11/8/6 and 54.
110 Wellington in *Hansard*, 3, vol. 4, cols 643–8 (4 July 1831) and ibid., vol. 112, cols 468–71 (27 June 1850); Disraeli in ibid., vol. 102, col. 541 (9 Feb. 1849), also his 'Memorandum on administrative reform' of Dec. 1855, in M. G. Wiebe et al. (eds), *Benjamin Disraeli Letters* (8 vols to date, Toronto, 1982–), vi, pp 546–55.
111 *Hansard*, 2, vol. 9, cols 1,232–5 (25 June 1823); Peel to Graham, 15 Dec. 1842 and to Eliot, 23 Dec. 1842, in Parker (ed.), *Peel*, iii, pp 40, 42.
112 Melbourne to Littleton, 18 Oct. 1833, Bodl., Melbourne Papers, 96.
113 Russell to Lansdowne, 4 May 1847, BL, [3rd marquess of] Lansdowne Papers, B102 (temporary reference); Russell's memorandum of June 1847, TNA, Russell Papers PRO30/22/6H; Hobhouse Diary, 17 May 1847, BL, Hobhouse [1st Baron Broughton] Papers, Add. Ms 43750; Russell to Queen Victoria, 21 Jan. 1850, Royal Archives [microfilm], A20/116.
114 Vincent (ed.), *Derby, Disraeli and the Conservative Party*, p. 169.
115 Grey to Russell, 10 Jan. 1851, TNA, Russell Papers, PRO30/22/9A; also Clarendon to Russell, 9 Mar. 1851, Bodl., Clarendon Papers, Irish Letter-Book VI.
116 *Hansard*, 3, vol. 146, cols 1,048–110 (7 July 1857) and vol. 149, cols 712–81 (25 Mar. 1858).
117 Carlisle to Palmerston, 26 June 1857, SUL, Broadlands Papers, GC/CA/496.
118 Deasy's Memorandum, 25 Oct. 1860, CH, Carlisle Papers, J19/11/13. The memoranda by Cardwell (8 Sept. 1860), Larcom (1 Oct. 1860), and Carlisle (18 Oct. 1860) are all in NLI, Larcom Papers, Ms 7504.
119 Spencer to Gladstone, 28 May 1871, BL, Gladstone Papers, Add. Ms 44307; Gladstone's Memorandum, 25 June 1871, ibid., Add. Ms 44760; Kimberley's Memorandum, 28 June 1871, ibid., Add. Ms 44224; Spencer's Memorandum of a conversation with Gladstone, 14 Oct. 1871, BL, Spencer Papers, Add. Ms 76850; Printed Cabinet Paper, 16 Oct. 1871, NLI, Larcom Papers, Ms 7504.
120 Spencer to Harcourt, 19 Jan. 1885, BL, Spencer Papers, Add. Ms 76933; Harcourt to

Spencer, 25 Jan. 1885, ibid.; Spencer to Gladstone, 26 Jan. 1885, BL, Gladstone Papers, Add. Ms 44312; Spencer's Cabinet Paper, 23 Mar. 1885, TNA, Cabinet Memoranda, CAB37/14/19; Carnarvon's 'Historical Notes', c.1885–6, BL, Carnarvon Papers, Add. Ms 60826; Smith to Ashbourne, 5 Feb. 1886, PA, Ashbourne Papers, B139/8.

121 Cadogan to Devonshire (Hartington), 20 Aug. 1895, ChH, Devonshire Papers, 340.2643; and to Salisbury, 20 Aug. 1895, HatH, Salisbury Papers, 3M/E; Salisbury to Cadogan, 20 Aug. 1895, PA, [5th Earl] Cadogan Papers, 717; Spencer to Campbell-Bannerman, 20 Aug. 1905, BL, Campbell-Bannerman Papers, Add. Ms 41229.

122 Derby to Disraeli, 6 Oct. 1867, Bodl., Disraeli Papers, 110/3.

123 Spencer to Gladstone, 29 Dec. 1868, BL, Gladstone Papers, Add. Ms 44306; Spencer to Gladstone, 6 June 1870, BL. Spencer Papers, Add. Ms 76849; Gladstone to Granville, 3 Dec. 1870, TNA, Granville Papers, PRO30/29/58; Hartington to Gladstone, 16 May 1871, ChH, Devonshire Papers, 340.465; Bessborough's Memorandum, 26 May [1871], BL, Gladstone Papers, Add. Ms 44430; Gladstone's Memorandum, 25 June 1871, ibid., Add. Ms 44760; Gladstone to Queen Victoria, 12 Oct. 1871 and 10 Dec. 1872, TNA, Royal Letters, CAB41/4/44 and 54; Gladstone to Hartington, 23 Sept. 1872, ChH, Devonshire Papers, 340.502; Biddulph (for Queen Victoria) to Spencer, 12 Nov. 1872, ibid., 340.506.

124 Ponsonby to Carnarvon, 11 Sept. 1885, TNA, Carnarvon Papers, PRO30/6/53; Cadogan to Salisbury, 5 Sept. 1897, HatH, Salisbury Papers, 3M/E; Salisbury to Cadogan, 7 Sept. 1897, PA, Cadogan Papers, 1,185; Cadogan to G. W. Balfour, 15 Nov. 1897, TNA, Balfour Papers, PRO30/60/18; and to Ashbourne, 17 Nov. 1897, PA, Ashbourne Papers, B22/6.

125 Wimborne to Redmond, 9 Jan. 1915, NLI, Redmond Papers, Ms 15232. Significantly, Wimborne's first overtures to his under-secretary were almost deferential: Wimborne to Nathan, 9 May 1915, Bodl., Nathan Papers, Ms 448.

126 Lawrence W. McBride, *The Greening of Dublin Castle: The Transformation of Bureaucratic and Judicial Personnel in Ireland, 1892–1922* (Washington, DC, 1991), p. 212; A. Chamberlain to Asquith, 22 June 1916, BL, Balfour Papers, Add. Ms 49732(2); Asquith to Redmond, 28 July 1916, NLI, Redmond Papers, Ms 15165 (Asquith here trotted out the old saw about the viceroy being 'a symbol of the separateness of Ireland'); Asquith's Cabinet Paper, 21 May 1916, TNA, Cabinet Memoranda, CAB37/148/18; Long to Campbell, 12 July 1916, WSA, Long Papers, 947/10/173.

127 *Royal Commission on the Rebellion in Ireland: Report of Commission*, HC 1916 [Cd 8279], xi, pp 173–4.

128 Asquith's Cabinet Paper, 21 May 1916, TNA, Cabinet Memoranda, CAB37/148/18. Lansdowne thought the same and wanted the viceroy to be 'replaced' by a secretary of state and more royal visits: Typescript Memorandum, 2 June 1916, PA, Lloyd George Papers, D/15/10.

129 Long to French, 15 Oct. 1918, WSA, Long Papers 947/9/231; French to Long, 17 Apr. 1919, ibid., 947/9/230; Long to Lloyd George, 23 Oct. 1919, ibid., 947/9/287; Eunan O'Halpin, *The Decline of the Union: British Government in Ireland 1892–1920* (Dublin, 1987), pp 206–7; Richard Holmes, *The Little Field Marshal: A Life of Sir John French* (London, 2004 ed.), pp 357–8.

130 O'Halpin, *The Decline of the Union*, pp 206–7; Memorandum by Greenwood, 5 July 1920, WSA, Long Papers, 947/9/240; Long to French, 6 July 1920, ibid., 947/9/231.

CHAPTER 8

A 'People's Viceroyalty'? Popularity, Theatre and Executive Politics 1835–47

Peter Gray

The Irish lord lieutenancy uneasily combined two roles – the headship of the executive government of Ireland and the office of viceroy, representing the person of the monarch at the apex of the Irish court. This dual position may always have been replete with tension; as the monarch's minister as well as his personal representative, the lord lieutenant was the agent of the governing ministry at Westminster, while simultaneously being expected to play a courtly role elevated above partisanship. Individual temperament led some holders of the office to emphasise one aspect over the other, and the fluctuating balance of executive experience and assertiveness between the lord lieutenant, chief secretary and home secretary frequently tilted the balance between the two. Others sought, with varying degrees of success, to exploit the elevated status of the viceroyalty to advance the political agenda of their lord lieutenancy. Periods of intense partisan polarisation in Dublin or Westminster, Irish political unrest, or strains in British-Irish relations tended also to highlight the ambiguities inherent in the office and to stir up debate about its very utility.[1] The 1830s–40s was one such period.

Both aspects of the lord lieutenancy posed problems for the institution's public popularity in Ireland during the nineteenth century. As the personification of both the ministry and the British Crown, the name and activities of the lord lieutenant were widely reported through the island through proclamations, the press and pamphlets as well as popular ballads and oral transmission. Residents of Dublin and its environs were most likely to have direct experience of his presence, not least through observation of the public pomp and ceremonial of viceregal reviews, processions and public entertainments. Lavish expenditure surrounding the viceregal court made many Dubliners defensive of the institution (especially in the wake of the reduction of aristocratic spending in the city after the Act of Union), but did not necessarily endear them to the office-holder or his politics. Beyond the capital, where the person of the lord lieutenant might only be observed during occasional provincial visits and reminders of his existence were manifested most frequently through his signature on proclamations announcing some new measure of coercion, indifference or hostility to both the office and its bearer was more likely, at least below the level of the local Protestant elite. As the fount of Irish political patronage, apogee of the Dublin court and representative of the monarch the lord lieutenant tended at least to command the respect of the bulk of the ascendancy class, though not without an admixture of suspicion arising from his perceived subservience to the British administration, even if a Tory one, and resentment on the part of disappointed patronage-seekers. Although generally 'managed' in the early nineteenth century by the powerful coterie of conservative Protestant officials at the Castle (most notably the long-serving William Gregory, under-secretary 1812–30), there remained a concern that English lords lieutenant were ultimately loyal to the interests of London rather than to the ascendancy, and that the 'Castle clique' of Irish Protestant officials held place only by viceregal sufferance.

For these reasons, the idea of a 'popular' viceroyalty in nineteenth-century Ireland seems an unlikely one. Nevertheless, the subject of this paper is the concerted attempt from the mid-1830s to popularise the institution, utilising both its 'decorative' and 'efficient' elements in an attempt to articulate and implement a popular liberal-unionist political project. This initiative, forming part of the broader 'justice to Ireland' policy agenda of the second Melbourne government, was remarkably successful, albeit temporarily and at a price – the thorough-going alienation of much of the landed and clerical establishment. Through his flamboyant and frequently theatrical efforts, the second earl of Mulgrave rendered himself the most popular lord lieutenant in the institution's history, while simultaneously making himself the most loathed in the eyes of its traditional defenders and associates. Mulgrave was not the first to seek to redefine the office through popularisation – but previous attempts (for example under Fitzwilliam in 1795, Bedford in 1806, Wellesley in 1821 and Anglesey in 1829) had been short-lived or half-hearted. Nor was he the last; his Whig successors Viscount Ebrington in 1839–41 and the fourth earl of Bessborough in 1846–7, also sought, but with more mixed success, to promote 'justice to Ireland' from the Viceregal Lodge and appeal beyond the confines of the Dublin court to the mass of the Irish population.

The novel tenor of the Mulgrave viceroyalty was dramatised by the new lord lieutenant's inaugural entry to Dublin in May 1835. As was customary, the event was marked by military display and a formal (albeit chilly) official welcome from the office-holders of Dublin Corporation. What distinguished this episode was both the viceroy's behaviour and the public's response. Having first been met by a delegation of liberal peers at Kingston pier, Mulgrave proceeded to the city on horseback, accompanied by a procession estimated at swelling to 120,000 strong, led by the trades union of Dublin and observed by even larger crowds expressing noisy enthusiasm. 'Some excellent amateur bands', playing 'national airs', accompanied the raucous procession to the capital. Controversy arose immediately from the participation of the radical trades and the green banners and placards displayed along the route and in the new viceroy's train, including texts such as 'The friend of your king and of the people', 'Justice' and 'A Free People', along with other trades' banners allegedly making reference to repeal of the Union (there was some suggestion that pro-Mulgrave inscriptions patched onto older placards had washed off in the heavy rain).[2]

For his part, Mulgrave played the part of the triumphal hero; despite the rain, he 'remained uncovered nearly the entire way, kindly acknowledging the salutations and cheers of the crowd as he proceeded'. An unofficial ceremony in his presence saw the radical orator Marcus Costello rename a new bridge 'Mulgrave Bridge', in defiance of the corporation's recent decision to name it after the previous Tory viceroy.[3] Irish Tories immediately reacted in print and in parliament, denouncing Mulgrave's followers as a 'rabble', identified the banners displayed as those of the Ribbonmen and O'Connellites, and demanded Mulgrave's prosecution under the party processions act, while the government papers preferred to interpret the predominant sentiment as one of a 'deep feeling of loyalty to the king, and affectionate respect for their sovereign's representative'.[4] From its inception it was clear that this viceroyalty would be intensely divisive and that Mulgrave's personal style, as much as the policies his administration adopted, would play a role in stoking both enthusiasm and repulsion.

Mulgrave's popular reception in May 1835 was made possible by a significant political realignment in the preceding months, itself dependent on the outcome of factional conflicts within the Whig-Liberal party. Earl Grey's administration of 1830–4 had pursued an ambiguous policy in Ireland, combining moderate reformist initiatives on education, public works and the established Church with the use of coercion against social and political agitation, while demonstrating reluctance to jettison traditional ruling cadres in the Castle administration and senior legal offices. Particularly during Edward Stanley's period as chief secretary, relations with Daniel O'Connell had been very poor, as the anti-tithe and repeal agitations had pitted the forces of the state against those of popular politics in much of the country. Grey's viceroys, the marquess of Anglesey and Marquess Wellesley, had both previously held that office under Tory administrations and, while both supporters of Catholic emancipation, lacked both the popular touch and much inclination to treat constructively with O'Connell as leader of the 'popular' party in the country.[5] Mulgrave's propagandists were quick to contrast their failure with the new beginning in 1835.[6]

The appropriation issue, pressed in the cabinet in spring 1834 by Lord John Russell, famously 'upset the reform coach' and led to secession of the 'Derby Dilly' Whig moderates (including Stanley) followed by the resignation of Grey himself. Melbourne's succeeding ministry was more forward on Irish policy, but it was not until the dismissal of the government by the king in late 1834, and its reformulation on the fall of Peel's short-lived ministry in April 1835 that the full consequences of this became manifest. Peter Mandler has characterised the 'Foxite Whig' faction, led by Russell, which emerged predominant from this period of upheaval, as marked both by a style of aristocratic populism and by a genuine commitment to thorough (albeit non-democratic) reform in the domestic sphere. Unusually for any group of British politicians, Ireland held a certain fascination and was a high political priority for the Foxites, and from 1835, with Russell at the home office, they both dominated Irish-related offices of state and dictated that reform of Irish tithes, municipal corporations, justice, poor relief and the franchise would be at the head of the incoming government's legislative agenda.[7] Preparatory to the ousting of the Peel administration, the Foxite Whigs negotiated the so-called 'Lichfield House compact' with O'Connell and the British radicals, ostensibly on the shibboleth of the appropriation of the surplus revenues of the Irish Church, but more substantially on a commitment to a thorough-going revolution in Irish governing practice as well as substantive reforming legislation.

Lichfield House, and O'Connell's subsequent commitment to a Whig alliance he believed best calculated to advance his own political objectives in Ireland at that time, thus paved the way for Mulgrave's reception in Dublin. Indeed the 'Liberator' assured his allies that on arrival the new lord lieutenant would 'get nothing but strength and comfort and confidence from the popular party'. Privately he praised the choice of Mulgrave as an ideal lord lieutenant, while expressing his consciousness that too close a public association with him might prove counterproductive for both parties.[8] For his part, Mulgrave had fewer qualms, and soon courted controversy with moderate Irish and British Whigs, and more ominously aroused the anger of the king, by inviting O'Connell to dinner at the Viceregal Lodge and to levees at Dublin Castle. However, he had the support of the home secretary in doing so, and, after 1837 was even emulated by the new queen in publicly receiving the much-demonised Irish leader.[9]

It does not follow, however, that Tory claims that 'O'Mulgrave' was merely the subservient tool of the manipulative Irish agitator were correct.[10] The Whigs and O'Connell sought to advance their separate, if overlapping, agendas through pragmatic collaboration in the face of a common enemy; this involved some sacrifice on O'Connell's part, suspending the popular campaign for repeal in return for substantive reforms and a sympathetic patronage regime – 'I have thrown away . . . my "talisman" – the Repeal', he observed in late 1834, and the size of his 'tail' of loyal MPs fell in subsequent elections to 1841.[11] At the same time the pact encumbered the Whigs with an easily caricatured connection with a man many in Britain regarded as a seditious demagogue, a heretical church and a barbarous populace, damaging them at the British (although not the Irish) polls.[12]

Political calculation played its part in the O'Connell-Whig alliance, but so also did political idealism, at least on the part of many of its Whig advocates, and also the bonds of personal trust. The latter element emanated principally from the genuine friendship between O'Connell and Lord Duncannon, heir to a County Kilkenny estate, an Irish earldom and headship of the 'patriot' Ponsonby family, and from the 1820s a key political organiser for the Whig-Liberal party and mainstay of the Foxite political grouping. Duncannon was the principal architect of Lichfield House – having begun detailed negotiations with O'Connell on an electoral pact in November 1834.[13] Duncannon also hosted Russell's fact-finding visit to Ireland in 1833 and was a key adviser to both the Mulgrave and Ebrington viceroyalties. He was subsequently the shaper of Foxite Irish policy in the 1830s and, as fourth earl of Bessborough, was himself viceroy in 1846–7, when he (along with O'Connell) sought in vain to revive the politics of 1835 in a much more hostile political and economic context.[14]

Mulgrave was an inspired choice for the first Foxite viceroy of Ireland. The son of a Tory cabinet minister, he exhibited the seal of the political convert. After making his earliest parliamentary speeches in support of Catholic Emancipation and parliamentary reform, he attached himself to Russell's circle, and was rewarded with appointment as governor of Jamaica in 1832 followed by the cabinet post of lord privy seal in 1834. His enthusiasms were not restricted to the political. He spent much of the 1820s resident in Tuscany, and devoted much of his energy there to theatrical and other cultural pursuits.[15] He was well known as a writer of fiction, publishing four romantic novels between 1825 and 1832, which attracted mixed reviews.[16] Returning to London, Mulgrave vigorously patronised the theatre, chairing the Drury Lane Theatrical Fund dinners in 1832 and 1835.[17] He carried this enthusiasm with him to Dublin, where he promoted both Rossini's operas and burlesque amateur theatricals.[18] The theatre in Dublin, however, embodied a political as well as a cultural dimension. Visits by previous viceroys had witnessed more intense drama around the viceregal box than on the stage, with Marquess Wellesley's December 1822 appearance sparking the infamous 'bottle riot' by Orangemen infuriated by his banning of the decoration of King William's statue on College Green, while Lord Haddington's in early 1835 had attracted attention by the provocative display of Orange paraphernalia in the box behind the lord lieutenant's head (albeit without his advance knowledge).[19] Lord and Lady Mulgrave's first visit to the Dublin theatre in May 1835 saw partisan disturbances in the stalls resulting in the appropriation of the auditorium space by his supporters, followed by 'the most enthusiastic plaudits of certainly the most dense assemblage [. . .] ever witnessed in a Dublin theatre' – these of course were directed at the viceroy rather than the performers.[20] For their part, 'the lord lieutenant and his lady carried off their roles remarkably well', noted a visiting diarist, 'bowing gracefully, and with apparent feeling, to the congratulation of the audience'.[21]

The politics of space and display were not restricted to the theatre. Although the viceroy had earlier been concerned that any encouragement of the 'day of license' that was St Patrick's Day might be used against the government, in 1837 large numbers of the public were admitted to Upper Castle Yard to hear military bands play Irish airs (including 'St Patrick's Day' and 'Garryowen'), witness the changing of the guard and cheer Mulgrave and members of the viceregal family, several of whom were adorned in green costume for the occasion.[22] This 'wearing of the green', both sartorially and rhetorically, was to be a particular trait of his regime. This was not entirely new; Bedford had revived the observance of St Patrick's Day in 1806, and both Wellesley and Anglesey had engaged in similar 'patriotic' displays, but Mulgrave took such emblematic activities to new lengths.[23] Moreover, with much of the Anglo-Irish gentry now boycotting the viceregal court, the focus of his attention was decidedly on the 'public' rather than the traditional courtly sphere of muted 'patriotism'.

Mulgrave's taste for the theatrical provided plentiful ammunition for his political opponents, and has tended to shape historical interpretations of his Irish administration. From R. R. Madden, writing in the mid-1840s, onwards, there has been a pattern of identifying the talented but sober under-secretary Thomas Drummond rather than his flamboyant aristocratic superiors as the moving genius of reforming government in Ireland. Perhaps as a consequence of his having died in office in 1840, and acquiring admiring biographers (John Ferguson McLennan in 1867, R. Barry O'Brien in 1889), Drummond has tended to be elevated in historical memory, while his political chiefs Mulgrave and the chief secretary Lord Morpeth suffered from the oscillations of their subsequent political careers and lacked nineteenth-century biographies.[24] Unquestionably popular (as demonstrated by the public obsequies in Ireland following his premature death), highly capable, and with an acute and extensive knowledge of Irish conditions, Drummond was an indispensable member of the administrative team, but it is frequently overlooked that he was a subordinate official and rarely the initiator as opposed to the executor of its public policy. Responsibility for the success or failure of the 1835–41 Irish government lay with the lord lieutenant, and secondarily with the chief secretary – the overemphasis on Drummond may reflect a historiographical preference for the bourgeois (and perhaps Scottish) virtues of professionalism and administrative efficiency over those of a more effervescent aristocratic political populism.[25]

If Mulgrave owed his initially favourable reception by 'popular' opinion in Ireland to O'Connell's goodwill, he was also in large part the architect of his own public persona. Dublin Castle projected his image through the use of favourable newspapers (especially the *Dublin Evening Post*) and regular periodical articles – Drummond commissioned at least six such eulogies for insertion in the newly-established *Dublin Review* (which was part-owned by O'Connell himself) in 1836–8 as well as two for the *Edinburgh*. Mulgrave's previous Jamaican experience was put to particularly good use as an emblem of the emancipatory moment he and Russell envisaged his viceroyalty as signifying for Ireland.[26] The fact that he had presided there over the implementation of the 1833 slavery abolition act was repeatedly enthused on in addresses to the viceroy, in his responses and in liberal commentary. In one of his earliest public responses, to a rather half-hearted address of welcome from Trinity College (where he had been 'groaned' at by the students), Mulgrave commented that 'it requires to have seen men slaves, fully to appreciate the happiness of leaving them free'.[27] In Belfast, where the abolitionist movement had been particularly active, liberals drummed up enthusiasm for Mulgrave's visit in 1835 by highlighting this element of his personal narrative.[28] Despite sectarian tensions and municipal hostility, the viceroy's visit to the town in October appears to have been a popular success, at least among the Catholic and large sections of the Presbyterian population, who feted him in the town's theatre (suitably enough). His statement that, while he came as the king's impartial representative, he believed that Ireland must be governed through the power of its 'public opinion', was particularly well received.[29] His anti-slavery record also played well with liberal unionists suspicious of O'Connellism – both the Presbyterian Synod of Ulster and the Seceding Synod congratulated Mulgrave on his appointment, making special reference to his 'conspicuous part' in the abolition of slavery as grounds for expressing confidence in his reforming administration of Ireland.[30]

The exchange of public addresses and viceregal responses was an important part of Mulgrave's public projection, especially as it was associated with the series of provincial tours he began shortly after arrival. Given the Whig government's commitment to radically reform the Irish municipal corporations, it is not surprising that addresses from the established corporate bodies tended to be curt and formulaic, or that many of these Tory-dominated bodies declined to issue invitations to the viceroy. Their place was taken (or rival addresses were prepared) by more informal parish, town and county meetings, or by voluntary associations. Of the 200 Irish addresses to Mulgrave collected and published together in 1836, eleven were from corporations, 120 from parishes and towns, and twenty-six drawn up by county or baronial meetings. Twenty-one came from Catholic clerical bodies, five from Presbyterians, one from a Wesleyan congregation in Donegal and none (hardly surprisingly) from the established Church. The contents of the addresses varied, but many were the product of local political organisation and combined professions of loyalty to the lord lieutenant and the monarch he represented with explicit demands for 'equality', especially in the administration of justice, and speedy implementation of Irish reforms. While careful to avoid sounding excessively partisan, Mulgrave's published answers were clearly sympathetic to such aspirations, again to the outrage of Conservative commentators.

Mulgrave's annual progresses throughout the island appear to have been much more extensive than those of his predecessors (who tended to regard them 'with undisguised horror'), and served a number of purposes.[31] At one level these were 'fact-finding' visits, to appraise the lord lieutenant of both local conditions and grievances. There is evidence that he took this responsibility seriously and that it informed policy-making. Mulgrave was the first lord lieutenant since the Union to visit County Donegal; he took the opportunity to report in detail to London on the social distress he witnessed there and provided a radical anti-landlordist social commentary as an interpretive gloss.[32] His personal efforts to investigate and alleviate local famine conditions further bolstered his local popularity, and was contrasted with the distant formality of his predecessors.[33]

The tours were also highly political, bolstering support for liberal and radical political interests in the localities and providing the lord lieutenant with the opportunity of engaging in the politics of spectacle before fresh audiences. The streets of towns he visited were frequently decorated with 'green boughs' and triumphal arches – such as that across the highway at Drumsna, County Leitrim, emblazoned 'Long live Lord Mulgrave, the Impartial Viceroy' and 'Justice to Ireland' – setting the scene for the politics of public gesture.[34] The viceroy appears to have enjoyed the lionising he received in the provinces, writing to Russell from Wexford that 'nobody who has not seen the wonderful outpouring of an Irish population of all ranks can have any idea of it'.[35] While Tory papers dismissed such scenes as the result of priestly rabble-rousing, the extent of popular excitement during these tours in the west and south, in the face of the hostility of the bulk of the gentry, could not be gainsaid.[36]

One of the most controversial aspects of Mulgrave's viceroyalty was his use of the prerogative power of clemency to mitigate sentences or release prisoners. This was in itself nothing new – the prerogative power had been widely used by previous incumbents and, as the liberal press pointed out, had actually been resorted to for larger numbers under Tory governments. Again, what marked out Mulgrave's regime was the very personal and direct mode with which this power was used. Some of the acts of clemency, such as the remission of Thomas Reynold's sentence for sedition in 1836, were explicitly political (in response to the perceived partisanship in his conviction and sentencing);[37] but others were more concerned with 'popularising' the administration of justice through a more arbitrary display of mercy to lesser malefactors. At Clonmel Gaol in August 1836, he ordered the release of fifty-seven prisoners; this was a risky proceeding given that each reoffending case was enthusiastically leapt on by his enemies.[38] In several instances Mulgrave staged public reconciliations between those convicted of faction fighting, while threatening vigorous prosecution of future such offences; at Carrick on Shannon the same month thirty-six men convicted of rioting were set free: 'Well then, boys,' he is reported as saying on hearing their profession to keep the peace in future, 'I accept your pledge – walk out'.[39] While hotly contested by his opponents, liberal writers hailed the positive consequences of this exercise of clemency, combined with moves towards the de-sectarianisation of policing and justice, as a personal triumph: 'Tipperary is deeply indebted for this remarkable improvement to the personal exertions of Lord Mulgrave . . .', wrote one pamphleteer, 'He visited the disturbed districts, and claimed in person the cooperation of the well-disposed of all classes in his exertions to restore order'.[40] Justifying himself against charges that the policy of clemency had been recklessly pursued, and had encouraged crime, Mulgrave insisted that close attention had been paid to the character, situation and nature of the offence in all cases, that leniency had been shown to those of all religious and political opinions, and that in general the policy was justified by the general tendency of Irish courts to impose excessive sentences.[41] The Irish crime statistics in the period were the subject of vituperative claim and counter-claim, but they appear generally to support the Whig contention that agrarian and political crime had fallen, and suggest that the drive to popularise the legal structures of Ireland was not without some success. While fully supported by his allies, however, Mulgrave's flamboyant style and manifestation of viceregal autonomy in this sphere concerned the more moderate prime minister, Viscount Melbourne, who felt privately that his pardons and progresses were 'too like the acts of an absolute sovereign and not in the character of a constitutional government'.[42]

While Mulgrave's chief cheerleaders were to be found among the liberal middle classes of Ireland, there is some evidence of genuine popularity, beyond the reports of cheering crowds drawn from the lower levels of Irish society. One surviving chapbook produced in the period, a text that was cheaply produced and probably widely circulated, accompanied a misogynist ballad on female entrapment of young men with a panegyric on 'Earl

Mulgrave's welcome to Waterford'. The verses stressing the key themes of the O' Connellite alliance, Mulgrave's emancipatory record in Jamaica and Ireland, viceregal patronage of local manufactures, and (of course) the importance of drinking his excellency's health. The vicereine's patronage of Irish products and display of Irish patriotic emblems was also singled out for praise:

You injured sons of Erin draw near until my theme
While I relate the praise of this worthy man of fame
Our noble Lord Lieutenant he is O'Connell's friend
And to regain our long lost rights is what he does intend.

CHORUS
It's what he does intend, it's what he does intend,
And to regain our long lost rights is what he does intend.

His visit into Waterford it was a glorious sight to see
Men of every rank and station they all now did agree
With heart and hand in unity their country for too free,
With colours fine he seemed inclined to be welcome here with green.

A new hope has sprung up for Erin and that you'll shortly see
If we but join our hearts together in love and unity
Sure our present Lord Lieutenant he ruled the Indian shore,
He repailed, the slaves broke off their chains, his loss they do deplore.
. . .

To encourage Irish manufacture his lady now she goes
And wears the shamrock on her breast it's seen in beaten gold.
Attended by each noble so splendid there she's seen
At each ball and assembly decorated all with green.
. . .

I wish I was endowed with learning or could direct my quill,
The praise of his Excellency some pages it would fill
Come fill up your flowing bumpers and drink with alacrity,
And toast to brave O'Connell and his Excellency.[43]

More 'respectable' demotic expressions of support came from the trades of the cities of Cork and Limerick and the Cork Mechanics Institute.[44] I have yet to discover, however, whether the reported call by a chairman of an O'Connell dinner that Irish mothers should christen one of their sons 'Mulgrave' has any effect on popular naming practices in the later 1830s.[45]

The legislative strategy of the 1835–9 administration was largely outside Mulgrave's hands, although he and his colleagues in Dublin Castle were consulted on the drafting of Irish legislation.[46] He was expected, however, to manage the anticipated negative reaction in Ireland to the continued rejection or belated and watered-down passage of the tithe and municipal reform measures. Patronage and appointment policy, the fields most firmly in the lord lieutenant's hands, were vigorously employed to promote 'popular' (frequently, but by no means predominantly Catholic) candidates to law offices, the magistracy and the administration and dismiss those overtly associated with Orange demonstrations.[47] Senior appointments in the reformed and centralised Irish Constabulary were also retained by the Castle, a fact which led to the resignation of the force's commander, Col. Shaw Kennedy, although he declined to condemn the appointments made when questioned by a parliamentary committee. The marked overlap between the appointments and those advocated by O'Connell inevitably opened the administration up to Conservative attack, although claims that they were made at the Irish agitator's dictation were untrue, and by 1841 only around one third of all judicial and administrative offices under the Crown were held by anti-Tories, and less than half of these were Catholics.[48] Mulgrave defended himself in person to the Lords on this key point:

> I fearlessly and utterly deny that the Government has been controlled by Mr O'Connell, or has consulted with Mr O'Connell as to any of the appointments that have been made; and as to the charge of the Government having the steady support of Mr O'Connell, I honestly confess that that is a circumstance, considering how much he carries with him the hearts and affections of the Irish people, that I can regard only as a great advantage, and as one that ought not to be made a matter of reproach. But that Mr O'Connell influences me – that he actuates me in the discharge of my duties, or that I am governed or actuated by any other than my own sense of right, I utterly and totally deny in the face of your Lordships, and of the noble Lord by whom the charge was brought forward.[49]

The executive decision to reject applications for the use of the police to enforce the collection of tithes and rent, and to publicly refuse the demand from local elites for the introduction of coercive measures (as manifest in Drummond's 1838 letter to the Tipperary magistrates, written at Mulgrave's direction), proved equally controversial.[50]

The price of Mulgrave's popularity amongst Catholics and liberal Protestants in Ireland was an intense degree of antagonism manifested against him throughout and indeed after his period in Dublin. Not only were the Conservative papers in both islands replete with hostile reports and leaders in virtually every issue, peers and MPs regularly initiated censure motions, which were particularly dangerous given the opposition majority in the Lords. This climaxed in 1839 when infuriated Irish Tories, led by Lord Roden, succeeded in initiating a full-scale parliamentary inquiry into his administration. The marquess of Normanby (as Mulgrave became on his promotion in the coronation honours of June 1838) was present to defend himself in the debates surrounding this motion, but had expressed dismay that the Whig leaders in the Lords had made only ineffective efforts to do so on previous occasions.[51] Unhappiness at his political exposure, along with his political ambition to return to the cabinet and growing weariness of the tedium of viceregal functions, eventually led to his decision to leave Ireland.[52] Lord Glenelg's resignation as colonial secretary in early 1839 provided the desired opportunity, and Normanby left Dublin after nearly four years, convinced that he had succeeded in attaining the objective set out in 1835 of establishing general tranquillity without resort to coercion.

While less boisterous than the viceregal arrival in 1835, the departure of the Normanbys in February 1839 was also marked not only by the usual formalities, but by public displays of emotion, effusive addresses from Dublin, Belfast and many other places, and a procession to Kingston that 'far eclipsed' that of his predecessors in 'numbers, respectability, without saying anything of popular enthusiasm'. The viceregal couple were reported to be moved to tears by the scenes they witnessed.[53] Only Russell's father, the duke of Bedford, in 1807, and Anglesey at the end of his first viceroyalty in 1829 – following his public conversion to Catholic emancipation – had received anything like such an emotive and popular send-off.[54] Typically, his critics again fastened on the theatricality of this staged departure. The Irish-born cartoonist John Doyle – ever an acidic commentator on the Whig-O'Connellite ménage – depicted a Dickensian quayside scene in which Normanby (in the persona of the departing Nicholas Nickleby) is embraced with studied theatricality by O'Connell as the impresario Vincent Crummles, while O'Connell's son John mimics his father with a nonplussed Lord Morpeth.[55]

This would be a hard act to follow, and the choice of Normanby's successor was complicated by the multiplicity of roles expected of the appointee and by the difficulty of identifying a replacement who could combine these as effectively as he had done. Normanby's own inclinations leant towards the appointment of a 'decorative' viceroy, with the executive functions devolving more on the experienced team of Morpeth (who would be raised to cabinet rank) and Drummond, and he favoured the queen's uncle, the duke of Sussex. However, the cabinet was not persuaded of the suitability of a royal appointment, not least given the fury with which Normanby had been assailed in the Lords; Lord John Russell's elder brother, Lord Tavistock, declined the offer, as did the radical Lord Radnor. Although a number of names were discussed, in the end the appointment went to another active

'Foxite Whig' peer, Viscount Ebrington, who was keen for personal reasons to take the post. Russell had entertained some doubts concerning Ebrington's ability to withstand sustained political pressure, and even considered the abolition of the office at this juncture, but in the end acceded to the argument that this would ensure continuity.[56]

The new viceroy's skills lay very much on the 'efficient' side of the scale; he was not personally charismatic and, despite a popular entry that echoed Mulgrave's in 1835, he lacked the almost automatic enthusiasm his predecessor had commanded.[57] Ebrington's political base was in Devon, but he was also an Irish landowner and had engaged in extensive back-channel negotiations with O'Connell in the previous years, and had fully approved Mulgrave's policy line.[58] He had a record for outspokenness on both the anti-slavery and Irish church questions, the latter immediately polarising opinion on him in the press and parliament.[59] Ebrington sought to maintain the same course, and was reinforced in this by Normanby's transfer to the home office in September 1839 after a mediocre spell as colonial secretary. The two worked closely together for the next two years, with Morpeth (now in the cabinet) serving as the third member of an unusually cohesive 'Irish' ministerial bloc.[60] The 'Liberator' expressed great reluctance to break with the government, but was under pressure from his own ranks to revivify the Repeal movement and prepare for what now appeared an inevitable return of the Conservatives to power.[61] Despite his best efforts, and insistence that unlike the Chartists O'Connell could be won back through conciliation, Ebrington was eventually obliged in 1840 to proscribe Repealers from government patronage and saw his Irish popularity diminish as a consequence.[62] The alliance held until 1841, but the 'popularity' that Normanby had attained proved ephemeral, as it was overly dependent both on the vagaries of individual personality as well as on a specific conjunction of political circumstances.

Despite this setback, and the further intensification of political antagonisms in Ireland associated with the full-blooded Repeal campaign of 1842–3, the Foxite Whigs were reluctant to abandon the liberal-unionist project of 'Justice to Ireland', and sought to revive it on returning to office, now with Russell as prime minister, in summer 1846. Again, the lord lieutenancy was seen as crucial to the attempt, and Duncannon, who had succeeded as 4th earl of Bessborough in 1844, undertook the office, with a relatively inexperienced chief secretary (Henry Labouchere) and, for the first time in the office's history, an Irish Catholic under-secretary (Thomas Redington). He was the first viceroy with predominantly Irish connections or residency since the 2nd duke of Ormond in 1714, and the last until Abercorn in 1866 and Londonderry in 1886.

After the state trials of 1844 and his brief imprisonment, O'Connell was again prepared to suspend Repeal in favour of reform, and to engineer the expulsion of the radical firebrands of Young Ireland from his ranks in order to attain this. The long-standing personal bonds between the two men facilitated a serious attempt to return to the politics of Lichfield House, but in the context of Ireland in 1846–7 this proved illusory.[63] Against expectation, famine conditions intensified and the Irish government lost control over this vital area of policy to the ideologues at the Treasury. Reluctant despite his bitter frustration with the Whigs to break with Bessborough, O'Connell's health collapsed in early 1847 and he died en route to Rome in May. Increasingly politically isolated, and with his own health declining, Bessborough too expired on 16 May, a day after his old friend – he was only the second lord lieutenant, after Rutland sixty years before, to have died in office.[64]

What appears extraordinary is the extent to which, despite the horrors of Irish mass mortality in the spring of 1847 – the very nadir of the Famine – Bessborough retained his personal popularity. Never a charismatic speaker or a theatrical personality, he was nevertheless well known to be the architect of the Irish reform strategy as well as one of the most sympathetic and generous of Irish landlords. The nationalist press, increasingly bitter about Whig 'betrayal' of Ireland in 1846–7, was careful to exempt him from responsibility; he had been 'thwarted and counteracted by the despotism of the Home Office, which . . . leaves no freedom of action to Lieutenant or Secretary', one Dublin paper observed, indeed he had 'struggled almost on his death bed to preserve the lives of the Irish people'. The provincial nationalist press agreed, with the *Galway Vindicator* praising him as 'a thorough Irishman in feeling and character', dedicated to 'promot[ing] the prosperity and welfare of Ireland'.[65] Eulogies came from O'Connell's son John in the Repeal Association and the provincial Catholic press, and were collected into a memorial volume.[66] Turning the realities of the viceregal office on its head, the author of the latter asserted that Bessborough's success had been due to the fact 'that his appointment appeared to be the unanimous election of a popular representative, rather than the nomination of a delegate of royal authority'.[67] According to the *Freeman's Journal*, the funeral cortege from the Castle to Kingsbridge Station was witnessed by a 'vast assemblage', all of whom 'seemed to feel the loss Ireland has sustained in the death of the excellent nobleman, who in life evinced the greatest desire to alleviate the distress which unhappily prevails in this country'.[68] The *Times* noted also the throngs of people who came to see the cortège arrive at Carlow by railway, and proceed onwards to Bessborough in his native County Kilkenny.[69]

This funeral, with O'Connell's some weeks later, marked the end of the Foxite Whig experiment in Ireland. Always in two minds about the utility of the lord lieutenancy, Russell now decided to initiate the abolition of the office and opt for the integration of the Irish executive into the British through the substitution of a fourth secretary of state. Consequently, Morpeth – who actively sought the viceroyalty – was passed over for the 4th earl of Clarendon, a moderate Whig heavyweight with no previous Irish associations, who acceded on the express understanding that he would be the last viceroy, paving the way for an abolition bill as soon as practicable.[70] A royal visit to Ireland in August 1849, the first since George IV's brief stop in 1821, was intended to be the first of many, which would obviate the need for a resident viceroy to represent the monarch in Ireland.[71] Although the abolition measure, when finally introduced in 1850, proved abortive, Clarendon's administration marked a sharp break with the recent past.[72] Uninterested in personal or political popularity, he took a much harder line against Repealers, oversaw the return of coercive legislation in 1847–8 and, while privately appealing for additional relief expenditure in Ireland, was publicly associated with the regressive poor-law based policy that marked the latter years of the Famine, as well as the Ecclesiastical Titles Bill fiasco of 1850–1 which alienated the Catholic clergy. Lichfield House was well and truly buried with Bessborough.

What explains the relative success of Whig lords lieutenant in the 1835–47 period in attracting 'popularity' in Ireland, and what legacy did this leave, if any, in British-Irish relations? The Mulgrave viceroyalty partially coincided, and bore marked similarities to, what might be described as the 'first Victorian moment' in British-Irish relations. The accession to the throne in 1837 of the nineteen-year-old Princess Victoria, unsullied as she then was with the negative political associations that attached to her predecessors (and indeed to herself in later years), offered an opportunity for the expression of widespread popular royalism among Irish Catholics. As James Murphy has highlighted, O'Connell himself enthused on the innocence and grace of the new queen, and sought to utilise the emotional power of royalty to outflank Irish Protestant 'loyalism' and advance the reformist alliance.[73] The queen's despatch to Mulgrave in July 1837, expressing total confidence in his conduct and 'recognis[ing] in her Irish subjects a spirit of loyalty and devotion towards her person and government', which was widely reprinted in the Irish press, reinforced this.[74] In the absence of a royal visit to Ireland before 1849, the viceroy offered some local substitute for the glamour of a popular monarchy. While many incumbents offered only a pale shadow of the original, the Mulgraves excelled in playing the part. Lady Mulgrave's place as one of the (controversially partisan) ladies of the royal bedchamber, and the status of the couple as royal favourites in Victoria's early years, no doubt enhanced this association.

Mulgrave proved himself a skilled practitioner of the politics of symbol and gesture, to a much greater extent than he was able to master a departmental brief after 1839. The importance of the theatrical and charismatic aspects of public politics in explaining the success of O'Connell's extraordinary mass mobilisations in this era has recently been investigated by Gary Owens.[75] Mulgrave was perhaps unique among nineteenth-century viceroys in his ability to echo O'Connell's political flourishes and harness the Irish popular movement (if briefly) to the carriage of British reforming politics. Although aspiring to the full political integration of Ireland within the Union, Russell grasped the benefits of Mulgrave's style at a crucial point in its evolution; he told the lord lieutenant in 1838,

> You have now established a name and an influence in Ireland, which is in itself a power, . . . in a country where the elements of government are so much wanting, and are only beginning to operate beneficially.[76]

In short, Mulgrave had dramatised the state as symbolically embodied in Ireland by the viceroy, as an entity quite distinct from and even at odds with the traditional elites which had previously dominated Dublin Castle and its court. The idea of a 'neutral' (or as his Conservative critics insisted, a pro-Catholic) state was thus popularised, creating a political space in which liberal Catholics and constitutional nationalists could act or aspire to participate.

For their part, large numbers of the Irish public responded with some enthusiasm to the Whig olive branch. One striking physical manifestation of this is the 'Morpeth Testimonial Roll' of June 1841, a huge document signed by up to 300,000 individuals and presented to the outgoing chief secretary in gratitude for his efforts for Irish reform since 1835. The creation of the document, pieced together from sheets sent in by local committees from many parts of the country, was undertaken by a body headed by the Whig duke of Leinster, but with the active cooperation of the O'Connellite political machine and with support from much of the Catholic parochial clergy.[77] Despite this manifestation, Morpeth's rather half-hearted attempt to revive his personal popularity in Ireland when he returned as lord lieutenant in 1855 (having succeeded as 7th earl of Carlisle in 1848), was not successful. Although genial and good-natured, in the very different post-Famine conditions of the 1850s, this was not enough, and any return to the viceregal politics of the 1830s proved impossible.[78]

Both the meliorist optimism of Foxite Whiggery and the demotic response accorded to the theatrical populism of Mulgrave, and the more restrained (and less polarising) reforming paternalism of Ebrington and Bessborough, owed something to the romantic cultural context in which it was played out. It is perhaps fitting that the last word here should go to the high priest of Irish sentimental romanticism, Tom Moore – who was also an acute political observer. Writing for a liberal public periodical in 1838, Moore declared that the Mulgrave administration had brought a new dawn to Ireland, principally due to his personal impact:

> His progresses through the provinces in the first year scattered the seeds of social improvement wide; the people received with open hearts and arms the first Lieutenant who presented the majesty of the law in its attractive attributes, and showed them the crown of Protestant Britain adorned with its best jewel. In the southern counties, long unaccustomed to those mild qualities in which the true force of government resides, his reception was enthusiastic; the insurgent delivered up his pike – the incendiary quenched his brand – the demagogue renounced his frantic projects: the founder of the dispensation of clemency and justice was hailed with the due honours of a patron and deliverer, wherever he bent his steps.[79]

While overstated for effect, and ignoring both the vulnerability of the achievement and the negative consequences of political polarisation, Moore's comments are a useful reminder of the importance of viceregal style and of the possibility, at least, of a popular lord lieutenancy, at least prior to the calamities of 1847.

Notes

1 For a Tory attack on the institution (as well as its 1835–9 incumbent), see [David Robinson], 'What is the use of a lord-lieutenant of Ireland?', *Fraser's Magazine*, 13 (Apr. 1836), pp 475–87.

2 *Freeman's Journal* (hereafter *FJ*), 12 May 1835, *Northern Whig* (hereafter *NW*), 14 May 1835.

3 *Times*, 14 May 1835; *Morning Chronicle* (hereafter *MC*), 14 May 1835.

4 *Times*, 14 May 1835; *MC*, 21 May 1835; *Hansard's Parliamentary Debates*, 3, vol. 27, cols 1,118–25 (15 May 1835); vol. 28, cols 1–14 (22 May 1835).

5 O'Connell had attended Castle levees in the early years of both Wellesley's and Anglesey's first administrations in 1821–2 and 1828 respectively, but this was not sustained once the early optimism about Catholic emancipation had receded, Joseph Robins, *Champagne and Silver Buckles: The Viceregal Court at Dublin Castle, 1700–1922* (Dublin, 2001), pp 105–6, 112.

6 [Anon.], 'Earl Mulgrave in Ireland', *Dublin Review*, 1: 1 (May 1836), pp 28–46.

7 For a full discussion, see Peter Mandler, *Aristocratic Government in the Age of Reform: Whigs and Liberals 1830–1852* (Oxford, 1990); Peter Gray, *Famine, Land and Politics: British Government and Irish Society 1843–50* (Dublin, 1999), pp 17–22. For the case that Mulgrave's policy embodied the spirit of Charles James Fox's aspirations, see [Edward Berwick], 'Lord Mulgrave's speech on the state of Ireland', *Edinburgh Review*, 66 (Jan. 1838), pp 457–8.

8 O'Connell to Duncannon, 28 Apr. 1835, West Sussex Record Office, Chichester (hereafter

WSRO), Bessborough Papers, F.201; O'Connell to FitzPatrick, 21 Apr. 1835, O'Connell to Ellice, 11 May 1835, in M. R. O'Connell (ed.), *Correspondence of Daniel O'Connell* (7 vols, Dublin, 1972–80), v., pp 293–5, 303–6.

9 *Times*, 12 Oct. 1835, 14 Jan. 1837, Melbourne to Mulgrave, 10, 19 Oct. 1835, Mulgrave Castle, N. Yorkshire (hereafter MuC), Normanby Papers, MM/48–49; Russell to Melbourne, 24 Oct. 1835, Southampton University Library (hereafter SUL), Broadlands (Melbourne) Papers, MEL/RU/ 11/1–2; Anon., *A Letter to the Earl of Mulgrave, Lord Lieutenant of Ireland. By a Dissatisfied Country Gentleman* (Dublin, 1836); James H. Murphy, *Abject Loyalty: Nationalism and Monarchy in Ireland during the Reign of Queen Victoria* (Washington DC, 2001), pp 14, 22–3.

10 The epithet 'O'Mulgrave' was heavily employed in satirical commentary on the viceroy's relations with O'Connell, see *The Age*, 17, 24 May 1835, etc.

11 O'Connell to Bessborough, 30 Nov. 1834, WSRO, Bessborough Papers, F.201.

12 For a study of John Doyle's satirical swipes on the Whig-O'Connell entente (as 'HB'), which frequently depicted Mulgrave as the dupe or flunky of the self-promoting Irish leader, see J. N. McCord, 'The image in England', in M. R. O'Connell (ed.), *Daniel O'Connell: Political Pioneer* (Dublin, 1991), pp 57–71.

13 O'Connell to Duncannon, 26, 30 Nov., 17 Dec. 1834, WSRO, Bessborough Papers, F.201.

14 K. Theodore Hoppen, 'John William Ponsonby', in *Dictionary of Irish Biography* (hereafter *DIB*) [www.dib.cambridge.org/viewReadPage.do?articleId=a7416]

15 Richard Davenport-Hines, 'Constantine Henry Phipps, first marquess of Normanby', *Oxford Dictionary of National Biography* (hereafter *ODNB*) [www.oxforddnb.com/view/article/22187]

16 *Examiner*, 5 May 1832. Contrast the view of one reviewer that he was 'the Froissart of fashion' with Disraeli's snide critique, [Anon.], 'Living literary characters (No. IX): the earl of Mulgrave', *New Monthly Magazine*, 32 (July 1831), pp 249–53, [Benjamin Disraeli], 'Gallery of literary characters, no. LXVI. Earl of Mulgrave', *Fraser's Magazine*, 12 (Nov. 1835), pp 540–1.

17 *MC*, 7 Apr. 1832, *Times*, 4 Apr. 1835.

18 *FJ*, 5 Jan., 21 Feb. 1837.

19 Brian Jenkins, *Era of Emancipation: British Government of Ireland, 1812–1830* (Kingston and Montreal, 1988), pp 186–7; *Hansard*, 3, vol. 27, col. 151 (23 Mar. 1835)

20 *Dublin Evening Post*, cited in *Examiner*, 24 May 1835; see also ibid., 5 July 1835.

21 Henry Heaney (ed.), *A Scottish Whig in Ireland, 1835–1838: The Irish Journals of Robert Graham of Redgorton* (Dublin, 1999), p. 21.

22 Mulgrave to Russell, 15 Mar. 1836, The National Archives, Kew (hereafter TNA), Russell Papers, PRO30/22/2A, fols 207–303; *FJ*, 18 Mar. 1837. None of this was new in itself – Richmond had insisted on Irish-made regalia, Wellesley had shamrocks impressed on his livery buttons and had revived Bedford's innovation of celebrating St Patrick's Day, and Anglesey had ordered the playing of Irish airs on public occasions – the difference lay in the extent to which the Mulgraves succeeded in winning over and keeping mass public support in Ireland, Edward Brynn, *Crown and Castle: British Rule in Ireland 1800–30* (Dublin, 1978), pp 101–2, 106.

23 Robins, *Champagne and Silver Buckles*, p. 99; Brynn, *Crown and Castle*, p. 106.

24 John Ferguson McLennan, *Memoir of Thomas Drummond: Under-Secretary to the Lord Lieutenant of Ireland, 1835 to 1840* (Edinburgh, 1867); R. Barry O'Brien, *Thomas Drummond: Under-secretary in Ireland, 1835–40: Life and Letters* (London, 1889). See also M. A. G. Ó Tuathaigh, *Thomas Drummond and the Government of Ireland, 1835–41* (Dublin, 1978).

25 McLennan claimed that 'men like Mulgrave and Morpeth were incapable of feeling, even for a moment, the power of inward impulse to action which regulated Drummond's whole life', *Memoir*, p. 250. Interestingly, Drummond's portrait was still on public display in the public rooms of Áras an Uachtaráin (the former Viceregal Lodge) in 2009, a rare survival from the colonial era in an official building of the Republic of Ireland.

26 Russell saw Mulgrave's course as essentially that of giving real effect to the 1829 Catholic Relief Act, and 'destroying extreme parties by shewing them how well they are to be treated under a just Government', Russell to Mulgrave, 5 Aug. 1836, MuC, Normanby Papers, M/835.

27 W. F. Wakefield (ed.), *Addresses Presented to His Excellency the Earl of Mulgrave, from the Different Parts of Ireland, During the Years 1835 and 1836, with His Excellency's Answers* (Dublin, 1836), p. 3; *MC*, 23 May 1835.

28 *NW*, 1 Oct. 1835.

29 *NW*, 26 Oct. 1835. While the visit was largely stage-managed by Belfast's middle-class liberals, demotic support was expressed in several places, including at the viceregal couple's tour of the model damask factory at Ardoyne; a more hostile Protestant crowd hissed at them at Sandy Row, ibid., 29 Oct. 1835.

30 Wakefield (ed.), *Addresses*, pp 93–5, 215–16. This image was enhanced by the presence in the viceregal household of John Mulgrave, a freed slave, who died in Dublin Castle in 1838.

31 Brynn, *Crown and Castle*, p. 106.

32 Peter Gray, *The Making of the Irish Poor Law, 1815–43* (Manchester, 2009), pp 160–1.

33 *NW*, 2 Nov. 1835; *FJ*, 29 Aug. 1836; Wakefield (ed.), *Addresses*, p. 339–40, 351–6.

34 *Times*, 29 Aug. 1836.

35 Mulgrave to Russell, 11 Aug. 1836, TNA, Russell Papers PRO30/22/2B, fols 302–4.

36 *Dublin Evening Mail*, repr. in *Times*, 13 Sept. 1838.

37 *Examiner*, 8 Nov. 1835.

38 *Times*, 16 Aug. 1836.

39 *FJ*, 29 Aug. 1836.

40 [M. W. Savage], *Ireland under Lord Mulgrave* (2nd edn, London, 1837), p. 16.

41 Mulgrave to Melbourne, 15 Feb. 1837, Royal Archives, Windsor (hereafter RA) [microfilm], Melbourne Papers, 100/20; this was contested, see *Times*, 24 Dec. 1839.

42 Melbourne to Russell, 3 Feb. 1837, SUL, Broadlands (Melbourne) Papers, MEL/RU/303.

43 Anon., *The Female Angler. To which are added Earl Mulgrave's Welcome to Waterford* (Waterford, [1835]). For a more sedate poetic appreciation of Mulgrave, see Anon., *Farewell: Being a Poem, Commemorative of the Administration of the Noble the Marquis of Normanby in Ireland. By a Lady* (Dublin, 1839).

44 Wakefield (ed.), *Addresses*, pp 72–5, 85–6.

45 *Times*, 25 Jan. 1839.

46 See for example Russell to Mulgrave, 25 Nov. 1836, MuC, Normanby Papers, M/846.

47 For the religious breakdown of Irish appointments in 1835–6, see [Anon.], 'Ireland and her calumniators', *Dublin Review*, 2: 4 (Apr. 1837), p. 434.

48 See Mulgrave to Drummond, Oct. 1836, in O'Brien, *Drummond*, p. 237; Oliver MacDonagh, *The Emancipist: Daniel O'Connell, 1830–47* (London, 1989), pp 127–31.

49 *Hansard*, 3, vol. 39, col. 247 (27 Nov. 1837).

50 Drummond to the Tipperary magistrates, 22 May 1838, in O'Brien (ed.), *Drummond*, pp 276–87.

51 Normanby to Melbourne, 28 July 1838, RA, Melbourne Papers, 100/83; *Hansard*, 3, vol. 46, cols 974–1,012 (21 Mar. 1839). Normanby's promotion, part of the coronation honours of 1838, was in reward for remaining so long in the viceroyalty, Melbourne to Russell, 3, 4 June 1838, SUL, Broadlands (Melbourne) Papers, MEL/RU/492–3.

52 Normanby to Russell, 29 July 1838, TNA, Russell Papers, PRO30/22/3B, fols 230–5.

53 *NW*, 19 Feb., *Times*, 19 Feb., *Examiner*, 24 Feb. 1839.

54 Brynn, *Crown and Castle*, p. 108.

55 'HB' (John Doyle), 'A leaf out of Nicholas Nickleby with slight variations: Nicholas quits the company – theatrical emotion of Mr Vincent Crummles', cartoon published in London, 26 Mar. 1839.

56 Normanby to Russell, 6 Sept. 1838, TNA, Russell Papers, PRO30/22/3B, fols 273–9; Russell to Mulgrave, 17, 28 Oct. 1838, MuC, Normanby Papers, M/922, 923; Normanby to Melbourne, 12 Feb. 1839, RA, Melbourne Papers, 101/19; Tavistock to Ebrington, 28 Feb. 1839, Devon Record Office, Exeter (hereafter DRO), Fortescue Papers, 1262M/LI/17.

57 See for example the polite but rather guarded welcome in *FJ*, 2 Mar. 1839; for the entry, see *Belfast Newsletter*, 9 Apr. 1839.

58 Ebrington to Mulgrave, 29 Oct. 1835, Morpeth to Mulgrave, 30 Oct. 1835, MuC, Normanby Papers, M/156, 490, Ebrington to O'Connell, 9 Dec. 1838, DRO, Fortescue Papers, 1262M/FC/94.

59 *NW*, 5, 9 Mar. 1839; *Hansard*, 3, vol. 45, cols 1,144–62 (4 Mar. 1839)

60 Ebrington to Normanby, 13 Aug. 1839, MuC, Normanby Papers, V/159; O'Connell was again entertained at the viceregal lodge, Ebrington to Normanby, 10 Jan. 1840, ibid., V/166.

61 O'Connell to Ebrington, 3 Jan. 1839, DRO, Fortescue Papers, 1262M/LI/1; Ebrington to Russell, 8 Sept. 1839, TNA, Russell Papers, PRO 30/22/3D, fols 23–6.

62 Ebrington to Normanby, 8 Sept. 1840, DRO, Fortescue Papers, 1262M/LI/160; *FJ*, 12 June, 24 Sept., 13 Oct. 1840.

63 For this period, see Gray, *Famine, Land and Politics*, pp 142–51.

64 Ibid., pp 163–8.

65 *FJ*, 18, 21 May 1847.

66 Anon., *Notices of the Viceroyalty of the late Earl of Besborough* (Dublin, 1847). In death, as in life, the viceregal ritual was organised with due pomp and ceremony by the Ulster king at arms, *FJ*, 19 May 1847.

67 *Notices*, p. 7.

68 *FJ*, 22 May 1847.

69 *Times*, 24 May 1847.

70 Morpeth to Russell, 2 May 1847; Russell, Memo on the post of Irish viceroy [May 1847], TNA, Russell Papers, PRO30/22/6C, fols 211–12, 6H, fols 372–3.

71 James Loughlin, 'Allegiance and illusion: Queen Victoria's Irish visit of 1849', *History*, 87 (2002), pp 491–513.

72 For the 1850 Bill in its context, see Peter Gray, '"Ireland's last fetter struck off": the lord lieutenancy debate 1800–67', in Terence McDonough (ed.), *Was Ireland a Colony? Economics, Politics and Culture in Nineteenth-Century Ireland* (Dublin, 2005), pp 87–101.

73 Murphy, *Abject Loyalty*, pp 20–31.

74 *NW*, 25 July 1837.

75 Gary Owens, 'Visualising the Liberator: self-fashioning, dramaturgy, and the construction of Daniel O'Connell', *Éire-Ireland*, 33–4 (1998), pp 103–30; 'Nationalism without words: symbolism and ritual behaviour in the Repeal "Monster Meetings" of 1843–5', in James S. Donnelly and Kerby A. Miller (eds), *Irish Popular Culture, 1650–1850* (Dublin, 1998), pp 242–70.

76 Russell to Normanby, 27 July 1838, TNA, Russell Papers, PRO30/22/3B, fols 215–16.

77 The Testimonial, which is part of the Castle Howard archives, is currently being conserved and interpreted at the National University of Ireland (hereafter NUI), Maynooth, see Patrick Cosgrove, 'The 1841 testimonial to Lord Morpeth: a remarkable new source for pre-Famine Ireland', (unpublished paper, NUI Maynooth, 2010).

78 Carlisle spent much of his viceroyalty promoting schemes of 'improvement' in education, the arts and agricultural development. These themes dominate the commemorative volume edited by J. J. Gaskin, *The Vice Regal Speeches and Addresses, Lectures and Poems of the Late Earl of Carlisle* (Dublin, 1865).

79 [Thomas Moore], 'Ireland', *Monthly Chronicle*, 2 (1839), pp 31–9.

CHAPTER 9

The British Monarchy and the Irish Viceroyalty: Politics, Architecture and Place, 1870–1914

James Loughlin

As an institution ostensibly mirroring the monarchy in Britain the Irish viceroyalty inevitably suffered by comparison. During the nineteenth century the monarchy developed as the hegemonic institution embodying national identity on a plane above party politics, while the viceroyalty's regal pretensions were often a subject of ridicule, its appointees politically determined by the government of the day, and its practical utility repeatedly questioned.[1] Yet against the expectations of many it survived until the end of the Union in 1922, and in this period (1870–1914), it had rather more political significance towards the end than it had at the beginning. The fortunes of the viceroyalty were shaped by a range of separate, though interacting, factors – socio-economic, political and constitutional. This chapter, focusing on the royal-viceregal relationship, will attempt to account for the ways in which they did so.

I

1870 was a landmark year in Irish politics. It saw the formation of the Home Rule movement that would dominate nationalist politics up to 1914 and which, in the formulation of autonomy provided by its founder, Isaac Butt, both the monarchy and viceroyalty had central roles in identifying Ireland's place in the British state.[2] At the same time, and with opposite intent, Gladstone's first administration sought to secure the existing Union through combining substantive reforms to address 'real' Irish problems with a royal project intended to engage the royal family more closely with the Irish people.[3] That the viceregal office was occupied by Lord Spencer, a convinced believer in its role as a monarchical surrogate, was significant in this context. In their different ways, both Butt and Gladstone regarded Irish attitudes to the monarchy as reflective of the relative success of their policies. The difficulties they faced, however, were formidable.

The proliferation of royal statuary throughout Britain in this period – stimulated by Queen Victoria's decade-long mourning for Prince Albert – may have indexed the hegemonic place of the monarchy as a British national signifier, but its absence in Ireland was no less telling, and especially vexing to the queen.[4] Royal or viceregal monuments and residences were almost entirely confined to the greater Dublin area, the chief exception being the recently constructed Albert memorial in loyalist Belfast. That policy success would be reflected in a proliferation of royal monuments in nationalist Ireland was unlikely; nevertheless, this period would evidence a clear linkage between political and policy developments and attitudes to viceregal and monarchical structures and locations, reflecting the complexity of the relationship between the monarchy, the viceroyalty and popular opinion. The viceroyalty itself – an anomalous colonial institution in a region integrated into the British state – suggested ambiguity about Ireland's constitutional standing, while public use of the Phoenix Park, a royal park and the location of the Viceregal Lodge, was an issue that could easily suggest that Ireland had an apparently inferior constitutional status.

The royal parks had been substantially remodelled between 1832 and 1849 according to plans designed and implemented by the architect, Decimus Burton, for St James's and Regent's Parks in London.[5] The Phoenix Park remodelling was more extensive than the others: at 1752 acres, it was larger than Regent's Park, Hyde Park, Kensington Gardens, St James's Park, Greenwich and Battersea Parks all combined.[6] But while its remodelling reinforced a royal identity with its London counterparts, the import of that remodelling was quite distinctive; the transformation of a landscape characterised by indeterminate boundaries and hilly aspects into one smoothed and ordered, carried, in the Irish context, 'civilising' connotations that did not apply in Britain. Unlike in Britain, royal monuments and locations in Ireland were less affirmations of constitutional security than *assertions* of it – contested more than accepted. The visit of the Prince and Princess of Wales, Edward and Alexandra, to Ireland in 1871 provides an illustration.

The visit was promoted by Gladstone as a mechanism for articulating the popular loyalty to the throne he believed his government's reform programme was inculcating in Ireland. However, an amnesty campaign for the release of Fenian prisoners was in progress, while Gladstone's land legislation of 1870 had fallen well short of tenant expectations and agrarian conflict was continuing. In this unsettled environment, the presence of the royal party in the Viceregal Lodge at the same time that an illegal amnesty meeting in the park was being violently dispersed, created a controversy establishing negative associations between the royal visitors, the viceroyalty and the issue of public rights in the use of royal parks in London and Dublin. A peaceful meeting had been savagely attacked in the Phoenix Park, at a time when, as the Amnesty Association claimed, in London parks 'the socialist and the infidel may freely address assemblages'.[7] Even *The Times* asked: 'Is there one law for Britain and another for Ireland?'[8] The controversy occasioned a hasty and undignified departure by the royal party from Dublin with the consequent impression of failure. Thereafter, and for the rest of the decade, Ireland was spared major public controversies associated with either the monarchy or the viceroyalty, though there were recurring concerns in Dublin Castle about viceregal abolition. Outwardly, in fact, the viceroyalty could be perceived as following a parallel line of development to the Crown in Britain.

David Cannadine has remarked on the degree to which royal ceremonial became more refined and elaborate in the later nineteenth century under the direction of Lord Esher.[9] While the royal pretensions of the Dublin social 'season' could provoke mockery, a similar process was developing in Dublin with respect to viceregal ceremonial under the direction of the viceroyalty's own Lord Esher, Ireland's chief heraldic officer, Sir Bernard Burke.[10] But whereas the refinement and elaboration of royal ceremonial in Britain reflected the primacy of the monarchy as a national institution, in Ireland it merely served, as the agricultural depression of the late 1870s took hold, to disguise temporarily a fundamental alienation between the mass of the population and the Castle authorities.

II

Despite the establishment of the Home Rule movement in 1870, its progress throughout the decade was lacklustre; only on the back of the agricultural crisis and its exploitation by the cadre of young dynamic radicals led by Parnell was it able to prosper. Parnell's critique of British rule was comprehensive, covering the constitutionally symbolic no less than the administrative, as a countrywide agitation for tenant rent reductions got under way. From 1879 to 1886 the monarchy and the viceroyalty were targets of attack. In 1880 Parnell claimed that the queen had donated nothing to famine relief in the 1840s, while the viceroyalty was condemned more generally: historically, as an institution of British oppression; politically, for its security policies; and even for its attempts to alleviate rural distress – that is, welfare monarchism by viceregal proxy.[11] The nationalist critique also found an architectural focus in the buildings associated with British rule, especially the royal palace of Dublin Castle, a structural embodiment, as it were, of the iniquities of British rule.[12] Such attacks were part of a wider campaign of denigration, which included a nationalist boycott of the Castle, and its representation in visual propaganda as a structure devoid of architectural nobility befitting the centre of Irish coercion. In so far as nationalist propaganda presented a holistic view of Dublin Castle in the mid-1880s it was an image of its ground-plan imposed on a map of Ireland, signifying the Castle's oppression of the country.[13]

A morally informed structural critique also came easily to foreign sympathisers with Irish nationalism. The French socialist, Pascal Grousset, regarded the Castle as a 'stronghold . . . forming a sort of separate city entrenched within its fortifications', and argued that the way it 'seems to hide "its diminished head" under a little hillock in the central quarters' was indicative of 'why the name of *Dublin Castle* is for the Irish synonymous with despotism and oppression.'[14] In a similar vein, C. P. Trevelyan, an ADC to the Liberal viceroy, Lord Houghton in 1892, remarked that the figure of justice situated over the state entrance to the Upper Castle Yard was positioned looking inward on the yard, with '*her back turned to the Irish people*.'[15] Even the situational criticisms of a non-political commentator such as the novelist, George Moore, who described the Castle as arising 'like an upas tree [a corrupt influence] amid ruins and death'[16] – a reference to its location in a slum district – was easily interpreted as a metaphor for the administration's relationship with the mass of the Irish people. The Castle compared unfavourably with royal palaces in Britain, reflecting the inauthenticity of the viceroyalty's regal pretensions.

The American journalist, George Smalley, was amazed to find 'that this third-rate barracks should really be Dublin Castle' and that

> in these paltry circumstances . . . the state and splendour of a viceregal establishment . . . are kept up. From the moment you enter to the moment you quit the Castle you are never allowed to forget you breathe the atmosphere of a Court.[17]

It invoked comparison with Holyrood Palace in Edinburgh, but negatively: 'Holyrood is really a palace' Smalley observed.[18] The ease with which it was possible to invest the structure of the Castle with negative moral connotations was facilitated by its rather ad hoc architectural history. From the early years of the nineteenth century the Castle's lack of 'uniformity of plan, and . . . dignity of appearance' were apparent to visitors.[19] Certainly it compared poorly with the impressive classical frontage of the Bank of Ireland in College Green, the old Irish parliament building and a venerated site for constitutional nationalists. No such structural or environmental critique could be easily applied to the Phoenix Park; nevertheless, the murders in its grounds of Lord Frederick Cavendish, a newly appointed chief secretary and Thomas Burke, the under-secretary at Dublin Castle, on 6 May 1882, effectively reconfigured its identity imaginatively and practically as an atrocity site and another arena of conflict. It was undoubtedly the park's notoriety that chiefly attracted visitors in the immediate aftermath. Henceforth, viceregal ritual and ceremonial were tense and heavily – if discreetly – militarised affairs.[20] More importantly, the murders occasioned a series of security initiatives that served enormously to enhance the powers of the viceroy, Lord Spencer.

Spencer had been appointed to succeed Lord Cowper, but with a greatly empowered role, taking on many of the security responsibilities of the chief secretary as well as the symbolic regal role of the monarch's surrogate. The Phoenix Park murders, however, together with a sustained nationalist campaign of personal vilification, forced Spencer to use his emergency powers much more often than he had originally intended. He would come to believe that in so doing he had effectively compromised his role as the monarch's surrogate in Ireland, and, by extension, also compromised the monarchy's relationship with the Irish people.[21] This was precisely what nationalists had intended: their campaign against the 'castle system' was directed as much against its constitutionally symbolic aspects as its coercive powers, a theme reflected in the introduction of an abortive bill for viceregal abolition in 1883.[22]

By 1885 the divergence between the position of the monarchy in Britain and its surrogate in Ireland was vast. In the former, the nationally emblematic and non-political function of the Crown was a given, and architecturally reflected in the public status of Buckingham Palace as a royal residence, as against the Palace of Westminster, the centre of government and political conflict. In Dublin, however, no such structural separation of functions existed: the Castle housed both the constitutionally symbolic and administrative/coercive arms of the regime, mirroring the combination of the administrative/coercive and symbolic roles that Spencer had brought together from 1882, and lending colour to Parnellite claims that the constitutional freedoms taken for granted in Britain were being denied to Ireland.[23] This was not an entirely new development. It was implicitly evident in nationalist complaints about differential rights in the public use of royal parks in London and Dublin in 1871. But it had far greater import in the 1880s, registering common ground between Parnellites and British Liberals supporting the agitation for Home Rule.[24] Appropriately enough, the conflict between Spencer and the Parnellite movement came to a head in April 1885, when the Prince and Princess of Wales again visited Ireland.

Intended by Spencer to demonstrate Irish loyalty to the throne, and opposed aggressively by Parnellites as a piece of Castle manipulation to deceive British opinion about Ireland, this visit was noteworthy among Irish royal visits in the nineteenth century for the civil disorder it occasioned; and brought the Parnellite-administration antagonism to a climax which did not cease until the Liberal government left office two months later. When a Tory administration assumed office in June 1885 with intimations of conceding Home Rule, the nationalist attitude towards the personnel and institutions of the state adjusted accordingly. The Tory viceroy, Lord Carnarvon, was welcomed where Spencer had been vilified. This enthusiasm was short-lived, and was reversed when Gladstone declared for Home Rule in January 1886.

III

To repair the ill-will and alienation of the Spencer years, Gladstone appointed Lord Aberdeen as viceroy with a remit, effectively, to conciliate nationalists, aided by the vicereine, the formidable Lady Aberdeen. In the short period from February to August 1886 this was successfully accomplished. Thereafter, the viceroyalty as a constitutional office would escape the kind of criticism from nationalists it had faced in the first half of the 1880s.

Before 1886 the role of the viceroyalty was to defeat nationalist agitation by cultivating loyalty to the existing Union of Great Britain and Ireland. From 1886, for the Liberal Party and Parnellites, it was to be an institution that, under Home Rule, would function to harmonise Irish patriotism with a wider British and imperial patriotism, facilitated by removal of the ban on Roman Catholic occupants that had been introduced in 1829 as an accompaniment to the Emancipation Act. From 1886 the nationalist critique of the Castle administration focused primarily on the chief secretary, something made easy by the fact that the Unionist viceroys of the period 1886–92, Lords Londonderry and Zetland, were 'King Logs', restricted to viceregal ceremonial and charitable activities. Likewise, despite Queen Victoria's openly Unionist sentiments, Parnellites sought carefully to negotiate royal occasions and personages. Nevertheless, for other reasons, the viceroyalty retained its place in the Home Rule controversy.

Long-standing Tory arguments for the abolition of the office were given a contemporary focus when Gladstone's scheme emerged: abolition would either compel him to recreate the viceroyalty or reproduce a measure in which the separatist nature of his Home Rule scheme, hitherto concealed by the viceroyalty, would be fully exposed.[25] This was highly misleading. The defining statement of the Unionist case, A. V. Dicey's *England's Case Against Home Rule*, had emphatically argued the reverse, that a Dublin parliament's powers would be restricted to purely internal Irish affairs, otherwise the terms of the Act of Union would remain unchanged. In fact, in Gladstone's bill the powers of the viceregal office were so vaguely defined that an ill-disposed Westminster government could easily retain executive authority over Ireland without breaching the Home Rule act.[26] Only in the context of a British public largely ignorant of Ireland, and a Unionist mindset which regarded the existence of the viceroyalty a bar to a more complete union,[27] does their focus on the office make sense.

For most Unionists, abolition of the viceroyalty and its replacement by a royal residence was the preferred option, though it was also recognised that the symbolically contaminated Dublin Castle was unsuitable for the purpose.[28] But two factors inhibited action by Unionist governments. Firstly, there were complications involving legislative abolition and administrative reordering in a packed parliamentary session, together with ongoing Irish agrarian agitation; and, secondly, the resolute opposition of the queen to the proposal. Defeat at the general election of 1892 closed off the option for the immediate future.

IV

Gladstone's return to office shifted attention away from debate about the existence of the viceroyalty to how it might best be used to further the Home Rule cause, but without significant effect. A concern to address the increasingly formidable Ulster problem motivated the appointment of Lord Houghton to the office. Seen as more politically 'centrist' than Aberdeen had been in 1886, Houghton, however, turned out to be rather too remote, 'too kingly,'[29] while being widowed, he lacked a vicereine to assist in the kind of welfarist activities associated with his office. His appointment merely disconcerted nationalists, for whom Lord Aberdeen had set the ideal standard of viceregal behaviour, without any compensating effect on Unionist opinion.[30] Accordingly, Dublin Castle, despite being a royal site, remained ostracised by nationalists, while despite Houghton's efforts, the Unionist communities, north and south, maintained their distance. Only with the return of a Unionist administration in 1895, committed to conciliation, was the viceroyalty to make a significant impact on popular opinion.

V

The first phase of Unionist conciliation in 1886–92 had been complicated by widespread agrarian strife, the need for stringent coercion measures, a Gladstonian campaign for Home Rule and a hegemonic nationalist movement. The absence of all these factors by 1895 provided an ideal context for the exercise of viceregal, and indeed, royal conciliation. Between 1895 and 1905, the duke of York (the future George V), Queen Victoria and Edward VII all made successful Irish visits.

The Parnellite split of 1890 had led to a fracturing and factionalising of constitutional nationalism and the apparent collapse of the Home Rule campaign in Ireland. Certainly following the defeat of the second Home Rule bill in1893 there was little evidence of popular enthusiasm for self-government, something that remained of concern to nationalist leaders well into the Edwardian period. At the same time, in the late 1890s, conciliation was enthusiastically driven by Gerald Balfour, a chief secretary who assumed office at the same time as the viceroy, Lord Cadogan.

At first sight it is easy to dismiss Cadogan as an intellectually challenged political lightweight. His own son described him as 'not of nimble mind.'[31] Nevertheless, while no intellectual, Cadogan combined meticulous attention to detail and routine with a willingness to engage with all sections of the community.[32] Conscious of his dual role as government appointee and royal surrogate, Cadogan adopted a flexible combination of regal formality and personal familiarity – 'as from man to man' – as each situation seemed to require, thereby doing much to conciliate moderate nationalist and Unionist opinion. Certainly Cadogan's practice as viceroy struck a more responsive public chord than that of his stiffly aloof Home Rule predecessor. Acting in accordance with the government's conciliation policy, Cadogan sought to appoint and promote eminent Catholics, such as the intellectually formidable Archbishop Walsh of Dublin to the public administration.[33] Moreover, controversially for a Unionist viceroy, Cadogan was a vocal advocate for a Roman Catholic university in Ireland.[34]

Cadogan's cultivation of the hierarchy was astute, sensing rightly that the church – the central institution of the Catholic community – was not, as such, committed to Home Rule. After five years of conciliation W. B. Yeats could conclude that government reformism had so diminished 'misrule' that without the advent of a major war, nationalism would have to be refounded on a new basis with the Irish language as its lever.[35] It was a context that allowed Cadogan to maximise the effect of his ceremonial and organisational skills. These found an appropriate focus during the celebrations for Queen Victoria's diamond jubilee on Jubilee Day, 21 June 1897, the Irish highlight of which was a visit by the duke and duchess of York.

The occasion would ensure an intensity of British media attention, with jubilee and royal ceremonial offering seductive and inevitably distorting prisms through which to assess the extent of Ireland's integration into the British state. Royal occasions always had this dimension, but arguably, against a favourable political background, the 1897 events were more persuasive, while the substantial Protestant population of the greater Dublin area – the dominant element in the city's business community – could be relied upon to ensure that the primary site of royal ceremonial and celebration, Dublin city centre, would produce the popular manifestation of loyalty appropriate to royal occasions.

Cadogan took account of the jubilee events, both in terms of approval and protest, in making preparations for the duke's visit a week later. The scene setting had been in train since the beginning of the year, with care taken to ensure cross-community involvement.[36] Cadogan also made known the duke's refusal of an address from the Orange Order.[37] Recent Irish royal visits had been negatively influenced, both in terms of route and scale, by the controversial visit of 1885. By 1897, however, political conditions had been so transformed that a countrywide tour was now envisaged with Dublin as its starting point. A centrepiece of the visit was the inauguration of the duke as a knight of the Most Illustrious Order of St Patrick, while an exhibition of Irish manufactures that Cadogan had initiated earlier in the year provided a suitable occasion for royal engagement when the duke performed the official opening.[38] In sum, the visit was highly successful and occasioned effusive testimony of Irish loyalty to the queen.[39]

And yet the visit, though it can be seen as an effective riposte to republican protesters, was nevertheless conditioned in some respects by their activities. While the state entry to Dublin and public duties in the city went off well, they were apparently conducted with rather less display and pomp than was usually associated with great state occasions; and during the visit Cadogan frequently referred to the duke, not as a royal personage and likely future king of Ireland, but merely as a 'tourist', a stranger travelling to see the country. It was a ploy to deter hostility by framing the occasion as personal, rather than constitutional, in character. Republicans, not unreasonably, thought the practice remarkable and an inhibiting effect of their protests.[40]

Arguably, Cadogan's presentation of the duke as merely a tourist reduced royal ritual and ceremonial to mere non-signifying public entertainment. Nevertheless, the visit had quite substantive results. As the first Irish visit by the duke as an adult, it clearly made a very favourable personal impression, and can reasonably be regarded as a significant influence determining his later attitude to Ireland as king – which was decidedly conciliatory during the troubled period from 1910 to 1922. More immediately, it convinced him that an Irish royal residence was necessary to cultivate the apparent loyalty already existing. But while the queen remained opposed to the proposal, the success of this visit and the encouragement of the duke of York that followed from it, were important factors influencing her decision to visit Ireland in April 1900.

In organising this occasion Cadogan faced a greater challenge than in 1897, coming as it did during the South African War, a subject on which there was significant division, not to say inconsistent attitudes, among constitutional nationalists, while republican groups could again be relied upon to attempt disruption. But with 1897 as a precedent, Cadogan responded energetically. He established a clampdown on the city, threatening tradespeople who might be inclined to protest with withdrawal of their business licences if they did so; bill-posting organisations and the press were pressurised not to handle opposition material; while Arthur Griffith's *United Irishman*, which carried an article by Maud Gonne describing the monarch as the 'Famine Queen', was suppressed; anti-royal symbols were removed, while groups suspected of planning hostile demonstrations were closely watched. An attempt to hold an oppositional torchlight procession on the night of the queen's arrival was met with uncompromising police action strong enough to incur accusations of brutality and a subsequent official explanation.[41]

Cadogan, moreover, combined situational coercion with news management; that is, organised and privileged access to the Dublin press in reporting royal events, and, as he had in 1897 with the duke of York, the queen's visit was described as being of a personal rather than a state nature, perhaps more persuasive in her case given the ordinary non-regal attire she preferred in later life. Also, a Catholic clerical boycott of the visit was undercut – at least for propaganda purposes – when some Catholic peers persuaded the gullible Cardinal Logue, primate of all Ireland, to attend a Castle banquet on the misleading premise that the queen would thereby facilitate the establishment of a Catholic university. Furthermore, the public ritual surrounding the queen's official entry to the city, while it provoked municipal dissension, was to all intents and purposes effectively executed.[42]

As a test of Cadogan's organisational skills the queen's visit was a great success, but it was also the last occasion on which they would be applied. Cadogan was essentially a viceroy for settled times, and when a period of agrarian agitation took off in late 1901 he aligned himself overtly with the Irish Unionist community and its demands for a coercive response. This was at odds with an Irish administration emphasising conciliation and reform, especially the chief secretary, Gerald Balfour, whom Cadogan resented for having failed to keep him informed on Irish legislation. This situation worsened under Balfour's successor. George Wyndham voiced his exasperation at explaining Irish legislation to an uncomprehending Cadogan thus: 'like speaking through a megaphone with a pudding in its orifice.'[43] Cadogan resigned in August 1902. Despite his limitations he had made a significant contribution to the role of the viceroyalty.

In a period when royal ceremonial in Britain was becoming more sophisticated and carefully organised so as to maximise its public appeal, in the Irish context – a much more problematic one than Britain – Cadogan's ceremonial stage-management functioned to create the image of popular loyalty for an administration whose reformist policies still appeared capable of establishing the reality to match the appearance. Against a background of lacklustre or aloof viceroys – Londonderry, Zetland, Houghton – the Cadogan viceroyalty set the institution on a path of forward popular engagement that would run through to 1914.

VI

Cadogan's resignation came at a time when developments were in train that would facilitate a decided advance in the viceroyalty's conciliationist role. With the death of Queen Victoria in 1901 the negative association of the monarchy with the Great Famine was removed. Her successor, Edward VII, was widely, though wrongly, believed to be supportive of Home Rule, and gave colour to the belief by consistently cultivating Irish goodwill. His reaction to the death of Pope Leo XIII in July 1903, just as his coronation visit to Ireland was beginning, was a masterclass in sympathetic engagement. The king, moreover, was wholly in sympathy with the enthusiastic reformism of Cadogan's successor.

Lord Dudley was one of the richest men in England, well equipped to carry the expenses of his office, and was so impressed by the popular enthusiasm attending his official entry to Dublin that he began immediately to consider how to improve Irish conditions, according to 'Irish ideas'.[44] It was a policy informed by an appreciation of contemporary Irish 'needs and aspirations and . . . the complex traditions of their past history',[45] and wholly in sympathy with the equally reformist chief secretary, George Wyndham. Wyndham had made known publicly his direct lineage from Lord Edward Fitzgerald, a leader of the United Irishmen, and had appointed the Catholic Sir Anthony McDonnell undersecretary at Dublin Castle, but with considerably more freedom of action than usually attended the position: 'more a colleague than a mere Undersecretary'.[46] Wyndham believed that there was now a 'more favourable opportunity [for the state] in Ireland [than] in a century.'[47] Certainly for the first time in this period government reformism was firmly underpinned by a royal-viceregal nexus of monarch, viceroy and chief secretary, the latter's position strengthened by a seat in cabinet.

In fact, although a Unionist-appointed viceroy, Dudley's early policy speeches were – in their concern to act in accordance with Irish national traditions – virtually at one with Gladstone's conception of the viceroyalty as the agency through which Irish patriotism and that of loyalty to the British state would be harmonised under Home Rule. The administration at Dublin Castle thus took on a decidedly pro-national, if not nationalist, hue. During the Dudley viceroyalty the land issue would be effectively settled by the Wyndham Act of 1903, while the conference of landlords and tenant representatives on which the act was based was also the basis of the ill-fated devolution bill of 1904–5. It was a measure of limited administrative, as opposed to legislative, reform, but raised a howl of protest from Ulster Unionists and Tory backbenchers.

Ulster Unionists in particular never warmed to Dudley's brand of conciliation, while there were also concerns about a king given the nickname 'Popish Ned' in the north.[48] That a moving figure in the devolution proposal was the Catholic McDonnell reinforced their anxieties. Edward Carson, indeed, was to claim that Dudley had actually expressed to him a desire to have Ireland governed through the agency of the Catholic Church, a claim Dudley denied and which led to a correspondence of accusation and denial in the press.[49] Their concerns were reflected in the creation of the Ulster Unionist Council (1905). However, while the devolution controversy damaged the reform process – McDonnell's claim that he had the tacit approval of Wyndham for his actions led to the latter's resignation[50] – the influence of the king ensured that Wyndham was the only casualty. There is no evidence that Edward VII opposed the devolution proposal and he effectively prevented Dudley's removal from Ireland.[51] What the anti-devolutionists gained, however, was the appointment of an anti-reformist chief secretary: Walter Long was appointed primarily to appease Ulster Unionist concerns about the 'nationalist' viceroy, Dudley, whose private secretary, Walter Callan, was the son of a well-known nationalist MP.[52] The consequence was a period of intra-administration conflict, as Long's coercive tendencies – supported by Edward Carson – met fierce resistance from Dudley, thereby putting the issue of the relative primacy of the offices of viceroy and chief secretary in contention.[53]

To the Ulster Unionist mindset Dudley had veered too closely towards nationalist sympathies. But while it is highly unlikely that Dudley expressed himself in favour of Romanist government in the way that Carson claimed, it was, nevertheless, the case that his speeches evidenced a concern to appeal chiefly to Ireland's Catholic and nationalist community, something which might have obscured his commitment to the existing Union of Britain and Ireland.[54] Moreover, the nationalist response to Dudley's speeches on governing according to Irish ideas would have reinforced Unionist anxieties. A political cartoon in the *Weekly Freeman* depicting Dudley waving the flag of 'Governing Ireland according to Irish Ideas' at Edward Carson, represented as the 'Bull of Orangeism',[55] reflected the widespread popular currency of the belief that the viceroy was supportive of Home Rule. Certainly for John Redmond, governing according to Irish ideas meant 'Home Rule, and . . . so [Dudley's speeches] were interpreted in Ireland.'[56] This was undoubtedly the case, in Ulster no less than the south and west. The devolution proposal of 1904–5 may have provoked some nationalists, concerned about its implications for the achievement of Home Rule, to remind the viceroy of the unrepresentative nature of the viceregal system.[57] But this was an indictment of the system in general and not Dudley as an individual. Moreover, having little time for religious bigotry and extremism, Dudley's repugnance found expression in a vehement condemnation of Carson's rhetorical 'violence': Carson levied 'blows as heavy and as effective [at the Union] as any as could be dealt to it by its avowed enemies.'[58] Nor did Dudley hesitate to venture north, reminding his loyalist audiences of the supposed common love of Ireland they shared with the island's Catholics and warning them against 'narrowness'.[59]

Given the zero-sum outlook of northern Unionism, Dudley's Ulster speeches were, to say the least, too lacking in nuance to have local appeal. They also arguably reflected the traditional mindset of Dublin administrations on the north; namely, that however much Unionists might complain, their support for the Union could be taken for granted, and that the primary task was to cultivate the loyalty of the Catholic and nationalist community. Certainly, despite the coercionist disposition of Walter Long, the combination of an evidently well-disposed monarch and viceroy, together with substantive reforms and progressive intentions, functioned to maintain the conciliationist identity of the viceroyalty, while facilitating a corresponding shift in nationalist attitudes.

From January 1905, for example, John Redmond's attacks on Dublin Castle tended to focus less on the history of British oppression than on a system of government whose main failings were lack of democratic accountability, inefficiency and extravagance. Quoting Lord Dunraven, Redmond told the Commons: the Castle system 'was not democratic, [but] it was not despotic, [and] it was not an oligarchy', though certainly not a suitable system of government in a democratic age.[60]

VII

The change of government at the general election of 1905 was a political landmark. The Liberal administration of Henry Campbell-Bannerman was elected on a landslide, with a legislative programme determined by British imperatives. It thus had no need of nationalist support and no necessity to move immediately on the difficult Home Rule issue. Nevertheless, a credible signifier of good faith on Home Rule was needed for nationalists, and this was provided by Lord Aberdeen's return to the viceroyalty. But Aberdeen was also important now in the Ulster context.

As a Scots Presbyterian he was, arguably, better placed to appeal to northern loyalists than his Liberal predecessor, Houghton, had been. Certainly he sought to assuage the northern Presbyterian sense of being discriminated against by the Anglican establishment by appointing Presbyterians to his household.[61] Aberdeen also made a point of including Ulster as an essential dimension of his viceregal tours. At the same time, the mutual goodwill between the viceroy and the nationalist people was underpinned by a wide range of reforms. At least fifty-seven substantial pieces of Irish legislation were implemented during his term of office – especially on land and the university question – mainly under the direction of Augustine Birrell, the chief secretary, who was viewed as the nationalist voice in the cabinet.[62]

The British-Irish amity Aberdeen and Birrell facilitated was reflected in the unproblematic inauguration of a controversial statue of Queen Victoria on Leinster Lawn in 1908, and more especially in changing popular perceptions of Dublin Castle. Justin McCarthy memorably described the Castle as a structure that 'may be taken as the architectural emblem of England's rule over Ireland', or 'a local and comical version of the Athenian Acropolis or the Pyramids of Egypt . . . It has in our present time lost, or voluntarily surrendered, much of its oppressive political power.'[63] In this context, it is worth noting that R. Barry O'Brien's indictment of the Irish administration, *Dublin Castle and the Irish People* – which was facilitated by access to the Castle and its personnel[64] – was overwhelmingly historical in its citations of oppression, finding in religious discrimination, from which Birrell and Aberdeen were absolved, the most significant contemporary example of popular grievance.[65] In fact, so important did Aberdeen and Birrell become for nationalists that during the third Home Rule crisis Redmond refused to countenance their removal from Dublin, fearing that this would be interpreted by Unionists as a serious weakening of the nationalist position.[66] Aberdeen remained in post despite a fraught relationship with King Edward VII, a consequence of the theft of the Irish Crown jewels in 1907, together with an embarrassing *faux pas* at the Dublin Exhibition of the same year, when the king moved to confer a knighthood on William Martin Murphy, the exhibition's main benefactor, who did not wish to receive it.[67] Nor initially, was Aberdeen's relationship after 1910 with George V much better. At the same time, Anglo-Irish harmony was not without complications for nationalists.

Keen as party leaders were to have Home Rule, popular attitudes did not quite match their commitment, something that had been a recurring problem since the early 1880s. When, during the controversy over the Irish Councils Bill of 1908, Redmond was taxed about party compliance with

Liberal inaction on Home Rule, he exclaimed: 'If Ireland does not choose to make the Irish question an urgent one by action in Ireland, in Parliament, and in England, then she herself is to blame.'[68] In the end, however, it was not Irish opinion that forced Home Rule on to the government's legislative agenda, but the outcome of the general elections of 1910, which left the Liberal Party dependent on nationalist support to remain in office.

VIII

Redmond's insistence on the introduction of a Home Rule bill would give a British constitutional crisis an Irish focus with an Ulster boiling point, as Unionists railed against nationalist dictation of government policy and rallied to 'loyal' Ulster's defence. Moreover, Unionists were baulked of a resolution of the constitutional crisis on their own terms with the accession to the throne of George V in 1910. The new king, though reluctantly, was supportive of the government's position on the constitutional issue, which saw the Lords' veto on Commons' legislation removed in favour of a suspensory power of two years, thus opening the way to Irish autonomy. Moreover, while Edward VII was personally opposed to Home Rule, George V accepted it and created a good impression with his Catholic subjects by refusing to open parliament until the deeply offensive anti-Catholic Declaration of Accession was changed. Accordingly, as preparations were in hand for George V's coronation visit to Ireland in July 1911 Irish opinion was in a receptive mood. Also, coincident with the political decontamination of Dublin Castle, the complex underwent substantial renovations, especially to its sanitary and drainage system.[69] It was thus now a fitting royal residence for the duration of a visit that was both the last to Ireland by a British monarch under the Union, and also arguably the most successful.

IX

The royal visit of 1911 offers a useful standpoint from which to assess the development of the viceroyalty from the later 1870s. Then, the contrast between the position of the monarchy in Britain and its surrogate in Ireland was stark: the monarchy was an institution emblematising the nation, with Buckingham Palace an architectural statement of the monarchy's place above party politics; the viceroyalty, in contrast, was symbolic of state coercion, alienated from nationalist opinion, with Dublin Castle a negative architectural and situational signifier. The coronation visit of 1911, however, registered the dramatic changes that had occurred since then; the product of an autonomy campaign which Parnell had prioritised from 1882 and which climaxed in Gladstone's Home Rule plan of 1886, and with its successor apparently soon to be implemented; the enthusiastic conciliation of both Unionist and Liberal appointed viceroys – together with the substantive reforms that underpinned that conciliation; and, not least, changes in the attitude of British monarchs towards Ireland, away from the trenchant Unionism of Queen Victoria to the objective facilitation of government policy that characterised George V. When he adopted Dublin Castle as the residence for his coronation visit in 1911 the king was less asserting the Castle's status as a royal palace than confirming it.

The period from 1911 to the outbreak of the Great War included developments that were far from congenial to nationalists, especially compromises on Ulster they never expected having to make, but the standing of the viceroyalty was largely unaffected. As an institution it was politically sidelined as the Home Rule crisis required the attention of the prime minister, while the nationalist relationship with the Crown was actually strengthened as the king's attempts to facilitate a settlement brought Redmond into personal contact with him, thereby enhancing the nationalist leader's already strong imperial allegiance. The outbreak of hostilities saw Redmond wholeheartedly commit Ireland to the British war effort, while Dublin Castle's identity was transformed: it was refitted as a military hospital with the support of the king, the Castle administration and the nationalist-controlled city corporation. A complete harmonisation of formerly antagonistic interests had apparently been achieved.

This, of course, would not last. The war brought developments that transformed the Irish political landscape, resulting in partition and also a far greater degree of national independence than was envisaged under Home Rule. Dublin Castle, nevertheless, retained its symbolic function. Just three days after the Dáil voted to support the Anglo-Irish Treaty in early January 1922, the Castle civil servant, Mark Sturgis, noted: it made 'a good propaganda appearance with its gates standing open for the first time for at least two years and soldiers busy removing barbed wire.'[70]

Notes

1 The monarchy as an institution embodying national identity is definitively stated in Walter Bagehot, *The English Constitution*, ed. Richard Crossman (1867/London, 1971). For ridicule of the regal pretensions of the viceroyalty by officeholders, see Angus Hawkins and John Powell (eds), *The Journal of John Wodehouse First Earl of Kimberley* (Cambridge, 1997), p. 144; Countess Cowper, *Earl Cowper KG: A Memoir* (London, 1913), p. 363; and for a more general account: A Native, *Memories of Dublin Castle and Dublin Society* (London, 1903).

2 Isaac Butt, *Irish Federalism! Its Meaning, Its Objects and Its Hopes* (Dublin, 1870), pp 27, 30, 54–55, 59, 67, 70.

3 For coverage of this subject see James Loughlin, *The British Monarchy and Ireland: 1800 to the Present* (paperback edn, Cambridge, 2011), chs 6 and 7.

4 Elizabeth Darby and Nicola Smith, *The Cult of the Prince Consort* (New Haven and London, 1983); David Duff, *Victoria Travels: Journeys of Queen Victoria between 1830 and 1900* (London, 1970), p. 187.

5 Dana Arnold, 'Trans-planting national cultures: the Phoenix Park Dublin (1832–49), an urban heterotopia?', in Dana Arnold (ed.), *Cultural Identities and the Aesthetics of Britishness* (Manchester, 2004), p. 171.

6 Maurice Craig, *Dublin 1660–1860: A Social and Architectural History* (Dublin, 1969), p.14.

7 Amnesty Association protest, reproduced in T. D. Sullivan, *Troubled Times in Irish Politics* (Dublin, 1905) p. 141.

8 *The Times*, cited ibid., p. 142.

9 David Cannadine, 'The context, performance and meaning of ritual: the British monarchy and the "invention of tradition" c.1820–1977', in Eric Hobsbawm and Terence Ranger (eds), *The Invention of Tradition* (Cambridge, 1983), pp 101–64.

10 The viceroyalty was savagely ridiculed by Thackeray: 'The Irish sketchbook [1843]' in W. M. Thackeray, *Sketchbooks* (London, 1902), pp 577–8; Susan Hood, *Royal Roots – Republican Inheritance: The Survival of the Office of Arms* (Dublin, 2002), pp 18–19.

11 For his references to the Queen and the Famine, see Parnell to the editor, *New York Herald*, 1 Feb. 1880 in P. J. Tynan, *The Irish National Invincibles and their Times* (London, 1894), pp 147–8. The term 'welfare monarchism' has been coined by Frank Prochaska (*Royal Bounty: The Making of a Welfare Monarchy* (New Haven and London, 1995) to denote how the British monarchy compensated for its loss of political power with a great increase in its social influence through a vast extension of charitable activities. Welfare monarchism was also a traditional feature of viceregal activities.

12 *The Nation*, 2 Jan. 1886.

13 'Under the rod', political cartoon in *Weekly Freeman*, 10 May 1884.

14 Pascal Grousset, *Ireland's Disease: The English in Ireland 1887*, Intro., Constance Connor (1888/ Belfast, 1986), p. 15.

15 Cited in A. J. A. Morris, *C. P. Trevelyan: Portrait of a Radical 1874–1958* (Belfast, 1977), p.14.

16 George Moore, *Parnell and His Island* (London, 1887), p. 20.

17 George Smalley, *London Letters* (2 vols, London, 1890), ii, pp 140–1.

18 Ibid., p. 144. The same negative comparison also occurred to Grousset, *Ireland's Disease*, p. 14.

19 Cited in Constantia Maxwell, *Dublin under the Georges 1714–1830* (London, 1956), p. 305.

20 See for example, Julia Roundell, 'From a diary at Dublin Castle during the Phoenix Park trial', *Fortnightly Review*, 60, no. 356 (Oct. 1906), pp 559–66; Elizabeth Countess of Fingall, *Seventy Years Young* (New York, 1939), pp 126–7.

21 See James Loughlin, 'Nationality and loyality: Parnellism, monarchy and the construction of Irish national identity 1880–1885', in D. G. Boyce and Alan O'Day (eds), *Ireland in Transition 1867–1925* (London, 2004), ch. 2.

22 See Justin McCarthy in *Hansard*, 3rd series, vol. 280, cols 1,076–83 (20 June 1883). Its defenders tended to be anti-Parnellite nationalists concerned about the movement's apparently socially destabilising effects. See Loughlin, *British Monarchy and Ireland*, ch. 8.

23 For graphic evidence, see the political cartoons 'Lev(ee)ying loyalty at the cawstle', *Pat*, 10 Feb. 1883; 'An old story re-told', *Weekly Freeman*, 10 Jan. 1885.

24 For a penetrating study of the values shared by Liberals and nationalists, see Eugenio Biagini, *British Democracy and Irish Nationalism 1876–1906* (Cambridge, 2007), passim.

25 St Loe Strachey, 'Shall we abolish the lord lieutenant?', *National Review*, 2 (Aug. 1888), pp 788–91.

26 A.V. Dicey, *England's Case against Home Rule* (London, 1886), p. 32; J. H. Morgan, 'The constitution: a commentary', in J. H. Morgan (ed.), *The New Irish Constitution: An Exposition and Some Arguments* (London, 1912), pp 32–3; Loughlin, *British Monarchy and Ireland*, pp 207–9.

27 House of Lords debate, *The Times*, 5 Jan. 1886; Lord Charles Beresford in *The Times*, 24 July 1897; *Memoirs of Admiral Lord Charles Beresford* (London, 1914), pp 412–14; Michael McDonnell, *Ireland and the Home Rule Movement* (Dublin, 1908), p. 6.

28 Strachey, 'Shall we abolish the Lord Lieutenant?', pp 788–91; St Loe Strachey, 'A royal residence for Ireland', *National Review*, 25 (Aug. 1895), pp 746–9.

29 Entry (17 Dec. 1892), Horace G. Hutchinson (ed.), *Private Diaries of Sir Algernon West* (London, 1922) p. 93.

30 Healy to the chief secretary, John Morley, 14 Sept. 1892, in T. M. Healy, *Letters and Leaders of My Day* (London, 1928), ii, p. 383; Parnell at Edinburgh, *The Times*, 22 July 1889; also *Nation*, 18 May 1889.

31 Sir Edward Cadogan, *Before the Deluge: Memoirs and Reflections 1880–1914* (London, 1961), p. 4.

32 Ibid., pp 4–5.

33 Walsh was appointed to at least two viceregal commissions, one on Manual and Practical Instruction in Primary Schools (1897); another on intermediate education (1899): M. J. F. McCarthy, *Five Years in Ireland 1895–1900* (London/Dublin, 1901), pp 245, 131. On Cadogan's enthusiasm for promoting eminent Catholic lawyers to the High Court Bench, see Sir John Ross, *Pilgrim Script* (London, 1927), pp 122–3.

34 McCarthy, *Five Years in Ireland*, pp 244–5, 398–9, 430.

35 See Warwick J. Gould et al. (eds), *The Collected Letters of W. B. Yeats, 1896–1900* (Oxford, 1997), ii, pp 562–3.

36 McCarthy, *Five Years in Ireland*, pp 244–6.

37 *Freeman's Journal* report in *Derry Journal*, 27 Aug. 1897.

38 *Derry Journal*, 30 Aug. 1897; McCarthy, *Five Years in Ireland*, pp 260–2.

39 Loughlin, *British Monarchy and Ireland*, p. 246.

40 On visit ceremonial, see *Derry Journal*, 20 Aug. 1897, and the republican response to Cadogan's description of the duke in *Shan Van Vocht*, 6 Sept. 1897.

41 Terence Denman, 'The campaign against army recruitment in Ireland', *Irish Historical Studies*, 29 (1994), pp 214–17; Loughlin, *British Monarchy and Ireland*, pp 250–1.

42 Ibid., pp 253–5.

43 Wyndham to Arthur Balfour, 20 Sept. 1901 in Elizabeth Muenger, *The British Military Dilemma in Ireland: Occupation Politics 1886–1914* (Lawrence, Kansas, 1991), p. 65.

44 Reply to address from Dublin Chamber of Commerce in Earl of Dudley, *Milestones on an Irish Journey: Some Speeches Delivered by the Earl of Dudley during His Vice-Royalty in Ireland* (Privately published, n. l., n. d. [1907]), p. 7. A copy is held in the National Library of Ireland (hereafter NLI).

45 Speech in reply to toast of 'The Lord Lieutenant and prosperity to Ireland', at the annual dinner of the Incorporated Law Society of Ireland, 20 Nov. 1902, in ibid., pp 9–10; Dudley cited in M. F. J. McDonnell, *Ireland and the Home Rule Movement* (Dublin, 1908),p. 158.

46 Ibid., p. 157.

47 Wyndham to Lord Knollys, 17 Feb. 1903, Royal Archives, Windsor, EDVII/W74/14. Material from the Royal Archives is used with the permission of Her Majesty Queen Elizabeth II.

48 Shane Leslie, *Long Shadows* (London, 1966), p. 130.

49 See Dudley-Carson correspondence, *Belfast Newsletter*, 19–20 Mar. 1906.

50 A. C. Hepburn, 'Devolution crisis', in S. J. Connolly (ed.), *The Oxford Companion to Irish History* (2nd edn, Oxford, 2002), p. 202.

51 Loughlin, *British Monarchy and Ireland*, pp 265–6.

52 Reginald Lucas, *Colonel Saunderson MP* (London, 1908), pp 334–6; McDonnell, *Ireland and the Home Rule Movement*, p. 159; Sir Henry Robinson, *Memories: Wise and Otherwise* (London, 1924), p. 149.

53 Dudley-Long correspondence, May–Aug. 1905, in Sir Charles Petrie, *Walter Long* (London, 1934), pp 89–90.

54 Dudley to Arthur Balfour, 7 Mar. 1905, in Muenger, *British Military Dilemma*, p. 66.

55 See 'The green flag to the bull', *Weekly Freeman*, 31 Mar. 1906.

56 Redmond in the Commons, 4 Feb. 1904 in John Redmond, *Home Rule Speeches*, ed. with introduction by R. Barry O'Brien (London, 1910), p. 159.

57 R. Barry O'Brien, *England's Title in Ireland: A Letter Addressed to His Excellency the Lord Lieutenant of Ireland* (London, 1905), pp 3–4.

58 Dudley quoted in McDonnell, *Ireland and the Home Rule Movement*, p. 161.

59 Dudley, *Milestones on an Irish Journey*, passim.

60 Redmond in the Commons, 19 Feb. 1906, in John Redmond, *Home Rule Speeches*, p. 181; also speech at Drumkeerin, County Leitrim, 27 Oct. 1907, in John Redmond, *Some Speeches on Home Rule* (Dublin, 1908), pp 58–60; John Redmond, *Irish Government: A Speech* (Dublin, 1907), pp 4–7; John Redmond, *Ireland's Financial Relations with England* ([Belfast], 1905), pp 4–5.

61 See J. R. B. McMinn (ed.), *Against the Tide: A Calendar of the Papers of Revd J. B. Armour, Irish Presbyterian Minister and Home Ruler 1869–1914* (Belfast, 1985), pp xxxiv, xlix.

62 Patricia Jalland, 'A liberal chief secretary and the Irish question: Augustine Birrell 1907–1914', *Historical Journal*, 16 (1976), pp 425–51.

63 Justin McCarthy, *Irish Recollections* (London, *n.d.*, [1909–10]), p. 155.

64 See preface in R. Barry O'Brien, *Dublin Castle and the Irish People* (2nd edn, London, 1912), p. vii.

65 Ibid. (1st edn, London, 1909), pp 78–80, 410.

66 Loughlin, *British Monarchy and Ireland*, p. 288.

67 Ibid., pp 272–3.

68 Redmond quoted in Denis Gwynn, *The Life of John Redmond* (Dublin, 1932), p. 156.

69 This was largely due to Lord Pirrie, a temporary convert to Home Rule: Lord and Lady Aberdeen, *More Cracks with 'We Twa'* (London, 1929), p. 144.

70 Michael Hopkinson (ed.), *The Last Years of Dublin Castle: The Mark Sturgis Diaries* (Dublin, 1999), p. 227 (10 Jan. 1922).

CHAPTER 10

Lady Microbe and the Kailyard Viceroy: The Aberdeen Viceroyalty, Welfare Monarchy, and the Politics of Philanthropy

Patrick Maume

The historian of philanthropy Frank Prochaska argues that as the political role of the British monarchy declined from the mid-nineteenth century, it found a new social role by increased patronage of charities. This 'welfare monarchy' remains central to its image as embodiment of shared national identity in familial terms.[1] This chapter suggests that in the late Victorian and Edwardian era a similar transformation of the lord lieutenancy was attempted and explores this thesis in relation to Lord and Lady Aberdeen. It expands on James Loughlin's discussion of the Aberdeens in relation to welfare monarchy by arguing that their version of the project drew on a specifically Scottish form of communitarianism embodied in the liberal-Presbyterian 'kailyard' mentality of the late nineteenth century, and by discussing how their separatist opponents sought to counteract their endeavours.[2]

By the later nineteenth century the lord lieutenant was politically eclipsed by the chief secretary (with a few exceptions, notably Lord Spencer's second viceregal term). Moreover, the lord lieutenant's status as quasi-monarch was impaired by his remaining a political appointee, leaving office with the government that appointed him. Some high-profile charitable activities of vicereines (such as the duchess of Marlborough's Famine Relief Committee in 1879–80,[3] or Lady Dudley's nursing scheme) suggest attempted reinterpretation of the viceroy as a 'welfare monarch', with the vicereine as stand-in for a maternally imagined Queen Victoria.

The longevity of the Aberdeen viceroyalties (1886, 1905–15), the extent of their philanthropic schemes, and their association with the Gladstonian project of incorporating Ireland into a wider British circle of reciprocal moral duty and sympathy by addressing genuine grievances – replacing an abstract, enforced and unloved union of laws by a spontaneous and mutually-felt union of hearts – make the Aberdeens the representatives par excellence of this approach. Indeed, their career in Ireland and other quasi-royal positions (such as the Lord High Commissionership to the General Assembly of the Church of Scotland and the Governor-Generalship of Canada), Lady Aberdeen's self-image as a sort of national mother, and the terms of the denunciations directed against her, replicate imagery associated with Queen Victoria.

The political and welfare activities of Lord and Lady Aberdeen also expressed the hopes and limitations of the 'kailyard' sensibility pervading late Victorian and Edwardian Scottish Liberal politics, and were open to some of the criticisms levelled against it: that its rural or semi-rural ambience ignored urbanisation and class differentiation, and that its flight from Calvinist rigour promoted a sentimental, anti-intellectual and conformist view of literature and society, censoring the avant-garde in the name of community standards and shunning exposes of the darker side of the idealised kailyard milieu.[4] Irish separatist denunciations of the Aberdeens were carried to absurd and unjust lengths, but they reflected wider critiques of the Gladstonian project as intended to fool the gullible Irish into believing the well being of Britain and of Ireland were compatible, and of proffering aristocratic philanthropy as a corrupting antithesis to republican virtue.

Nationalist politicians warned of 'killing home rule with kindness'; radical nationalists extended the critique to pro-Home Rule viceroys. Denouncing Aberdeen's second appointment as viceroy, Arthur Griffith complained:

> The business of the British Lord Lieutenant in Ireland . . . is to keep this country acquiescent in its plunder and oppression in return for £20,000 a year, taken out of our pockets, and the business of his wife is to act as a political souper. Lady Aberdeen's interest in our health, like Lady Dudley's interest in our nursing, Lady Cadogan's interest in our moral welfare, and Lady Londonderry's interest in our industries, are part of the game . . . when the Irish people are asked to regard as a philanthropist a foreign lady for whose board and lodging they are compelled to pay, we presume they may shrug their shoulders.[5]

Griffith and his associates drew on the traditional republican ideology of active citizenship, on awareness of the workings of the Dublin Castle patronage machine underlying Viceregal civic displays, and on miasmatist theories of disease as product of degraded environments rather than infection, to represent welfare monarchism as the ideology of a monstrous stepmother, exploiting while pretending to nurture and promoting dependency through jobbery and mystification.

I

Most accounts of the Aberdeens begin with Lady Aberdeen (née Ishbel Marjoribanks, 1857–1939), but the attractions of the kailyard mindset are best understood through the family background of her husband, John Campbell Gordon (1847–1934), seventh earl of Aberdeen. His grandfather, the long-serving foreign secretary George Gordon, fourth earl of Aberdeen (1784–1860), was haunted by the death of his first wife and their three daughters from tuberculosis, and by witnessing the Battle of Leipzig in 1813 as ambassador to Vienna. He was the only Victorian prime minister to see a battlefield at close quarters; this made his failure to prevent the Crimean War all the more bitter.[6]

His son, the fifth earl, was an evangelical of morbidly puritanical views (he disapproved of theatres and many childhood amusements); the future viceroy ascribed his lifelong detestation of coarse language to paternal admonitions when sent to public school.[7] His death in 1864, aged 47, may have been due to tuberculosis. John was his third son; the second son died in an accident (possibly suicide) in 1868, while the eldest, the sixth earl, abandoned his social position and emigrated to America, became a sea captain under an assumed name and drowned in 1870. Love of technical pursuits recurred in the family. The fifth earl insisted his children make their own toys, Aberdeen had a lifelong interest in railways, and his second son became an engineer.[8]

Aberdeen was subject to fits of depression; until the age of 48 he feared he would die at his father's age,[9] and he acquired a lifelong nervous twitch which led to the nickname 'Jumping Jack'. One recourse for this gloom was charitable work in the East End of London. Another was the friendship of Ishbel Marjoribanks, ten years his junior, the forceful daughter of a London banker, who acquired a romanticised image of her Scottish heritage from childhood holidays in the Highlands and later brought this fascination with the Gael to the west of Ireland.[10] This nostalgic image of paternal chieftains ruling over faithful retainers shared with the more lowland-oriented kailyard mentality a sentimentalised and evasive version of the Scottish Enlightenment preoccupation with the social bondings which combine with and meliorate rational self-interest in holding society together. Aberdeen discovered after some years that Ishbel wished to marry him and he believed he had a duty to comply. They married in 1877 and had five children of whom four survived to adulthood.

Ishbel admired Gladstone (cooperating in his rescue work with London prostitutes) and under her influence Aberdeen moved from lukewarm Toryism to calling Liberalism 'the Christianity of politics'.[11] In his later career Gladstone used their house on the north-western outskirts of London as his

London base. Gladstone appointed Aberdeen high commissioner to the General Assembly of the Church of Scotland (i.e. the monarch's representative) in 1881–5. The Aberdeens promoted reconciliation between the established Church of Scotland and the Free Church, which had seceded from it in 1843; they liked to recall that one of Aberdeen's ancestors was a Covenanting martyr while another was executed as a Cavalier, thus symbolising how time healed divisions.[12] Free Church representatives were invited to functions in connection with the General Assembly and the Aberdeens organised discussions on reunion.

The Aberdeens moved from evangelicalism to a more nebulous liberal Protestantism under the influence of the Free Church theologian Henry Drummond (1851–97), who maintained evolution was a divinely directed force working for the progressive betterment of humanity, to be attained through philanthropy amongst other things. Drummond cooperated with the Aberdeens' charitable endeavours, forming an intense emotional relationship with Ishbel which Aberdeen accepted placidly.[13] This theological liberalism was accompanied by artistic pursuits strict evangelicals would have shunned. Presbyterians traditionally disapproved of instrumental music in worship; Aberdeen developed an interest in pipe-organs and installed one in the estate chapel. The Aberdeens came to see theatre (particularly Henry Irving's Shakespeare productions) as a force for moral and educational uplift. Their fondness for collecting and publishing jokes (which they insisted should not be 'broad' and which later commentators found tedious),[14] reflected a belief that humour made the whole world akin, and provided therapy for Aberdeen's depressions.

The Aberdeens' cultural pursuits exemplify the mentality of the 'kailyard' literature popular in Scotland in the late nineteenth and early twentieth centuries, and subsequently denounced by Scottish Renaissance writers such as Hugh MacDiarmuid.[15] Kailyard literature was strongly associated with Liberal politics, nonconformist religion, and movement from strict scholastic Calvinism to a vaguer liberal Protestantism based on social benevolence. Leading kailyard authors were Presbyterian ministers such as S. R. Crockett and Ian McLaren; its chief promoter was the Aberdeenshire-born Free Church minister turned journalist William Robertson Nicoll (who encouraged the Aberdeens to write their memoirs).[16]

The kailyard portrayed Scotland in terms of rural and small-town communities (hence 'kailyard' or cabbage garden, from a poem by Burns) governed by tacit social norms based on common sense and undenominational Christian morality. Inequality and social hierarchy were acceptable if the upper classes remained in contact with their subordinates and thus open to human feelings prompting them to acknowledge obligations towards the less fortunate. This can be related to the Gladstonian image of the philanthropic duties required if the upper classes personally, and the state as a whole, were not to become self-seeking and corrupt, and the related Gladstonian concept of the inspired statesman appealing to the latent moral sense of the masses to provide a mandate for necessary reform.

The administration of the Aberdeens' estate was overseen by Ishbel, since Aberdeen had little business ability and she wished to shield him from stress.[17] They emphasised family traditions of enlightened landlordism, and boasted that they built many houses and increased the number of small-holdings rather than consolidating them. The estate was not very profitable, partly because of agricultural depression, and Aberdeen's heirs mourned the expense of Ishbel's charitable pursuits.[18] Ishbel's work with prostitutes made her aware that many were former domestic servants; the Aberdeens responded by trying to replace the periodic 'sprees' of farm and other servants on leave with supervised entertainments, and promoting their moral and practical education. They formed the 'Onward and Upward Club' among the servants at Haddo House, and were elected president and vice-president by a vote of the servants. The club developed into a nationwide association held together by a journal, also called *Onward and Upward* (assisted by advice from W. T. Stead), combining educational correspondence courses with edifying stories, household hints and jokes. This exemplified the Aberdeens' combination of self-promotion with an eye on the educative value of publicity. Though the club and magazine were genuinely popular, the Aberdeens' dealings with servants produced much comment and ridicule in high society.[19] They were sensitive to claims that J. M. Barrie's 1902 play *The Admirable Crichton* (where liberal aristocrats ostentatiously describe servants as equals but when wrecked on a desert island are humiliated when their butler takes charge) satirised them.[20]

The Aberdeens' work with prostitutes, and belief that self-control was inseparable from social reform, also inspired Aberdeen's lifelong connection with the National Vigilance Association (NVA), which campaigned for literary censorship; indeed, Aberdeen's last public address was a 1934 radio appeal for the NVA.[21] In 1911 an Irish Vigilance Association (modelled on the NVA) campaigned against allegedly indecent British popular newspapers, including destruction of newspapers at railway stations and pickets on newsagents. Although the IVA was overwhelmingly Catholic, Aberdeen led an official IVA delegation which lobbied for censorship legislation. The contemporary refusal of the Maunsell publishing house to publish James Joyce's *Dubliners* is generally attributed to Joyce's refusal to remove derogatory references to Queen Victoria and Edward VII, but Aberdeen's high-profile involvement with the IVA helped to make the publisher nervous.[22] Lucy McDiarmuid suggests that the way Aberdeen was outmanoeuvred in conversation with Lady Gregory about the 1909 Abbey premiere of Shaw's *The*

Shewing up of Blanco Posnett reflected his expectation of a shared sense of aristocratic propriety, but he may also have assumed that his own views about the moral and educational function of theatre were shared by everyone of goodwill.[23]

The Aberdeens first came to Ireland when he was appointed lord lieutenant by Gladstone in 1886. Aberdeen, who believed Home Rule necessary,[24] accepted without consulting Ishbel, whose general opinion of Ireland had been unfavourable. The previous Liberal viceroy, Lord Spencer, stuck rigidly to official etiquette and his vicereine rarely appeared in public (the Aberdeens' later comments gloss over the fact that this reflected fear of assassination). Ishbel appeared in the procession marking the viceregal entry into Dublin in an open carriage accompanied by her children, and staged a series of highly publicised events aimed at promoting Irish craft industries.[25] 'Whether by instinct or luck Ishbel . . . at once struck the newer, informal, practical tone that we now associate with royalty and its representatives', her daughter commented in 1952.[26] Aberdeen overcame the division between the viceroyalty and the lord mayor of Dublin as official representative of nationalism by attending a lord mayoral meeting for the relief of distress; he pledged a generous contribution and shook hands with Michael Davitt. Aberdeen's memoirs downplay the radicalism of this step by claiming Davitt was only imprisoned for speeches.[27] When Gladstone's administration fell, the Aberdeens' departure was accompanied by a great demonstration of popular sympathy.[28]

Thereafter Ishbel visited Ireland regularly to promote home industries, while Aberdeen appeared on platforms with prominent nationalists in Britain – symbolising national reconciliation. While their reception in Dublin had been a triumph, it was less unalloyed than they assumed. They were excluded from most administrative matters and from the drafting of the Home Rule bill by John Morley, who saw them as meddling in affairs which should be reserved for the chief secretary. When Gladstone returned to power in 1892, Morley insisted Aberdeen should not be reappointed, partly because he felt that their identification with nationalist Ireland would antagonise Irish Protestants. Gladstone told the Aberdeens, not entirely convincingly, that he felt he could not override the wishes of the responsible departmental minister; they were fobbed off with the Governor Generalship of Canada when it fell vacant in 1893.[29]

The Aberdeens' positive reception in 1886 also reflected orders from Parnell and his lieutenants. Arthur Griffith, a lifelong separatist who was fifteen in 1886, recalled this as a national humiliation:

> Twenty years ago the order was given to Ireland by its Parliamentarian leaders to abase itself beneath the lines of British bayonets and beneath the folds of the Union Jack, and the degradation of the 3rd of August, 1886 [Aberdeen's

ceremonial departure] followed. We remember that shameful day, and we remember his Excellency as he passed the Irish Parliament House, baring his head and dramatically saluting the silent Senate House, amid the frenzied cheers of the deluded Irish people.[30]

Such views were more widely expressed after the Parnell split led Parnellites as well as separatists to call the professed union of hearts a sham, pursuing power for the Liberals by gulling Irish nationalists with pretended benevolence. The Aberdeens' reception in 1886 had been shaped as much by the first wave of nationalist enthusiasm for Gladstone's conversion to Home Rule and by a prestigious and united nationalist leadership consciously seeking to make a good impression on British opinion, as by their own initiatives, however symbolically potent these might have been. When they returned, twenty years older, to the viceroyalty in 1905 it would be as representatives of a Liberal government conspicuously devoid of the Gladstonian enthusiasm for the Home Rule cause which they themselves still cherished. They now encountered a nationalist movement divided, no longer expecting imminent victory, and deeply influenced by the Parnellite view that the Gladstonian crusade, and the more half-hearted Irish commitments of Gladstone's Liberal ministerial successors, had been a cynical political dodge which had left Irish nationalism demoralised, divided, and weakened by jobbery.

Where the Aberdeens saw the Gladstonian project and their own philanthropic work as generously helping Ireland to help herself, separatists claimed it undermined self-respect by bribing recipients to compromise their inborn nationalism, like 'soupers' engaged in religious proselytism (who also called their activities philanthropy towards social inferiors).[31] In 1908 the Protestant separatist and former Parnellite Alice Milligan published a poem comparing Lady Aberdeen to the soul-buying demon merchants in Yeats' play *The Countess Cathleen* and recipients of her aid to the Biblical Esau selling his birthright.[32] This provoked an indignant protest from the secretary of Lady Aberdeen's anti-tuberculosis campaign (discussed later in this chapter).[33] Milligan's reply, as well as attributing Irish ill health to past and present British misgovernment, recalled the 1890s:

> [Some may] argue that it is . . . possible to meet Lady Aberdeen, the philanthropist, apart from the viceroy's wife and diplomat . . . Some fourteen years ago, I suffered from this delusion . . . Lady Aberdeen, whose husband then held no government office [although the Liberals were in power], was in Ireland on a tour of inspection of Irish industries . . . A district in Donegal had suffered the horrors of an eviction campaign . . . encouraged and stirred up largely by Liberal politicians [i.e. during the Plan of Campaign]. Many natives of Gweedore were in prison, others as evicted tenants were in rude huts on the

> hillsides, waiting for promised relief from the Liberals. I expected Lady Aberdeen the philanthropist would have steered straight to Gweedore to bring relief to the sufferers, but Lady Aberdeen, the diplomatist, found it necessary to confine her survey to a district where the Congested Districts Board had something to display for her edification, and where there were no evicted tenants. . . . Then . . . she all of a sudden was transformed from being a mere philanthropist, by the announcement that Lord Aberdeen had been appointed Viceroy of Canada. The lady who was innocently inspecting knitting in the Glenties store became thereupon a representative of British sovereignty, and as such was about to enter into the circle of Irish Irreconcilables in Chicago [staging an Irish industries exhibition at the World's Fair], a benefactor of Ireland, a messenger of peace . . . I saw a very fine piece of diplomacy was about to be enacted . . . and was never again found as a humble unit in the working of the diplomatic machinery.[34]

This reflects the core radical-nationalist critique of the Gladstonian project; what the Aberdeens saw as national reconciliation showing differences between Britain and Ireland were surmountable by goodwill, radical nationalists called corruption concealing insurmountable conflicts of interest.

In Canada, the Aberdeens similarly positioned themselves as bridging conflicts, holding viceregal functions in provincial capitals as well as Ontario cities, using French as well as English on state occasions, visiting churchmen and institutions of all denominations. Ishbel founded the Victorian Order of Nurses (working in remote rural areas) to mark Queen Victoria's jubilee and supplied reading matter to remote settlers.[35] These works, and unfortunate investments in the interests of two of Ishbel's brothers, further eroded the Aberdeens' finances by the time of their return to Britain in 1898.

Although the Aberdeens engaged in philanthropic activities for the rest of their lives (Ishbel, for instance, was president of the International Congress of Women 1893–9 and 1904–36), these were underpinned by Aberdeen's unawareness of their financial predicament and Ishbel's Gladstone-like belief that the Holy Spirit personally inspired her endeavours and might thus provide funds.[36] Inability to spend more than their official salary, as was expected of viceroys, gave their second viceregal term in 1905–15 a penny-pinched air, remarked on by unionists and by hostile nationalists.[37] This was seen by Griffith as mirroring continuing Irish decline under British rule: '"The Home Rule Viceroy" . . . returns to a country which has expended in the interim half-a-million of money on Parliamentarianism and received . . . an annual addition of several million-pounds in taxation, some new poorhouses, an additional service of emigrant ships, and cattle to graze where men and women lived.'[38]

The Aberdeens' second viceregal term began with an aristocratic boycott of the Viceregal Lodge, which the Aberdeens sought to remedy by attracting a wider range of middle-class invitees, who they expected to participate in their philanthropic campaigns. Even moderate nationalists such as Ishbel's correspondent Stephen Gwynn, however, avoided the Viceregal Lodge,[39] while Griffith suggested Aberdeen had been reappointed so belief in his personal probity would quieten Irish opposition to Liberal abandonment of Home Rule for more limited devolution.[40] 'Every mushroom society and eating and drinking club which will accept his presence can command a visit from the Liberal Lord Lieutenant', he asserted, 'The Irish jig has become fashionable at the Castle'.[41] In fact the Aberdeens showed flexibility in promoting Irish cultural revival as an equivalent to Balmoral tartanry. An Irish dancer denounced by Griffith for giving a display at the Castle explained that he had insisted 'God Save the King' should not be played and that no recognition of the Aberdeens' official position was involved; Griffith replied that the dancer should not give bad example.[42]

A 1906 viceregal tour of the country, addressing meetings and receiving addresses, was denounced as 'Aberdeenism . . . the Soft Soap policy'. Ishbel's remarks about emigration to Canada were noted with scorn, and Griffith imaginatively suggested cheers were supplied by pensioners, soldiers on leave for the occasion, and detectives in women's clothing.[43] 'Many people have speculated what the maintenance of a mock British King and a mock British Court in Ireland means', he added, 'It means corruption. The British Lord Lieutenant is maintained in Ireland as a fount for all that is slimy in our national life.'[44]

Lady Aberdeen emerged as the principal focus of criticism, because she was clearly the dominant partner, because her cultivation of loyal addresses and similar honours, despite its political implications, was presented as an act of personal courtesy towards a woman, and opposition to it as discourteous (similar claims about courtesy had been made by promoters of loyal addresses during Queen Victoria's 1900 visit). 'If any public body, class, or association in Ireland . . . desire to present addresses to ladies, there are a million ladies in Ireland . . . to whom to present them. When they have finished presenting addresses to the million, the case of Lady Aberdeen might be considered.'[45] One anonymous writer presented her as 'Lady Jellaby', luring gullible and snobbish females to drag long-suffering husbands to showy social events.[46] The fact that these occasions were accompanied by the usual methods employed to secure support for official displays and glossed over by the Aberdeens (such as threatening local councillors that charitable projects would be diverted elsewhere if they failed to show support),[47] was highlighted. Ishbel's imaginative use of modern publicity methods to promote her causes (such as the theatrical element in her use of Irish dress and the travelling wagon, drawn by a widely-renowned 'spotted horse' which publicised the anti-tuberculosis crusade which dominated the Aberdeens' second term),[48] was presented as systematic deception.[49]

When Ishbel addressed a teachers' conference on TB, a correspondent remarked: 'It is the duty of every teacher in Ireland to train their pupils for the fight against the "white plague" but it is also their duty to teach them that some of our beloved philanthropists are the representatives of a foreign plague, to which Ireland annually sacrifices a greater number of her sons and daughters [through emigration] than she has lost in half a century by consumption'.[50] The image of Ishbel as causing or embodying plague recurs in Griffith's papers; a cartoonist shows a crowned female figure wielding a sword labelled 'Anglicisation' as 'The Real Plague', and a parody of Swinburne's poem 'Dolores' (about a dominatrix) presents Ishbel as 'Our Lady of Pain', embodiment not only of British misrule and exploitation but of a mimsy Puritanism which by sapping the robust life-force found in eighteenth-century Ireland promoted TB.[51]

Ishbel's maternalist failure to distinguish between personal and official preferences led her to place protégés in official positions, producing such contretemps as the widely denounced appointment of Isabella Degani (rather than the better-qualified Helena Concannon) as professor of Spanish and Italian in University College Dublin.[52] The publicisation by separatists of a homosexual scandal in connection with the 1907 theft of the Irish crown jewels, and unfounded suggestions that the Aberdeens' eldest son was implicated,[53] was an attempt to resuscitate the 1884 Dublin Castle scandal (thereby equating the Aberdeen regime with the coercive Spencer viceroyalty),[54] and to attack the maternalist and familialist image projected by the Aberdeens.

The Aberdeens' claim to promote Irish industries was described as wishing to 'co-opt them out of existence',[55] particularly when the Aberdeens associated themselves with the 1907 International Exhibition organised by William Martin Murphy and opened by Edward VII. Presented as displaying Ireland's modernisation and claiming her rightful place within the empire, the exhibition was denounced by separatists as seducing Irish consumers by displaying foreign goods.[56] The Aberdeens' cultivation of Murphy and the eulogies his *Irish Independent* offered to the TB crusade were presented by Griffith as evidence that tycoon and vicereine alike embodied a demoralising Anglicised consumerism, undermining Irish producerist virtue and corrupting national consciousness through mindless advertising.[57]

The political outlook of Griffithite Sinn Féin was to a considerable extent that of Griffith's own artisan class, emphasising the difference between the hard-working deserving poor, unfairly snubbed and patronised by wealthy snobs and whose honest endeavours should be assisted by an Irish government, and those corrupted by patronage – aristocrats, Castle Catholic professionals, the lumpenproletariat. 'A thousand sentimentalists and ten thousand job-hunters and tuft-hunters will rise as one worm', to defend Ishbel, Griffith sneered in a parody of Burke on Marie-Antoinette.[58] This opposition between corrupt patronage and active citizenship clearly opposed paternalist philanthropy. It also included a certain distrust of the cult of the bureaucratic expert (at least under British rule) as mystification intended to breed passivity and dependence. The Aberdeens' project of bringing the kailyard spirit to modern government could be seen as combining the worst of old corruption and new regimentation.

Griffith and other radical nationalists denounced Ishbel's anti-tuberculosis campaign as conspiracy against Irish industry, making overseas customers believe Irish goods were infected.[59] Her erection of a sanatorium at Peamount, County Dublin, was described as endangering the paper industry carried on nearby (it was also suggested she personally profited from the state's acquisition of the site).[60]

The Aberdeens' reminiscences contain self-consciously quaint descriptions of country people being persuaded of the existence of microbes. This was less straightforward than they suggest; Brian O'Higgins's verse satires on 'Lady Microbe', imply microbes are imaginary creatures devised to spread anxiety:

> There were microbes all about us – on our fingers an' our toes,
> An' every man had millions o' them climbin' up his nose;
> There were billions o' them livin' with us, mornin', noon an' night,
> There were thrillions o' them floatin' there between us an' the light;
> An' no one ever saw them until Mrs Aberdeen
> Came down with some suggestions an' a blessin' from her queen.
> She saw the awful state of us an' spoke to us most kind,
> An' turned matthers over in her philanthropic mind,
> An' mutthered most melodiously – an' fingered with her gown –
> ''Twill take me all my time to make them loyal to the Crown;
> I wondher what'll fetch the women – that's the bloomin' rub! –
> Och! I'll chuck the Sanatorium an' start a Babies' Club'.[61]

This opposition drew intermittently on the arguments of the contemporaneous British anti-vaccination movement, a significant political presence in this period which only died away after conscientious objectors were exempted from vaccinating their children in the Edwardian period.[62] Like their British counterparts, some of Ishbel's separatist critics were suspicious of germ theory as mystification intended to facilitate the extension of state power over the citizenry on the pretext of its superior professional expertise (hence the mocking nickname 'Lady Microbe').[63] They alleged that the TB crusade was a pretext for the Treasury ('the Treasury microbe') to evade its financial obligations to Ireland in such matters as undertaking arterial drainage,[64] and favoured the miasmatic theory of disease as part of a radical social critique of the toleration of bad wages and slum conditions by local and national elites.[65] The Irish separatists presented this as a critique of a specifically colonial state; economic revival under Irish self-government would remove the root causes of disease.

Although Griffith reprinted material produced by British anti-vaccinationists,[66] his emphasis on living conditions, poverty and climate and his scornful remarks about the 'viceregal microbe' did not amount to doctrinaire miasmatism. At times he expressly described TB as infectious, for example when commending Dr Seamus O'Beirne's Connemara anti-TB campaign as Sinn Féin policy in practice.[67] His attitude was that no good could come from Dublin Castle and any stick was good enough to hit it. Griffith's most doctrinaire anti-vaccinationist contributor was one F. Ó hUaithne, who combined reproduction of British anti-vaccinationist claims that the practice propagated the diseases it professed to cure, with claims that its practice in Ireland was a sign of the national slave mind; he extended this to experimental vaccination with tuberculin as well as the more usual target of smallpox vaccination.[68]

Ishbel's forays into town-planning, culminating in a 1914 civic exhibition devised by the Scottish planner Patrick Geddes to show how Dublin might be remodelled under Home Rule,[69] attracted similar opposition; establishing a boys' camp at the old Ormond Market as part of a scheme to provide children's playgrounds was denounced as spreading tuberculosis in central Dublin,[70] while her complaints about noxious odours from factories in the Liberties (reflecting interest in town planning) were denounced as killing Irish industry.[71]

In their last viceregal years the Aberdeens faced increasing financial strain and political marginalisation. A 1908 attempt to bridge Dublin's developing labour conflict by meeting Larkin on his release from prison failed to reprise their symbolic success with Davitt in 1886; Larkin publicly denounced the Aberdeens as patronising know-nothings, while Griffith cited the meeting as evidence that Larkin was part of the conspiracy against Irish industry.[72] William Martin Murphy's involvement with the Aberdeens' philanthropic projects did not make him responsive to private appeals for compromise in the 1913–14 lockout. Aberdeen privately favoured a strong line against the UVF and opposed compromise on partition, but carried no political weight.[73] The struggle to hold onto the viceroyalty finally ended after Griffith's paper (shortly before its suppression after the outbreak of the First World War) published an intercepted letter from Ishbel to the editor of the *Freeman's Journal,* indiscreetly describing the need to overcome Unionist opposition to a separate Irish Red Cross.[74]

On retirement in 1915, Aberdeen received a marquessate; he chose the title 'Aberdeen and Tara', changed to the Ossianic 'Temair' after protests by some unionists and nationalists. The Aberdeens spent the remainder of the war in America raising funds for their charities, accompanied by accusations from diehard unionists that they had conspired with Sinn Féin.[75] In 1920 they resigned their much-diminished estate to their eldest son and retired to a dower house. Ishbel regularly returned to Dublin in connection with Peamount Sanatorium and other philanthropic work until her death in 1939.

The Aberdeens' reinvention of the lord-lieutenancy as a surrogate 'welfare monarchy' failed to have a lasting effect. It would be unfair to dismiss their critics without acknowledging that the Aberdeens' paternalism was distinctly suffocating and their understanding of Ireland contained significant elements of condescension and wishful thinking; but the new Ireland was less free of these vices than their opponents had hoped. Like the wider Gladstonian project in which they participated, Lady Microbe and the kailyard viceroy may not have achieved their professed aims, but did something to make Anglo-Irish relations better than they might otherwise have been.

Notes

1 Frank Prochaska, *Royal Bounty: The Making of a Welfare Monarchy* (New Haven, 1995).

2 James Loughlin, *The British Monarchy and Ireland: 1800 to the Present* (Cambridge, 2007), pp 210–12, 271–83, 288–9.

3 Margaret E. Forster, *Churchill's Grandmamma* (London, 2010).

4 C.f. Ewen A. Cameron, *Impaled upon a Thistle: Scotland since 1880* (Edinburgh, 2010), pp 9–11; Roderick Watson, *The Literature of Scotland* (London, 1984), pp 290, 314–19.

5 *Sinn Féin* (hereafter *SF*), 25 Jan. 1908.

6 Lucille Iremonger, *Lord Aberdeen* (London, 1978).

7 Marquess and Marchioness of Aberdeen and Temair, *We Twa* (2 vols, London, 1925), i, p. 6.

8 Ibid., i, pp 32–6.

9 Marjorie Pentland, *A Bonnie Fechter: The Life of Ishbel, Marchioness of Aberdeen and Temair* (London, 1952), p. 114.

10 Maureen Keane, *Ishbel: Lady Aberdeen in Ireland* (Newtownards, 1999), p. 15.

11 Aberdeen, *We Twa*, i, p. 272.

12 Pentland, *Bonnie Fechter*, p. 42; Aberdeen, *We Twa*, i, pp 7, 215.

13 Keane, *Ishbel*, pp 24–7.

14 Lord Aberdeen, *Tell Me Another* (London, 1925); Aberdeen, *We Twa*, i, pp 237–9.

15 Watson, *Literature of Scotland*, pp 314–19, 332–9, 345–6, 349–60. Interesting discussions of the version of 'kailyard' literature which developed among Ulster Presbyterians in the late nineteenth and early twentieth centuries, which provide significant insights into the overall kailyard phenomenon, are Norman Vance. '"Kailyard" stories in Ulster: northern fiction after Carleton', in Frank Ferguson and Andrew R. Holmes (eds), *Revising Robert Burns and Ulster: Literature, Religion and Politics, c.1770–1920* (Dublin, 2009), pp 148–64; Colin Walker, 'A bibliography of Presbyterianism in Ulster fiction, 1780–1920', ibid., pp 165–90.
16 Aberdeen, *We Twa*, i, p. v.
17 Pentland, *Bonnie Fechter*, pp 240–1.
18 Doris French, *Ishbel and the Empire: A Biography of Lady Aberdeen* (Toronto & Oxford, 1998), pp 299–301.
19 Aberdeen, *We Twa*, ii, pp 1–5; James Drummond (ed.), *Onward and Upward: Extracts (1891–96) from the Magazine of the Onward and Upward Association founded by Lady Aberdeen for the Material, Mental and Moral Elevation of Women* (Aberdeen, 1983).
20 According to Peter Hollindale (ed.), *Peter Pan and Other Plays by J. M. Barrie* (Oxford, 2008), it was inspired by the earl and countess of Carlisle.
21 Pentland, *Bonnie Fechter*, p. 213; Peter Keating, *The Haunted Study: A Social History of the English Novel 1875–1914* (London, 1989).
22 L. M. Cullen, *Eason and Son: A History* (Dublin, 1998), pp 248–50, 255; *Irish Times*, 16 Mar. 2011.
23 Lucy McDiarmuid, *The Irish Art of Controversy* (Ithaca, 2005), pp 87–122.
24 Pentland, *Bonnie Fechter*, p. 57.
25 Aberdeen, *We Twa*, i, pp 252–3, 259, 264; Pentland, *Bonnie Fechter*, pp 55–6; Janice Helland, *British and Irish Home Arts and Industries 1880–1914: Marketing Craft, Making Fashion* (Dublin, 2007).
26 Pentland, *Bonnie Fechter*, p. 57.
27 Aberdeen, *We Twa*, i, p. 256; Keane, *Ishbel*, pp 42–4, 54–5. Loughlin, *British Monarchy*, pp 212–13, notes Aberdeen was afraid to inform Queen Victoria directly of his actions.
28 French, *Ishbel and the Empire*, pp 79–80; Loughlin, *British Monarchy*, pp 212–13.
29 Keane, *Ishbel*, pp 71–3; Loughlin, *British Monarchy*, pp 236–7.
30 *United Irishman* (hereafter *UI*), 10 Feb. 1906; for a sceptical loyalist description see Loughlin, *British Monarchy*, p. 213.
31 *SF*, 28 Mar. 1908.
32 Ibid.,18 Jan. 1908.
33 Ibid., 25 Jan. 1908.
34 Ibid., 1 Feb. 1908. Milligan also describes her own experiences of assisting TB patients.
35 Aberdeen, *We Twa*, ii, pp 46–8, 114–33.
36 Pentland, *Bonnie Fechter*, pp 145–6.
37 *SF*, 30 June, 4 Aug. 1906, 24 Feb. 1912.
38 *UI*, 10 Feb. 1906.
39 Pentland, *Bonnie Fechter*, pp 154–5.

40 *UI*, 16 Dec. 1905.
41 Ibid., 31 Mar. 1906.
42 *SF*, 11 May 1912.
43 Ibid., 16 June, 14 July 1906.
44 Ibid., 4 Aug. 1906.
45 *UI*, 16 July 1906.
46 *SF*, 19 Sept. 1908. In Dickens's *Bleak House* the philanthropic Mrs Jellyby neglects her own household while pursuing the well being of Africans.
47 *SF*, 1 Feb. 1908; for coercive measures to secure signatures for a 1911 Women's Address to Queen Mary sponsored by Ishbel, see ibid., 18 Mar., 15, 22 Apr., 20 May 1911.
48 Pentland, *Bonnie Fechter*, pp 160–1. Public service advertising by such figures as Horace Plunkett and Ishbel is an underexplored aspect of the last decades of Dublin Castle administration; see Colum Kenny, *Irish Patriot, Publisher and Advertising Agent: Kevin J. Kenny (1881–1954)* (Dublin, 2011), pp 33–7, 46–58, 86–90, for one advertiser's work with the Aberdeens.
49 C.f. Griffith's claim that the British-built wagon gave 'less work for the consumers [Irish workmen] and [hence] more for consumption', *SF*, 26 June 1909.
50 Ibid., 28 Mar. 1909.
51 Ibid., 25 Sept., 23 Oct. 1909 – the style and sentiments of the latter suggest Oliver St John Gogarty, whose criticisms of the Aberdeen campaign for neglecting school medical inspection are reported ibid., 18 Nov. 1911.
52 Ibid., 29 Apr., 6 May, 5, 12, 19, 26 Aug., 2 Sept. 1911.
53 Ibid., 24 July 1909, 'Lady Crown Jewels, whose philanthropic work on behalf of criminals in Ireland is so well known'.
54 Ibid.,18 May 1912.
55 Ibid., 16 June 1906, 21 Nov. 1908.
56 Ibid., 4 Aug. 1906, 27 Apr. 1907, 11 May 1907.
57 Ibid., 20, 27 Mar., 9 Oct. 1909.
58 Ibid., 14 Mar. 1914.
59 Ibid., 26 June, 17 July 1909, 24 May 1913, 14 Mar. 1914. For the Aberdeens' private response to such accusations see J. R. B. McMinn (ed.), *Against the Tide: J. B. Armour, Irish Presbyterian Minister and Home Ruler* (Belfast, 1985), p. 70.
60 *SF*, 3 Aug. 1912; Griffith's opposition to sanatoria as 'concentration camps for consumptives' pre-dated the Aberdeen viceroyalty, *UI*, 28 Oct. 1905.
61 Brian O'Higgins, *Wolfe Tone Annual 1950: 1916, Before and After* (Dublin, 1950), pp 31, 40–1. James Stephens, 'The old philosopher discourses on the viceregal microbe', *SF*, 11 Sept. 1908, is a piece of surreal political whimsy rather than actually denying the existence of microbes.
62 Nadia Durbach, *Bodily Matters: The Anti-Vaccination Movement in England, 1853–1907* (Durham and London, 2005).
63 *SF*, 24 July 1909.

64 Ibid., 9 Oct. 1909, 17 June 1911.

65 E.g. ibid., 19 Dec. 1908 (Belfast textile workers' working conditions contrasted with employers' support for Ishbel on TB), 17 July 1909 (local councils spread TB by shoddy construction of labourers' cottages).

66 E.g. J. R. Williamson, quoted in *SF*, 9 Feb. 1907.

67 Ibid., 27 July 1907; Aiden Foley and Lawrence William White, 'Seamas O'Beirne', *Dictionary of Irish Biography* (hereafter *DIB*). [www.dib.cambridge.org/viewFullScreen.do?filename=/app/dib/production/content/html/9780521633314_6447.htm]

68 *SF*, 12 July 1913, 'Health, nationality and vaccination', ibid., 19 Jan. 1907 (but a pro-vaccination reply was published 2 Feb. 1907); 3, 10 June 1911, 17 Aug. 1912.

69 Helen Miller, *Patrick Geddes: Social Evolutionist and City Planner* (London, 1990), pp 182–9. See also Pentland, *Bonnie Fechter*, p. 51, Aberdeen, *We Twa*, ii, pp 188–90.

70 Pentland, *Bonnie Fechter*, p. 164; *SF*, 14 Apr. 1912.

71 *SF*, 18 May 1912.

72 Ibid., 26 Dec. 1908, 30 Sept., 7, 14 Oct. 1911, 3 Feb. 1912.

73 McMinn (ed.), *Against the Tide*, p. 196; A. T. Q. Stewart, *The Ulster Crisis* (London, 1967), p. 213.

74 *SF*, 17 Oct. 1914. One of the Aberdeens' last projects was a war hospital in Dublin Castle, with Murphy chairing the finance committee, Aberdeen, *We Twa*, ii, p. 240.

75 E.g. *Plain English*, 10 July 1920, pp 7–9.

CHAPTER 11

Vizekönigerdämmerung: Lords French and FitzAlan at the Lodge, 1918–22

Keith Jeffery

It is a curiosity in the history of the Irish lord lieutenancy that, at precisely the moment when the office was rapidly sinking into irrelevance, the appointment of the last two incumbents was in each case meant to infuse considerable significance to its function. Lord French, viceroy from May 1918 until April 1921 and who regarded himself as an Irishman (unlike many of his predecessors), was a high-ranking soldier and supposed to reassure the population that Home Rule would be implemented, as well as bringing the stamp of firm military government to Ireland. By the appointment of Lord Edmund Talbot (who was created Viscount FitzAlan), the highest-ranking English Catholic layman of the day, and the first Catholic viceroy since the seventeenth century, it was hoped to stem the ebbing power and influence of the British administration. In neither case can it be said that the experiment was much of a success.

Insofar as historians have reflected at all on the last two lords lieutenant they have not given them much of a good press. FitzAlan, indeed, is notable for his absence from nearly every history of the period, which presumably reflects historians' implicit judgment of his importance, if not also his actual significance. Dorothy Macardle, indeed, while dismissing any notion that Irish nationalists might have taken the appointment of a Catholic viceroy as a conciliatory gesture, even got his name wrong.[1] As for French, the best that could be said of him (as Eunan O'Halpin has argued) is that 'a bluff old soldier could not be expected to master the intricacies of Irish politics', that illness in early 1919 debilitated him and that he 'was entirely in the hands of his [Unionist diehard] private secretary [Edward] Saunderson'. O'Halpin's damning conclusion, indeed, is that in 1918–19 French actually made the situation 'far worse', and that by the summer of 1920 he 'was little more than a mendacious blusterer, irrelevant to the administration of which he was technically still head'.[2] Despite the apparent failure of the last two viceroys, however, it is worth revisiting the circumstances of their appointments and the history of their tenure since this can illuminate much about British attitudes towards Ireland, as well as the sometimes neglected British context of Irish policy-making and the administration of Ireland during what might be called the 'end-game' of British rule over at least most of the island.

'Johnnie' French was appointed lord lieutenant on 7 May 1918 in succession to Lord Wimborne, who had occupied the office since February 1915 (with a gap between May and August 1916 when he had resigned pending the official review of events during the 1916 Rising). French was a genuine military hero who had made his name as a dashing and successful cavalry commander during the South African War of 1899–1902.[3] Back home, he rapidly rose to the top of the reformed army staff, becoming Chief of the Imperial General Staff (CIGS), the professional head of the army, in March 1912. At the beginning of the First World War, French was an automatic choice to be the Commander-in-Chief of the British Expeditionary Force which was despatched to support France against Germany in August 1914. This was the climax of his career as a military commander. He did not cope well with the new mass, industrialised conflict or the costly horrors of trench warfare and was forced to resign in December 1915 to be replaced by Sir Douglas Haig. From January 1916 French served in the newly created post of Commander-in-Chief of Home Forces, with responsibilities for defence against invasion, military training and military aid to the civil power throughout the United Kingdom.

Although his branch of the family had lived in England since the eighteenth century, and was himself born in Kent, French came from Irish lineage and, according to his biographer, Richard Holmes, was 'proud of his Irish ancestry'. Not only was he intensely interested in Ireland and matters Irish, but he was convinced that his family background left him with a 'special understanding' of the problems of Ireland.[4] French joined the army initially through the Suffolk Artillery Militia, but in 1874 he transferred to the 19th Hussars. Stationed in Ireland in the late 1870s, his regiment was sent to provide support for Lord Erne's famous agent, Captain Boycott, and so he witnessed at first hand the agrarian unrest of the Land War. In 1881 he was posted back to England and spent no continuous time in Ireland thereafter until his appointment as viceroy in 1918 (though he did visit the country several times while he had the Home Forces Command). He clearly, nevertheless, retained a keen (and apparently growing) affection for Ireland. When he was raised to the peerage in 1915 (at the time he ceased being Commander-in-Chief of the Expeditionary Force), he took the title Viscount French of Ypres and High Lake (County Roscommon). In 1917 he bought a small country house at Drumdoe in Roscommon, a remote location north of

Boyle in the Irish midlands. Here he 'started buildings and extensions' which, Sir Henry Robinson (Vice-President of the Local Government Board) noted 'must have cost a mint of money, with a full intention of settling down and making it his home'.[5]

During the 'Ulster Crisis' of 1912–14, when he was CIGS, French could not avoid getting caught up in the consequences of Irish political affairs. He was not much of an overtly political animal, but (perhaps unexpectedly) by no means shared the unquestioning unionism espoused by so many of his fellow army officers. In November 1913 he told Brigadier Henry Wilson (the Director of Military Operations and a fierce unionist) that while he was nervous about the likelihood of civil war in Ireland, he would 'obey the King's Orders' (whatever they might be).[6] The following spring, by which time Asquith's Liberal government were tiring of what they perceived to be the militant and threatening posturings of Unionists, they asked French to organise the deployment of troops in Ulster. But the arrangements for this were badly mismanaged, and the combination of a windy and unpredictable Commander-in-Chief in Ireland, Sir Arthur Paget, with fervently unionist Anglo-Irish officers under his command, precipitated the so-called 'Curragh Mutiny', when on 20 March 1914 over sixty officers resigned their commissions rather than (as they thought) be mobilised to act against Ulster Unionists. When the leader of the 'mutineers', Brigadier Hubert Gough, was summoned to London, French erroneously gave him an assurance that his troops would 'not be called upon to enforce the present Home Rule Bill on Ulster'.[7] Since the government subsequently repudiated this statement, French was obliged to resign as CIGS. Asquith, however, assured him that he would still take command of any expeditionary force which Britain might send abroad, as happened just a few months later.

Among other things, Asquith seems to have been reassured that French was, at the very least, not a die-hard unionist like Henry Wilson, Hubert Gough and many others. Asquith's wife, Margot, indeed, regarded French as a 'hot Liberal', though there is little evidence at this stage that French had any particular party leanings.[8] Nevertheless, while remaining politically colourless, he stood firmly by the correct constitutional principle (challenged by Wilson, Gough and others) that his duty was simply to follow the 'King's orders' as handed down by the elected government of the day. By 1918, however, his opinions on Ireland had become sufficiently explicit for Lloyd George (who had succeeded Asquith as Prime Minister in December 1916) to describe him to C. P. Scott (editor of the *Manchester Guardian*) as 'excellent for the job [of viceroy] – of good judgment, an Irishman and a Home Ruler'.[9]

But there was more to it than that. The great German spring offensive, launched on 21 March 1918, quickly pushed the Allied armies (principally British units) back forty miles. Although losing momentum, further enemy attacks in April and May kept the pressure on the British, who hurriedly moved reinforcements from home and other parts of the Front, as well as the Italian theatre. It also provoked a manpower crisis at home. Boy soldiers were despatched to France; 'combing out' of men from industrial occupations was stepped up; and the upper age limit for conscription was raised. Ireland was thought to represent a prime source of manpower. Vehement nationalist objections had led Ireland to be excluded when conscription was introduced in Great Britain in January 1916. In 1918, however, the urgent military demand for troops on the Western Front, combined with a sense in British unionist circles that conscription, bringing a 'stamp of firm government' and siphoning off youthful potential troublemakers, might do some good in Ireland, put Irish conscription once more on the political agenda. Johnnie French was certainly in favour of imposing both firm government and conscription. On his return from a tour of Ireland early in March 1918 he told Henry Wilson that the country was 'in the most shocking pic [*sic*] but from a military point of view safe because aeroplanes, armoured cars, maxims etc terrify the natives'.[10] After the German offensive had commenced and the War Cabinet had begun to contemplate the extension of conscription, French (like Wilson, who was now CIGS) was one of those strongly in support.

Not everyone favoured the measure. At a Cabinet meeting on 28 March Sir James Campbell (a Unionist and the Irish Lord Chief Justice) 'was convinced that conscription could only now be enforced in Ireland at the cost of tremendous bloodshed'. Sir Edward Carson, too, had his doubts, but the opposition of these men, although clearly in touch with opinion in Ireland, was overridden. In the end the measure was agreed, but the Cabinet linked it to progress in the direction of Home Rule. The hope (though this was pretty forlorn) was that some political accommodation might emerge from the Irish Convention which had been meeting since the previous summer and was about to report. Noting that the government were 'pledged to Home Rule', it was believed that 'the logical order would be to first pass Home Rule, so removing a wrong, or an imaginary wrong, to the people of Ireland, and then to bring in conscription'.[11] As it turned out, in fact, even the threat of conscription was enough to create a pan-nationalist opposition, with Catholic Church support, which powerfully boosted Sinn Féin's political fortunes and effectively torpedoed those of the constitutional nationalists, whose conditional support for the war effort had by then ceased to resonate with the great mass of Irish nationalist opinion.

While Home Rule was evidently the carrot, Lord French was appointed to wield the stick. In February 1918, anticipating 'trouble' in Ireland, Lord Derby, the Secretary for War, had raised the possibility of French being sent to Ireland as viceroy and Commander-in-Chief.[12] In April Lloyd George thought of replacing the lord lieutenant with three 'Lord Justices': James

Campbell; Lord Midleton, the leading southern Irish Unionist (and a former Secretary of State for India); and French, but this came to nothing as the three men could not agree on policy, Campbell, for example, still being opposed to conscription. In the end French accepted appointment as lord lieutenant on the understanding that he would be head of a 'quasi-military government'.[13] In a departure from normal practice, he was given a seat in the Cabinet alongside a new chief secretary, the inexperienced Edward Shortt, a Liberal MP whose first government post this was.

From the start French appears to have been convinced that conscription could be imposed on Ireland, whether or not any feasible Home Rule measure was also introduced. On 6 May Henry Wilson dined with Lloyd George, French, Winston Churchill and H. A. L. Fisher (President of the Board of Education, who was 'drafting the H. R. Bill'). There was

> a long talk about how Johnnie ought to carry on as Viceroy. L. G. impressed on Johnnie the wisdom of putting the onus for first shooting on to the rebels; but L. G. was not in the least opposed to shooting.[14]

French was also sure that much of the sedition in Ireland was the result of German machinations. The Irish, he told Lord Esher, were 'so infernally emotional', but 'if they could only be got to realise the true character of such leaders as de Valera', he felt sure that they 'would cast them out like the swine they are'. His 'first great effort', moreover, was 'to stamp out German intrigue'.[15]

French's belief in enemy intrigue appeared to be confirmed by the discovery in April 1918 of a so-called 'German plot' to support another rising apparently timed to take place in June. Assured by Admiral 'Blinker' Hall, the Director of Naval Intelligence, that the plot was genuine, French was pressed to take action against Sinn Féin, and a large number of activists were arrested on the night of 17–18 May. But it soon became clear that the government could produce no convincing evidence to support their actions, and it was widely assumed in nationalist circles that the arrests were merely punishment for opposing conscription.[16] French was unswayed by the continuing Irish opposition to conscription and in both July and August told Henry Wilson he did not think there would 'be any real difficulty' in applying it.[17] In fact, the appointment of French as viceroy, the continued threat of conscription and the attempted suppression of Sinn Féin was, as Charles Townshend has observed, a 'gift to nationalist propagandists' and powerfully contributed to the virtual annihilation of the Irish Parliamentary Party in the 1918 general election.[18]

French attempted to improve the administration of Ireland with a number of innovations, including the creation in May 1918 of an 'Executive

Council' which soon became a 'die-hard's club' of Unionists committed more to coercion than any sort of conciliation. A 'military council', formed in July, was supposed to systematise security policy-making, but ended up as little more than a conduit for French's own inconsistent ideas. A third innovation was the 'Viceroy's Advisory Council', which was supposed to comprise a representative range of Irish opinion and keep the viceroy in touch with the feelings of the people. This never materialised, and a plan for it to take on some executive functions foundered on the opposition of the chief secretary. French, too, fell under the influence of his thorough-going unionist private secretary, Edward Saunderson, and was clearly out of his depth in the dangerous waters of Irish politics.[19] His soldierly instincts, which inclined him towards a draconian approach to security, were tempered by his sentimental conviction that with kind treatment the great mass of Irish people could be seduced away from the baleful influence of republican separatists. While he continued to believe in Home Rule, it was (at most) only limited devolution of the old sort, within the United Kingdom, which was becoming increasingly remote from anything which would satisfy even moderate nationalist opinion.

French, of course, was not alone in clinging to out-of-date solutions for the 'Irish problem', but since he was, to a considerable extent, in charge, this mattered more than it might otherwise have done. Especially during the first half of 1919, while most British politicians (and the Prime Minister in particular) were focused on the peace negotiations in Paris, Ireland slipped down the political agenda and French's wayward approach contributed to a sense of drift in Irish policy making. As early as January 1919, Edward Shortt told H. A. L. Fisher that French was 'now entirely under the influence of Saunderson' and 'a little knot of Kildare Club men'.[20] In February 1919 French fell ill with influenza which developed into pneumonia. This kept him out of Ireland for nearly two months and while he was away Ian Macpherson, another Liberal who had replaced Shortt in January, recovered some of the initiative from him. But he had not much to offer beyond more of the kind of helpless hand-wringing with which British politicians habitually responded to Irish difficulties. 'The state of the country was never worse than it is today', he told Lloyd George in April, and, though he claimed to be 'a thorough-going & consistent Home Ruler', he did 'not see how you can at the present moment surrender it [Ireland] to the inimical forces of Sinn Fein'.[21]

Despite the conventional dating of the start of the 'Irish War of Independence' to the Soloheadbeg ambush on 21 January 1919, when two policemen guarding a consignment of quarry explosives were killed by party of Irish Volunteers, for most of 1919 it was a very restricted type of 'war', marked, certainly, by a gradually rising tempo of violence, but one which was sporadic and for the most part highly localised. Although early in 1919

Sir Henry Wilson noted that Johnnie French and Sir Frederick Shaw (the army commander) were worried about 'the serious situation in Ireland',[22] there was not much from a purely 'law and order' perspective to suggest that any part of the country was becoming ungovernable. Assuming, as many did, that violence was endemic in Ireland, it was possible in 1919 to dismiss attacks on policemen and police barracks as just one more of the periodic bursts of 'outrages' which Ireland seemed fated to suffer. That being the case, a firm security policy (such as French favoured) might be all that was required.

But a failed attempt to assassinate French late in 1919 dramatically demonstrated how the security situation was rapidly deteriorating. Although, in fact, the 1919–21 conflict was characterised by an absence of political assassination – as Peter Hart has observed, 'no Unionist, Irish Party or British politicians were assassinated in 1919–21 (1922–3 was another story)' – there was an abundance of plans for such operations.[23] Dan Breen asserted that some dozen schemes were contemplated to kill French. 'Against the old soldier himself we had no personal spite,' he wrote, but 'we knew that his death would arouse the world to interest itself in our fight for freedom.'[24] One of them was to 'plug' French on the College Green review stand for the Armistice Day parade on 11 November 1919, the attack to be conducted possibly by a single sniper (a volunteer who 'would not come back') located in an office opposite the Bank of Ireland. The operation was called off at the last minute. In one version, either Cathal Brugha or Richard Mulcahy asserted that 'the people would not stand for it'; in another, Brugha vetoed it because it endangered civilian bystanders. According to Vinnie Byrne, a member of Collins's 'Squad', another suggestion was to kill French at the Viceregal Lodge 'where he was believed to take a daily stroll around the grounds'. But after Byrne and two other Squad members scouted the location they rejected the plan as completely unfeasible. An attempted attack was organised for a visit by French to Trinity College Dublin. A large group of gunman assembled, but the viceroy's party evaded them by unexpectedly slipping out through a side-gate.[25]

On 19 December 1919 the IRA made their most serious attempt to kill French. Tipped off by Collins's 'spy in the Castle', Ned Broy, about the viceroy's journey back to Dublin after spending a few days at Drumdoe, a party of eleven men gathered at a pub near Ashtown railway station on the north side of Phoenix Park. Alerted to the imminent arrival of French's train by the passage of a convoy of cars to take him to the Lodge, the gunmen hurriedly took up their positions. A bomb was thrown into the second car, in which French was supposed to be travelling, and there was a lively exchange of fire with the military escort. Although one soldier told the attackers that French had been 'blown to bits in the car', he had in fact been in the first vehicle. French's personal detective, who had been sitting beside the driver, was wounded but French escaped unscathed. One of the attackers, Michael Savage, was killed.[26] The unionist press greeted the incident with much shock and outrage ('Murderous attack near Ashtown Station'; 'Well-known Detective Sergeant wounded'; 'Thrilling story of His Excellency's Escape'),[27] while other observers were less moved. Lloyd George mordantly remarked 'they are bad shots'.[28]

During the Treaty negotiations in London late in 1921, the ambitious society hostess Hazel Lavery (wife of the painter Sir John Lavery) had both French and Michael Collins to dinner. French is reported to have said, 'This is the first time I have had the pleasure of meeting you, Mr Collins', to which Collins replied, 'It is not the first time I have seen your Lordship, for a couple of months ago [this cannot have been quite true, as French had left Ireland some seven months earlier] you were by yourself near the Lodge and the boys surrounded you; but I called them off, I thought it so brave of you.'[29]

George Bernard Shaw used the December 1919 attack to reflect on the wider British imperial context. 'The incident,' he wrote,

> was no more surprising than an outbreak of smallpox would be in a district where the Public Health Authority had not only neglected its duties, but sedulously introduced and enforced a series of anti-sanitary measures.

Nationalist Irish tempers, he claimed, had been inflamed by recently circulated reports about 'the proceedings of General Dyer at Amritsar in India', where in April 1919 troops under his command had fired on an illegal demonstration, killing over three hundred people. 'This,' asserted Shaw, 'made every citizen of the world who valued liberty and human dignity see red', and had the result in Ireland 'that Lord French, safe enough a week before, found himself under fire again at closer quarters than at Ypres'.[30]

There was not much French could propose except more police and troops, and an intensified security policy. By the end of 1919, moreover, he was getting increasingly frustrated at the lack of political progress. Late in November he told Lord Riddell (the proprietor of the *News of the World* and an important confidant of Lloyd George's) 'that Irish conditions were very bad and that more serious measures would have to be adopted'. He assured Riddell that Home Rule was 'an absolute necessity', but that the Irish government at Dublin Castle was 'as bad as it can be. I don't mean that the system is corrupt,' he continued, 'but it is bad. There is no proper control. It is impossible to make a satisfactory alteration under existing conditions.'[31] This showed some perspicacity, and widespread concerns about the 'Castle' administration led to the permanent under-secretary at the Treasury, Sir Warren Fisher, being sent over to conduct an enquiry in the early spring of

1920. 'The Castle administration does not administer', he sharply concluded in a damning report delivered in May.[32] Although Fisher's primary focus was the civil service side of things, in a supplementary note for Lloyd George and his closest advisers, he recommended 'one small change' which would, he believed, 'have a psychological effect out of all proportion to its intrinsic importance . . . the abolition of the Lord Lieutenancy'. Fisher thought that the post's 'atmosphere of pinchbeck royalty' had 'associations which do nothing but harm in the tenacious memories of the Irish people'. 'Its abolition,' he asserted, 'would have a spectacular touch which appeals to their temperament.'[33]

Fisher's proposal to abolish the lord lieutenancy reflected how irrelevant the office had become by the spring of 1920. French himself seems effectively to have given up any pretence of knowing what to do, beyond the soldier's solution of military rule. In January 1920 Saunderson had complained to Henry Wilson that French was 'brave as a lion but so erratic & unbalanced'.[34] After the Irish administration was stiffened in the spring of 1920 by the appointment of a new chief secretary (a bluff Canadian called Hamar Greenwood); a new army commander-in-chief, Sir Nevil Macready; and a new English under-secretary, Sir John Anderson, French's importance receded even further. Macready told Walter Long in April 1920 that French 'appeared to me to have been forced into an entirely false position, and to be made to do the work of a departmental junior'.[35] In July at a cabinet Irish committee H. A. L. Fisher thought he was 'a shadow of his former self and quite useless'.[36] In September Henry Wilson observed he had become 'a complete cypher'.[37] Reflecting afterwards on the change of French's circumstances, G. C. Duggan (who had worked in the Castle) asserted that 'power had gone from his hands, and he was kept in ignorance of most things that were happening. Yet like a true knight he would not turn from his post.'[38]

French's role in the appointment of the very able and politically astute Nevil Macready to the Irish Command may have been his most outstanding and beneficial contribution to the Irish situation. Macready claimed in his memoirs that he only accepted the job because French persuaded him to do so. On 23 March 1920 he had been summoned to 10 Downing Street from lunching at the Garrick Club to a meeting with Lloyd George, Bonar Law, Walter Long and Lord French where he was offered the command of the forces in Ireland. The 'only deciding factor' in leading him to accept, asserted Macready, 'indeed the only one that weighed with me, was the evident desire of my old Chief, Lord French, that I should take the appointment'. Apart from that, he claimed, 'nothing would have induced me to return to a country to which I was never attracted, or to take up a task which I instinctively felt would be affected by every variation of the political weather cock, and in which it was doubtful if any satisfactory result could be attained'.[39]

Although he had Irish ancestry himself, Macready had consistently been reluctant to have anything at all to do with Ireland, despite the fact (or perhaps *because* of it) that in 1914 at the height of the Ulster Crisis he had been earmarked to take over as 'Military Governor' in Belfast. Having been Commissioner of the Metropolitan Police in London since 1918 and possessing Liberal political sympathies (including favouring Irish Home Rule), made him especially well qualified for the Irish job. When Ian Macpherson had been appointed chief secretary in January 1919, Macready had written to him in startlingly acerbic terms: 'I cannot say I envy you for I loathe the country you are going to and its people with a depth deeper than the sea and more violent than that which I feel against the Boche'. But, continued Macready, there would be one compensation for he would 'be associated with one of the most lovable men I have ever met, my old Chief Lord French, and that alone to me would compensate for a very great deal'. Macready hoped that Macpherson would find in French 'one of the most loyal and true-hearted individuals you are ever likely to come across'.[40]

French's domestic arrangements while viceroy prompted some comment. Although married since 1880 to his second wife Eleanora (a brief and unhappy first marriage had ended in divorce), for years he had indulged in a series of spectacular affairs, and had been cited as co-respondent in one divorce action. Eleanora, meanwhile, put up with the situation, motivated, according to Richard Holmes, 'by a curious mixture of loyalty, affection and abhorrence of scandal'.[41] In 1915 French began an affair with Winifred Bennett, after her lover the Hon. Arthur 'Jack' Annesley (another cavalry officer and also from an Anglo-Irish family) was killed near Ypres in November 1914. French, a short man now in his early 60s, and Mrs Bennett, who was markedly taller than him, made an odd couple. While Lady French did not follow her husband to Ireland, Mrs Bennett was a regular guest at the Lodge. Saunderson described her as 'the wreck of a Continental Harlot'.[42] In December 1920 Mark Sturgis reported Sylvia Mulholland (the wife of French's military secretary) demonstrating her wit by 'alluding to His Ex and the beautiful Mrs Bennett walking in the Vice Regal Garden as "Pinkie and the Fairy"'.[43]

Another embarrassment for French came from his radical activist sister Charlotte – Lottie – Mrs Despard. Widowed and left independently wealthy in 1890, Lottie became a very well known socialist, pacifist and campaigner for women's rights. Strongly sympathetic to Sinn Féin, and by now in her mid-seventies, she regularly visited Ireland and spoke at political meetings with Maud Gonne among others. Gonne took keen pleasure in the puzzlement of 'the officers and Black and Tans, who continually held up our car, when Mrs Despard said she was the Viceroy's sister'.[44] Mary Colum even alleged French had had an affair with Maud Gonne, though Richard Holmes dismisses the story as having 'no foundation'.[45]

Whatever else he may have been, French was a social success among ascendancy types, at least at the start of his time. He raised the morale of fellow landowners by giving the impression that the 'good old days' had perhaps not entirely disappeared. He delighted Miss Margaret ffolliott of Holybrook, a 'lonely locality' in County Roscommon, by paying her a visit in August 1918 and she reported to a friend that 'he appears to take a genuine interest in his new job, and to be bent on carrying it out with more firmness and discretion than we have been accustomed to of late years'.[46] French himself tried to reinforce this impression by keeping overt security measures to a minimum. Lady Londonderry, a noted gardener, recalled two visits he made in 1918 to her house at Mount Stewart, near Newtownards, County Down. 'Sentries,' she wrote, 'had to be posted everywhere, but so averse was he to precautionary measures for his own safety that they had to be concealed. You would see a tin helmet glinting through large clumps of New Zealand flax, or catch a glimpse of steel from the back of some large rhododendrons; and when His Excellency went down to the sea loch, the sentries were seen going to ground in groves of *veronica* and *grissolinia*!'[47]

Although there was no return to prewar levels of entertainment at the Viceregal Lodge, indeed it remained very much on a wartime footing with the ADCs in khaki uniform and stringent security measures, French gave quite a few dances and dinners and maintained tolerably high standards of hospitality.[48] When Maurice Headlam, the senior British Treasury official in Ireland, attempted to reduce the lord lieutenant's entertainment allowance, a tax-free annual sum of £15,000 (which in contemporary values amounts to something over £500,000),[49] he recalled that the 'only result' was 'an excellent lunch with His Excellency, and a discourse afterwards in his private room on the expense of everything and especially of good champagne, Lord French insisting (quite rightly) "and of course one must have good champagne"; and with this I was dismissed'.[50]

A glum parallel can be drawn between French's experience as commander-in-chief of the British Expeditionary Force in 1914–15 and his time as Irish viceroy in 1918–21. In both cases he was a widely supported candidate for the job and was himself clearly raring to go. In both cases he soon found himself out of his depth. The dreary, costly and morale-sapping static trench warfare of the Western Front ground him down. Successive efforts to break through the German lines and develop the sort of war of movement with which he was more familiar, literally ran into the ground, dashed against the concrete and barbed wire of the enemy defences. The Irish political quagmire, similarly beyond his ken – G. C. Duggan remarked that French was 'by training unfitted to cope with the delicacy of the political situation'[51] – proved predictably unresponsive to the simple soldierly solutions he hoped would sufficiently restore order to enable a limited Home Rule settlement to be established in Ireland. The well-dug-in trench warfare of Irish politics defeated him as surely as the Western Front variety had done.

By the spring of 1921 French's time as viceroy was running out. At the beginning of March Nevil Macready remarked to Henry Wilson that French was increasingly being ignored. 'The poor little man,' he wrote, 'feels very deeply not only the studied neglect of Hamar [Greenwood], who of course has not the manners of a hog, but also that the great ones in Downing Street pay him no attention.'[52] At the end of the month French was told by Lloyd George that he was to be replaced by Lord Edmund Talbot, a Catholic who was thought would be more acceptable to Irish opinion.[53] Talbot, the uncle of the Duke of Norfolk, was the leading Catholic layman in England (while his nephew was a minor). He had been a Conservative MP since 1894 and was an unquestioned Unionist. Gregarious and well liked, he had been the Conservative chief whip since 1913, and had played an important part in the mobilising of Unionist parliamentary forces during the Ulster Crisis. In 1921 he no doubt seemed a perfect choice for the viceroyalty: Catholic to appease the Irish; unionist to reassure the unionists; aristocratic to endow the post with suitable grandeur. He was also prepared to take the job and was raised to the peerage as Viscount FitzAlan. At a presentation to FitzAlan to mark his long years as Unionist whip, Lloyd George remarked that he 'had had a difficult task as Chief Whip under a Coalition, and had discharged it to perfection'. He had 'now earned his rest, so he had been made viceroy of Ireland, by way of giving him a nice, quiet, tranquil task free from all anxiety'. Touching on the motivation behind FitzAlan's appointment, Lloyd George added that 'we look forward to the inauguration of an era of peace, the closing of a great feud between two nations which have been cast by Providence side by side in these islands. There is no-one better qualified for that great task.'[54]

Talbot evidently accepted the post through a keen sense of duty. 'Devotion to public duty alone', wrote Winston Churchill, 'inspired him to undertake so melancholy a task.'[55] He described his fate as 'an awful business' and told fellow-Tory Robert Sanders he 'tried to get out of it, but then felt I could not refuse'. He took soundings in Catholic circles before deciding. As George Younger (Chairman of the Conservative Party) reported to Sanders on 4 April, when Talbot and his wife had first spoken of the possibility to him 'some weeks ago', Talbot had been 'quite convinced it was his duty to go if he got the promise of every help from Rome, but she was doubtful and rather turned against it'. Now, apparently, this was 'all changed'. Rome had 'spoken quite clearly and both are quite happy'. Sanders noted that Talbot had 'the full backing of Rome'.[56] His old friend the arch-unionist Henry Wilson was clearly not reassured and wrote to him asking 'how could you do it, how could you?' Demonstrating his belief that the honour of his regiment was at stake, Talbot replied: 'Because I was brought up with cherry breeches not with a green coat'. He had served in the 11th Hussars, the 'Cherry Pickers', known for their crimson trousers, while Wilson's regiment was the Rifle Brigade, or 'Greenjackets'.[57] Wilson furthermore was gloomy about Talbot's prospects. 'There isn't a decenter, honester Christian alive', he wrote to Macready. 'But the poor man he is a Pope and he is in Ireland *hinc illae lacrimae*.'[58]

Whatever might have been the case in previous years, the appointment of a Catholic to the lord lieutenancy came too late to be of any political use. Eoin MacNeill liked to tell the story of Cardinal Logue's reply to congratulations on the appointment of a Catholic viceroy: 'I suppose the next thing they will send us will be a Catholic hangman.'[59] Reflecting on the reaction of the *Freeman's Journal* to the appointment, Mark Sturgis wrote 'That he is a Catholic is outweighed in their view by the facts that he is an Englishman, and a Tory politician, and Irish RCs dislike English RCs anyway'.[60] In the 1930s Sir John Lavery (himself a Belfast-born Catholic) related Lloyd George's secretary and mistress, Frances Stevenson, sharing a story which FitzAlan himself liked to tell. On becoming viceroy he had been 'taken up by one of the Castle officials to see the view from the top. "You can see for 30 miles, Your Excellency", said the man, "and there's not a bloody Papist in sight."'[61]

Lady Londonderry claimed in her memoirs that the FitzAlans's determination to attend all the important Catholic religious functions in Dublin 'was a source of deep resentment and annoyance to the Irish authorities, who could not overlook the fact that the lord lieutenant represented the King, and was head of the Government in Ireland'. When FitzAlan expressed his wish to attend a solemn requiem mass being held for the late Pope Pius IX, the archbishop of Dublin made it known that it would not be well regarded if FitzAlan did so. FitzAlan countered that, as he was the head of the Catholics in England, it would be highly improper for him *not* to attend the service. A compromise was eventually settled whereby the FitzAlans 'should attend the service as themselves in mufti, with only one gentleman in waiting'. They would, moreover, enter the church 'immediately following the choir and clergy, which meant that the congregation would be standing, and ensure proper respect'. Lady Londonderry alleged (though there is no way of confirming this, and the story may very well have grown in the telling) that 'on the opposite side to where Lord FitzAlan sat alone with Lady FitzAlan were seated in serried rows a whole number of gunmen fully armed, Michael Collins amongst them'. She further asserted that the FitzAlans 'left the cathedral amidst the plaudits of the crowd, who, whatever their political feelings, admire a brave man'.[62] Beyond special occasions like this, the FitzAlans were regular in their religious devotions. According to the 'Court and Personal' column of the *Irish Times*, on Maundy Thursday 1922, for example, Lord and Lady FitzAlan, accompanied by their only son, Henry FizAlan-Howard (who acted as the viceroy's assistant private secretary), Magdalen FitzAlan-Howard (one of their daughters), and an aide-de-camp, attended mass at the University Church in St Stephen's Green. That afternoon the FitzAlans visited St Gabriel's Catholic Church in Aughrim Street, and in the evening they were present at the Tenebrae service in the Pro-Cathedral, Marlborough Street.[63]

While Cardinal Logue may have dismissed the appointment of a Catholic as of no significance, FitzAlan himself made efforts to protect Logue from harassment by the Northern Ireland police. After the funeral of a priest in County Armagh in July 1922 had been stopped by the security forces and the clergy involved (including Logue) searched in what the (Catholic) press reported as a 'needlessly insulting' manner, FitzAlan protested formally to the Northern Ireland prime minister, Sir James Craig. 'I find it difficult, if not impossible,' he wrote, 'to imagine what real necessity there could be for such conduct.' Craig replied that he would personally request a report on the incident from the Minister of Home Affairs, but complained privately to Mark Sturgis at Dublin Castle that Logue was 'very difficult to deal with'. As it turned out, it was the army, not the police, who had been involved, so there was little Craig could do, though the police in Armagh provided Logue with a pass and they were ordered not to interfere with him on his travels.[64]

Describing the appointment of the new lord lieutenant, the unionist-sympathising contemporary historian W. Alison Phillips, Lecky Professor of Modern History at Trinity College, observed that on 2 May 1921 FitzAlan 'took the oath of office in Dublin Castle with all the old-world ceremonial. There had, however, been no state entry into the capital, as in happier days.' Now, he continued, the viceroy 'lived entrenched in the Viceregal Lodge in Phoenix Park, and could only venture abroad with infinite precaution'.[65] There were certainly republican plans to assassinate FitzAlan, and one actual attack was bungled.[66]

Over the summer of 1921 and during the negotiations which culminated in the Treaty of 6 December 1921, FitzAlan was consistently on the side of conciliation and the endeavour to find an accommodation with the Irish nationalists, even though this sometimes separated him from some of his Unionist colleagues.[67] In August, when the likelihood of any meaningful talks seemed remote, he reassured the sceptical Robert Sanders (a Unionist junior minister) that there 'would not be war again'.[68] On 14 November 1921 Tim Healy reported that FitzAlan had been 'lobbying like a Trojan on the Irish side'.[69] The viceroy, however, was no longer a principal in discussions concerning Ireland. In a kind of metaphor for the reduced viceregal role, during the night of 5/6 December 1921, when the Treaty negotiations came to a climax, as one of Lloyd George's secretaries recalled, FitzAlan was not part of the main action at 10 Downing Street, but merely stayed 'waiting in the secretary's room'.[70] And there was not much for FitzAlan to do thereafter, though he had a year to serve as lord lieutenant following the Treaty. In August 1922 he told Robert Sandars he 'was not going back to Ireland till October as no one consulted him there at present and he was better out of the way'. Typically, nevertheless, he remained an optimist and took a more hopeful view of the position there: 'he thinks well of Griffith and hopes for the best from Collins'.[71]

Lord French had intended to settle in Ireland after he gave up the viceroyalty and had purchased a second country house, Hollybrook, near Boyle, in addition to Drumdoe. But in March 1922 FitzAlan bluntly told him that he could not return to Roscommon, or, in the meantime, Ireland at all. 'I consider that your presence in Ireland would now be a disturbing factor', he wrote. 'The very fact of the presence of an ex-viceroy would be a real temptation to these gentlemen.'[72] G. C. Duggan remarked that French's 'last action before quitting Ireland was pathetic'. Before he left, 'unknown save to a few, he spent a couple of days in the house that possibly he might not visit again'. Thus Johnnie French departed, with perhaps only his title – Viscount French of Ypres and High Lake – to remind him of the home he might have enjoyed in (as Duggan put it) 'the evening of his life'.[73] In contrast to the 'might-have-been' of French's leaving was the actuality of FitzAlan's, who ceased being lord lieutenant in December 1922. Not, like French, seeking to put down roots himself, before his departure for England, FitzAlan planted two copper beeches at the Viceregal Lodge, to join other commemoration trees (such as the Giant Sequoia planted by Queen Victoria).[74] We do not know if the last viceroy of Ireland was much exercised by the symbolism of the particular trees he planted, but it might be observed that a noteworthy feature of some varieties of copper beech is that when the leaves first break they are intensely green, but as they reach maturity their emerald vividness is replaced by darker, more sombre hues. Perhaps this modest contribution to the grounds of what was about to become the official governor general's residence in a not-quite-independent Irish Free State, was as appropriate a legacy as might be wished for the Irish viceroyalty after its centuries of colourful and contested existence.

Notes

1 She calls him 'James Talbot', Dorothy Macardle, *The Irish Republic* (Corgi Books edn, London, 1968), p. 415.

2 Eunan O'Halpin, *The Decline of the Union: British Government in Ireland 1892–1920* (Dublin, 1987), pp 206–7. This remains the best single survey of the administration of Ireland during the last years of British rule.

3 The best biographical source for French (on which I have drawn extensively) is Richard Holmes, *The Little Field-Marshal: Sir John French* (London, 1981).

4 Ibid., p. 15.

5 Henry Robinson, *Memories: Wise and Otherwise* (London, 1923), p. 262.

6 Wilson diary, 4 Nov. 1913, Imperial War Museum, London (hereafter IWM), Wilson Papers.

7 Ian F. W. Beckett (ed.), *The Army and the Curragh Incident, 1914* (London, 1986), pp 218–19. The best account of these events is to be found in this book.

8 Holmes, *The Little Field-Marshal*, p. 168.

9 Trevor Wilson (ed.), *The Political Diaries of C. P. Scott, 1911–1928* (London, 1970), p. 342 (entry for 19–21 Apr. 1918).

10 Wilson diary, 8 Mar. 1918, IWM, Wilson Papers.

11 War Cabinet minutes, 28 Mar. 1918, The National Archives, Kew (hereafter TNA), CAB 23/5, WC376).

12 Wilson diary, 22 Feb. 1918, IWM, Wilson Papers.

13 French to Lloyd George, 5 May 1918, quoted in O'Halpin, *Decline of the Union*, p. 158.

14 Wilson diary, 6 May 1918, IWM, Wilson Papers.

15 French to Esher, 20 May 1918, quoted in Holmes, *The Little Field-Marshal*, p. 339.

16 Eunan O'Halpin, 'British intelligence in Ireland, 1914–1921', in Christopher Andrew and David Dilks (eds), *The Missing Dimension: Governments and Intelligence Communities in the Twentieth Century* (London, 1984), pp 65–8.

17 Wilson diary, 24 July and 16 Aug. 1918, IWM, Wilson Papers.

18 Charles Townshend, *Ireland in the Twentieth Century* (London, 1999), p. 84; idem., *Political Violence in Ireland: Government and Resistance since 1848* (Oxford, 1983), pp 324–5.

19 O'Halpin, *Decline of the Union*, pp 161–79 provides a stimulating critical analysis of French's role in 1918–19. Holmes, *The Little Field-Marshal*, pp 338–53, is more sympathetic.

20 Fisher diary, 8 Jan. 1919, Bodleian Library, Oxford (hereafter Bodl.), Fisher Papers, MS Fisher Box 8A.

21 Macpherson to Lloyd George, 14 Apr. 1919, Parliamentary Archives, London (hereafter PA), Lloyd George Papers, F/46/1/2.

22 Keith Jeffery, *Field Marshal Sir Henry Wilson: A Political Soldier* (Oxford, 2006), p. 257.

23 Peter Hart, *Mick: The Real Michael Collins* (London, 2005), p. 220.

24 Dan Breen, *My Fight for Irish Freedom* (Dublin, 1924), pp 120, 125.

25 Hart, *Mick*, pp 220–1; Michael T. Foy, *Michael Collins's Intelligence War: The Struggle Between the British and the IRA 1919–1921* (Stroud, 2006), pp 31–2.

26 The most complete account of the ambush from the republican side is in Foy, *Michael Collins's Intelligence War*, pp 32–3.

27 *Irish Times*, 20 Dec. 1919.

28 Note by Macpherson, 2 Dec. 1919, quoted in Charles Townshend, *The British Campaign in Ireland 1919–1921: The Development of Political and Military Policies* (London, 1975), p. 49.

29 John Lavery, *The Life of a Painter* (London, 1940), p. 214.

30 'The reign of terror', *Irish Statesman*, 3 Jan. 1920, reprinted in George Bernard Shaw, *The Matter with Ireland* (London, 1962), pp 232–4.

31 J. M. McEwen (ed.), *The Riddell Diaries, 1908–1923* (London, 1986), p. 296 (entry for 26 Nov. 1919).

32 Report by Sir Warren Fisher, 12 May 1920, PA, Lloyd George Papers, F/31/1/32.

33 Ibid., 15 May 1920, ibid., F/31/1/33.

34 Wilson diary, 13 Jan. 1920, IWM, Wilson Papers.

35 Macready to Long, 23 Apr. 1920 (copy), PA, Lloyd George Papers, F/34/1/19.

36 Fisher diary, 22 July 1920, Bodl., Fisher Papers, MS Fisher Box 8A.

37 Wilson diary, 6 Sept. 1920, IWM, Wilson Papers.

38 'Periscope' [G. C. Duggan], 'The last days of Dublin Castle', *Blackwood's Magazine*, 212 (Aug. 1922), p. 156.

39 Nevil Macready, *Annals of an Active Life* (London, n.d. [1924]), ii, p. 425.

40 Macready to Macpherson, 11 Jan. 1920, quoted in Townshend, *The British Campaign in Ireland*, p. 20; and Holmes, *The Little Field-Marshal*, p. 2.

41 Holmes, *The Little Field-Marshal*, p. 28.

42 Saunderson to Walter Long, 28 July 1920, quoted in O'Halpin, *Decline of the Union*, p. 205.

43 Michael Hopkinson (ed.), *The Last Days of Dublin Castle: The Mark Sturgis Diaries* (Dublin, 1999), p. 96 (entry for 20 Dec. 1920).

44 Andro Linklater, *An Unhusbanded Life: Charlotte Despard, Suffragette, Socialist, Sinn Feiner* (London, 1980), pp 217–18.

45 Mary Colum, *Life and the Dream* (rev. edn, Dublin, 1966), pp 130, 245–6; Holmes, *Little Field-Marshal*, pp 17, 370 n. 4.

46 Patrick Buckland, *The Anglo-Irish and the New Ireland, 1885–1922* (Dublin, 1972), pp 133, 140.

47 The Marchioness of Londonderry, *Retrospect* (London, 1938), p. 170.

48 Mark Bence-Jones, *Twilight of the Ascendancy* (London, 1987), p. 193.

49 This calculation is based on the Retail Price Index, as indicated in www.measuringworth.com (accessed 17 Aug. 2010).

50 Maurice Headlam, *Irish Reminiscences* (London, 1947), p. 75.

51 'Periscope', 'The last days of Dublin Castle', p. 139.

52 Macready to Wilson, 1 Mar. 1921, IWM, Wilson Papers, HHW 2/2C/41.

53 Holmes, *Little Field-Marshal*, p. 358.

54 *The Times*, 29 July 1921.

55 Winston S. Churchill, *The Aftermath* (London, 1941), p. 292.

56 John Ramsden (ed.), *Real Old Tory Politics: The Political Diaries of Robert Sanders, Lord Bayford, 1910–35* (London, 1984), pp 150–2 (entry for 24 Mar.; Talbot to Sanders, 1 Apr.; Younger to Sanders, 4 Apr. 1921).

57 Ibid., p. 154 (entry for 1 May 1921).

58 Wilson to Macready, 5 May 1921, IWM, Wilson Papers, HHW 2/2D/48. The Latin quotation, 'hence these tears', is from the Roman writer Terence's play *Andria*.

59 Michael Tierney, *Eoin MacNeill: Scholar and Man of Action, 1867–1945* (Oxford, 1980), p. 288.

60 Hopkinson (ed.), *The Last Days of Dublin Castle*, p. 152 (entry for 1 Apr. 1921).

61 A. J. P. Taylor (ed.), *Lloyd George: A Diary by Frances Stevenson* (London, 1971), p. 280 (entry for 4 Oct. 1934).

62 Londonderry, *Retrospect*, pp 195–6.

63 *Irish Times*, 15 Apr. 1922.

64 John Privilege, *Michael Logue and the Catholic Church in Ireland, 1879–1925* (Manchester, 2009), pp 182–3.

65 W. Alison Phillips, *The Revolution in Ireland, 1906–1923* (London, 1923), p. 203.

66 Peter Hart, *The IRA at War 1916–1923* (Oxford, 2003), pp 149, 198–9.

67 See, for example, Tom Jones's diary note of 6 Sept. 1921, in Thomas Jones, *Whitehall Diary, 1916–25* (London, 1969), i, p. 170.

68 Ramsden (ed.), *Real Old Tory Politics*, p. 159 (Sanders diary entry for 21 Aug. 1921).

69 Healy to William O'Brien, quoted in Frank Callanan, *T. M. Healy* (Cork, 1996), p. 573.

70 Geoffrey Shakespeare, *Let Candles Be Brought In* (London, 1949), p. 89.

71 Ramsden (ed.), *Real Old Tory Politics*, p. 180 (Sanders diary entry for 4 Aug. 1922).

72 FitzAlan to French, 5 Mar. 1922, quoted in Holmes, *The Little Field-Marshal*, p. 363.

73 'Periscope', 'The last days of Dublin Castle', p. 181.

74 *Irish Times*, 6 Dec. 1922.

The Chief Governors of Ireland 1541–1922

L – Lord Lieutenant; D – Lord Deputy	Date of appointment[1]
Sir Anthony St Leger, D	7 July 1540
Sir Edward Bellingham, D	22 Apr. 1548
Sir Anthony St Leger, D	4 Aug. 1550
Sir James Croft, D	29 Apr. 1551
Sir Anthony St Leger, D	1 Sept. 1553
Thomas Radcliffe, Viscount Fitzwalter, (3rd earl of Sussex, 1557), D, L (1560)	27 Apr. 1556
Sir Henry Sidney, D	13 Oct. 1565
Sir William Fitzwilliam, D	11 Dec. 1571
Sir Henry Sidney, D	5 Aug. 1575
Arthur Grey, 14th Baron Grey de Wilton, D	15 July 1580
Sir John Perrot, D	7 Jan. 1584
Sir William Fitzwilliam, D	17 Feb. 1588
Sir William Russell, D	16 May 1594
Thomas, Lord Burgh, D	5 Mar. 1597
Robert Devereux, 2nd earl of Essex, L	12 Mar. 1599
Charles Blount, 8th Baron Mountjoy, (cr. earl of Devonshire, 1603), D, L (1603)	21 Jan. 1600
Sir George Carey, D	30 May 1603
Sir Arthur Chichester, (cr. Baron Chichester of Belfast, 1613), D	15 Oct. 1604
Sir Oliver St John, (cr. Viscount Grandison of Limerick, 1621), D	2 July 1616
Henry Cary, 1st Viscount Falkland, D	4 Feb. 1622

Thomas, Viscount Wentworth,	
(cr. earl of Strafford, 1640), D, L (1640)	3 July 1633
Christopher Wandesford, D	1 Apr. 1640
Robert Sidney, 2nd earl of Leicester, L	14 June 1641
James Butler, 1st marquess of Ormond, L	13 Nov. 1643
Philip Sidney, Viscount Lisle, L[2]	21 Jan. 1646
Oliver Cromwell, L	22 June 1649
Henry Ireton, D	26 May 1650
Ulick Burke, 1st marquess of Clanricard, D[3]	6 Dec. 1650
John Lambert, D	30 Jan. 1652
Charles Fleetwood, D	c.27 Aug. 1654
Henry Cromwell, D, L (1658)	17 Nov. 1657
George Monck, Baron Monck,	
(cr. duke of Albemarle, 1660), L	June 1660
John Robartes, 2nd Baron Robartes, D	25 July 1660
James Butler, 1st duke of Ormond, L	21 Feb. 1662
Thomas Butler, 6th earl of Ossory, D	6 May 1664
Duke of Ormond, L	3 Sept. 1665
Earl of Ossory, D	7 Feb. 1668
Baron Robartes, L	3 May 1669
John Berkeley, 1st Baron Berkeley of Stratton, L	4 Feb. 1670
Arthur Capel, 1st earl of Essex, L	21 May 1672
Duke of Ormond, L	24 May 1677
Richard Butler, 1st earl of Arran, D	13 Apr. 1682
Duke of Ormond, L	19 Aug. 1684
Henry Hyde, 2nd earl of Clarendon, L	1 Oct. 1685
Richard Talbot, earl of Tyrconnell	
(cr. duke of Tyrconnell, 1689), D, L (1691)	8 Jan. 1687
(James II in Ireland	12 Mar. 1689 – 4 July 1690)
(William III in Ireland	14 June – 4 July 1690)[4]
Henry, Viscount Sidney, L	18 Mar. 1692
Henry, 1st Baron Capel of Tewkesbury, D[5]	9 May 1695
Laurence Hyde, 1st earl of Rochester, L	28 Dec. 1700
James Butler, 2nd duke of Ormond, L	19 Feb. 1703
Thomas Herbert, 8th earl of Pembroke and	
5th earl of Montgomery, L	30 Apr. 1707
Thomas Wharton, 1st earl of Wharton, L	4 Dec. 1708
Duke of Ormond, L	26 Oct. 1710
Charles Talbot, duke of Shrewsbury, L	22 Sept. 1713
Charles Spencer, 3rd earl of Sunderland, L	21 Sept. 1714
Charles, 2nd Viscount Townshend, L	13 Feb. 1717

Charles Paulet, 2nd duke of Bolton, L	27 Apr. 1717
Charles FitzRoy, 2nd duke of Grafton, L	18 June 1720
John Carteret, 2nd Baron Carteret, L	6 May 1724
Lionel Cranfield Sackville, 1st duke of Dorset, L	23 June 1730
William Cavendish, 3rd duke of Devonshire, L	9 Apr. 1737
Philip Dormer Stanhope, 4th earl of Chesterfield, L	8 Jan. 1745
William Stanhope, 1st earl of Harrington, L	15 Nov. 1746
Duke of Dorset	15 Dec. 1750
William Cavendish, marquess of Hartington (4th duke of Devonshire, 1755), L	2 Apr. 1755
John Russell, 4th duke of Bedford, L	3 Jan. 1757
George Montague-Dunk, 2nd earl of Halifax, L	3 Apr. 1761
Hugh Percy, 1st duke of Northumberland, L	27 Apr. 1763
Thomas Thynne, 3rd Viscount Weymouth, L	5 June 1765
Francis Seymour-Conway, 1st earl of Hertford, L	7 Aug. 1765
George William Hervey, 2nd earl of Bristol, L	6 Oct. 1766
George Townshend, 4th Viscount Townshend, L	19 Aug. 1767
Simon Harcourt, 1st Earl Harcourt, L	29 Oct. 1772
John Hobart, 2nd earl of Buckinghamshire, L	7 Dec. 1776
Frederick Howard, 5th earl of Carlisle, L	29 Nov. 1780
William Henry Cavendish Bentinck, 3rd duke of Portland, L	8 Apr. 1782
George Nugent-Temple-Grenville, 3rd Earl Temple, L	15 Aug. 1782
Robert Henley, 2nd earl of Northington, L	3 May 1783
Charles Manners, 4th duke of Rutland, L[6]	12 Feb. 1784
George Nugent-Temple-Grenville, 1st marquess of Buckingham, L	6 Nov. 1787
John Fane, 10th earl of Westmorland, L	24 Oct. 1789
William Wentworth Fitzwilliam, 2nd Earl Fitzwilliam, L	13 Dec. 1794
John Jeffreys Pratt, 2nd Earl Camden, L	13 Mar. 1795
Charles Cornwallis, 1st Marquess Cornwallis, L	14 June 1798
Philip Yorke, 3rd earl of Hardwicke, L	17 Mar. 1801
Edward Clive, 1st earl of Powis, L	21 Nov. 1805
John Russell, 6th duke of Bedford, L	12 Feb. 1806
Charles Lennox, 4th duke of Richmond, L	1 Apr. 1807
Charles Whitworth, Baron Whitworth, (cr. Viscount Whitworth, 1813, Earl Whitworth 1815), L	13 June 1813

Charles Chetwynd Talbot, 2nd Earl Talbot, L	17 Sept. 1817
Richard Wellesley, 1st Marquess Wellesley, L	10 Dec. 1821
Henry William Paget, 1st marquess of Anglesey, L	27 Feb. 1828
Hugh Percy, 3rd duke of Northumberland, L	2 Feb. 1829
Marquess of Anglesey, L	22 Nov. 1830
Marquess Wellesley, L	11 Sept. 1833
Thomas Hamilton, 9th earl of Haddington, L	29 Dec. 1834
Constantine Henry Phipps, 6th earl of Mulgrave, (cr. marquess of Normanby, 1838), L	23 Apr. 1835
Hugh Fortescue, Viscount Ebrington, (2nd Earl Fortescue, 1841), L	1 Mar. 1839
Thomas Philip de Grey, 2nd Earl de Grey, L	3 Sept. 1841
William A'Court, 1st Baron Heytesbury, L	10 July 1844
John William Ponsonby, 4th earl of Bessborough, L[7]	6 July 1846
George William Frederick Villiers, 4th earl of Clarendon, L	20 May 1847
Archibald William Montgomerie, 13th earl of Eglinton, L	27 Feb. 1852
Edward Granville Eliot, 3rd earl of St Germans, L	4 Jan. 1853
George William Frederick Howard, 7th earl of Carlisle, L	28 Feb. 1855
Earl of Eglinton (cr. earl of Winton, 1859), L	26 Feb. 1858
Earl of Carlisle, L	18 June 1859
John Wodehouse, 3rd Baron Wodehouse, (cr. earl of Kimberley, 1866), L	1 Nov. 1864
James Hamilton, 2nd marquess of Abercorn (cr. duke of Abercorn, 1868), L	6 July 1866
John Poyntz Spencer, 5th Earl Spencer, L	12 Dec. 1868
Duke of Abercorn, L	2 Mar. 1874
John Winston Spencer Churchill, 7th duke of Marlborough, L	28 Nov. 1876
Francis Thomas de Grey Cowper, 7th Earl Cowper, L	3 May 1880
Earl Spencer, L	3 May 1882
Henry Howard Molyneaux Herbert, 4th earl of Carnarvon, L	27 June 1885
John Campbell Hamilton Gordon, 7th earl of Aberdeen, L	6 Feb. 1886

Charles Stewart Vane-Tempest-Stewart, 6th marquess of Londonderry, L	3 Aug. 1886
Lawrence Dundas, 3rd earl of Zetland, L	30 July 1889
Robert Offley Ashburton Milnes, 2nd Baron Houghton, L	18 Aug. 1892
George Henry Cadogan, 5th Earl Cadogan, L	29 June 1895
William Humble Ward, 3rd earl of Dudley, L	11 Aug. 1902
Earl of Aberdeen, L	11 Dec. 1905
Ivor Churchill Guest, 2nd Baron Wimborne, L	16 Feb. 1915
John Denton Pinkstone French, 1st Viscount French, L	7 May 1918
Lord Edmund Bernard Talbot, (cr. Viscount FitzAlan of Derwent, 1921), L	22 Apr. 1921
Office abolished	6–8 Dec. 1922[8]

Notes

1 For complete annotated lists, including the date of swearing-in, and inclusion of the lords justices who presided in the absence of or between appointment of chief governors, see J. G. Simms, 'Chief governors, 1534–1800', and C. J. Woods, 'Chief governors, 1801–1922', in T. W. Moody, F. X. Martin and F. J. Byrne (eds), *A New History of Ireland, vol ix: Maps, Genealogies, Lists* (Oxford, 1989), pp 486–500.

2 Lisle was appointed by parliament as a rival lord lieutenant to the royalist Ormond, who remained in Ireland until 1647.

3 Royalist appointment, made in opposition to Ireton.

4 Following William's return to England, Ireland was government by lords justices until the appointment of Sidney as lord lieutenant in 1692.

5 Died in office, May 1696.

6 Died in office, Oct. 1787.

7 Died in office, May 1847.

8 The lord lieutenancy was abolished in accordance with the provisions of the Irish Free State Constitution Act, 1922 and the Irish Free State (Consequential Provisions) Act, 1922, with the powers of the lord lieutenant lapsing in the Irish Free State on 6 December, and in Northern Ireland on 8 December 1922.

Index